The Teaching of The Buddha

Being Happy Now

David Paul Boaz

Waterside Productions

Printed in the United States of America

First Printing, 2020

ISBN-13: 978-1-947637-53-5 print edition
ISBN-13: 978-1-947637-54-2 ebook edition

Waterside Productions
2055 Oxford Ave
Cardiff, CA 92007
www.waterside.com

For
Carol A. Hoy
Gendun Drolma
and for the
Happiness
of
All Beings

Table of Contents

Preface
Light from The County Jail

Notes from Students of David Paul Boaz

Dear Dr. Boaz,

"Your lecture 'The Good News About Suicidal Ideation' literally saved my life. I know now that God has given me a precious gift. I pray that I will figure out how to use it…"

"Thank you for your book and the meditation practices and inspired teaching I have received from you…You have helped me to free myself of serious obstructions to my thinking that for many years have caused me and my family great emotional pain."

"I wanted to let you know how your mindfulness of breathing meditation and the mantra prayer have helped me to get off psych meds and sleep better…(This) mantra of inner peace is in my mind day and night…I 'Let it be as it is'…Thank you for the Jesus picture."

Thank you for giving us the Buddhist Refuge. I am, per your request leading our meditation meetings every morning. I read aloud from your book. There are 18 of us practicing here in F4. F6, D2, and E4 have about the same…We bow to one another… We all have the Dalai Lama picture in our cells…We miss your humor, and the guided meditations…"

"Using your secular (I'm not into religion) mindfulness practice instructions I have actually learned to cultivate a peaceful, sometimes happy mind…My panic attacks and anger problems are a thing of the past (almost)…I am sharing your course with my family."

"Your humorous responses to my inane questions have allowed me to see that the 'prodigious drama of your life' should not be taken too seriously. You said, 'See it all as a divine comedy'... So 'I' am not the center of the universe after all. What a relief!"

"Thank you so much...You have taught me that Jesus and Buddha both came to earth to save us from the sin of ignoring our own *inner* Christ Nature...I know I am not an awful (person)...I am Presence of God!...This has forever changed my life for the better."

"The teaching you have given me is priceless, light and simple to apply in my life...My quiet mind presence is quickly found and the result is to me a very personal feeling of peace and gratitude for, as you often say 'the great gift of your life just as it is now'."

"If God forbids killing that means it's a sin to kill yourself...I tried it three times already...God gave me my life. So I can't take it away...I believe that (now)."

"The teaching of the Buddha that you have given us feels so familiar, as if it is a constant reminder of who I am...this Presence!...It's all so clear and obvious...Thank you!"

"Thank you for presenting your 'Awareness Management' strategy to our staff...We use your mindfulness handout with our patients in the PAC (Psychiatric Acute Care). The mindfulness practice has proven to be of considerable benefit for those with anxiety and sleep disorder, which are all too prevalent here... We very much appreciate your effort..."

Your mind training work with our PAC inmates has been exemplary...I appreciate your practical knowledge of General Psychiatry in a 'spiritual' context; not to mention your irreverent but not irrelevant humor...'Keep 'em laughing'...Thank you for your commitment to us...Thanks for the Jesus and Buddha photos, and all the books for our library."

"Joey---in PAC-1 is having a very bad day. Please see him on your rounds." —Chaplain

"I hope that your Tibetan is better than your Sanskrit! Let me help you with the latter... That said, your teaching has prepared me to take Refuge with the Tibetan Lama who visits here...You have helped me to understand that my intellectual arrogance is a rather nasty form of ignorance...Thank you for your guidance on this prickly path to wisdom."

"Your advice to see everyone as Buddha has helped me from being so insanely judgmental...Does that mean I am Buddha too?...Thank you for the awareness of all this..."

"After many years of (sleep disorder) I am sleeping normally thanks to the 'practice of the night' that you teach...I am willingly sharing it with others in the POD...Thank you..."

"After years of misery and hatred and mental breakdowns I have 'surrendered' as you call it, everything to my spiritual practice...It is the most valuable and important thing in my life...Your teaching has saved my life!...*OM AH HUM*...I want to meet *your* Lama..."

"I feel my connection to mother earth and the whole cosmos...I don't feel separate anymore...Strange peace...I practice bodhicitta for my fellow inmates...Ironic that I am given jail to meet you and change my life...In mantra prayer I feel my *Diné* roots...Everything is so bright...I feel your presence often, especially in *inipi.* I always will."

I am incredibly thankful for your introduction to me of the Buddha Presence that I am. It has changed everything for me... 'Who am I? That I Am!' You have taught me *that.*"

"My mantra prayer goes on almost by itself, without trying... Walking meditation has been my saving grace because I cannot sit for long without (anxiety)...I am peaceful for the first time in my life, even in the din of this hellish place...Someday I will teach this."

Your book and guided meditations are a Godsend! Thank you my *Kalyanamitta* for mirroring to me my own happiness, 'always already present in this very moment now'. So I stay present to it instead of suffering over something I can't control, which is just about everything...When I forget I come back to my mantra breath. It's everything I need."

"The light of your selfless Buddha mind makes my own teaching, such as it is, real…I remain present to the luminous mindstream of His Holiness, and of Lord Buddha through your kind, and not always so subtle wisdom counsel…I very much miss our talks and your guided meditation…You are always with me. *Lama Khyen, Lama Khyen.*"

Introduction
Being Happy Now

In these propitious but difficult times, a diverse array of intelligent people have become interested in the study and practice of Buddhism with its calming mindfulness meditation practices, and its selfless, kind, compassionate activity for the benefit of others.

What then is the teaching of the Buddha, and how may it help you to be authentically happy in your present busy life, not later, but right here and now?

My intention and my hope is that this little book will serve as an all too brief, practical, non-scholarly introduction to the profound and very practical teaching of the Buddha of this present age, Siddartha Gautama Shakyamuni the Buddha.

I pray that you, good Reader, will let it be an opening into recognition, then ultimate realization of the always already present *Presence* of your indwelling love-wisdom Buddha nature/ Buddha mind, by any name, that abides deep within your heart of hearts, and at the spiritual heart of each and every human being—without a single exception. That is the Buddha nature that you are now. And that is the Buddha's teaching for the ages.

Perhaps this is asking too much. So, at the very least, let this sublime teaching and practice reduce your stress, bring you peace of mind, and bestow patient loving acceptance of yourself, just as you are now, and through that, acceptance of others—especially those that you love.

This bright, selfless, indwelling love-wisdom mind Presence that you always already are is after all, the "innermost secret" teaching of all the Christ-buddhas, *mahasiddhas*, saints and sages of our great Primordial Wisdom Tradition; the open secret of both *relative* human happiness, and of *ultimate* liberation from suffering that is the fully awakened happiness that cannot be lost—Happiness Itself. Know now that your happiness is already present. It is That to which you awaken. Let it be so. How then shall we understand this great truth?

Who am I? All of the love-wisdom masters of the three times—past, present, future—have told it: *"That I Am"*, selfless innermost Presence of that vast boundless whole, non-conceptual, nondual primordial ground—by whatever name or concept—in which, or in whom this all arises and participates. We are all luminous instantiations of That!

How may you come to *directly* experience, feel, and know—beyond your concepts and beliefs *about* it—this profound Presence? That is the teaching of the Buddha that you shall herein engage, and understand—step by mindful step—via the growth of the practice of the your Path. Should your present practice be stalled, or nonexistent, that too is practice. Buddhist or not, all of your experience is love-wisdom practice. Buddha has some potent suggestions for you.

How do we know these truths? Who is it that knows? Ego? Wisdom mind? A profound, global understanding requires an open mind—Zen Mind, beginner's mind—mostly free of attachment to our limiting concepts, beliefs and biases; our not so comfortable cognitive comfort zones by which we have encaged our always present bright wisdom mind.

Buddha told it well: upon the mindful breath, relax into, then rest in your love-wisdom mind Presence—"brief moments, many times", day and night. Your direct, basic love-wisdom practice with its instant mantra prayer touchstone, makes it so. You can do it!

There is wisdom in these pages for those merely curious about the teaching of the Buddha; and as well, for Buddhist, and non-Buddhist practitioners of all stripes and levels who may have already established their own quiescent mindfulness practice, or other practices, yet feel a need to more deeply engage the Buddha's subtle wisdom mindstream.

Therefore, we shall explore the subtle many dimensional teaching of the View, the Meditation/Path, and the Action/Conduct—Buddhist philosophy and ethics—of the three Buddhist teaching vehicles, including *Dzogchen* and Essence *Mahamudra*, the subtlest and "highest" pinnacles of the teaching of the Buddha.

We shall engage Buddhist wisdom and practice on both an objective conceptual level, and a subjective non-conceptual, even nondual (subject/object unity) directly experiential strata of knowing—far above and beyond our dualistic Greek materialist deep cultural background "global web of belief" that has now colonized the Western mind. This destructive world view often harms our love for living beings, including our Mother Earth. There is little lasting happiness here.

Herein we shall experience our two human wisdom voices, objective and subjective—this noetic cognitive doublet—unified at once in a singlet peaceful, blissful mind state. It's not so difficult, as obsessive thinking mind begins to surrender to innermost wisdom mind.

We shall indeed learn to tame and train this anxious and angry, often destructive "wild horse of the mind" by awakening our already present deep inner peace—bright Presence of That—through Buddha's "mindfulness of breathing", beyond, yet embracing our mere thinking mind. It is this very practice that resulted in Buddha's own awakening so long ago. It is this very Presence that bestows the freedom that *chooses* to respond to the inevitable adversity of the world, not with fear and anger, but with patience and grace.

Thus shall we learn to connect to, then skillfully utilize our innate, indwelling love-wisdom mind, our "supreme identity" with that vast primordial whole in whom it arises. And all of this toward the compassionate thought, intention, and action to benefit living beings. It is this altruistic practice of compassionate, engaged "*bodhicitta*" that is, on the accord of the teaching of all the buddhas, the primary cause of our own human happiness.

Why is this difficult? Fearful self-ego-I gets in the way. So Buddha taught a simple, practical no-self help remedy—not to denigrate, deny, nor transcend ego-I—but to skillfully merge self into selfless wisdom mind, like a mother protects her child. It is after all, our intelligent, courageous self who *chooses* to establish the practice that reflexively awakens itself into its own love-wisdom mind Presence. Self/no-self are a prior, already present wisdom unity.

Thus it is, we learn to *connect* to our selfless, peaceful, bias-free Zen mind/wisdom mind in order to suspend or "bracket" our habitual attachment to that skeptical, often misleading sociocultural global web of concept and belief that would derail our wisdom practice experience.

So now, with your empty, quiescent Zen mind at the ready, and your biases and preconceptions wisely placed in abeyance, let us begin to lift this dark cloud of unknowing that mortal flesh is heir to, and open to receive the teaching of the Buddha, that it may bestow abundant happiness, and the causes of happiness, for each one of us, each moment now.

The Buddhist View of Human Happiness: The Four Noble Truths

For no light matter is at stake. The question concerns
the very way that human life is to be lived.
> —Plato, The Republic, Book I

The Buddha's primary concern was not philosophy, but peaceful, mindful practice and ethical discipline. He offered, to those with eyes to see and ears to hear, a logical, pragmatic and powerful no-self help remedy for the primary problem of human existence—the omnipresent problem of the suffering of living beings. What is this teaching? What is this fundamental Buddhist *logos, ethos,* and *mythos* that was to be the foundation of 25 centuries of Buddhist wisdom? From the early 1st century *Pali Canon,* the clear words of Gautama the Buddha:

> Do no harm.
> Practice what is skillful
> in benefiting beings.
> Purify your mind.
> That is my teaching.

These 17 words express the entire teaching of the Buddha.

In the Buddha's Four Noble Truths we have an impeccable unbroken linage of transmission of this boundless teaching—philosophical, moral, and contemplative—from the Buddha to all of us, here and now.

So, let us now both conceptually, and non-conceptually unpack the profound meaning of this bountiful teaching; and what to do with our lives in order to accomplish it.

Siddartha Gautama Shakyamuni the Buddha told that the open secret of freedom from suffering (*dhukha*, Tib. *dukkha*) and the causes of suffering, lies in his foundational *Four Noble Truths*—the Four Truths for one who would be noble of body, mind, and spirit. These four great truths pervade all three of the Buddha's teaching vehicles, and their various schools. Again, the luminous speech of the Buddha:

> Why do I not teach the nature of cosmos, and of self? Because this is not fundamental to awakening. What *is* taught by me?...It is only suffering and its cessation that I teach...There is suffering; there is the origin of suffering; there is the end of suffering; there is the path that causes the end of suffering...Why do I teach these four? Because this is the cause of awakening (*Majjhima Nikaya 65*).

Translation Note: I feel that "awakening" translates "*bodhi*" more clearly than "enlightenment" which is too easily conflated with the idealized and valorized Cartesian *cogito* "thinking I" of the 17th-19th century European Enlightenment—The Age of Reason.

Yes. This great teaching is the cause of awakening to who it is that we actually are, our always already present "supreme identity", bright Presence of That, prior to our thoughts, concepts and beliefs *about* it. This awaking does not require academic philosophy, nor science, nor cosmology, nor psychology, nor even heady Buddhist dialectics to liberate us from suffering, so that we may recognize, then realize our indwelling now present Buddha nature/Buddha mind.

Well then, what shall we do with this precious gift of the mind? From the *Diamond Sutra* (*Vajrachedika Prajnaparamita Sutra, 1900 Dunhuang manuscripts*):

The mind should remain independent of any thoughts that arise within it...The bodhisattva must develop a pure, lucid mind that does not depend upon any thought or sensory experience that arises within it...a mind that alights nowhere.

For humanity's Primordial Wisdom Tradition this luminous, numinous primordial Presence of the boundless whole that abides deep within us has many names. In the Third Turning of the Wheel of Dharma (*dharmachakra*) the Buddha referred to this always present Presence as Buddha nature (*tathagatagarbha*)—our innermost love-wisdom *bodhi* mind that is utterly indivisible from the vast awareness-consciousness all-embracing whole itself in whom this all arises and participates. It is always already present in all human beings, in all sentient beings, and indeed, for most of the Buddhist Mahayana, in all appearing phenomena, living or inanimate. As the Buddha told, "Wonder of wonders, all beings are Buddha". Holistic view indeed. It's all Buddha!

Hence, *bodhi* mind cannot be "attained" through the prodigious seeking strategies of self-ego-I. Rather, we awaken to it, step by mindful step, through assiduous engagement with the *two voices of wisdom*—this noetic doublet that is: 1) exoteric, physical, objective, thinking mind; and 2) esoteric, subjective, non-conceptual, direct contemplative experience (*yogi pratyaksa*). These two voices comprise the practice of Buddha's *relative* Path to the *ultimate* awakening that is Happiness Itself. "The only way to ultimate happiness is through the relative Path. Practice these two as a unity" (Guru Rinpoche, Padmasambhava).

It is this subtle clear light knowing, feeling awareness unity of our innate Buddha mind—bright Presence of That—that makes these Four Noble Truths so fundamental, and so urgent to authentic human happiness. How shall we understand this?

Human Happiness. All human beings aspire to happiness, and desire to avoid suffering and unhappiness. H.H. Dalai Lama

(2007) told, "From the time that human life began until the present day every single human being has wished only to be happy and to escape suffering". Might we consider this factoid a rare universal categorical truth regarding our *humanität*, our shared human nature? Moreover, this omnipresent universal human desire for the avoidance of suffering, and the experience of happiness admits of no empirical scientific, nor mathematical, nor deductive logical proof. How is this so?

Definitive "scientific proof", if it can be said to exist at all, is confined to the realm of relative conventional truth—Suzuki Roshi's "Small Mind". It has, *ipso facto*, no *definitive* meaning in the awakened post-empirical mind of nondual Ultimate Truth— Roshi's "Big Mind that includes everything within itself". For those who enter in and abide here, there is considerably less concern for the conventional, biased concept and belief of the "Small Mind" dimension of relative-conventional truth (*Ch. VI*, "The Fundamental Two Truths").

Yet, we still show up for work; take out the trash, and be kind to living beings.

However, as human beings with a foot in each of these worlds, the wise will diligently inquire into the *ultimate* nature of this earthly dimensional mansion of spacetime Relative Truth for it determines the happiness of our very being here as embodied living beings.

We human beings wish to know of our origin, our identity, and our destiny. It is through such relative being in time that we may *choose* to enter in diaphanous world of perfectly subjective "supreme source" of this wondrous whole shebang. Perhaps it is here that we shall discover the path to our ultimate "supreme identity"—and the prior unity of these two dimensional realms— spacetime Relative Truth, and Ultimate Truth that transcends yet embraces it.

As to the domain of mostly conceptual Relative Truth, our prevailing cultural metaphysic in the West, this is our much valorized *lebenswelt*, or "form of life" (Wittgenstein), to wit, prosaic Scientific Materialism/Physicalism. Indeed, even in the physical and conceptual dimension of astoundingly quantifiable scientific truth, there abides a perpetual uncertainty. The metaphysical abstractions that comprise the various memes of Science provide no absolute certainty. Even formal mathematical logic, that presumed exemplar of absolute objective certainty, is riddled with intrinsically vexing conceptually unsolvable logical paradoxes. Conceptual uncertainty is the norm; and indeed, the rule. That conceptual uncertainty pervades the hitherto logical certainty of the axioms of mathematics and of formal logic is now well recognized by its practitioners, and by philosophers of physics and mathematics.

If I may be permitted one more "rare universal categorical truth" in this our spacetime domain of relative conventional cognition: all scientific theories, even the great paradigmatic scientific truths—Newtonian Mechanics, Special and General Relativity Theory, Quantum Theory—are inherently uncertain and incomplete (Heisenberg's Uncertainty/Incompleteness Principle), apprehensively awaiting that next more inclusive theory; and with a bit of luck, and by grace, an exciting, yet still incomplete new knowledge paradigm (Thomas Kuhn, *The Structure of Scientific Revolutions*, 1962).

Justly famous for his two Incompleteness Theorems (1931), mathematician/logician Kurt Gödel demonstrated that no consistent logical or mathematical axiomatic system is capable of proving its own logical consistency! All relative conventional theory/belief necessarily refers beyond itself to other "higher" interdependent variables in the vast causal matrix of this "boundless implicate order of the whole" (David Bohm). Our centuries old quest to discover a singular complete and logically consistent set of axioms for all mathematical systems has been shown to be but a pipe dream. (Boaz 2021b, excerpt "Post-Quantum Logic" davidpaulboaz.org)

Thus have the inherent limits of logic, along with philosophy of science and philosophy of mathematics, if not always our common sense folk wisdom, revealed that even the empirical truths of science—physical, biological, and social—and even the axiomatic truths of formal logic and mathematics can never be more than provisional and uncertain relative conventional truths. It seems that our atavistic grail quest for absolute *objective* certainty is forever *kaput*! The resulting good news: we perforce enter in new realms of consciousness where anything is possible, even post-empirical, contemplative perfect certainty, as we shall come to see in these pages.

Therefore, if we wish to proceed with our quest for certainty it will require an adventure into the post-empirical, trans-objective, *subjective* "many mansions" of our human consciousness as we arise and participate as luminous conscious instantiations of this vast all embracing whole that is primordial awareness-consciousness itself. Indeed, that adventure shall be our program for this little book.

Be that as it may, happiness is that end in itself toward which the desire and activity—unconscious, preconscious, conscious and supra-conscious—of our human lives evolve. So, happiness is both origin and aim of human action. The joyous unfolding of this unquantifiable, immeasurable primordially enfolded process is the natural, often ironic dialectic of the human condition. We live in these two worlds at once! Discovering our individual and collective clarity and balance is the conscious and unconscious intention of this inherently happy process.

> Where got I that truth?
> Out of the medium's mouth,
> Out of nothing it came,
> Out of the forest loam,
> Out of dark night where lay
> The crowns of Nineveh.
> —W.B. Yeats, from *Fragments*

The Causes of Happiness and the Causes of Suffering. On the accord of the Buddha, both human happiness and human suffering result from a vast interdependent causal matrix of prior causes and conditions. This karmic relationship of thoughts, intentions and actions is described by the Buddha as "dependent arising" (*pratitya samutpada*). This seminal principle is the Buddha's Middle Way between the epistemic extremes of strict causal Laplacian determinism, wherein human free will is precluded, and a flaky random acausal indeterminism. Buddha's view of causality allows for enough free will to choose to enter in, and practice the Path. The Buddha speaks on the causal logic of the interdependent arising of form from its primordial base (*gzhi*) or *dharmakaya* ground:

> This being, that becomes. From the arising of this, that arises. This not being, that does not become. From the ceasing of this, that ceases (*Majjhima Nikaya* II, 32).

There are causes that result in human suffering; and causes that result in human happiness; cause and effect—in a word, karma. We shall see that most of these are very much within our control. We shall herein learn how to manage them, and as well, how to handle the natural adversity of being here in time and form that is not within our control.

We human beings may *choose* what causes of action to approach, and what causes to avoid. Choosing the causes that promote suffering of self and others arise from ignorance (*avidya, ma rigpa*) of the causes that promote authentic happiness.

Actions that "skillfully benefit" living beings are the principle causes of human happiness. Such is the "mind of enlightenment" or *bodhicitta*—selfless altruistic thought, intention, and action for the benefit of living beings. Actions that "harm" beings arise from serving only the self-ego-I and are the principle causes of our suffering. To understand and accomplish this primordial teaching requires the "skillful practice" of the Path that "purifies" the mind of such ignorance, delusion, and false views. The Buddha's prodigious Four Noble Truths offer the diagnosis, and the cure for human suffering, as we shall soon see.

Ignorance or *avidya* then, is the root afflictive condition to be diagnosed, so that its cause may be removed, thus effecting the cure. Cessation of suffering, opening into both *relative* conventional happiness, and liberating *ultimate* happiness, is the promised result.

Still, many diseases are quite insidious. We must diagnose the illness before we can effect the cure. And then we must have confidence that the cure is not worse than the disease. Uncertainty and doubt precede the relief and release that is the confident certainty that arises from effecting the cure.

So, while it's true that life's adversity is all too natural and real, we must understand that our *choices* of skillful response to inexorable adversity largely determine the extent of our suffering. We shall see that it is not adversity per se that is the problem. Rather, it is our habitual *reaction* to adversity—fear and anger—that is the common cause of suffering. We shall see that these afflictive emotions are within our control far more than we might presently believe.

Now, each of The Four Noble Truths implies an imperative. To accomplish the cessation of suffering we must understand the causes of suffering; these causes must be surrendered; and the Path—the cure must be engaged—all the way to the end of it.

The causes of our *individual* suffering—painful anxiety, anger, ill will, impatience, hostile biased judgementalism toward self and others, egocentric narcissism, emotional disconnects with others, and general dissatisfaction with our present lifeworld—become the causes of our *collective* suffering, namely, bigoted parochial hostility toward out-groups, human alienation, despotism, and war. Human suffering is not a pretty picture. Wonder of wonders, its resolution is already present within us, as we saw in our *Introduction*.

Students of human behavior now understand that these causes of our individual and collective suffering are not "normal" necessary genetic, epigenetic, nor psychologically fixed set points (Begley 2007). Human alienation and evil is not a foregone conclusion!

These causes of our suffering are rather an adventitious emotional cage from which we may *choose* to free ourselves. How? By settling this obsessively busy, mostly negative narcissistic "wild horse of the mind" into the quiescent peace of our already present indwelling Buddha mind. Random, non-directed conceptual thinking is loaded with negative destructive emotions—*Aversion*: fear, anger, hatred, and *Attachment*: furious sense desire, greed, and egocentric pride.

Thus do we train the mind through "mindfulness of breathing" and mantra prayer in placement of attention/awareness upon "instant presence" (*vidya, rigpa*) of our already present peaceful, compassionate Buddha mind (*buddhajnana*). This then is the Buddha's meaning of "purify your mind" in the quotation on page three above.

Therefore, if we are to effect the cure for human suffering, we must recognize that we, along with so many others, are suffering unnatural, avoidable unhappiness. If this were not the truth of the matter the Buddha's great teaching of the Four Noble Truths with its Path to freedom and happiness will seem cynical and pessimistic indeed.

The more profoundly we understand the nature and the causes of our suffering, the deeper our commitment to its cessation. The more awareness we bring to the causes of our suffering—our ego defense mechanisms, these subtle, mostly unconscious strategies of self-ego-I aggrandizement and self imprisonment—the more readily we awaken to our already present indwelling happiness.

Therefore, happiness is already the case! As we awaken to it through mindful contemplative practice, expressed in action as altruistic "loving-kindness" or *bodhicitta*, we—as loving bodhisattvas (we Buddhas in training)—learn to be gentle and kind to our prodigal self-ego-I; like the love of the mother for her child. Practicing loving-kindness for oneself is a cause for doing so for others. This skill set requires purifying and pacifying the "wild horse of the mind". In the noble words of the Buddha:

> Neither abide with the purity of the cause of affliction, nor with the purity of the cause of purification...The view of 'I' and 'mine' is a cause of affliction. Inner pacification and outer stillness is a cause of purification (Sutra of The Ornament of Light Awareness, 1.72).

Thus it is, we purify the troubled mind—self-ego-I—of emotional affliction, not by dwelling on "Why am I like this", or "What causes me to be so impatient", but by taming the chattering, obsessive concept mind through the very "cause of purification", namely, the "inner pacification" that is quiescent abiding in the clear light awareness of our primordial wisdom mind. Then, in "outer stillness" may we gently, skillfully and selflessly act to benefit living beings.

A Very Brief History of the Teaching of the Buddha. Buddha is often seen as the great physician who's prescription for liberation from suffering causes the actual cessation of suffering that opens into both relative and ultimate human happiness. Step by mindful step. This view of the Four Noble Truths is shared by all three extant Buddhist teaching vehicles—Hinayana/Theravada, Mahayana, and Tibetan Vajrayana. (Nyingma, Kagyu, Gelug, and Sakya schools constitute the Tibetan Vajrayana teaching vehicle.)

Just so, the view that non-recognition of the Four Noble Truths is ignorance (*avidya*), or delusion (*moha*) that is the root cause of human suffering, is also shared by all three Buddhist wisdom vehicles.

The *Three Turnings of the Wheel* (the *dharmachakra*) of the buddhadharma map nicely onto these Three Buddhist teaching vehicles.

The first scriptural reference to the Three Turnings is usually considered to be the *Dharmachakra parvartana*, "Setting the Wheel of the Dharma in Motion". The Yogachara *Samdhi Nirmocana Sutra* elaborates all three turnings in accordance with the "Mind Only" (*chittamatra*) view. (*Ch. V*).

Thus did Gautama the Buddha, and indeed all buddhas, express their supreme love for all living beings—without exception—through their desire that all beings, and especially human beings, be free of the suffering that inexorably arises from ignorance (*avidya, ma rigpa*) of the impermanent and interdependent way that appearing reality actually is. So things are not as they appear. What to do?

In Siddhartha Gautama the Buddha's first teaching, the *First Turning of the Wheel* of Dharma at the Deer Park in Sarnath, seven weeks following his full *bodhi* awakening at Bodh Gaya in Northern India, he taught the Four Noble Truths. He was 31 years old.

There is little scholarly agreement as to the Buddha's actual dates, but we often see the older "Corrected Long Chronology" of c. 563-483 BCE. Modern scholars prefer c. 480-400 BCE. There is general agreement that he lived in embodied form for 80 years.

In the First Turning of the Wheel Buddha presents not only the Four Noble Truths. He also presents his foundational Middle Way view of the Buddhist Path. As to ethics and the practice of the Path, the Middle Way avoids the extremes of asceticism and indulgence. Metaphysically, the Middle Way avoids the ontic extremes of materialist physicalism/eternalism, and idealist nihilism. The Four Noble Truths, and the Madhyamaka Middle Way. An auspicious beginning!

In the *Second Turning of the Wheel,* at Vulture Peak Mountain in Rajagriha, Buddha presented his *Prajnaparamita Heart of Wisdom Sutra* teaching of emptiness, the Two Truths—emptiness and form—and on the compassion that spontaneously arises from this noble unified understanding.

This Second Turning occurred about 500 years after the First Turning, so the Buddha was not present in his physically embodied form. Rather, he appeared as a "Kosmic" Buddha whose lucent teaching was transmitted to the great Bodhisattva

Mahasattva Avalokiteshvara, who then instantly transmitted it to the retinue of bodhisattvas, monks, and nuns who were present.

In this Second turning The Buddha teaches that the Path is much more than the personal liberation of the noble Shravakayana *Arhat.* Indeed, the Path is nothing less than the liberation from samsaric suffering of all living beings! That gracious calling is now known as the Mahayana Bodhisattva Ideal of altruistic *bodhicitta,* the heart-mind of compassion (*karuna*).

Bodhicitta, the heart of Buddhist ethics, is the unity of the wisdom of emptiness and selfless compassion—the two limbs of the entire buddhadharma—heart of the Mahayana vehicle. *Bodhicitta* may be understood as the thought, intention, and action for the relative and ultimate benefit of all living beings, including our precious Mother Earth. And that is the secret of our own happiness. *Bodhicitta* is the skillful means (*upaya*) of the Great Compassion (*Mahakaruna*).

And how is it that we arouse and generate *bodhicitta?* By observing, then deeply *feeling* the omnipresent suffering of living beings. We are all together interdependently connected. The terrible physical and mental suffering of others, if we open our hearts and *feel* it, compassion will spontaneously arise in our mindstream. Then we must find skillful and practical means to help. And that begins with "purifying" our own minds of the "afflictive" emotions of fear/anger, obsessive sensory desire, greed and egocentric pride.

We have thus far witnessed the evolution of Buddhism from the early Hinayana or Shravakayana vehicle to the Mahayana teaching vehicle (*Ch. VII*).

The Second Turning seems to represent a turning away from the clear conceptual logic of the First Turning, namely, the Four Noble Truths, and the Middle Way. This spooky nondual teaching of the *Heart of Wisdom Sutra* with its utterly non-conceptual emptiness of all conceptual entities seems to negate the existence of the Buddha's teaching of the First Turning of the Wheel.

We must utilize both of our given human cognitive modalities—exoteric objective, conceptual; and esoteric, subjective, contemplative. The First Turning gives us an *objective* Path to freedom from the ignorance that is the cause of suffering. The Second Turning apparently negates that noble Path via the *subjectivity* of the wisdom of emptiness (*shunyata*). Can the Third Turning affirm this trans-conceptual, nondual negation of the hitherto objective Path of the First Turning, and still offer a cogent soteriology (liberation/salvation)?

In other words, the First Turning gives us the Relative Truth causal conceptual logic of liberation. The teaching really exists here in relative time and space. If it did not exist, why bother to practice it? We need a payoff, do we not? Then the Second Turning altogether negates this pragmatic use of relative conceptual logic. It seems to negate Buddha's First Turning teaching of the Four Noble Truths, and the Middle Way Path to liberation from suffering. Here, all concepts, including concepts *about* Buddhist teachings, are utterly absent and empty of inherent existence! From the wise and scary *Prajnaparamita Heart of Wisdom Sutra*:

> There is no impurity, and no purity...
> no ignorance, no end of ignorance...
> no suffering, no origin of suffering,
> no cessation of suffering,
> no path, no wisdom, no attainment,
> and no non-attainment.

Can the Third Turning of the Wheel of Dharma offer a pragmatic Ultimate Truth "logic of the non-conceptual" that restores the *objective* skillful practice of the Buddha's Path to awakening?

It's useful here to recall that Buddha's dharma teaching differs in accordance with the need and capacity of the student located in sociocultural space and time. Outer, common sense folks have always required a logical, objective teaching. Those who have begun to realize that phenomenal reality, and the self-ego-I that apprehends it, is not at all as it appears require a subtler, trans-conceptual teaching. Committed practitioners of the Path—bodhisattvas—have developed a capacity for nondual understanding, and the innermost Presence of the primordial ground, boundless whole in whom this all arises. Such a one is able to receive direct mind to mind *buddic* transmission (*yogi pratyaksa*) from a buddha, or meditation master.

Our human cognition inherently includes the entire consciousness processional of: 1) pre-conscious direct perception; 2) objective conceptual cognition; 3) subjective contemplative-meditative cognition; and 4) perfectly subjective nondual (subject-object unity) cognition. That is our human potential. That great multidimensional potential is not exhausted by mere conceptual cognition, nor even by crowning intellectual virtuosity.

In the *Third Turning of the Dharma Wheel* Buddha's teaching of the first and second turnings are finally and completely unified. Here, the Two Truths, relative and ultimate, conceptual and nondual, syncretically bring together that which has been torn asunder by adventitious ignorance (*avidya, marigpa, ajnana*) of the way that reality actually is as a prior unity of all four of our human cognitive dimensions. The Buddha referred to such an understanding as Buddha wisdom mind (*buddhajnana*). Bright *buddic* Presence of That.

The human mind cannot understand, and the Heart cannot realize the nondual Ultimate Truth that is the intrinsic emptiness of our appearing spacetime realities, before being relatively, conceptually clear on just how and why it is that these realities exist. We need the first two turnings to bestow understanding that things are not as they appear, and how this is so. Then we can selflessly, deeply understand the Buddha's subtle nondual teaching of the Two Truths in his *Heart of Wisdom Sutra* of the Second Turning:

> Form is empty, emptiness is form.
> Form is not other than emptiness.
> Emptiness is not other than form.

Form really exists, relatively, conventionally. Only a fool would deny this truth of form. But form is utterly absent and empty of any whit of inherent absolute or ultimate existence. We need our *relative* conceptual mind to constantly remind us of this great truth of the *ultimate* nonexistence of form. Thus is our practice of the Buddha's path established in a conscious choice to enter in to it.

Now we are prepared to open the mind and the heart to receive the non-conceptual Ultimate Truth of Buddha's Path to awakening that is indwelling, "innermost secret" Presence of our always present Buddha nature/Buddha mind—the very nature of mind, by whatever name.

Thus, in the Third Turning of the Wheel we encounter the wondrous teaching of Buddha nature (*tathagatagarbha*)—that human beings are intrinsically endowed with all-pervading innermost wisdom *bodhi* mind (*buddhajnana*), our deep, subtle, always present love-wisdom mind Presence that is nothing less than our "supreme identity"; who it is that we actually are. We connect to That through mindful mantra practice.

But more than that; all living beings, and all spacetime form—mountains, rivers, trees, people, stars—are instantiations of that basal primordial Buddha essence. It's not that we and all of this arising stuff *have* Buddha nature. Rather, this all already *is* Buddha nature, prior to our thinking and beliefs *about* it. And there is a living Presence of That that always already abides at the human "spiritual" Heartmind (*hridyam*). Thus it is, that all-embracing Presence is the inherent *ultimate* Buddha nature of mind, and everything experienced through *relative* conventional mind—direct attention/perception, and obsessively thinking self-ego-I. That is the Buddha's teaching for the ages. Indeed, that is the essential nondual teaching of all the great masters of all our wisdom traditions who have incarnated in time to lighten the suffering of human beings. But don't *believe* this. As Buddha told, "Come and see".

We've seen that one of the earliest sutra sources for the Three Turnings of the Wheel is the foundational sutra of the Yogachara/ Mind Only Middle Way Madhyamaka school, namely, the *Samdhi Nirmocana Sutra*, which holds that the *Three Natures*, 1) relative imputed, 2) relative dependent, and 3) perfect/ultimate; with the Mind Only doctrine, and the *alaya vijnana* or storehouse consciousness altogether explain the Buddha's Two Truths (*Ch. V*).

Moreover, the Vajrayana considers the Tibetan tantras to be included in the Third Turning of the Wheel of Dharma—or else a Fourth Turning of the Wheel. For some Nyingma School Lamas the *Dzogchen* tantras are included in the Third Turning; or even constitute a Fourth Turning.

Other Buddhist Mahayana schools—Japanese *Sanron* Madhyamaka, Chinese and Japanese Pure Land School, Chinese *T'ien-T'ai* Lotus School (*Tendai* in Japan), and others—all have their own similar versions of the Buddha's Three Turnings.

It seems the Buddha's *dharmachakra* depends, from the view of Relative Truth, upon the conceptual view of the dharma eye of the beholder. From the nondual view of Ultimate Truth the Three Turnings of the Dharma Wheel may be seen as a prior and always present trans-conceptual, nondual ultimate unity of all the Buddhist schools of the three teaching vehicles (Buddha bodies/*yanas*).

Thus it is, Buddha's teaching in his *dharmachakra* has integrated our non-conceptual, even nondual cognition with our dualistic thinking mind. We have seen how it is that this unified noetic (body, mind, spirit unity) doublet abides as our aphoristic "two voices of wisdom": 1) objective, conceptual/intellectual experience; and 2) subjective, trans-conceptual, direct contemplative, even nonlocal, nondual experience.

This concludes our brief wisdom survey of the Three Turnings of the Wheel of Dharma.

For 45 years Buddha taught his profound and subtle dharma teaching to thousands of followers, both lay and monastic, both men and women, throughout Northern India.

We've seen that, as with all great avatars, Buddha taught love-wisdom in "many ways at once". For the masses and those of lesser capacity he taught in exoteric parable and metaphor. For yogi and yogini disciples of middling capacity he taught esoteric contemplative relative discriminating wisdom (*prajna*); and for disciples of superior capacity the Buddha taught not only conceptually and contemplatively, but by direct *Dzogchen*-like mind to mind transmission of nondual primordial wisdom (*jnana, yeshe, gnosis*). *(Dzogchen, Ch. VIII)*.

In the *Lankavatara Sutra* Buddha told, "To help beings I teach in many different ways". Good to remember when considering "contradictions" in the great Sage's teaching; for example his seemingly differing views on self/*atman* and no-self/*anatman*.

Thus does the *buddhadharma* transcend yet embrace the dualistic mind of self-ego-I. These Two Truths of relative understanding and ultimate wisdom are always an ontic prior, yet epistemic present inseparable unity (*"The Two Truths", Ch. VI*).

Buddha's teaching arose in the Northern Indian country of Magadha whose capitol was Rajagriha. Siddartha Gautama (his family name) spoke and taught in the local language of *Magadhi*, a dialect of *Sanskrit*. As a Shakya Clan Prince he would also have known *Sanskrit*, the 3500 year old precise and beautiful Indo-Aryan liturgical language of the Indian intelligentsia—the *brahmins*, and *panditas*.

This early foundational teaching that constitutes the Three Turnings of the Wheel of Dharma was transmitted orally by monks and nuns in the Indo-Aryan *prakrit* languages, which includes Buddha's *Magadhi* language. His teaching was first chronicled in *Pali* language texts, then Chinese, and then Tibetan texts.

The *Pali Canon* was recorded in the 1st century BCE in Ceylon (Sri Lanka), and from it the Buddhist Theravada textual tradition arose. Until the decline of Buddhism in India, whose presence ended in the 12th century, Sanskrit was the primary textual tradition in India. Many Mahayana Sutras were translated from Sanskrit into the Chinese and Tibetan Canons (*Taisho and Kangyur Canons* respectively). Some are now extant only in the Chinese translations.

From the 3rd century BCE *Pali Canon* Shravakayana (Hinayana) teaching spread from India and Ceylon (Sri Lanka) to Thailand, Burma (Myanmar) and Cambodia where it is now extant as Theravada Buddhism. Buddhist Mahayana entered China in the 1st century CE, then Japan, Vietnam, Korea, and in the 8th century, Tibet and the Himalayan Kingdoms of Bhutan, Nepal, and Sikkim. Mahayana arrived in Western Europe, then the United States in mid-19th century.

Therefore, to lead human beings to the happiness inherent in awakening to the wisdom of emptiness and compassion that is the interdependent unity of the Buddhist Two Truths (*Ch. VI*)—relative form and ultimate emptiness—Buddha's great gift to us arises as the Four Noble Truths: The Truth of Suffering; The Truth of the Cause of Suffering; The Truth of the Cessation of Suffering; and The Truth of the Eightfold Path that results in the cessation of suffering.

Let us now all to briefly engage the great Hinayana vehicle teaching of Gautama Shakumuni our historical *nirmanakaya* Buddha; the core teaching that is the very foundation of all that was to come.

The Truth of Suffering

Life is filled with suffering (*duhkha, Skt.; dukkha, Tib.*). Suffering is one of the Buddha's "three marks of conditioned existence" (*trilakshana*): impermanence (*anitya*), and egolessness (*anatman*) being the other two. Everything that arises that is not the full *bodhi* of liberation from suffering, is a cause of suffering. The Five Aggregates (*skandhas*) of relative existence—physical form,

Sensation-feeling, perception, mental formations, and personal consciousness (the six consciousnesses). All are all causes of suffering. "Birth, aging, sickness, dying, care, distress, affliction, despair, unfulfilled needs and desires; all of this is suffering". For we humans living in relative time suffering has three faces.

1) There is the "suffering of suffering"; the general dissatisfaction and uncertainty of life, physical and emotional pain; birth, sickness, old age and death. All that is born will die. We will lose everything that we love. And in between the endless cycles of birth and death awaits the slings and arrows of outrageous *samsara* that mortal flesh is heir to. In this brief *bardo* of life we don't get much of what we want. And we get way too much of what we don't want. It seems that life's porridge is always either too hot or too cold; never just right.

2) Then there is "the suffering of change" that results from fear/anxiety of our impermanence (*anitya*) and mortality in the face of continuous change/time. We and all that we love arises in emptiness, abides there for a brief time, and returns again to emptiness leaving, in Buddha's words, only "sorrow, lamentation, pain, grief and despair". What is initially pleasurable, even joyous, in due course changes into dissatisfaction and pain. Passion becomes aggression. Beauty fades. Beauty, goodness and truth become their opposites. Human suffering is indeed, not a pretty picture.

3) Finally, Buddha recognized the subtle "all pervasive suffering" of conditional existence that arises from the anxious, fearful uncertainty of the inherent impermanence (*anitya*) of all beings, and the things that we love; self and other, the things to which we attach, and to which we cling—all of the things that make us happy.

All-pervasive suffering is the fundamental fear that exists whether we're feeling happy or down. All of our feelings are pervaded by this fundamental fear, which is why it is called all pervasive suffering. But what is this fear? It is the fear of losing something that is very dear and beloved, something to which you have become attached. It is also the fear of gaining something that is unpleasant, that you don't want.

—Dzogchen Ponlop Rinpoche (*Buddhadharma Quarterly*; Spring, 2005)

A Brief Note On All-Pervasive Quantum Impermanence. The Buddhas, and quantum cosmologists agree, in the fullness of time all physical and mental forms shall pass away into the Great Emptiness, *Mahashunyata*; then arise again in a never ending cycle of countless, timeless eons. Physical and mental form arising from the vast primordial whole (*dharmadhatu*) of its emptiness/*shunyata* ground is inherently impermanent (*anitya*)—utterly absent and empty of permanent immutable existence.

Human and other beings upon the earth shall pass. Our precious Mother Earth shall pass. Our solar system and our home galaxy, the Milky Way shall, in due course, merge cataclysmically with our sister galaxy Andromeda. Many solar systems will perish. The great galaxy cluster in which this new galaxy abides shall in due course pass away. The physical and mental universe itself, and indeed all of the universes of the endless, infinite cyclic multiverse shall all expand into quantum emptiness and quite naturally cease to exist as matter-energy entropy thermodynamically peters out at absolute zero in the proverbial "Big Chill". All energy-motion is now *kaput*! Understanding that dark truth, there is nothing solid in heaven nor in earth to which we may cling. That is quantum *Kosmic* suffering writ large!

But wait! The buddhas and recent quantum cosmology have both told that from the emptiness of the vast expanse of space, and the zero motion of seemingly random non-physical "zero point energy" (ZPE) quantum vacuum field fluctuations—similar to "space particles" of Buddhist *Abidharma*—spontaneously arise proto-matter as new form. Hope springs eternal!

What does "quantum zero point energy" mean? The total energy density of this universe equals zero because the total mass of the universe is positively charged; and the total gravity of the universe is negatively charged. The positive charged mass exactly cancels the negative charged gravity, equaling zero. Therefore, the total universe energy density is zero. Sounds almost mystical; a conclusion resisted by both Buddhism and physics.

This endless process of the arising of physical form from its primordial quantum/*buddic* emptiness zero ground state is a continuity (the meaning of tantra) of infinite gravitational attraction and repulsion. Great gravity is thus, in the gloss of the Hindu *Bhagavad Gita*, the awful "creator and destroyer of worlds".

According to quantum pioneer Werner Heisenberg's Principle of Uncertainty, all matter particle fields, and every point in space undergoes random quantum fluctuations, even in its zero point energy "ground state". Sooner or later new matter/mass will fluctuate into existence. There is an eternity in which this may happen.

Einstein's equivalence of mass and energy, described by his Special Relativity equation $E = mc^2$, means that any zero point in space that has this quantum energy potential has mass. So, every point in space has potential mass to spontaneously give rise to quantum fluctuations of new "virtual particles" of physical form.

Thus, there is virtual motion/form inherent even in zero point emptiness; even at the zero atomic/molecular motion of absolute zero, at the end of time when all matter has finally lost its motion to the vacuum of nearly empty space. The properties of this newly arising matter-mass then, are nothing but quasi-empty vacuum random quantum fluctuations of the zero point energy field. In physics it is assumed that there can be no "perfectly empty vacuum". Empty space is not perfectly empty.

"Virtual particles" enter and exit spacetime existence continuously. Quantum Field Theory (QFT) predicts them, and their effects are observable.

It has now become scientifically acceptable to question mainstream physics insistence on the existence of the quite problematic, diaphanous, altogether unfindable "dark sector"—dark matter and dark energy. What is it? What is its origin? No one knows. If General Relativity is deceiving us at intergalactic time/distance scales, then perhaps we do not need spooky dark energy to fathom the exponentially increasing acceleration of the universe.

Perhaps the most promising, but least popular resolution is the ghastly notion that a modification to our much beloved and exceedingly accurate (at mere galactic distance scales) General Relativity Theory of Albert Einstein is in order. Evidence from the quantum theory is accumulating that GRT is incomplete at vast cosmic distance scales, such as the "Big Chill" at the thermodynamic entropic end of the universe.

Needless to say, any tweaking of GRT is anathema to the wondrous Lambda Cold Dark Matter (ΛCDM) Standard Model orthodoxy of modern physics. Still, there is significant work on "modified gravity" theories presently under way. (Boaz 2021a; excerpted at davidpaulboaz.org)

So, by the lights of both Buddhist metaphysics and recent astrophysical metaphysics, spacetime stuff really exists, at least relatively, and it is (almost) empty of inherent existence—just as Gautama the Buddha told so long ago. Yet, from quantum emptiness, spacetime form continues to arise; abide; then return again to emptiness, without ever departing its *Kosmic* primordial emptiness ground, vast boundless whole (*dharmadhatu*/basic space)—continuously and forever.

Yes, nothing lasts. Relative spacetime form is utterly impermanent (*anitya*). For embodied beings in form this causes great suffering.

There is much more to be said on the matter. Still, "Form is empty; emptiness is form". The Buddha understood the objective, and subjective emptiness nature of relative physical spacetime form, 25 centuries before Einstein and Heisenberg. (For more on "Quantum Emptiness and Buddhist Impermanence" please see *Appendix B*).

This concludes our brief excursus into all-pervasive quantum suffering.

Moreover, in addition to all-pervading quantum suffering, human beings suffer from ignorance (*avidya, marigpa*) and delusion (*moha*); this cloud of unknowing, uncertainty, and fear from living in the constant presence of our death. Buddha and Sigmund Freud agree, this fear/anxiety/worry about our impermanence is the root cause of most of our pathological emotions that result in suffering—furious sensory desire and grasping at self-ego-I with its attendant anger, aggression, hostility, impatience, greed, and pride. Under sway of this fundamental ignorance we suffer its catastrophic karmic cause and effect consequences.

As the Buddhist Wheel of Life (*bhavachakra*) so vividly pictures, the six dominions of relative worldly cyclic existence—the realms of the gods, demi-gods, humans, animals, hungry ghosts, and hell realms—are all enveloped in the proverbial jaws, and claws of death. Yama—underworld god of death. Yama, symbolizes our deep psychic background utter impermanence (*anitya*) of this local foreground of relative-conventional spacetime existence. He holds the entire Wheel of Life in his deathly embrace. "All pervasive suffering" indeed.

So, we are told by both Buddhist masters and by psychoanalysts that for we human beings the fear of death is all pervasive. Our entire life world is conditioned by its subtle, more or less unconscious anxiety, and sometimes all too conscious panic and terror. Then we suppress, repress and deny, through the busy distractions of our lives, the impermanence of things and relationships, especially our mortality, by conceptually imputing and reifying, then grasping at and clinging to a hoped for permanent, substantial, even eternal reality and an enduring self-ego-I to experience it.

In summary. According to the Buddha, the root cause of our suffering is fear: from stark terror to anxiety and worry. Our fearful "denial of death" via distraction, sublimation, suppression, repression gives rise to the poisonous "afflictive" pathological emotions: anger/hatred, raging sense desire, greed and the nearly entirely unconscious compensatory pride of self-ego-I. This entire odious process of denial and distraction is called, in the Buddhist view, ignorance or delusion (*avidya, marigpa, ajnana*). In The Christian tradition it is *hamartia,* or sin. By whatever name or concept our common experience is the "all pervasive suffering" of impermanent, conditional spacetime existence.

Indeed, all of the five *skandhas* or aggregates that constitute our human existence—form, sensation, perception, mental formation, and personal consciousness—are causes of suffering. How shall we deliver ourselves from this difficult human lot?

The good news? On the accord of the Buddhist Middle Way Madhyamaka Two Truths trope, relative and ultimate, self-ego-I and its all too real conceptually reified and imputed really real but impermanent *relative* spacetime realities—our "real world out there" (RWOT)—continuously arises in this infinitely vast perfectly subjective causal matrix of wholly interdependently arising (*pratitya samutpada*) causes and conditions. That is our gift of spacetime reality in which we have a bit of relative time to open into our already present selfless, fearless Buddha nature.

The bad news? Deluded self-ego-I, caged as it is in cyclic samsaric existence, obsessively grasps at impossible physically and emotionally stable permanence. If the multiverse is impermanent, so are we.

More good news. From the ultimate view, this continuum of arising phenomena is empty of any *ultimate* intrinsic existence—absent any real qualities or attributes of existence. Rather, appearing spacetime phenomena are impermanent (*anitya*), essenceless or selfless (*anatman*), and interdependent (*pratitya samutpada*), continuously causally, dependently arising, evolving and changing in time, then passing away—roughly analogous, as we have seen, to the quantum vacuum zero point energy field (ZPE)—foundational quantum qbits arising spontaneously, continuously in the vast emptiness of the primordial perfect space of *dharmakaya*.

Form is empty. Form is good. Form gives the brief gift of time in which to awaken to our human happiness now.

Life and death, the existence and nonexistence of all the stuff we know and love, are necessarily complementary faces of the *whole* interdependent truth of the matter. As the old Broadway song goes, "You can't have one without the other." Our noetic (body, mind, spirit unity) imperative: we must widen our view so that we see (*vipashyana, samadhi*) the interdependence and inclusion of we, the parts, in the vast unbounded primordial whole. This all embracing whole is indeed larger than the sum of its participating parts.

So now, the really good news. Deep trans-conceptual contemplative wisdom understanding of this miraculous process of nondual unity interrupts the awful cycle of fear and aggression, and brings peace to the troubled mind. Buddha told it thus: "Let it be as it is and rest your weary mind; all things are perfect exactly as they are." We shall see that the understanding of this deep unity of the Two Truths that are form and emptiness is good news indeed for our busy anxious minds. But, as Buddha told, "Don't believe this; come and see". The practice of the Path makes it so.

Buddha's profound Two Truths teaching (*Ch. VI*) in his great *Prajnaparamita Heart of Wisdom Sutra*: "Form is empty (*shunya, stongpa*); emptiness (*shunyata, stongpa nyi*) is form. Form is not other than emptiness; emptiness is not other than form". Clearly, this difficult truth of suffering requires some additional truths, lest it be but cynical folly.

This concludes our exploration of the Buddha's noble Truth of Suffering.

The Truth of the Cause of Suffering

The Second of the Buddha's Four Truths for one who would be noble of body, mind and spirit tells us that suffering is caused by fundamental primal ignorance (*avidya, marigpa, ajnana*) of the way things actually exist. From this in turn arises *moha*—delusion, confusion, and the "wrong views" of human self-ego-I as to the three foundational principles of the way that appearing reality—and the self that experiences it—truly exists. These three principles are *impermanence, selflessness*, and *interdependence*. They constitute Buddha's "definitive" teachings. Let us then first explore this rather offputting notion of the Buddha's *anatman*: selflessness, or no-self, or not-self.

Our challenge: how in heaven and earth can a self respecting relative conventional person not be a self? There are people everywhere. But no selves? How does the Buddha's doctrine of *anatman* avoid a dubious nihilism? This question impacts the Buddhist view of the person (*pudgala*), and of the basal consciousness "groundless ground" in whom such a self arises. This question has animated Buddhist philosophy and ethical practice for 25 centuries.

We shall engage the learned academic history of Buddhist dialectics in Chapter V, but perhaps we can here prepare a thoughtful foundation for the Buddha's profound Middle Way teaching that arises in the Third Turning of the Dharma Wheel—the Tibetan Vajrayana.

The Metaphysics of Substance. Since the beginning of human cognition, philosophy and exoteric religion have generally embedded themselves in the mostly preconscious *metaphysics of substance*, the belief that all arising and appearing reality, and the seemingly permanent objective person/self experiencing it, are ultimately grounded in a pre-given objective, physical, material base. In this prevailing substance metaphysic spacetime stuff is inherently, ultimately physical.

As philosophy departed religion and cast its metaphysical lot with science, 400 years of European Modernity has bequeathed to us monistic Metaphysical Scientific Materialism/Physicalism. This belief system has now entirely colonized the Western mind. Through it mental, emotional, psychological, and spiritual dimensions of human being in time are reduced (scientific reductionism) to mere physical, electro-chemical brain states—Louis Carroll's and Alice's "Nothing but a bag of neurons". Fundamentalist Scientism writ large.

This one dimensional monistic physicalist ontology is especially prevalent in Western analytic and continental philosophy, founded as it is in Greek Metaphysical Realism/Metaphysical Materialism. Western Abrahamic Monotheism (Hebrew, Christian, Islam) is also grounded in Metaphysical Physicalism.

This not unnatural metaphysical bias has been called by contemporary philosophers "the myth of the given". For obsessively objective Western mind physical *substance* is a given. Here, appearing stuff is *either* material substance, *or* mental substance that is reducible to physical (brain) substance, or it doesn't exist. *Either* material existence, *or* nihilistic non-existence. Take your pick. Buddhists have argued for 25 centuries that this absolute duality of existence or nonexistence is a misleading false dichotomy. This little book is an exploration of a Buddhist centrist Middle Way.

From the metaphysical ontology you choose arises the phenomenal world you deserve. We shall see that this false dichotomy is rejected by Mahayana Middle Way Madhyamaka Buddhism.

The metaphysical presumption that material substance is the ultimate reality of all human experience is antithetical to, and incommensurate with Absolute Metaphysical Idealism, and as well, with most esoteric trans-material religion/spirituality.

We shall see in Chapter VI, in our brief engagement with the Buddhist Two Truths motif, how it is that Mahayana Middle Way Prasangika Madhyamaka obviates this metaphysical materialist bias by decoupling an *ultimately* real enduring intrinsic self

(*Atman*) from a *relative* conventionally real experiencing person (*anatman*).

No small matter is at stake here. To paraphrase Plato, the question of the actual nature of appearing form, and the self-ego-I that experiences it, "concerns the very way in which human life is to be lived" (Republic Book I). The relative and ultimate nature of the self, in both the East and the West, asks the most fundamental metaphysical question of science, philosophy, and religion—what is the ultimate nature of being in form and time—in relation to its ultimate source or ground? What is our origin, our aim, and our end?

What is the ultimate nature of form, and mind that apprehends it? Is it merely physical substance, as our prevailing metaphysic of monistic Scientific Materialism demands; or is everything mental, as both Western and Eastern Metaphysical Idealism require; or a nice Cartesian dualism of both; or perhaps a monotheistic all-inclusive Creator Godhead? So many questions.

But wait! Why can't we just practice dharma through our wonderful mindfulness meditation, and our deity practices? Do we really need all this conceptual metaphysical drama? Isn't the intellect just a trap that distracts us from the real work of transcending samsaric suffering via our heavenly meditation? Anyway, I just don't have time to study (reading Buddhist scripture and philosophy is a low priority for me at this busy time in my life).

Perhaps too many Buddhist scholars neglect their trans-conceptual contemplative practice in pursuit of a deeper conceptual understanding. Conversely, some of us resist a deeper conceptual understanding of the buddhadharma that we presume to practice more or less blindly. Buddha offered a "middle path".

Human cognition has at least two relative voices: 1) outer, exoteric, objective, conceptual; and 2) inner, esoteric, subjective, contemplative. Utilizing *both* of these cognitive modalities seems a sane and wise approach to dharma, and to being here in time and space—what we need to know, and how. We each must find our own balance in manifesting the unity of these two precious gifts for the benefit of living beings, and thereby for ourselves; as if these two voices were somehow separate. As a suitable balance is struck we begin to enter in a third voice of our human cognition, namely, innermost esoteric nondual, perfectly subjective Buddha mind (*buddhajnana*)—bright Presence of That. And that was the Buddha's answer to our relentless question as to the nature of mind and its experience.

The masters of our great Primordial Wisdom Tradition have told it well. We must commit to a firm conceptual understanding of just what it is that we are receiving through non-conceptual wisdom transmission from our spiritual lineage, our Lama, Ajahn, or Roshi, and our meditation practice; and how to use it wisely. Thus do we learn to unify and express this gift of our two relative cognitive voices—the noetic doublet that is our objective and subjective mind.

Who is it that is practicing dharma? What is it that all the Buddhas and *mahasiddhas* have offered us? How is it that our self-ego-I may derail our practice through self, and no-self deception? Outer and inner guru ask that we understand what it is that we presume to practice.

Self and No-Self. If we are to understand the noble Truth of the Cause of Suffering, we must engage the often vexing Buddhist disjunction of relative self-ego-I (*atman*), and ultimate selfless egolessness (*anatman*).

The iconoclastic Buddhist understanding of *relative* conventional human mind (Suzuki Roshi's Small Mind), and selfless *ultimate* primordial Buddha nature of mind (Roshi's Big Mind) in which, or in whom it arises and participates, is grounded in the Buddha's Two Truths, Relative and Ultimate (*Ch. IV*). It is here that we find the Buddhist doctrine of no-self or not-self, or selflessness/egolessness (Skt. *anatman*, Pali *anatta*).

In this view, human experience is not based merely in the cognitive activity of local spacetime located physical, *observer-independent*, enduring, permanent *atman* self-ego-I agency. Nor is it based in physical brain structure and function; nor in linguistic parlance of the grammatical personal pronouns I, you, they, it; nor in any other relative conceptual semiotic convention or ideological construct.

Ultimate *anatman* no-self abides beyond, or ontologically prior to our relative-conventional collective "global web of belief" (Quine 1969). Yet, paradoxically to our concept-mind, but not to our Buddha wisdom mind, *anatman* is an already prior, yet always present Two Truths unity. Relative *Atman* self, and ultimate *anatman* no-self together at last—a nondual, "ontologically relative" subject-object unity.

Ontological relativity is, broadly construed, the notion that arising and appearing phenomenal spacetime being in form from its primordial emptiness ground, is relative to the *frame of reference* of the observer (Quine 1969; Einstein, Special Theory of Relativity).

It makes little sense to ask, what is *really* real—self or no-self, existence or nonexistence, subject or object. Ultimately, such dichotomies are an interdependent complementary unity. Relatively, it depends on the view. And no particular relative view is privileged in any ultimately meaningful sense (the Buddha, Quine, Einstein).

So, on this relative, perspectival view, there is no absolute purely objective reality "out there", or in here. There are only the causal relations of objects to one another. Yes, we require scientific and philosophical relational theories to describe and predict the behavior of relatively real spacetime physical objects, micro and macro. That is the pragmatic beauty of human thinking mind. But these objects of appearing reality, and the self that engages them, are absent and empty of any inherent, ultimate, permanent objective existence in and of themselves—"from their own side". They are *ontologically relative* to the perceptual and conceptual, linguistic reference frame of we impermanent observer/perceivers.

That, in any case, is the *perspectival* view (experienced reality is dependent upon the observers' relative perspective) of

Middle Way Buddhism, and of the relativistic Quantum Field Theory of Albert Einstein and of Niels Bohr. The Buddha, Einstein, and Bohr all understood the panpsychic/cosmopsychic interdependent arising of spacetime form from its primordial "quantum zero point energy" emptiness ground. Good company indeed.

Therefore, on this propitious relativistic centrist view that bestrides the cognitive ontic extremes of either an ultimate physical reality (Metaphysical Scientific Realism/Materialism), or an ultimate mental reality (Metaphysical Idealism), abides a Two Truths Middle Way, to wit, ultimately non-existent primordial emptiness arises and appears as real, relatively existent form. "Form is empty; emptiness is form".

And this great gift of a really real phenomenal reality is observer-dependent; dependent upon our *relative* reifying perceptions and concepts—our relative frame of reference. Spacetime stuff is not *ultimately* observer-independent, existing somehow in a separate "real world out there" (RWOT).

When we choose to translate—under sway of the reifying impulse of a two-valued (*either* true *or* false) language—an unfindable phantom entity we call "I" into a truly, absolutely existing and enduring self-ego-I—we ignore what W.V.O. Quine (1969) called the "indeterminacy of translation" (indeterminacy of reference). Our semiotic linguistic terms and their conceptual referents are inherently indeterminant. Which is to say, the appearing really real reality of this permanent self that we have come to know and love is *ontologically relative*—relative to and observer-dependent upon the conceptual frame of an observer/perceiver. So, our arising realities really are relatively real; we can act to help other beings in this relative world. Still, this realm is not absolutely, or ultimately, or eternally real, existing beyond our concepts and beliefs about it.

This brief lexical explanation represents a Western *perspectival* philosophical analog of the Buddhist Two Truths Middle Way philosophy.

Thus did the Buddha reveal, 25 centuries ago, that there is a complementary middle way between such false dichotomies as true and false, existence and nonexistence, appearance and reality, subject and object, self and other, self and no-self.

Scientific and religious dominant cultural paradigms demonstrate a cognitive attachment, based in strong belief, to one or the other pole of an ontological dilemma. For example, metaphysical monistic Monotheism, monistic Scientific Materialism/Physicalism, and monistic Idealism resolve the dilemma of our being here in time via differing absolutist views of appearing reality. Monistic ontologies are sometimes replaced by polytheism, or pantheism strategies. These strategies to provide absolute answers to conceptually unanswerable questions all seem to evolve into dogmatic absolutism. Countervailing centrist ontic strategies are taboo. Such a one may well be cast out into the outer darkness; or lose tenure.

The wise will discover a centrist middle way between such ontic extremes. Given our human cognitive propensity for dogmatic belief, perhaps it is preferable to have questions that can't be answered, than to have answers that can't be questioned.

Should you, dear Reader, venture into the heady ornamental abstractions of Buddhist self/no-self metaphysical dialectics, please remain close to this healing, unifying nondual consideration: "Form is empty; emptiness is form": relative form, and its ultimate emptiness ground—present *buddic* Presence of that ground. These are the perennial Two Truths of our great Primordial Wisdom Tradition that science, philosophy, ethics, and government must, in our 21st century Noetic Revolution (Boaz 2021b), finally engage.

So, in the Buddhist view, our arising local spacetime reality is not objectively *independent* of an observer-experiencer existing in a separate RWOT. Rather, the perceptual and mental dimensions of human experience are viewed as an *observer-dependent* process of interdependent, interconnected causes and conditions arising within a vast interdependently arising causal matrix—the numinous, primordial all embracing unbounded whole itself (Skt. *dharmadhatu, cittadhatu,* Bön *mahabindu*). Once again, on the Mahayana Buddhist view our experience of appearing reality is observer-dependent, and ontologically relative. Stuff is utterly interdependent and interconnected; and fabricated by our relative-conventional concepts and beliefs about it.

This involutionary form-making and form manifesting process is known to Buddhists of all stripes as interdependent arising, or dependent origination, or interbeing (*pratitya samutpada*). It is the process of impermanent (*anitya*) relative spacetime form arising from, while never departing, its all embracing, basal ultimate luminous emptiness "groundless ground". "Form is empty; emptiness is form". Emptiness *is* dependent arising. The relation is one of identity.

So, this self/no-self dialectic is the very foundation of Buddhist philosophy, and of Buddhist ethics. It pervades all Buddhist vehicles, and their various schools. The Buddha himself taught that no-self—beyond our prosaic concepts about it—with its metaphysical deconstruction of the five *skandhas* of human experience, provides the cessation of the core human problem of ubiquitous human suffering. After all, grasping at self—I, Me, Mine—is the root cause of the afflictive emotions (fear, anger, ill will, sense desire, hatred, greed, pride, and the rest) that cause suffering.

Thus does thought, intention, and action grounded in transconceptual *anatman*/no-self—beyond our doctrinaire concepts and beliefs about it—provide not only a resolution to our primary metaphysical problem as to the nature of both relative "Small Mind", and ultimate "Big Mind" and their unified relationship of identity, but as well an altruistic ethic of compassionate *bodhicitta* that lessens the suffering of beings. That's a primordial wisdom "twofer" if ever there was one.

But wait! There's more. This deep nondual understanding and practice of *anatman* liberates the Buddhist practitioner from the ignorance (*avidya, marigpa, ajnana*) that causes suffering, and that obscures and obstructs ultimate full *bodhi* mind/Buddha mind awakening or enlightenment. *Anatman/no-self* provides the Buddhist soteriology (salvation) that is ultimate happiness itself! *Mahasukhaho!*

Recent Buddhist scholars are far from agreement on a definitive conceptual interpretation of *anatman* doctrine. We shall see in Chapter V that this relative fact does not preclude an ultimate, deep no-self wisdom mind understanding of this seminal teaching of the Buddha.

Now, because ego-I is brimming with self (*atman*), it is the primary actor in the chain of human ignorance that causes suffering. What more should be said as to the Mahayana view of self? How does it differ from the earlier foundational Hinayana *Pali Canon* view of self?

For Chinese Chan and Japanese Zen Buddhist teaching *Wu* (Jap. *Mu*) constitutes a radical non-affirming denial of our materialist conceptual presupposition of a necessary grounding relation of all appearing stuff in an objective physical basis. This includes the experiencing self. The Great Mahayana Zen Soto School founder Master Dōgen Zenji (1200-1253) expresses this great Mahayana insight in the following wisdom pith (*Shobogenzo*, Tanahashi and Welch 1985):

> To study Buddhism is to study the self.
> To study the self is to forget the self.
> To forget the self is to be enlightened
> by myriad things. To be enlightened by
> all things is to drop away body and mind.
> Now no trace of enlightenment remains.
> This no trace continues endlessly...

> Of existence, there is enlightenment
> and delusion, life and death, Buddhas
> and ordinary people. Of existence
> without self, there is no delusion, no
> enlightenment, no Buddhas, no ordinary
> people, no life and no death.

Self-ego-I is here an adventitious, ultimately illusory, though relatively all too real aggregate of various and sundry perceptions, thoughts, feelings, and emotions that constitute human "personality". These are known in the Buddhist gloss as the *skandhas,* the five "heaps" or "the five aggregates of attachment": physical form, sensation/feeling, perception, mental formation/fabrication, and personal consciousness (the six consciousnesses). "Consciousness" here means personal awareness participation of the human sensory, perceptual, and the mental dimensions that arises in all-inclusive aboriginal awareness-consciousness itself—*dharmakaya,* whose very nature is emptiness/*mahashunyata.* Grasping ego desire (*trishna*) attaches itself to any and all of them making them *causes of suffering.*

However, the early (1st century) Hinayana *Pali Canon* expresses what appears to be a more realistic and relative view of *anatman.* In the clear words of the Buddha:

> O monks, the common person who has no discipline and no regard for dharma clings to (the five aggregates/ *skandhas*) that are assumed to be a substantial and permanent self...so he cannot be freed of suffering—and so ultimate happiness eludes him... These five are no-self. (*Samyutta Nikaya* 22:99, 22:59)

> O monks, what is not yours, let it go. Your letting go will be your long-term welfare and happiness...And what is it that is not yours? Form, feeling, perception, mental fabrication, and consciousness are not yours. Let them go. (*Majjhima Nikaya* 22)

Such *Pali Canon* "right understanding" of no-self/*anatman* prepares the Buddhist practitioner to surrender that which cannot be controlled, namely, the five *skandhas* of attachment, and to use skillful means to control that which can be controlled. And what can we control? We can, as a relative self-ego-I acting in the relative phenomenal world, use wise skillful means to control our actions/conduct, our response and reactions to inevitable adversity, and the clarity/purity of our own mind (Thanissaro 2011).

For Buddhist Mahayana, from the empty *impermanence* of the self that experiences the five *skandhas* of attachment is inferred the absence or nonexistence of a Hindu "higher" or Atman Ultimate Self; but not, as we shall see, the relative conventional existence of a nominal embodied self-ego-I that functions to allow us to survive in a merely *relative* real world out there (RWOT).

A close reading of the Mahayana view that considers the prior unity of relative self and ultimate no-self narrows the conceptual explanatory gap between what is too often a false dichotomy of a present self in the *Pali Canon,* and an absent self in the Mahayana. The wise avoid attaching to either view. We shall see that the truth of the matter lies in a centrist, middle way view that is the complementary unity of both relative self-ego-I, and ultimate no-self or *anatman.*

Again, the compelling non-entity that is self-ego-I has no *ultimate* existence; but we still have to show up for work; and choose skillful compassionate action that disarms the destructive narcissistic self. So, once again, be kind to your ego. Don't beat your ego self up. After all, it is this strange amalgam of self-centered desire and attachment that chooses to enter in and practice the Path toward liberation from suffering that opens into our selfless relative and ultimate happiness. It is this narcissistic self that loves its loved ones, and learns *bodhicitta,* the thought, intention, and action to benefit living beings.

Therefore, in Mahayana doctrine the *skandhas,* the five "aggregates of attachment" that lead to suffering fail to constitute an ultimately real self-entity. Self in time, while relatively real, is in the ultimate view, as Albert Einstein told, "an illusion, but a very persistent one".

We must understand here that these five aggregates of attachment are not in themselves the causes of human suffering. We suffer because, under sway of ignorance (*avidya*), we attach and cling to them. Adversity happens! It is our choice of response—fear, anger or mindful equanimity—to inevitable adversity that determines the extent of our suffering (*Ch. IV*). How is this so?

Gautama the Buddha teaches, as we have just seen,

What is not yours, let it go. Letting go will be your long term welfare and happiness. And what is it that is not yours?

In the ultimate view, none of the precious things to which we cling are ours. Our marriage, family, home, money, career, relationships, health, our very lives—by grace do we have them at all. Not a whit of it do we own or possess. None of it belongs to the self. All of it is, in the ultimate view of our wisdom mind, primordial selfless no-self. All of it is, in the big picture, selfless (*anatman*), impermanent (*anitya*), and causally interdependent (*pratitya samutpada*). These three basal principles are the conceptual foundation of emptiness/*shunyata*. And emptiness is the essence of primordial *dharmakaya* (*Ch.V*).

It is good and proper to love and provide for ourselves and our family, and for others in need. It is wise to honor, appreciate and protect the many blessings that we have been given to receive. And when inevitable adversity arises and we lose the ones that we love, and the things to which we have become attached, it is good and proper to grieve.

Recall, the Buddha's First Noble Truth is the Truth of Suffering. Life is pervaded by suffering. The wise will choose to lighten this burden by deeply engaging Buddha's great truth of *anatman* or selflessness. "What is not yours, let it go". Such a practice will perforce reveal our ultimate liberation from suffering—Happiness Itself—which is, as *Dzogchen* founder Garab Dorje told, "already present from the very beginning". It is That to which we awaken through the Path.

We accomplish such a multidimensional understanding at first conceptually, as we are doing here, then contemplatively, upon the mindful mantra breath (*Appendix A*), beyond our current web of concept and belief. It is here that we connect to our indwelling innermost love-wisdom Buddha mind—bright selfless Presence of That. So we assiduously practice that. Practice makes it—if not perfect—real, and here, and now. Practice is not "just sitting" on the cushion. Practice is the whole of our experience, everything we think, intend, and do.

The qualities or characteristics of these five aggregates or *skandhas* of attachment are birth, sickness, old age, death, and constant change. These qualities are, on the accord of Nagarjuna (2nd century), utterly absent "any shred" of *essential* existence and are thus impermanent (*anitya*), selfless (*anatman*), empty (*shunya*), and loaded with suffering (*duhkha*).

It bears repeating, the "definitive" basic principles that we shall explore in Chapter V as to arising and appearing spacetime reality are that it is, in all the Buddhist vehicles: 1) ultimately impermanent (*anitya*); 2) our realities are *ultimately* selfless or absent/empty of absolute *intrinsic* existence (*anatman*); and 3) all appearing reality experience arises in dependence upon a vast nexus or matrix of prior and present interdependent, interconnected causes and conditions (dependent arising or *pratitya samutpada*). These three foundational principles of Buddhist *shunyata/* emptiness constitute the basis of all Buddhist metaphysics, which support Buddhist ethics—which are, in a word, *bodichitta*—the luminous, compassionate heartmind of enlightenment.

From ignorance of these three foundational metaphysical principles arises self-ego-I *attraction/attachment* and *aversion/hostility*— and from that, much suffering for we human beings being here in form and time. Thus are the "three poisons"—ignorance, attachment, and aversion—the root causes of human suffering.

The 1st century *Pali Canon* record of Gautama the Buddha's early teaching is the basis of the Theravada, the only extant

Hinayana School. *Pali* is an Indian dialect derived from the *Sanskrit* language. From the *Pali Canon* arises the Buddha's foundational teaching of The Four Noble Truths which include his teaching on selflessness, emptiness, and the Eightfold Path. His teaching on our indwelling Buddha nature of mind arises in the Tibetan Vajrayana Third Turning of the Wheel.

We've seen that this Hinayana *Pali Canon* pre-Mahayana teaching vehicle is the very foundation of all of the Buddhist teaching vehicles—Theravada, Mahayana, and Tibetan Vajrayana and their various schools of doctrine. Hinayana adds doctrinal insight to what is sometimes mistakenly considered a pejorative denial of a relatively functioning self-ego-I that we sometimes find in the later Mahayana/Vajrayana traditions. In the Theravada view this was not the Buddha's intention. In this view he taught that self must be worked with and lifted into its true selfless identity. How? Assiduous practice of the Path.

We are well advised to remember that self (*atman*), and no-self (*anatman*) are, to our nondual clear light wisdom mind, already an ontic prior, and epistemic present unity. No dilemma. No duality. No problem at all.

Well then, is our choice to submit to the rule of unruly self-ego-I over our human cognition and action a dark Faustian bargain with primal ignorance? Must we somehow dump our nasty narcissistic egos to be saved from this difficult lot that is cyclic samsaric existence? In order to awaken to the inherent happiness of our innermost Buddha mind, must self be entirely transcended; or annihilated?

No. It is misleading to parrot "I and everything else are no-self; the self does not exist." Or, "The *Kosmos* itself is Supreme Self, eternal, permanent, and unchanging". These are but two of many in the conceptual "thicket of views" regarding the logically possible relation of self to no-self. The Buddha refuted them all (Thanissaro 2011). So, the question remains: what is the *ultimate* relation of self to no-self?

We must work with, and lift, and integrate *relative* self with our *ultimate* selfless Buddha mind. Thus do we practice the already present unity of Buddha's Two Truths.

We shall soon see that our aboriginal primordial love-wisdom Buddha mind is quite naturally free of this misleading conceptual duality, this false dichotomy of self and no-self. Recall, relative conceptual duality is always embraced and subsumed in nonlocal, nondual truth—vast unbounded implicate order of the boundless whole—*dharmakaya, dharmadhatu, mahabindu (Ch. IX)*.

Our *concepts* of self and no-self represent complementary identities. Like day and night, existence and nonexistence, good and evil, male and female, particle and wave—you can't have one without the other. This complete process arises in boundless emptiness, abides in emptiness, and returns again to emptiness. Indeed, form is always already emptiness. It has always been thus. As Buddha told so long ago, "Form is empty; emptiness is form". Once again, in the ultimate view, self and no-self are a prior and present unity. But from the relative view, self and no-self must work together as a wisdom team. Selfless no-self (*anatman*) embraces and guides self-ego-I.

Most students of Buddhism have considered the question: "If there is no self, who is it that acts, and who is it that receives the karmic result of our actions?" What is the meaning of karma without a self? Who is it that is liberated? That benefits from *bodhicitta?*

Clearly, the annihilation of the self-ego-I was not the Buddha's intention as it has come down to us through ancient *Pali Canon* scriptures. Yet, we have seen that the three principle metaphysical tenets of Buddhism are: impermanence, no-self/selflessness, and interdependence. What then shall we make—ultimately—of this perennial creative dialectical tension between Buddhist self and no-self? We have yet to complete our answer this question.

The Buddha himself declined to define self and no-self "because this is not fundamental to awakening". Buddha did not say that there is no self. Nor did he say that there is a self. Speaking of what Buddhist scholars now refer to as the relative self that abides in the dimension of everyday conventional Relative Truth, the Buddha told:

> Your own self is your mainstay, for who else could it be?
> With you yourself well trained, you obtain a mainstay hard
> to obtain (Dhammapada 160).

So, Buddha's teaching includes the ego strength of a healthy and mindful ego. An intelligent, trained, discriminating relative self-ego-I (*atman*) is required to understand ultimate selflessness (*anatman*), and the interdependent relationship that constitutes the trans-conceptual unity of these two seemingly separate, yet complementary notions. *One need not give up one's ego-I!* We practice in order to align and lift the inherent narcissism of self-ego-I into the wisdom light of altruistic *bodhicitta*.

Therefore, be present to yourself, moment to moment, here and now. Meta-cognitively, reflexively, mindfully witness your mindstream, whatever arises, negative or positive, free of any criticism. Accept yourself just as you are now. Offer thanks for this precious gift of your life, just as it is now. Know now, and feel that you are always embraced in loving Presence of your always already present Buddha mind, even when you forget. Such is reflexive mindfulness practice. Do it now for a few seconds, and again later, "brief moments many times" until it becomes a bright continuity of mindful awareness.

Hence, we need not be concerned that Buddhism ignores the importance of self esteem, and motivation for "success" in life, and the other attributes of the "fuller functioning self" of modern Western "ego psychology". Perhaps the antidote to the modern affliction of low self esteem is no-self esteem!

Conversely, we need not construe Buddhist no-self/selfless-ness doctrine as a rationalization for self-loathing, for beating ourselves up, for paralyzing guilt, shame and blame. Nor is it an excuse for what Thanissaro (2011) calls "spiritual bypassing"—the unconscious, unskillful, yet all too common game among Buddhist practitioners wherein we deny and so remain attached to our basic psycho-emotional "unfinished business". Is not most psychopathology pathology of the self?

Buddhist practice will, in due course, under the guidance of a living master, and in the good company of the *sangha*, reveal many of our emotional hang ups and disconnects; but it is not a panacea to be used to deny, repress and avoid them. Transpersonal or other therapeutic intervention may be indicated to further the loving acceptance of yourself, so that you may truly benefit others, especially those that you love. And benefiting others—family and "other" living beings, including our precious Mother Earth—is after all the very secret of human happiness.

Thus did the Buddha consider with his disciples the exoteric, *relative* conventional self-ego-I and its necessary activity, not only for survival, but for the choice to enter the Path, and to "practice what is beneficial to beings". Who is it after all that *chooses* the practice of the Path that results in human happiness. Just so, Buddha considered with his disciples esoteric no-self/selflessness/*anatman*—the utter emptiness and ultimate absence of an intrinsically existing self-ego-I. And, as all great love-wisdom masters have done, he taught these two, and many other levels of understanding to disciples of different capacities.

Sometimes the Buddha teaches the reality of the "well trained" *relative* self that chooses to enter and practice the Path; and sometimes he teaches that self is altogether absent and empty of intrinsic *ultimate* existence. There is no anomaly here. Again, these are two interdependent dimensions of realizing the singular nondual whole that embraces our relative conceptual dialectic of self and no-self. Buddha told, "To liberate myriad beings I teach in many ways at once" (*Lankavatara Sutra*).

In short, the Buddha's teaching on *atman* self and *anatman* no-self includes instruction for us as to the training of the relative self with its scattered and undisciplined mind; and instruction as to the ultimate nature of that selfsame self. These two are not at all contradictory. Indeed, this twofold understanding is the very root of the Buddhist Two Truths motif—the prior unity of Relative Truth with Ultimate Truth—*one truth*, nondual and invariant throughout our entire human awareness-consciousness processional that includes, as we have seen, the cognitive dimensions of 1) pre-conceptual immediate attention/perception; 2) objective, conceptual, physical, 3) subjective emotional, intuitive, contemplative, and 4) "innermost secret", perfectly subjective nondual (*Ch. VI*).

Hence, we must conclude that our notions and concepts about self and no-self may easily become a false dichotomy. "To be or not to be", and "Which self is my true self" are not the proper questions. In this all too real world of relative conventional space-time existence, being and becoming, self and no-self must, and indeed do work together. We utilize the intelligence of relative self-ego-I to accomplish the ultimate selflessness that is the peace and compassion of *anatman*. We utilize ego's power of reason and self-analysis to reflexively critique itself, in order to realize trans-rational truth. We utilize mindfully trained ego's discipline to be constantly, mindfully, gently present to self. Both self and no-self are strategies of the Path to awakening to innermost Presence of our already present luminous clear light Buddha mind/Buddha nature. "Practice these two as a unity".

Now, we understand that our innate love-wisdom Buddha mind embraces both self and no-self. Ultimate nondual wisdom (*jnana, yeshe*) is utterly free of such conceptual false dichotomies.

Well and good. How then shall we use such wisdom to free ourselves from this dreadful cognitive cage of suffering that ignorance has forged, that we may know and share the inherent happiness that is our innermost *bodhi* mind that abides always within our spiritual heart of hearts?

This concludes our exploration of the Buddha's noble Truth of the Cause of Suffering.

The Truth of the Cessation of Suffering

If there is a cause of suffering, the cure should be removal of that cause. Hope springs eternal! Here Buddhist metaphysical ontology meets logically pragmatic Buddhist ethical or moral philosophy—lifeworld practice of *bodhicitta*, the beautiful wisdom of kindness. The cessation of suffering is accomplished by freeing or liberating the deluded largely negative desire-concept-mind of self-ego-I from the primeval, but unnecessary ignorance (*avidya/hamartia*/sin) that is the root cause of our suffering.

How do we do this? In a word, *surrender.* Through assiduous practice of the Noble Eightfold Path to liberation/enlightenment we train the "wild horse of the mind" to surrender its obsessive narcissistic effort in service of self-ego-I and gradually shift our attention to benefiting other beings. For Buddhists, especially in the Mahayana/Vajrayana tradition, that very attitude of *bodhicitta* is the primary cause of human happiness.

This love-wisdom Path is manifested through both exoteric, objective, conceptual understanding, and esoteric, subjective contemplative direct *realization* of the unity of primordial *wisdom of emptiness/shunyata* merged with compassionate *activity* or conduct, in a word, *bodhicitta*—the generous thought, intention, and action for the benefit of all living beings, human and otherwise, including our Mother Earth.

H.H. Dalai Lama has termed these two voices of human cognition *conceptual* and *experiential.* The latter is direct "felt experience", the easy feeling sense in the physical body of the heartmind Presence of our very Buddha nature of mind. The directness of such "feeling experience" is not transcendent experience, beyond physical space and time; nor is it necessarily mystical experience. It is not metaphysical—beyond physical body and ordinary mind. The location of happiness is the human body, and our ordinary human mind! Our all too human bodymind is where Buddha mind Presence happens, then acts.

Yes, we may approach the understanding of the ultimate nature of appearing reality—the wisdom of emptiness—through both the critical analysis of reason, and through trans-conceptual direct contemplative experience (*yogi pratyaksa*), both of which we experience in this perfect present moment now. And we *feel* it in the body, through the five senses, mirrored in human consciousness—these beautiful myriad instantiations of primordial awareness-consciousness itself, luminous Buddha mind Presence (*vidya, rigpa*) of That. That said, we must open wide our heartmind to receive it, well beyond our current concepts and beliefs *about* it.

Yes, scriptural authority and philosophical understanding point the way to accomplishing these two modes—objective conceptual and subjective experiential—of our human understanding. However, authority and reasoned concept/belief are not enough. As Buddha told, "Do not believe what I teach out of respect for me. Come and see".

Therefore, in good times and in bad times, sit or lie under a tree, or under the vast empty sky, or on a cushion, or on a straight-backed chair, or walk in the woods or the garden and simply *feel* whatever arises here and now. Just be here now, fully present and awake as you practice these precious words of the Buddha:

> Breathing in, I am aware of breathing in.
> Breathing out, I am aware of breathing out...
> Breathing in, my body and mind are peace.
> Breathing out, my body and mind are peace...
> Breathing in, I am happy.
> Breathing out, I am happy...
> Breathing in, I liberate activity of my mind.
> Breathing out, I liberate activity of my mind...
> Breathing in, I observe my surrender of all things.
> Breathing out, I observe my surrender of all things...
> Breathing in, I observe cessation of all things.
> Breathing out, I observe cessation of all things.
> —Anapanasati Sutta; Satipatthana Sutta

You are alive! Now in this present moment, feel luminous *prana/ lung* life current pervade your being here in time and form. Awareness upon the breath in the body is being awake to that living Presence in this very moment now. Notice the subtle feeling of delight. Of fearless peace. That is the very foundation of love, and wisdom, and skillful thought, intention and action for the benefit of living beings; and so of your own happiness. Your happiness rides the breath. As the busy mind arises, return again and again to the breath. Remain close to the breath. That is the original teaching of all the Buddhas of the three times—past, present, future—on the cessation of human suffering. Take a break and do it now for two or three minutes.

Whatever you are doing now, that is the most important thing. Now is the best time to do it. Who you are with now is the best person, or persons to do it with. Being here in this present moment now is the happiest thing you can do. Breathing mindfully is how you do it.

We've seen that the Buddha did not teach abstract conceptual metaphysical speculation, nor transcendent mysticism, nor even meditation upon "emptiness", nor upon "*dharmakaya*", nor upon "the nature of mind". He declined to comment on such metaphysical questions from his disciples. He told that such conceptual metaphysical speculation does not directly facilitate awakening; nor does it help to reduce the suffering of living beings. Nor did he teach concept and belief about an abstract separate theistic God, or "higher" Atman God-Self. Nor did he teach denigration or denial of self-ego-I who habitually pursues such conceptual abstract distractions.

We've seen that this constant relative conceptual duality of self/no-self must be viewed strategically as the path to awakening. Again, as Guru Padmasambhava told, we utilize the dualistic practice of the realm of Relative Truth—the Path—to accomplish non-conceptual, nondual Ultimate Truth, the Fruit or Result. Our awakened state is, ultimately, free of concepts about both self and no-self, even in the very midst of such distractions. No dilemma. No problem whatsoever! *Emaho!*

What then did the Buddha teach? He taught that we must learn to relax our obsessively busy minds and rest in the life force *prana* wind (*prana vayu*, breath of life) of the mindful breath (*shamatha, sati*), and thereby open to receive our always present Buddha love-wisdom mind that instantly imbues self with nonlocal, non-conceptual no-self Presence of That. Self must be nurtured and guided by That, like the mother loves, nurtures, guides and corrects her selfish child.

Thus does the buddhadharma cultivate a strong, intelligent, courageous ego who *chooses*, step by mindful step, to *surrender* itself to always present primordial Buddha mind Presence so that one may rest in natural peaceful equanimity (*upeksha*), then express it as the loving-kindness (*maitri*), compassion (*karuna*), and joy (*mudita*) that is *bodhicitta. It requires a strong ego to deconstruct itself.* And that takes a bit of practice. That is the heart of the prodigious teaching of Gautama the Buddha as to self and no-self.

Be that as it may, we've seen that Buddha taught selflessness/ *anatman*; impermanence/ *anitya*; and interdependence/*pratitya samutpada*. These are the three "definitive teaching" principles that liberate us from suffering. It is That that is to be realized, conceptually, and upon trans-conceptual quiescent mantra (e.g. *OM AH HUM*) with "mindfulness of breathing" (*Appendix A*).

"Do not depend on logic, inference, analogies, scripture, probability, or agreeable views" (*Kalama Sutra* 3:15). Dharma practice is a compassionate skill set taught by the Buddha; and all the Buddhas of the three times; and all of the primordial wisdom masters of humankind. It furthers one to learn, and practice *shamatha, sati,* the mindfulness of breathing of Gautama Shakyamuni the Buddha, and Tibetan mantra practice. These are the foundation of love, wisdom, and happiness.

Therefore, as we explore Mahayana philosophy and ethical practice with its opulent metaphysical abstractions we must remember the foundational *Pali Canon* "source sutras", especially the *Anapanasati* and *Satipatthana Suttas* which do not stray far from the breath of life. Once again, the early Hinayana *Pali Canon* is the very source and foundation of all that was to come in the monumental Mahayana Revolution (*Ch. VII*).

Meanwhile, the nondual ultimate primordial source and nature of mind is always already present—as *Dzogchen* View and Practice reveals—in the unelaborated "bare attention" of our "ordinary direct perception", upon the mindful breath, just prior to the superimposition of abstract concepts and beliefs *about* it (*Ch. VIII*).

Thus does Buddhist meditation have two contemplative voices: 1) *shamatha* or *sati*—quiescence or calm abiding—calming the "wild horse of the mind" through "full awareness of breathing"— so that we may then directly *see* (*samadhi*) with the deep direct penetrating wisdom insight of 2) *vipashyana* into the luminous empty nature of mind, nonlocal (beyond spacetime), nondual (beyond the subject-object split), ultimate nature of appearing reality itself, "exactly as it is". It is the unity of these two wisdom voices, quiescent mindfulness and deep penetrating insight, that pervades the three vehicles of the Buddhist Path—Hinayana/ Theravada, Mahayana, and Vajrayana—with their various inter- pretative practice schools.

We enter this wondrous Path by engaging the precious Three Jewels—*the Buddha* seen as the Lama, or Ajahn, or Roshi; *the dharma* teaching of the Buddha; and the *sangha* or spiritual community (*Ch. IV*).

That now said, on the accord of Vajrayana Middle Way Prasangika Madhyamaka, the *Middle Way Consequence School* founded by 2nd century Nagarjuna, the truth of the intrinsic emptiness of arising form to human perception is also present to human understanding through the process of logical analyti- cal reasoning.

Just so, liberation (*moksha, nirodha*) from the suffering of ig- norance may be principally known through enlightened reason, because, as Nagarjuna tells us, liberation is not other than the complete release or cessation of ignorance (*avidya*), both subtle and gross. This august Mahayana tradition of engagement with the *logic of the non-conceptual* is the great legacy of Nagarjuna and his heart son Aryadeva to all of us. It is alive and well in the four schools of the Vajrayana wisdom tradition—Nyingma, Kagyu, Gelug, and Sakya (*Ch. V*).

Thus, for early Vajrayana Middle Way Madhyamaka—both Prasangika and Yogachara—freedom from suffering, the cessation of suffering, is logically dependent upon the many mansions of our depth of understanding of Buddha's realization of emptiness—the absence of "any shred" of intrinsic or *ultimate* existence (Ultimate Truth) of *relative* arising phenomenal form (Relative Truth) from its emptiness "groundless ground", spacious *dharmakaya* itself.

However, it is urgent to understand that the "object of negation" here is not the *relative* conventional existence of space-time form, but its intrinsic *ultimate* existence. Stuff really exists relatively; just not intrinsically, absolutely or ultimately. Thus the object of negation for Prasangika is the *intrinsic existence* of relatively really real appearing, impermanent reality; a middle way centrist view that bestrides the ontic absolutist extremes of *nonexistence*, to wit, nihilistic Metaphysical Absolute Idealism, both Eastern and Western; and *existence*, the observer-independent realist eternalism and solid permanence of absolute monistic Metaphysical Materialism/Physicalism—the proto-religion of which is fundamentalist "Scientism".

As Buddha told in his lapidary *Heart of Wisdom Sutra*: "Form is empty; emptiness is form. Form is not other than emptiness; emptiness is not other than form." This is the perennial Two Truths. The cessation of suffering is the direct knowing-feeling realization of the prior and always present unity of this great nondual truth (*Ch. VI*).

We've also seen that in Mahayana Buddhism the two limbs of Buddha's teaching on freedom from suffering are the wisdom of emptiness, and compassion. In the Mahayana, compassion is much more than a feeling—sympathy, kind thoughts, even an intention or commitment to act. Compassion is selfless *karuna*, the *engaged action* to lessen the suffering of beings. The "*kar*" in *karuna* means action. And since we're all in this adverse reality boat together, we lessen our own suffering through altruistic *bodhicitta*. Thus is selfless *bodhicitta* the primary cause of our own happiness. *Mahasukaho!*

Please consider, human happiness is always already the case, already present—but only in this present moment now. The past is gone; but a present memory. The future has not yet arisen; but a present anticipation. Though we must learn from the past, and consider the future, everything happens only in this present moment now, which itself is already future. The Buddha's "middle path" abides in the present nondual unity of these "three times"—past, present. future.

Therefore, we cannot *become* happy in some future mind state. But we can *be* happy here and now. How? Not through rejection of ego, but via step by step *surrender*—with loving acceptance of narcissistic ego-I, that we may more readily help others to their own happiness.

It must be noted here that the Buddhist Path to ultimate human happiness does not end human adversity—"the heartache, and the thousand natural shocks that flesh is heir to". Adversity happens! It is part of this whole shebang that is human life being here in time and form. That's the deal we signed up for in the beginning; is it not?

However, adversity does not necessarily mean suffering. Suffering does not arise from adversity per se, but from our habitual confused emotional reactions to adverse experience. Once again, with practice, under the guidance of a qualified master, we learn to *choose our responses*—e.g. fearful-hostile or kind-compassionate—to the inevitable adversity of being here as guests of the phenomenal world. How shall we understand this?

From ignorance—with its attachment and aversion—arise the afflictive emotions—fear, anger, hostility, hatred, greed, guilt and pride—both individual, and collective cultural. From these pathological emotions arises adventitious adversity—human alienation, despotism and war.

As the "wild horse of the mind" is trained through *shamatha/* mindfulness, mantra prayer, and the cultivation of altruistic *bodhicitta*—and as we surrender more and more of narcissistic self-ego-I and align self with our Buddha mind Presence we can, step by mindful step, *choose* creative selfless compassionate responses to the endless adversity of life. Self and no-self work together. After all, adversity afflicts a self. No-self is, *ipso facto*, immune from it. We learn to abide in a balanced centrist middle way.

The mindful, skillful selflessness that is *bodhicitta* is a learned response, through the practice of Buddha's Eightfold Path, and the Six Perfections of the Mahayana—for those who would choose to engage it. It is this Path that, via skillful means, offers the *ultimate* cessation of suffering; and in the mean time an abundance of *relative* happiness in our busy lives.

This concludes our exploration of the Buddha's noble Truth of the Cessation of Suffering.

The Truth of the Path

The Cessation of Suffering is accomplished through the Truth of the Path. Buddha's very practical no-self help mind training life practice accomplishes our awakening through Wisdom, Ethics, and Meditation. This prodigious Buddhist Path is the cause of human flourishing that is relative hedonic happiness (*eudaemonia, felicitas*), and as well, the cause of the fruition of ultimate Happiness Itself (*mahasuka, paramananda, beatitudo*), karma-free harmless happiness that cannot be lost—our indwelling already present Buddha mind Presence, always here now. Yes, it is that liberated happiness to which we awaken through this joyous and difficult process of the Path.

Human happiness grounded in the Buddha's Eightfold Path requires apprenticeship, then mastery of eight interdependent

disciplines that remedy ignorance (*avidya, ma rigpa*), and delusion (*moha*), the root causes of human suffering. These eight are
expressed in three cognitive-behavioral wisdom categories—
Wisdom, Ethics, and Meditation thusly:

Wisdom: 1) right view or understanding; 2) right intention
or aspiration.
Ethics: 3) right speech; 4) right action or conduct; 5) right
livelihood.
Meditation: 6) right effort; 7) right mindfulness; 8) right
wisdom.

The Six Perfections. In the Buddhist Mahayana vehicle, the
Buddha's Eightfold Path to perfect happiness—liberation from
suffering, enlightenment itself—includes and requires skillful
practice of the Six Perfections (*Paramitas*) in which arise the precious *bodhicitta*—altruistic compassionate thought, intention and
action for the benefit of all living beings. These six naturally and
logically arise from the Buddha's Eightfold Path of the Hinayana
vehicle in the ancient *Pali Canon*—the cause of the cessation of
human suffering. The Six *Paramitas* abide in a relationship of
interdependence that constitutes the singular unified whole
of the Buddhist Path.

We discover in the early *Pali Canon* that following the Buddha's
awakening under the Bodhi Tree (*Ficus religiosa*) he continued
his meditation on the perfection of wisdom and the Four Noble
Truths that dissolve ignorance and cause an end to suffering. We
are told that he practiced for seven weeks (or seven days) through
continuous meditation on the *paramitas* before he accomplished
his full *mahabodhi samyak-sambuddha* final awakening—his ultimate
realization of the indivisible unity of the Two Truths, relative
form, and ultimate emptiness (*mahashunyata*). It is said that at
the moment of the knowing/feeling *samadhi* of this prior and
present unity of the Two Truths, Buddha was forever liberated
from the *samsara* of conditioned cyclic existence.

He then embarked upon his first teaching—the First Turning of Wheel of the buddhadharma (*dharmachakra*)—at the Deer Park near Sarnath, in Northern India. It was here that he taught the Four Noble Truths—utterly profound and subtle foundation of all that was to come.

The first four of the Six Perfections are Buddha's teaching of loving skillful means (*upaya*); the last two are his teaching of the practice, and realization of wisdom—discriminating *prajna* and nondual *jnana*. This wondrous union of skillful compassionate means and primordial wisdom of emptiness is the heart essence of the entire Buddhist Path. The "two limbs" of the Buddha's teaching then are wisdom and compassion. They are a prior and present unity.

The *Six Paramitas* include all of the Buddhist means-methods and wisdom that free human beings from conditioned suffering. How is this so? Through taming and training the "wild horse of the mind" (self-ego-I) we may authentically benefit living beings. And that is our own happiness. The *Six Paramitas* describe the actual primordial nature, the Buddha nature (*tathagatagarbha*), Buddha mind (*buddhajnana*). Thus do we recognize, then realize and compassionately express through altruistic *bodhicitta* our own love-wisdom Buddha mind—bright always already present Presence of That. And That is the open secret of human happiness.

In accordance with the Two Truths, there are two ways of understanding the Buddha's teaching in Mahayana Buddhism—relative and ultimate (*Ch. VI*). Therefore:

> For bodhisattva mahasattvas who are beginners one must explain the Six Perfections with a reference point, with the notion that suchness (*tathata, dharmata*) is expressible. That is to say, they must understand the nature of the elements to be arising and perishing. Only then should they familiarize with the idea that all phenomena are in essence inexpressible, non-arising, non-ceasing, not perceptible, and not ultimately existing.
>
> —*Akashagarbha Sutra* 1.15

Thus do these six primary virtues, perfected by the bodhisattva's (we Buddhas in training) skillful love-wisdom Path include the *Six Paramitas*:

1) *The Perfection of Generosity (dana)*: From our innate *bodhicitta* naturally and spontaneously arises selfless thought, intention, and action to reduce the suffering, and increase the happiness of living beings. Generosity is sharing and giving freely, selflessly, skillfully, and wisely of our money, time, love, encouragement with generous praise and kind words, and the nonjudgmental purity of love (*maitri*) toward oneself and others—with *purity of intention*—little or no desire for recognition or reward.

   Generous receiving of loving kindness for oneself is a prerequisite for generosity toward others. Take total responsibility—not just your share of it—for your emotional disconnects (*parche*) with others. Consider an apology, even when you're sure you were right. In the greatest view there is no blame. Through your own always present Buddha nature, recognize Buddha nature in everyone, and in everything. This will make others happy, which makes you happy. *Buddha mind sees only Buddha. Course mind sees insult and trouble (Ch. IV).*

2) *The Perfection of Ethical Discipline (sila)*: The development and perfection of morality; selfless, kind virtue, loving, compassionate thought, intention and conduct for the benefit of living beings, including oneself; that is the perfection of ethics. Buddhist morality is the skillful practice of right speech, right livelihood, and right action. *Sila* is not mere automatic obedience to a set of rules. A bodhisattva *responds* (not reacts) spontaneously and effortlessly (*Wu-Wei*) to moral situations with selfless, wise, skillful compassion, without need to refer to a codified set of rules. Such ethical self discipline generates a subtle and profound understanding of karma—inexorable cause and

effect of our human action—which reduces one's negative karmic burden, and enhances one's "good karma", and happiness (*Ch. IV*).

3) *The Perfection of Patience*: (*ksānti*): Patience is gentle, kind nonjudgmental tolerance, acceptance, forbearance—in a word equanimity—in face of inane, often destructive thought intention and action of oneself and of others. The flipside of patience is destructive impatience and anger toward self and others. With patient practice impatience becomes compassionate equanimity. Primordial love-wisdom alchemy indeed.

The assiduous cultivation of patience toward oneself dissolves the self destructive unconscious projection of poisonous anger and hostility onto others, especially loved ones, and authority figures, before it does its damage. Patience forestalls and surrenders our *attachment/attraction*, and *aversion/ hostility*—toward both self and others.

Patience has three faces: 1) patience and strength in the fraught face of life's inevitable adversity, 2) patience with one's self-ego-I and all of its hang-ups, and 3) the patience to develop a multidimensional, both conceptual and contemplative understanding of the teaching of the Buddha: his Four Noble Truths, and his truth of emptiness, (impermanence, selflessness, interdependence), and his truth of our innate indwelling Buddha nature (*Ch. V*).

And now, a bit of annoying no-self help. Gentle, kind patience toward oneself, and forgiveness and acceptance of one's own egocentric narcissistic destructive actions, is almost as difficult, and as rare, as acknowledging pride in oneself. But from such balanced gentle acceptance of oneself follows patience with others, just as night follows day. As angry, self-righteous ego-defenses rise up to defend this odd nonentity we call self from the unjust attacks of wisdom, enjoy a bit of self-deprecating humor.

In the greater view the all-important drama-story of self-ego-I may not be as urgent as we think. Ego cannot be disrespected without our permission. Disrespect and rudeness from another cannot harm us. So, we cultivate a little patience, and don't take ego-self so seriously. It's good to remember that this entire reality display is but the spontaneous play of *Vidya Maya,* whose ultimate identity is our primordial wisdom mind—*jnana, yeshe*—luminous Presence (*vidya, rigpa*) of That.

4) *The Perfection of Diligence (virya):* Diligence is the skillful means (*upaya*), effort, energy, intensity, vigor, assiduity, constancy, mindful perseverance and courage required to continue, then complete the Path—all the way to the end of it. *Virya*—the courageous heroic effort and intention to accomplish our innate *bodhi* mind/love-wisdom mind for the benefit of living beings—is the etymological root of the English word virile. It means hero in ancient Hindi. Perfecting diligence requires real courage.

Further, diligence requires the intelligence to skillfully and spontaneously act from *Wu-Wei*—natural, sustained, unforced effortless altruistic action for the benefit of living beings—arising from, and identical to, already present numinous, luminous primordial love-wisdom Buddha nature/Buddha mind that animates all being and action. From the *Tao Te Ching,* "Perseverance furthers".

Reasons to quit or "take a break" from one's practice are never ending. The practice of the Path includes all of them, and everything else that you think or do; or think you can't do. All experience is practice. One cannot so easily quit experience. "Being here now" upon this joyous, difficult path requires the hero's courage. And we all have it. Zen Master Suzuki Roshi told it well, "The only mistake you can make in your practice is to quit".

Please consider for a moment, but don't believe, this universal proposition: All human beings are, by virtue of our humanity, love-wisdom mind Buddha nature/Buddha mind—by whatever name or concept—bright, always now present, numinous indwelling Presence of That. Whether we choose to believe it, or not. It is the diligent practice of the Path through which we awaken to that great truth.

Therefore, the *goal* of practice is not some remote future enlightened condition or mind state, but diligent skillful method and conduct, and joy in this present moment here and now. "We are betrayed by destinations", as Welsh poet Dylan Thomas told.

How is this so? Buddha told it thus: "Let it be as it is and rest your weary mind; all things are perfect exactly as they are". Here and now. As it is abundantly clear that in the relative domain of *samsaric* existence, things are not quite so perfect, this lovely pith describes the subtle innermost dimension of Buddha's nondual Ultimate Truth in which, or in whom this all arises and appears. In the inscrutable words of 19th century ecumenical *Rimé Dzogchen* master Patrul Rinpoche, teacher of Ju Mipham, "Things are not as they appear; nor are they otherwise".

Happiness, liberation from suffering—is always already present at the knowing-feeling spiritual heart (*hridaym*)— luminous clear light Presence of That. Yes, it is that *timeless* wisdom truth to which we awaken through the diligent practice of the Path.

But wait! Don't we require a dualistic cause and effect path here in spacetime to awaken to this great truth of the nondual Path? And doesn't the Law of Karma—the law of cause and effect— require time, a past and a future in which to play out?

Yes, and yes. And, as usual, it depends upon the view—relative or ultimate. As Zen Master Dōgen, founder of Soto Zen told, "The three times, past, present, future, are arrayed for us simultaneously". So, we must learn from the past; and consider the future as we abide imperfectly in this present moment now. Everything happens now. The Buddha's timeless Six Perfections—enlightened *Wu-Wei* action—only happen in this present moment now. Where else could it happen? Thus are the Buddha's relative three times and Two Truths ultimately a present unity.

Buddha taught, "What you are is what you have been; what you will be is what you do now". Our past action has resulted in the condition of our present lifeworld. Our future results from our acts in the present now. Inexorable Law of Cause and Effect, in a word, karma.

The Relative Truth of dualistic, and even nondual practice of the Path gradually awakens our sleep-waiting minds to always present nondual fruit of the Path, knowing feeling love-wisdom mind Buddha mind Presence that was "already present from the very beginning". *We practice the relative Path to realize the Ultimate Truth of our Buddha mind that is already present now.* Padmasambhava advises us to view this wondrous process as indivisible and nondual. Diligently, patiently, ethically, and generously "Practice these two as a unity".

Therefore, as Karma Kagu *vidyadhara* Chögyam Trungpa said, "Make the goal the path".

5) *The Perfection of Meditation (dhyana, samadhi)*: Contemplative practice in all of the primary wisdom traditions of our species begins and ends with the right effort of right mindfulness (*shamatha, sati, smriti*). Buddha told that *shamatha/sati* is the quiescent foundation of all meditation practice, which provides the skillful means of awaking to, then engaging our always already present Buddha mind/love-wisdom mind. Meditation is the foundation of, and pervades all the myriad practices of the Buddhist love-wisdom Path. *Bodhi* mind-wisdom mind is a continuity of such mindful awareness Presence, "brief moments many times", between the many distractions that mortal flesh

is heir to. *Dhyana/samadhi* is the foundation of the perfection of wisdom (*Ch. III and Appendix A*).

6) *The Perfection of Wisdom* (*prajna, yeshe, jnana*): Right wisdom is the wisdom of emptiness—*Prajnaparamita*, perfection of wisdom. The perfection of wisdom is 1) the selfless realization of the ground that is boundless emptiness/ *shunyata*—that appearing phenomenal reality is utterly absent and empty of any trace of *independent, ultimate* self-existence—and 2) our indwelling luminous perfect clear light Buddha nature of mind: primordial wisdom, and compassionate Buddha nature.

Such ultimate wisdom transcends yet embraces all of the Six Perfections. It is the end of the perennial cognitive-emotional duality that is the split of knowing subject and its objects known—the end of the painful duality of a lonely separate "self" from everyone, and everything else. Thus is the unifying Perfection of Wisdom the cessation of human suffering.

Ultimate primordial intrinsic awareness wisdom (*jnana, yeshe*) is the very essence of the whole of the Buddha's teaching. How then shall we perfect it? Not by relative conventional conceptual understanding alone, but by the mindful perfection of trans-conceptual, nondual meditation—shamatha and vipashyana—along with the assiduous practice of compassionate generosity, selfless ethics, diligent effort, and plenty of patience.

This concludes our brief review of the Buddha's Eightfold Path and his *Six Paramitas.*

Subtle Considerations of The Path. As we *choose* to practice the Noble Truth of The Path of the Buddha we begin to understand the noetic doublet that is the prior and always present unity of Buddha's Two Truths—ultimate and relative—Suzuki Roshi's all embracing Big Mind, and relative conventional Small Mind arising and participating therein (*Ch. VI*).

Thus does the wisdom of the Path have two voices: skillful, discriminating nonjudgmental *relative* wisdom that is *prajna*, and non-conceptual, nondual intrinsic pristine *ultimate* primordial awareness wisdom (*jnana, yeshe*) that is the ground of *prajna*, namely, the wisdom of *shunyata*/emptiness, essence of *dharmakaya*; vast boundless whole itself (*dharmadhatu, mahabindu*); full *bodhi* mind, love wisdom mind, our indwelling, always already present Presence of That.

Therefore, *bodhi* mind/wisdom mind gradually lifts the dark cloud of unknowing and doubt that benights bright Presence of our always already present primordial wisdom mind.

It is wisdom that moves us from aspirational *bodhicitta* to the engaged selfless *bodhicitta* of intention and action. Wisdom is the absence of the false superimposition of an independent self-ego-I onto our cognition and action such that we may directly, non-conceptually experience both self and other as impermanent, selfless, and utterly interdependent.

Wisdom of the Path nurtures and protects the bodhisattva practitioner's mind and gentle, loving conduct—*bodhicitta*—the root cause of both relative human flourishing (*eudaimonea, felicitas*) and liberation from suffering, ultimate Happiness Itself (*mahasuka, paramananda, beatitudo*), the harmless happiness that forges no karma; the happiness that cannot be lost.

In the Tibetan Buddhist Vajrayana tantric evolution of Mahayana, *jnanaparamita* is the expression of ultimate wisdom—nondual primordial wisdom (*jnana, yeshe*)—that embraces and subsumes the "skillful means" of *Wu-Wei*, relative discriminating *prajna*.

The knowing-feeling, felt sense *awareness* of love-wisdom be-speaks our always already present Buddha wisdom mind Presence (*vidya, rigpa*), dynamic intrinsic awareness Presence (*gzhi rigpa*) of the empty, basal primordial "groundless ground" of all that arises and plays for all of us being here in relative time and space.

In whom does this all arise? On the accord of H.H. Dalai Lama, all states of consciousness, negative or positive, indeed all beings are pervaded by this, our clear light self-reflexively aware aboriginal Buddha wisdom mind (*rang rig yeshe, svasamvedana-jnana*), always "already present from the very beginning" (Garab Dorje). For 20th century *Dzogchen* master Adzom Rinpoche,

> All the limbs of Buddha's teaching have this one great purpose; to lead beings to the nondual primordial wisdom. This innermost secret wisdom mind pervades all views and paths for one who is capable of accessing it (private retreat at Tara Mandala, NM 2002).

Viewed relatively and conventionally this Buddhist love-wisdom Eightfold Path with its *Six Paramitas* transforms primeval igno-rance (*avidya, marigpa*) into primordial wisdom (*vidya, yeshe, jnana*), nondual numinous indwelling Presence (*vidya, rigpa*) of That. In the greater more inclusive *ultimate* view, wisdom's two voices, relative discriminating *prajna* and nondual *jnana/yeshe* are always a prior and present indivisible unity. Once again, as Guru Padmasambhava told, "Practice these two as a unity".

Yes. Ultimate wisdom grounds, embraces and pervades rela-tive wisdom. Just so, Ultimate Truth embraces Relative Truth. As Buddha told, "Form is empty (*shunya, stong pa*); emptiness (*shunyata, stong pa nyi*) is form". On this view, this great *one truth unity*, invariant throughout the many mansions of human cognition—exoteric, objective, conceptual; esoteric, subjective, trans-conceptual, contemplative; and perfectly subjective "in-nermost secret" nondual—is the heart essence of this Buddhist Two Truths dominant trope. (*Ch. VI*).

Primordial dynamic intrinsic awareness wisdom manifests for beings being here in time and space as *grace*, our great gift (*jinlob, euengelion*) of absolute or *ultimate bodhicitta*, given again through sentient beings in form as the kind *bodhicitta of aspiration*, and the engaged compassionate *bodhicitta of action*.

Thus is precious *bodhicitta* the very cause of human happi-ness, both relative human flourishing, and ultimate Happiness

Itself—liberation from suffering, and in due course and by grace, full *bodhi* mind Presence, nameless by any name. Thus is *bodhicitta* the skillful means/method of the bodhisattva (wisdom being) in fulfilling the enlightened promise of the Buddha's Four Noble Truths—for the benefit, not of self, but for all living beings. That is the Buddha's teaching; and that is the very secret of human happiness.

Rainer Maria Rilke recognized this lucent sidereal presence that is always present, deep within each one of us:

> A billion stars spin through the night,
> blazing high above your head. Deep
> within you is the presence that will be,
> when all the stars are dead.

This concludes our exploration of the Buddha's Four Noble Truths.

Buddhist Meditation: Shamatha and Vipashyana

Without past, present, future; empty awake mind.

—Ju Mipham

The nature of mind is the unity of awareness and emptiness.
The nature of mind is clear light.

—Gautama the Buddha

Meditation is the necessary means and method for awakening to, and compassionate expression of our always present indwelling Buddha mind/love-wisdom mind (*buddhajnana*)—subtle numinous Presence of That, by whatever name. Buddhist meditation practice—mind training—has two voices, *shamatha* mindfulness, and *vipashyana*, or penetrating insight, both imperative to engaging and accomplishing the Buddhist Path.

So, the first question. What is meditation?

Meditation is a simple non-conceptual conscious cognitive activity that opens a finite human awareness portal into the infinite vast expanse of all embracing primordial awareness-consciousness being itself in whom we arise and participate. This fecund *Kosmic* consciousness womb is the unbounded unbroken whole in which, or in whom meditator, and everything else that arises to our experience is embraced and included. It is this infinite order of all-pervading *ultimate* reality in whom all enfolded *relative* finite spacetime reality unfolds, arises, participates, and is thereby instantiated—including all of us. Thus is finite meditation our instant and continuous connection to that nondual infinite whole. This is more or less the nondual Primordial Wisdom view as it has arisen in cognitive history of our species.

By virtue of our indivisible prior and always present love-wisdom mind unity of inclusion in the vast whole, there abides here a bright, numinous *Presence* (*vidya, rigpa*) of this primordial reality ground—by whatever name or conceptually contrived concept—necessarily always already present at the heart of the participant, whether in a meditative "state of Presence", or in a state of distraction. It is this prodigious practice of mindful meditation that awakens the practitioner to the nondual (subject-object unity) innermost truth of the matter.

Thus does the practice of meditation offer a finite cognitive link or connection to the prior, infinite primordial awareness-consciousness ground that is indivisible unity of we finite participating parts with our infinite, all inclusive whole itself. The short term, and long term experiential result of such contemplative practice is an emotional sense of peace, well being, and connectedness, even bliss—which is life-changing as it becomes integrated into the lifeworld.

The second question. Just who is it that meditates?

While it is the self-ego-I who *chooses* to establish a meditation practice, and who chooses the *placement of attention* upon the object of meditation—the breath, or emptinesss/buddha nature—it is our basal, primordial love-wisdom Buddha mind (*buddhajnana*) itself that meditates. The mind of self-ego-I, Suzuki Roshi's "Small Mind", is already included and embraced by primordial Buddha mind/wisdom mind—"Big Mind". It is this vast primordial mind that assimilates the physical, perceptual, mental, and emotional raw data of experience, then wondrously organizes it all into nonjudgmental, non-conceptual, nonlocal, nondual "primordially present" love and wisdom—in short, our always present love-wisdom mind—bright Presence of That. We learn to relax into and gently rest in that original primordial Buddha nature of mind.

It is *relative*, conventional mindful mantra prayer, upon the life-giving *prana* wind of the breath, that *connects* to ultimate meaning which embraces relative meaning in the whole of this contemplative process. This post-conceptual, dualistic Small Mind-stabilizing process reflexively refers beyond itself to nondual, all embracing Big Mind which embraces and includes it. Such a penetrating unifying process demonstrates the mythopoetic nondual "logic of the non-conceptual" which transcends and includes our dualistic discursive mind (Klein 2006).

As the hyper-judgmental "wild horse" of conceptual mind simmers down and rests in wisdom mind Presence of the very primordial Buddha *nature of mind*, already present love-wisdom arises as peaceful, loving kindness ethical conduct toward all living beings—including oneself. In the Mahayana tradition such altruistic compassionate thought, intention, and action for the benefit of human and other living beings—including our Mother Earth—is known as *bodhicitta*.

No small matter is at stake in our consideration of the what and the who of meditation. All the buddhas and *mahasiddhas* have told it. The loving kindness of altruistic *bodhicitta* is the primary cause of human happiness, as we have so often seen in these pages.

Indeed, by the lights of some recent Postmodern cultural anthropology, it is survival of the kindest—Late Paleolithic Homo proto-altruism—that is the primary cause of the rise and success of the otherwise unexceptional species *H. sapiens*, the only extant species of the genus Homo.

So, we learn to counter our harsh judgments of self and others with loving kindness; we accept whatever arises in Small Mind—the senses, concepts, and feelings—exactly as it is. No need to try to change anything. No need to fix anything. No need to try to stop thinking; nor to try to accomplish "positive thinking". Simply witness, without evaluation, your thoughts and feelings as they come and go. Witness this display of the mind with gentle loving compassion, like the mother sees her child at play.

Meta-cognitively, reflexively be aware of your awareness in this moment now. No need to change or censor any of it. No need to grasp or reject or react to any of it. Thoughts are merely thoughts. Thoughts cannot harm us. They need not become harmful negative emotions. Thoughts possess only the power that we choose to bestow upon them. It's all the magical display of the mind. No need to like or dislike your experience. All that arises in the mind is utterly natural. The mind and all its stuff are always a prior and present unity with its perfectly subjective primordial source/ground. No problem at all.

The Buddha told it well, "Let it be as it is and rest your weary mind, all things are perfect exactly as they are". Your *ultimate* Buddha mind/wisdom mind Presence already knows this. Let us learn to connect to it through our *relative* imperfect meditation practice. Peace of mind is the wondrous result.

It is through this radical skillful "right understanding" and self-acceptance that meditation effects its miraculous result. Such nondual wisdom cannot be told in words. Wisdom mind experiences it through *feeling* awareness—this "peace that passes all understanding". So, we simply practice opening to receive that lucent already present Presence—without expecting anything at all. Who am I? All the avatars who have incarnated into earth time have told it: living Presence of That I Am!

Therefore, your primary responsibility is *awareness management*. So, right now be reflexively meta-cognitively aware of your present awareness. As compassionate, non-judging witness Presence, monitor whatever arises in the mind—sights, sounds, smells, your breath, feelings of love, sense desire, anger, thinking, guilt and past regret, worry about the future, present mood states, anxiety, impatience, gratitude. There's plenty to worry about. And lots to be happy about. From the view of your loving Buddha mind, observe the whole show—without evaluating or judging any of it. That is the View. That is the Meditation. So, settle in upon the mindful breath, with a mantra if you have one, and rest in the Buddha nature of your mind. Do it now for two minutes (*Appendix A*).

Your psychological attitude now is *shoshin*—Zen Mind/ Beginner's Mind—placing in abeyance questions, judgments, the grasping/attachment and aversion/avoidance that is the constant activity of the busy mind of your self-ego-I. Enjoy your open awareness with a minimum of self-identification. Such "open monitoring meditation" is the first step of *shamatha*, "focused attention meditation". Who is it that meditates? It is your Big Mind love-wisdom mind—clear light now present Presence of That.

Shamatha (*sati, smriti, bhavana*)—calm abiding—may be seen as the foundation of Buddhist contemplative and ethical practice. *Shamatha* literally means calm or quiescence. It is the Buddhist antidote to the distracting mind states of *excitation* or obsessive sensory desire and stimulation, and *laxity* or failure of focused attention on the breath, or other object of meditation.

By cultivating quiescent, non-conceptual *shamatha* or "calm abiding" we utilize the breath, or other meditation object, to settle the "wild horse of the mind" into, and then rest in clear peace of the vast expanse of emptiness/*shunyata*—the very nature of *dharmakaya*—nonlocal, nondual Buddha nature of mind.

Shamatha is, as Buddha told, "mindfulness of breathing"—the gentle *placement of attention* upon the movement of the breath in the belly; the *feeling* of the breath, over and above mere *thinking* about it. Meditation is not a higher form of thinking. Wisdom mind Presence is not a "higher self" upgrade of our habitually thinking self-ego-I. Contemplative practice is mostly trans-rational, non-conceptual, nonlocal, even nondual, beyond the destructive duality or separation of knowing subject and its objects known. As quantum pioneer Werner Heisenberg told, "Subject and object are only one".

Such quiescent mindfulness develops focused attentional stability and a bright vivid acuity of the mind upon its contemplative object—the movement of the breath, emptiness/Buddha nature/

Buddha mind, or an image of the Buddha, or tantric meditation deity, or for Christians, the luminous Presence of the Christ.

Indeed, Buddha, by his own account, accomplished his final *bodhi* mind love-wisdom mind awakening through engaging the mantra seed syllable *OM* while abiding in undistracted, selfless "mindfulness of breathing" (*Appendix A*).

"Mindfulness of breathing" (*sati*) is then the skillful method or means for accomplishing *shamatha* or meditative quiescence. Moreover, on the accord of Buddhist scholar-practitioner B. Alan Wallace (2007):

> Mindfulness...must be accompanied by the mental faculty of introspection...the function of monitoring the meditative process... a type of metacognition...in the development of *shamatha*, swiftly detecting the occurrence of either excitation or laxity.

As subtle introspective awareness detects that the mind has wandered from its object of meditation, through one or another thinking/feeling distraction, attentional awareness is immediately returned to the peaceful quiescent breath—again, and again, and again.

The practitioner gradually "progresses" through the nine stages of *shamatha*. Its ultimate accomplishment leaves only pure awareness, luminosity, and bliss. Thoughts continue to arise but "self-liberate" at or near the instant of their arising, leaving no karmic imprint. The mind is now prepared to "rest in its natural state", free of any attentional object of meditational support, for example the breath, or mantra, or image presence of a deity. Meanwhile, use the supports.

Potential distractions arise as before, and pass away as they will, without intervention, introspection, judgment or antidote. The mind rests in the always already present purity of its own nonlocal, nondual natural state of original primordial awareness-consciousness itself, the very Buddha nature of mind. The result is peaceful bliss (*Ch. VIII, Dzogchen*). But, in the meantime, remain close to the breath, and get a mantra (e.g. *OM AH HUM*). The mind that is filled with the light and sound of mantra has no remaining space for afflictive thoughts and emotions.

That all said, most of this "no-self help" is mere idealized concepts and beliefs *about* meditation, until one enters into it by establishing an effective practice. Let a qualified teacher help you establish your practice, then introduce you to a qualified meditation master, and a like-minded community.

An effective meditation practice cannot be learned from a book, not even this one, nor from a DVD series by a famous spiritual person. Still, books and tapes by Buddhist masters, and yogis and yoginis may be helpful in clarifying basic principles—how it all fits together; and why bother in the first place?

Thus it is, mindfulness practice—fully realized or not—transforms the habitually self-referencing "selfing" mind via training in deep inner peace. The gradual result is a loving, happy, always imperfectly stable mind. Thus does *shamatha* provide support for the vivid clarity and direct wisdom of true *vipashana* realization.

Vipashyana literally means "extraordinary seeing"—penetrating direct clear seeing that is the primordial purity of yogic direct perception (*yogi pratyaksa*)—prior to the reflexive superimposition (*vikshepa*) of discursive conceptual mind. *Vipashyana* is "analytic insight meditation".

Such insight is direct, non-conceptual, transpersonal seeing (*samadhi, kensho/satori*) of the empty absence of "any shred" of ultimate intrinsic existence of all spacetime phenomena; to wit, the *ultimate* emptiness of all the *relatively* real appearing physical and mental stuff of our busy life-world realities. We shall see in these pages that this initially rather offputting radical emptiness notion becomes the main source of our human happiness. And yes, it requires a bit of patience.

So, *vipashyana* insight transcends but embraces clear thinking through clear *direct* seeing. Here the knowing subject does not merely intend its object of knowledge, but is aware of the direct *feeling* experience of being already present in it, with no distance or separation at all. Again, just for a moment, settle into the breath in the belly and *feel* the bright delight of seeing without thinking!

Hence, *shamatha* and *vipashyana* meditation liberate perception and conception from their habitual and constricted experience of the myriad objects arising in objective time, with all their random and wandering distractions, thereby permitting the gaze of the mind to settle into, and rest in its subjective, innermost body of present moment, here now bright "feeling experience". This is the bodily location of human happiness. It happens upon the breath. Remain close to the breath.

English poet William Blake called this healing purification of awareness of our constant objective inherently dualistic thinking—"cleansing the doors of perception".

In this way are Aldous Huxley's "doors of perception" opened wide to the "micro-phenomenological" purity of our inter-subjective, direct present moment blissful "feeling experience", prior to the dualistic semiotic conceptual contraction that is our all too human deep cultural background (unconscious) materialist "global web of belief" (Quine 1969).

Thus, upon an encounter with a lovely red rose, we drop our "expectational bias" about its objective meaning—"Yes, that's a red rose"—and encounter it intimately with all of our sensory, aesthetic, and affective feeling awareness. It is by way of meditation that we "stop to smell the roses" of our feeling nature—our affective, awake and delightful "lived experience". Stop and see.

This intrapersonal *awareness management skill set* changes everything. It enriches the dance of both verbal and nonverbal interpersonal awareness in our relationships with those within our sphere; and especially with our most beloved. Greatly enhanced human happiness and well being is the wondrous result, as many of you well know.

In this way our arising realities become the subtle feeling experience of poetry. Thus does the shaman-poet dwelling in mythtime, at the root of attention and just prior to the world, sing,

Everything is alive!
Trees, grasses, wind dancing,
guides me. I understand
the songs of the birds!

"The poet's eye, in a fine frenzy rolling, doth glance from heaven to earth, from earth to heaven" (Wm. Shakespeare). Thus do we unify the lucent heaven of our divine nature with the fervent earth of our bodily existence.

Wisdom Mind No-Self Help. But wait! If I "change my mind, and so change my brain" (Begley 2007) by meditation, I fear that I might "tune in and drop out" of life, quit my job, leave my family as did the Buddha, join some cult, get on drugs, and wind up on the streets, or worse.

Psychologists have a name for such fearful cognition: "catastrophic expectations". We're all a little frightened of change. Not to worry. As the prodigious self-ego-I becomes *gradually* aligned with your compassionate love-wisdom mind Presence of this vast primordial whole, committed meditation practitioners still show up for work, pay the bills, and change diapers. All the attractive and aversive stuff of always thinking, furiously desirous self-ego-I that we have come to know and love still exists in abundance in a conventional, *relatively*, really real "real world out there" (RWOT).

It's just that all this stuff of form doesn't exist absolutely or *ultimately*. In the really big picture, as Buddha told, "Form is empty; emptiness is form". So we, as a separate self, need not get hung up on the absolute reality of it. We learn to chill out and stop taking our ego life drama so seriously. We learn to drop our spooky "conformational bias"—that all new data are interpreted as supporting our current skeptical "global web of belief—and adopt the refreshingly open *shoshin* cognitive posture of our already present peaceful Zen mind. Perhaps we are not the center of the universe after all. Now that's a scary thought!

In other words, all of this *relative* form is absent and empty of any permanent *ultimate* existence. Appearing spacetime reality is not as it appears! Our self-ego-I is not nearly as real as it appears! We change our view of reality a bit, and a lot of our suffering drops away.

Really understanding this unity of Buddha's Two Truths (*Ch. VI*)—relative form and its ultimate emptiness—imperfectly frees us from fear and anger, and thus opens our hearts and minds to our always present Presence of *bodhicitta*—benefiting living beings—which is after all, the very secret of human happiness. And this places the unruly narcissistic self in its "supreme identity"—our primordial Buddha love-wisdom mind—bright always present Presence of That. Everyone in our sphere of influence benefits, especially those we love the most.

As Buddha told so long ago, "Wonder of wonders, all beings are Buddha".

So, that is more or less the Mahayana view of the Path of meditation. We align an amorphous empirically unfindable and unprovable yet conventionally real unruly self with selfless Buddha mind Presence, more or less moment to moment, and skillfully work and play in a beautiful, relatively real, but not ultimately real world with often imperfect peace, and great happiness. Contrary to an all too common misperception about Buddhism, we are not required to give up, put down, or otherwise abolish our self-ego-I! Buddha's way is to work with it, lift and align it with our always present Buddha love-wisdom mind, all the while remaining aware of ego's very subtle duplicity. Buddha mind "is already accomplished from the very beginning", deep within us, here and now. It is That to which we awaken—step by step—upon the Buddhist Path.

Therefore, "Leave it alone and let it be as it is". Now, just for this precious moment, experience profound thankfulness for your precious life, just as it is now, imperfections and all. Feel that gratitude within your heart of hearts. Then feel your good will intention to benefit living beings, however imperfectly. No need to fabricate it. It's already present. Open and receive it. Begin and end each day with this selfless affirmation: "Thank you for the gift of my life, just as it is now". This will help you to stay present to Presence of your Buddha nature/Buddha mind—your already present Heart's desire.

Through such wisdom mind considerations we come to see clearly that our habitual thoughts and feelings have no real substance in themselves—but are rather an apparitional will-o'-the-wisp, utterly dependent upon our constantly changing distracted mind states. Thus arises all important loving self-acceptance, like the love of the mother for her fearful child.

We begin to see the humor of our absurd, obsessive self-referential story-narrative—why I-Me-Mine is always right, never wrong; and always the center of the universe. If everyone acted like that the world would be in a real mess. The bad news: everyone *does* act like that! And the world *is* in a real mess. We need your help. We're all in this reality thing together.

True, some of the slings and arrows of outrageous samsara are abated as our compassionate intrapersonal relationship with our indwelling love-wisdom mind Presence grows, and through that our interpersonal relationships flourish (even with "difficult people").

Still, much of the natural adversity that mortal flesh is heir to remains unabated. We never get enough of the stuff we want; and we get far too much of what we don't want. And we're still impermanent (*anitya*), living in the constant presence of our death. And that requires a bunch of courage; the courage not to fall into readily available ego defenses that sublimate our powerful inner fear of nonexistence into endless outer distractions of work and play. So *stop* and smell the roses. Love-wisdom mind Presence, it is said, has a very subtle aroma of roses.

Awareness Management. What is it that changes with "mindfulness of breathing"? It is our habitual *reaction* to adversity; and our *response* to that opportunity! Anxiety, anger, and dread lose most of their power over us. That is to say, we no longer *choose* to submit to the negative stuff. We choose instead to place our awareness—in between myriad distractions—upon our mantra breath, always present mindful Presence of That. That is the simple practice of the Path. What a relief!

With our attention nearly always placed upon wisdom Buddha mind Presence that rides each mantra breath we are, however imperfectly, at peace. *Thus is human happiness very much a matter of awareness management. Human happiness is, very pragmatically, a direct result of where we choose to place our present attention, here and now!* We have more control over our present mind state than we may have imagined possible. Mindful attention practice, "brief moments, many times", makes it so.

Abiding calmly in this centrist Middle Way view and practice, things aren't nearly so worrisome. Our lived experience is all the more vivid and beautiful. Ultimately, in the proverbial final analysis, even as we live in the uncertainty and impermanence of this "dark cloud of unknowing", "there is no problem whatsoever in this world" (Suzuki Roshi). That is the aboriginal wisdom of the all embracing dimension of Ultimate Truth, our Big Mind that pervades and embraces this all too real world of conventional Relative Truth, Small Mind (*Ch. VI*).

Just so, these two reality realms are utterly indivisible, an always already prior and present non-conceptual, nondual inseparable unity—bright Presence of That. Such a peace may be beyond discursive, conceptual understanding; but it is readily present to our contemplative indwelling love-wisdom Buddha mind, when we to open and to receive it. So, breathe mindfully right now for a few moments. Rest in that bright mind space between your thoughts. Now is the time.

Therefore, the key principle that grounds contemplative practice is this: human happiness, and human suffering, arise from our present mind state. So, we consciously manage our awareness by training the "wild horse of the mind" in placement of attention on our innermost indwelling wisdom mind Presence (vidya, rigpa). In Buddhism this process of the Path begins with calm abiding upon the breath, beyond our thoughts and beliefs about it.

Basic Mindfulness Practice: Quieting the Wild Horse of the Mind. Well, wouldn't it be nice to *directly* experience that primordial love-wisdom mind Presence that you already are? There's no time like the present. Therefore, bracket for a moment your present quiescent practice, if you have one, and all your questions—just for this precious moment now—and give yourself *two minutes* of peace. It's easier than you think. If you find it useful the Buddha has some surprising suggestions to deepen your practice, and enhance your present happiness. You cannot learn, nor experience mindfulness by reading about it.

"Without past, present, future; empty awake mind" (Ju Mipham Rinpoche).

Sit up straight, uncross your legs, cast your partially closed eyes down slightly so that your neck is straight, and place your attention upon the breath in your belly. Relax jaw, neck, gut. Feel the breath naturally rising and falling in the belly.

1. *Thank you!* First, very briefly experience deep gratitude for your life exactly as it is now. Then feel your great good will intention that your life may benefit living beings. This affirmation is most important. It opens the heart and mind to receive selfless grace by shifting attention from self.

2. *Attention!* Now gather the "wild horse of the mind" by *placement of attention* upon your breath as it rhythmically, naturally arises in your belly. Breathe normally. Just for this moment—without grasping at, or rejecting anything— witness your awareness. Be reflexively aware of your awareness; of the *prana* life force current that animates you with each and every breath.

   The Polyvagal Breath. Now breathe in normally for five seconds; then out for seven seconds, through pursed lips, like breathing out through a small straw. Practice this for three, seven, or nine times, as you wish. Then breathe normally. Polyvagal breathing interrupts the production of cortisol, the stress hormone, produced by the adrenal cortex. This inhibits its flow along the vagus nerve (CNX) which innervates all the organs of the parasympathetic nervous system—heart, lungs, digestive—instantly reducing the "fight or flight" stress response.

Now, with each breath feel your busy mind settle into its natural state of wakefulness—your clear light love-wisdom mind Presence—that aspect of you that is utterly one with the great source of everything—your safe place, free of thoughts, concepts, beliefs; free of past and future; free of judgment, fear, anger, guilt, and pride; momentarily free of narcissistic self-ego-I. No need to think about it, or fabricate it. Open and feel it. Be that stillness now. *Feel the peace that passes all understanding.*

3. Now feel life force energy of gentle *prana* spirit wind—the very "breath of life"—as it enters in upon the breath, then pervades every space of your body and mind—all physical, mental, emotional, spiritual structures. *Prana, c'hi, pneuma*-Holy Spirit is the subtle form of gross spacetime physical light energy/matter form ($E = mc^2$) arising continuously from formless, spacious, vast boundless whole, primordial awareness-consciousness ground itself in whom you, and all of this arises, participates, and is happily instantiated.

    Enjoy this feeling of delight within you. Feel your connectedness to everything. No need to try to create it. Your mindful Presence upon the breath is always already present. That is your "supreme identity". Who am I? That I Am! Feel That. Awaken to That.

4. Now, with your gaze still slightly downward, briefly close your eyes, raise your eyebrows and focus attention behind your forehead. Feel a subtle, focused fullness in your forebrain. You are now *directly* experiencing subtle, but observable waking alpha and theta brain rhythm—the

non-conceptual "relaxation response", which replaces "fight or flight" stress response. Breathe and enjoy. Notice here the profound sense of your luminous wisdom mind Presence. Amplify it. No need to think about it; simply feel the lush texture of it.

5. As the mind begins to wander from the breath, thoughts and feelings naturally arise. No problem. Whatever arises, let it be as it is. No need to grasp at, or reject anything at all. No need to try to "meditate"; or to stop thinking; or to block troublesome thoughts; or to *try* to do anything at all. There is no goal. Just breathe. Always return to the breath in the belly. Simply remain present to your breath.

    Without your attention, thoughts and feelings "self liberate" at the very instant of their arising. They dissolve and pass on the out breath. Or watch them gently flow by like a cloud in the vast empty sky, leaving no trace. *Choose* to transfer your attention to That, again and again.

    More or less absent thoughts and concepts, and the emotions they induce, your non-conceptual Buddha mind Presence is revealed just as it is—luminous and clear. Kind compassionate activity of love spontaneously arises from That. As your mind is filled with spacious, unifying clear light wisdom of love, no room remains for the negative stuff.

    Let it be so. As Buddha told so long ago, "Let it be as it is and rest your weary mind; all things are perfect, exactly as they are....Wonder of wonders, all beings are Buddha".

    So, briefly greet whatever arises—positive, negative, neutral—then label it "distraction", and return your *attention* to the breath, again and again. Happiness and peace ride the mindful breath. Now *feel* your present connection to indwelling love-wisdom Presence that you actually are, by whatever name, right here upon each mindful breath. Rest now for a couple of minutes, or more, in the spacious primordial essence and nature of mind—your always already present Buddha mind. Directly experience, and enjoy.

6. If you wish to add the great Buddhist mantra *OM AH HUM* (*Ch. IX*; *Appendix A*) to your alpha breath practice, please do so. It's a touchstone that will aid in managing distractions, and subtly, instantly connect you to the inherent power of your *bodhi* mind Presence. Remain present to it—"brief moments, many times"—in your cognitive foreground or background throughout the day and night. Please give yourself this gift of light, one minute, several times a day, and night.

7. Practice immediately upon rising for 10-30 minutes; and for ten minutes, or more just before sleep. This is especially important if you have sleep troubles. *Be* the entire night in your love-wisdom mind. Let this be your love-wisdom lullaby and good night.

8. Dream work. Upon arising, before meditation, very briefly write down important dream images. No need to" analyze" the dream; or try to figure out "what it means". "Work the dream" in the first person tense. Speak as the key person or image in the dream thusly: "*I am----*, and *I feel----*. Do this with a loved one if possible. You will find it quite revealing. Now practice your morning meditation as usual. Be present to key dream images as you practice.

9. Now, close this and all of your meditation sessions— whether a minute, or an hour, or a day—with this great aspiration: "*May all beings be free of suffering, and the causes of suffering. May all beings have happiness, and the causes of happiness*". This bodhisattva *bodhicitta* intention shifts self-centered practice from merely benefiting self—which it most certainly does—to the benefit of both self and all other beings. Astonishingly, this is the best way to be happy yourself.

10. Spontaneously practice this "alpha mantra breath" for about 60 seconds several times a day, and night. Let the opening prayers and initial settling of steps 1-6 be accomplished in the first minute. For brief 60 second meditations these steps happen in the first 36 seconds of mindful breathing. Then, simply rest in your Buddha nature of mind. Such patience and diligence will establish a deep, subtle and abiding continuity of your love-wisdom mind—luminous Presence of That. *Emaho*! How wonderful! *Mahasukaho*! Ultimate happiness!

(For the complete Brief Course, visit *Appendix A*, "Let It Be: Basic Mindfulness Meditation".)

Review of The View. The analytic "penetrating insight" that is liberating *vipashyana* reveals this great nonlocal (beyond time and space), nondual (subject-object unity) truth of the *buddic* wisdom of emptiness, that we may utilize it in selfless service of sentient beings—compassionate *bodhicitta*—here in time and form (*Ch. V*).

For Tibetan Vajrayana practice, *vipashyana* and *bodhicitta* are the View and Path that bears the Fruit or Result of realization of the inseparable, indivisible unity of: 1) arising, appearing phenomena and emptiness; 2) of vivid clarity and emptiness; and 3) of bliss and emptiness.

Therefore, *shamatha* mindfulness bestows peace of mind that opens into *vipashyana* (and many other practices)—selfless open awareness Presence (*vidya, rigpa*) that facilitates entering in direct penetrating insight of the very nature of mind—intimate, mostly concept free liberation that is our "supreme identity" with the vast spacious, empty boundless whole (*dharmadhatu*) of appearing reality itself. *Emaho*!

In whom does this all arise? It is this ultimate primordial awareness-consciousness itself, numinous vast whole in whom relative human awareness-consciousness is always a luminous instantiation. We are never separate from That. Good to know.

The Neuroscience of Meditation and Our Experience of Self. What are the neurobiological influences of mindfulness meditation on human behavior; how do these influences effect our sense of self-ego-I; our brain structure and function; relative human flourishing; and the ultimate happiness and freedom of liberation from suffering, enlightenment, and Buddhahood?

Buddhist masters and neuroscientists agree, "mindfulness of breathing" ("focused attention meditation"), and "compassion meditation" both facilitate 1) a beneficial shift of attention from obsessive, usually fraught *self-referential thinking* and concern for "I, Me, Mine"; which 2) bestows a sense of inner peace and self-acceptance; which 3) reduces anxiety and anger toward self and others; which 4) enhances altruistic thought, intention and action for the benefit of other beings, 5) enhancing well being and happiness. How shall we understand this amazing contemplative process in the gloss of neurobiology?

Unfocused, ruminating, wandering mind, under sway of the brain's "default mode network"—the medial prefrontal cortex (MPFC) and posterior cingulate cortex (PCC)—significantly increase self-referential attention—"selfing"—with its always present fear/anxiety, anger/hostility, greed/pride, and negative judgments about self, which are then projected onto others. The micro-cognitive result of such afflictive negative emotion in the individual is stress and unhappiness. The macro-cognitive result in the human sociocultural cognosphere is alienation, despotism, and endless war.

Scientific meta-research, synthesizing data from thousands of research projects since 1970, reveal that all three of the classes of meditation—1) mindfulness focused attention (usually upon the breath); 2) open monitoring mindfulness (witnessing whatever arises in awareness without judging, grasping or rejecting); and 3) loving-kindness compassion meditation (feeling our natural empathy for living beings)—conclusively reduced or deactivated processing in some physical brain structures, while enhancing activity in others. Just so:

1) Meditation reduced processing in the default mode network (PCC and MPFC) of the "selfing" wandering mind; which 2) reduced self-ego-I self-referential processing— habitual attention and concern about I-Me-Mine with its attendant anxiety, anger and ill-will mind states; 3) reduced activity in, and reduced physical size of the amygdala which is responsible for fear and anger ("fight or flight"); 3) reduced stress related cortisol production by the adrenal cortex while blocking cortisol circulation throughout the upper body upon the autonomic vagus nerve (CN X); 4) enhanced beneficial brain alpha, theta, and high amplitude gamma band oscillations (25 to 42 hertz), while reducing excessive beta activity; 5) reduced activity in the right prefrontal cortex which is active in fear, anger, and ill-will mind states; 6) greatly increased left prefrontal cortex processing which enhances feelings of altruism, compassion and forgiveness toward self and others; 7) induced increased, long term frontal cortex gyrification (neuroplasticity), which is permanent, even when contemplative practice ceases (Siegel 2013; Porges 2014; Begley 2007; Wallace 2007, 2009; *Scientific American,* November, 2014).

The no longer surprising result of this neuroscientific meta-research is greatly reduced preoccupation with self and its obsessive narcissistic self-narrative; reduced psycho-emotional stress; induced and enhanced subjective feelings of connection, well being, good will, and subjective reports of increased happiness.

Thus does mindfulness and other types of meditation train the "wild horse of the mind" in the *placement of attention,* and continued focus of attention upon immediate, non-conceptual, present moment to moment sensory/ feeling experience, upon the mindful breath—our eternal here and now connection—while shifting attention away from chronic unfocused wandering mind with its obsessive and unhappy attachment to self-ego-I.

Therefore, meditation clearly reduces or suspends the "selfing" that causes the terrible suffering secondary to our pervasive sense of a lonely, separate, mortal self. And all of this through a program of mind training in present moment, trans-conceptual *feeling awareness* upon the breath—the placement and maintenance of attention upon the breath which settles the "wild horse of the mind" upon the very source and "nature of mind", boundless all embracing whole, nondual wisdom mind Presence of That, by whatever name or concept.

Yes, neuroscientific research demonstrates the profound value of meditation—especially *shamatha* calm abiding, and loving-kindness compassion meditation—in support of human flourishing and happiness. Indeed, there is a "mindfulness revolution" now abroad in the Western mind and its culture. Mindfulness training is alive and well in most of our institutions: education, medicine, psychology, the social sciences, business, government, military, and corrections.

Our Western mindfulness cognitive reconstruction has even entered monotheistic organized religion—Judaism, Christianity, Islam. Abrahamic Monotheism has lost, under sway of the dominant cognitive paradigm that is Greek animated Scientific Materialism/Physicalism (which has now colonized the Western mind), much of its foundation in the contemplative mythos and praxis of the highest nondual (subject-object unity) teaching of our great Primordial Wisdom Tradition (*e.g.* Buddhism, Hinduism, Taoism).

On this neurobiological view then, human happiness is very much dependent upon an *awareness management skill set*—where, when, and how we *choose* to place our attention. In short, both happiness and unhappiness are the result of our *choices* as to present *placement of attention*—negative emotion or love-wisdom mind Presence—each moment now.

Cognitive neuroscience has identified two ways of experiencing the self—two modes of self-reference: 1) *narrative focus upon self*, our urgent all consuming story-drama about ourselves; and 2) *experiential focus*, bodily proprioceptive sense experience, with direct trans-conceptual feeling experience. These two modes are often hypothesized by cognitive scientists to be neurologically distinct. Buddhism has unified them.

Once again, volumes of research have demonstrated that in both meditators and non-meditators the *experiential focus* mode involving non-conceptual "mindfulness of breathing" as the Buddha called it, reduced egocentric narrative self-referential activity, in a word "selfing", in the MPFC and PCC of the default mode network. However, for highly skilled meditators habitual fantasy-reverie self-referential thinking of the untrained mind is absent during sitting meditation, and for varying periods of time following formal sitting meditation. Here, processing activity of the default mode network is nearly quiescent (Siegel 2013). These skilled practitioners abide in a "walking meditation" mind state most of the time. And this calm state persists through several sleep states during the night.

In short, "advanced" meditators have demonstrated in many studies (Begley 2007; Siegel 2013) the capacity to maintain such stable contemplative mind states, with their corresponding brain rhythms (theta and gamma) in "post-meditation" activities—while "hewing wood and carrying water", and driving, talking, loving, and even creative thinking!

Therefore, meditation practice for established meditators seems to facilitate the *choice* of a fluent cognitive ambulation from conceptual self narrative mode to a peaceful, even blissful non-conceptual experiential mode, almost at will. Indeed, the mind states of the nondual mode are usually experienced as pervading and embracing conceptual self narrative mind states. There is no appreciable difference.

The global result of meditation practice is calm abiding quiescent peace of mind, and a happy felt sense of connection and interdependence with all living things; and indeed, with the unbroken whole of *Kosmos* itself—even as inexorable adversity continues to arise.

Mindful Thinking About Science and Spirit. We've just seen that hundreds of scientific studies with highly advanced Buddhist meditators, as well as beginning meditators, have demonstrated that subjective meditation states have objective neural correlates in the brain. Does this fact mean that trans-physical, post-empirical meditation experience can be reduced to merely physical brain states, as acolytes of our modern prevailing materialist metaphysic—the "scientific reductionism" of fundamentalist "Scientism"—believe?

Does the fact that Buddhist modernists, for example H.H. Dalai Lama, correctly state that Buddhism is, and has always been a contemplative "science of mind" mean that the Buddhist understanding of mind, and the very nondual Buddha nature of mind, is also an objective science of mind in the same way that experimental psychology, or physics is?

It does not. Is the "mind of enlightenment" taught by all of the buddhas reducible to the mere EEG brightening of the left prefrontal cortex during an advanced meditator's heartfelt compassion for a living being in terrible pain? It is not.

It is useful here to remember that the spectrum of human knowledge—from the objective conceptual understanding of mathematical physics, to the deep subjectivity of Buddha mind—is, when engaged by discursive concept mind—pervaded by metaphysical, or ontological speculation. Philosophers of science and Buddhist Lamas agree: that appearing spacetime reality is *ultimately* objective and material/physical is an unproven, unprovable metaphysical belief. That reality is ultimately subjective and illusory is equally so. That reality is a centrist middle way between these two metaphysical extremes is still provisional, uncertain, fallible concept and belief. No problem at all. And the trans-conceptual definitive contemplative certainty of nondual Buddha mind? Clearly, that is beyond belief. We are thus naturally referred to deeper, post-empirical contemplative strata of cognitive formation (*Ch. V*).

Metaphysical scientific reductionism—the ontological reduction of all appearing reality to mere physical phenomena—is the dogmatic hand maid to the prevailing Western cultural "global web of belief", namely, the much valorized and idealized metaphysic of Scientific Materialism/Physicalism.

The "scientific method"—systematic objective observation, measurement, experiment, and the experimental formulation and testing of hypotheses—is wondrously capable of revealing truths in the conceptual dimension of objective, physical spacetime appearing reality; the world of physics, cosmology, mathematics, and biology. Yet, such a monistic metaphysic, *ipso facto*, methodologically ignores the entire dimension of subjective, non-conceptual, non-physical human experience, to wit: 1) the feeling emotional experience of personal and spiritual love; 2) the trans-conceptual contemplative experience of the perfectly subjective nondual primordial wisdom of the Buddha and the Christ; and 3) the great nondual Primordial Wisdom Tradition of humankind that transcends yet embraces and includes the objective realm of modern science.

Physical science and contemplative science must work together to pragmatically unify our essential human cognitive capacities—objective conceptual, and subjective contemplative—that is so profoundly displayed through these two complementary sciences. That is our joyous urgent wisdom project as we enter in the 21st century Noetic Revolution that is now upon us. (Boaz 2021b, excerpted at davidpaulboaz.org)

Therefore, subtle primordial wisdom, beyond but including conceptual knowledge, requires that we human beings utilize our innate *noetic cognitive doublet* that constitutes both the objective and subjective voices of the nonlocal, nondual whole of our human wisdom mind. We must understand that these two are an ontologically prior, yet an epistemologically and phenomenologically present complementary, indivisible unity. We utilize this handy cognitive doublet to ascertain both provisional and definitive truth, both relative and ultimate truth, and the ontic prior but always present indivisible unity of these two human cognitive modalities.

Philosophy—*philo-sophia*—Western or Eastern is so much more than sterile academic philosophy. Traditionally, philosophy is the love of wisdom. Ultimately, philosophy is the prior and present unity of love and wisdom. For the spiritual practitioner philosophy is understanding the practical, skillful expression in compassionate conduct of this love-wisdom unity for the benefit of living beings. That is how we may *be* happy now. And that is what Buddhist philosophy is about (*Ch.V*).

Kuhnian (Thomas Kuhn's 1961 *Structure of Scientific Revolutions*) scientific "paradigm shifts" produce "scientific revolutions" every generation or two. Cases in point: the 17th century Newtonian Revolution utilized, but enhanced Galileo's theory of relativity; Einstein's Special Relativity Theory (SRT) replaced Newton's relativity, and established the present relativistic scientific paradigm. Quantum electrodynamics (QED) corrected and included Einstein's Special and General Relativity Theory (GRT) establishing the prevailing physics Standard Model (ΛCDM) of particles and fields, revealing in the process its own quantum incompleteness, as Einstein was quick to point out (*Appendix B*).

We are now perched rather precariously upon the cusp of a new knowledge/wisdom paradigm, a Noetic Revolution in matter, mind and spirit (Boaz 2021b) that begins to heal the relentless subject-object split between our objective and subjective cognitive modes of experience. Buddhist contemplative studies is facilitating this process as dialog continues between physicists, philosophers of physics, and practicing Buddhist scholars. And we need a lot more of it.

Therefore, lest we valorize too much in our clinging to the descending "scientific" metaphysic that is modern Scientific Materialism/Physicalism ("Scientism" in its fundamentalist cloak) let us understand that all scientific theories are fallible, provisional and incomplete; impatiently awaiting that next more inclusive, syncretic but ever incomplete theory. Just so, Buddhist dialectics is incomplete. Such is the destiny of conceptual, dialectical, relative conventional truth, whether scientific or religious. Absolute *objective* certainty is a pipe dream.

Clearly, the neuroscientific implications of meditation for the reduction of human suffering and for human happiness are profound. Mindfulness meditation and loving-kindness meditation offer skillful regulation of negative emotional response to life's inexorable adversity by transforming the painful narcissistic self-narrative into peaceable, and altruistic states of mind.

We have now seen that through the assiduous practice of the Buddhist Path we learn to place our present moment to moment awareness—our *attention*—upon our direct trans-conceptual *feeling experience.* This contemplative process opens a finite awareness portal into infinity wherein we connect with an aspect of ourselves that is selfless, non-conceptual, and profound. We come to understand that we need not believe and defend our adventitious dreary and destructive negative ego-centric thoughts and feelings; stress is reduced; and human happiness is enhanced.

The psychological/emotional takeaway here is this: our thoughts and feelings—positive and negative—are fleeting, inherently evanescent, ever changing, and impermanent (*anitya*).

Understanding this, we, as self-ego-I, give them as much power as we choose. We do have this choice. Perhaps we might take ourselves less seriously, and with a bit of ego-self-effacing humor.

Thus does the noble Truth of the Path to the happiness of liberation from ignorance (*avidya, ma rigpa*) that is the root cause of suffering—with its Mahayana Six Perfections, and ethic of *bodhicitta*—provide a contemplative way to remain present, moment to moment, to our already present, innermost Buddha mind—happy bright Presence of That. That is the Buddha's promise of primordial awakening to all of us—without a single exception. Meditation practice makes it so.

This concludes our exploration of Buddhist meditation.

Buddhist Ethics

> No small matter is at stake. The question concerns the
> very way that human life is to be lived.
>
> —Plato, *The Republic*, Book I

Self and No-Self. That Buddhism bespeaks the ultimate absence
or emptiness (*shunyata*) of an intrinsically existent permanent self
(*atman*) is axiomatic. This is the ubiquitous Buddhist view of the
emptiness of self, or *anatman*. On this metaphysical principle the
three Buddhist vehicles—Hinayana/Theravada, Mahayana, and
Tibetan Vajrayana—and their various doctrinal schools agree.
From such a metaphysic arises Buddhist ethics. How shall we
understand this?

In the earlier Buddhist Hinayana teaching vehicle the
Arhat in training cultivates the wisdom of selflessness—the
emptiness of self (*anatman*)—through the practice of avoiding
the Ten Nonvirtuous Actions—killing, stealing, sexual misconduct, lying, slander, gossip, abusive speech, greed/pride,
vindictiveness, and wrong views. In the Mahayana these ten
are reduced to the Five Buddhist Precepts, as we shall soon
see. The Buddha's Eightfold Path to the ultimate cessation
of human suffering is seen by the early Hinayana vehicle as a
"middle path", or middle way (*madhyama-pratipad*) that avoids
the behavioral extremes of sensory indulgence and extreme
asceticism. From the *Pali Canon:*

The Perfect One avoided these two extremes and found the Middle Path which opens the eyes, produces knowledge and leads to peace, insight, enlightenment, and nirvana...
—*Samyutta-nikaya* 56,11

In the 1st century C.E. the Mahayana Vehicle begin to evolve from the Indian Hinayana *Sarvastivada* and *Mahasanghika* schools, then in the 2nd century, Mahayana developed Nagarjuna's Middle Way Madhyamaka, and in the 4th century Asanga and his half brother Vasubandu founded the mentalist Mind Only (*chittamatra*) Yogachara school. These two—Middle Way Madhyamaka and Middle Way Yogachara—are the not entirely commensurate centrist interpretations of Buddha's Middle Way teaching. They represent the two main schools of the Mahayana Great Vehicle. They spread from India to China, Japan, Korea, and in the 8th century to Tibet, to become the Tibetan Buddhist Vajrayana/Mantrayana Secret Mantra teaching vehicle.

In the early 6th century Indian Mahayana Buddhism was introduced by Bodhidharma, the first Ch'an/Zen patriarch, to China, which merged with Chinese Taoism to become the illustrious Ch'an Buddhist tradition. Two of these traditions—Rinzai (with Eisai Zenji) and Soto (with Dōgen Zenji)—then entered Japan in the late 12th century to become the Zen tradition, now extant throughout the world. In the mid 20th century Suzuki Roshi firmly established Soto Zen in the United States. (More history in *Ch. I.*)

Zen is notorious among the Mayayana schools for its emphasis on the nondual *direct* yogic experience (*yogi pratyaksa*) of awakened Buddha mind—*kensho, satori*—over ritual and liturgy, deity practice, and conceptual doctrinal analysis; although Zen utilizes a bit of all three. For Zen Buddhism the path to enlightenment—awakening to the wisdom of emptiness—is mostly *zazen*, "simply sitting" in meditation on emptiness. More on Zen in Chapter V.

The Indian Mahayana Vehicle, which includes the Tibetan Secret Mantra Vajrayana—added to this seed principle of the wisdom of the *emptiness of self*, the wisdom of the *emptiness of "other" phenomena* appearing to such a self-imputed self. This added complexity thickened the Mahayana dialectical plot. Thus we now have two domains of self emptiness in the Tibetan Vajrayana: 1) emptiness of self, or *intrinsic emptiness*—the *Rangtong* view of Middle Way Prasangika Madhyamaka, and 2) emptiness of phenomena "other" than self, or *extrinsic emptiness*—the *Shentong* view of Middle Way Yogachara Svatantrika. We shall briefly survey these views in Chapter V.

The compassionate Mahayana/Vajrayana Bodhisattva (we Buddhas in training) aims to ascertain not only the absence or emptiness of any trace of *atman* self-ego-I, but to go beyond the noble *Arhat's* understanding, to the inherent emptiness of all appearing spacetime phenomena, both "self", *Rangtong* and "other" phenomena, *Shentong*. So, the wisdom of emptiness of the Vajrayana teaching vehicle, in that view, transcends yet includes the foundational wisdom of the Hinayana/Theravada vehicle.

The Hinayana, or "lesser vehicle" does not, not surprisingly, agree that it is a lesser vehicle. To respect the Hinayana extant Theravada school the pejorative epithet "Hinayana" is often, rightly replaced by the term "Shravakayana". The Hinayana vehicle is ,after all, the very foundational teaching of all the later teaching vehicles and their various schools.

Thus, that which is to be negated (the *negandum*) for the Mahayana, or "greater vehicle", is all appearing phenomena, and the *atman* self that perceives it. The Buddha told it thus: "*Sabbe dharma anatta*"—"All appearing phenomena are no-self". All spacetime stuff, and its sentient perceivers are ultimately empty of any whit of essential *ultimate* self-existence (*svabhava*).

We shall see in Chapter V, "Buddhist Philosophy", that in order to avoid the apparent negative nihilism of this view, Mahayana Middle Way Madhyamaka sees appearing reality as *relatively*, conventionally existent, just not *ultimately* inherently existent.

Relative Truth and Ultimate Truth—relative form and its ultimate emptiness—Suzuki Roshi's Small Mind Big Mind unity is the Mahayana Two Truths motif (*Ch. VI*) whose understanding is the foundation of *bodhicitta*, heart of Buddhist Mahayana and Vajrayana ethics. *Bodhicitta* may be seen as the basis of human happiness, both relative human flourishing, and liberation from suffering—Happiness Itself. We accomplish the happiness of our ultimate Buddha wisdom mind—the wisdom of emptiness—via the assiduous practice of the dualistic relative Path.

Therefore, "Practice these two as a unity" (Padmasambhava). "And all the *tathagatas* will rejoice" (from Buddha's *Heart of Wisdom Sutra*).

Quieting the Busy Mind and Arousing *Bodhicitta*. A very brief rehearsal of our quiescent mindfulness practice from Chapter III is in order. In order to *directly* experience the trans-conceptual clarity and peace that abides within all these words and concepts, in this very moment now: sit up straight, cast your gaze slightly downward, partially close your eyes, uncross your legs, and place your mindful attention upon your breath in the belly. Practice the polyvagal breath (five seconds in; seven seconds out through pursed lips) for a minute or two. Simply witness your mind, your natural awareness. Be aware of your present awareness. As thoughts and feelings naturally arise, briefly greet them, label whatever arises "distraction", and return your attention to the quiescent peaceful breath, again and again. No need to think about it. Let it be as it is. Simply *feel* your breath for a minute. Please do it now.

Now meditate, as before, on *bodhicitta*, your natural good will innate compassion for living beings everywhere, including our Mother Earth—that they may be happy, and have the causes of happiness. Let it be as it is. *Feel* what arises. Practice for another a minute or two.

Now, meditate briefly on the clarity and luminosity of empty space of *dharmakaya*—vast boundless primordial whole itself in whom this all arises and participates, by whatever name or concept (*Appendix A*: "Let It Be: Basic Mindfulness Meditation")

Thus it is, the monumental, direct yogic-contemplative (*yogi pratyaksa*) cognitive coupling of these Two Truth dimensions—relative form and its ultimate emptiness—reveals directly the ontic prior, and epistemic and phenomenal already present unity of this very pragmatic conceptual duality. The resultant indivisible primordial unity is the trans-conceptual one truth, with all its many names, that is invariant throughout our entire human cognitive processional—1) pre-conceptual direct perception; 2) exoteric, objective, conceptual; 3) esoteric, subjective, contemplative; and 4) "innermost secret" perfectly subjective nondual.

No small matter is at stake here. It is said that at the instant of his final nondual realization of the primordial identity of these two truth dimensions—relative form and its ultimate emptiness—Siddartha Gautama became the Buddha (*Ch. VI*).

The realization of this nondual (*advaya, nyid med*; "not two, not one" subject-object unity) wisdom of emptiness (*jnana, yeshe, gnosis*) of the intrinsic Buddha nature of mind (*tathagatagarbha*) and its phenomenal contents is requisite for awakening to the intimate knowing, feeling and luminous clarity of our indwelling innate clear light Buddha *bodhi* mind (*buddhajnana*)—innermost Presence of That. And that is none other than primordial *dharmakaya*—always already present at the spiritual heart (*hridyam*) of human beings. Lots of big words for that Presence in your Heart.

Therefore, in due course, and by grace (*jinlob, euengelion*) the prodigious result of this nondual view and practice is the ultimate realization of buddhahood—reflexively aware primordial wisdom (*rang rig yeshe*)—Presence (*vidya/rigpa*) that cognizes at once the already present unity of the Two Truths—full *bodhi* enlightenment that is ultimate human Happiness Itself!

In the West we might call such primordial wisdom, after Spinoza, *sub specie aeternitatus*—selfless That (*Tathata*, "*suchness*", "*thatness*") which is ultimately true—Ultimate Truth itself, *dharmakaya* that is both origin and aim of the spacetime dimension of Relative Truth. It is That in whom this all arises, participates, and is instantiated.

Be That as it may, the ethical foundation of the Mahayana Path with its "bodhisattva ideal" is *bodhicitta*, "heartmind of enlightenment", the altruistic, compassionate thought, intention, and action for the benefit of living beings—beyond, on the Mahayana view—the less complete compassion of the noble Hinayana *Arhat*. The heart essence of *bodhicitta* is *mahakaruna*, the Great Compassion that naturally, spontaneously, and skillfully expresses itself in myriad ways for the benefit of all sentient beings.

The *bodhisattva* practices choosing to avoid the *Pali Canon* Hinayana ten non-virtues through the practice of the Mahayana *Six Paramitas* (Perfections)—generosity, ethics, patience, diligence, meditation, wisdom—as we shall see later in this chapter.

Awakening Our Buddha Mind. These Six Perfections of wisdom are, relatively, causally viewed, the very causes of realization of ultimate unity of the three buddha bodies of light—the *Trikaya* of the Base, namely, the *rupakaya* form bodies that are *nirmanakaya* (emanation body of spacetime manifesting buddhas), *sambhogakaya* (delightful light body of the transcendent yet ever present tantric deities), and nondual ultimate wisdom body that is primordial whole of *dharmakaya*, the perfect nondual, innate luminosity of our clear light wisdom mind (*samatajnana, buddhajnana*) that is identical to that of a fully realized buddha. It is That to which we awaken, step by step, through the assiduous practice of the Buddhist Path.

Our always already present Buddha mind—trans-conceptual, direct nondual luminous Presence of That—is, in the Mahayana Causal Vehicle, the cessation of the causes of the afflictive emotions (*kleshas*) that are rooted in basic ignorance (*avidya*), and delusion (*moha*). It is these destructive emotions—fear, anger, hatred, obsessive sense desire, greed, pride—that are the causes of human suffering (*dukkha*). These three buddha bodies of light, when considered as a conceptually inexpressible unity are sometimes called *svabhavakakaya*.

Thus is the Mahayana Path often seen as the Paramitayana, the Causal Vehicle of the Perfections of Wisdom—*Prajnaparamita*. Cause and effect. Practice these virtuous causes, and reap the happy love-wisdom effect. The assiduous practice of the *Six Paramitas*, with devotion to the guiding living Vajra Master, is the practical cause of full *bodhi* awakening to the primordial wisdom of emptiness.

The Perfection of Wisdom. The earliest (circa 100 B.C.E.), and perhaps the primary Mahayana teaching is the great, and long, *Prajnaparamita sutra*—the *Perfection of Wisdom Sutra*. The heart essence of Gautama Shakamuni the Buddha's teaching on the *ultimate* absence or emptiness of self, and of all spacetime physical and mental phenomenal forms is stated in his *Heart of Wisdom Sutra*. At about 500 words, it is the briefest of the prodigious 8000 verse *Prajnaparamita* corpus. In this wondrous *Heart Sutra* the Buddha reveals the justly famous "fourfold profundity" that strikes the essence of the entire Mahayana *Prajnaparamita* teaching linage:

> Form is empty; emptiness is form.
> Form is not other than emptiness;
> Emptiness is not other than form.

Relative form and its ultimate emptiness: the Two Truths of the Buddha's teaching in eighteen words. We've seen that emptiness/*shunyata* has a twofold nature: 1) emptiness of self, and emptiness of all phenomena "other" than self; and, 2) because emptiness is the primordial ultimate, emptiness even of nondual Buddha nature. Realization of the wisdom of emptiness (*dharmakaya, primordial Adi Buddha Samantabhadra*) is not other than the awakening to our innate, indwelling, already present Buddha nature/Buddha mind. We accomplish this by "purifying the mind" of afflictive emotions—both *Attraction*: pride, greed, obsessive sense desire; and *Aversion*: fear, anger, ill will, hatred.

Please recall from Chapter II the Buddha's statement as to the heart essence of his teaching. From the *Pali Canon*:

> Do no harm.
> Practice what is skillful
> in benefiting beings.
> Purify your mind.
> That is my teaching.

The essence of Gautama the Buddha's entire teaching in seventeen words.

We can find general agreement in the commentarial corpus of the Indo-Tibetan Buddhist traditions that these above two sublime piths—the first from the Mahayana sutra tradition, the second from the Hinayana tradition of the *Pali Canon*—express the supreme wisdom of both the Buddha's philosophical teaching, and his ethical teaching—the teaching of the selfless nondual wisdom of ultimate emptiness/*shunyata*, and the precious *bodhicitta* that arises as the natural expression of our luminous but empty Buddha nature, being here in relative time. The practice of purifying the mind of the obscurations of ignorance (*avidya, ma rigpa, ajnana*) makes possible our awakening to this profound teaching.

This foundational teaching on emptiness grounded later seminal Mahayana metaphysical and ethical developments—the Second and Third Turnings of the Wheel of Dharma (*dharmachakra*)—the Two Truths, and our innate Buddha nature respectively in whom naturally arises the compassionate *bodhicitta* of aspiration, and of action—the very secret and primary cause of human happiness.

From the *Prajnaparamita* legacy arose Nagarjuna's seminal *Fundamental Wisdom of the Middle Way* (*Mulamadhyamakakarika*), foundation of the Indian Middle Way Madhyamaka school, established by Nagarjuna and his student Aryadeva in the 2nd century C.E. Another student of Nagarjuna, Buddhapalita developed the Nalanda University Madhyamaka Middle Way Consequence School—Prasangika Madhyamaka, the very foundation of *Dzogchen* according to the Nyingmapas. Buddhapalita (5th century), Chandrakirti and Shantideva (8th century) further contributed to the Prasangika legacy. Tsongkhapa (14th century), founder of the Gelug School of Tibetan Buddhism, formulated what is usually considered the definitive view of Prasangika Madhyamaka.

In the 5th century Bhavaviveka adapted the *Rangtong* Middle Way Prasangika understanding to the idealist, mentalist Mind Only (chittamatra) metaphysics of the Yogachara School. The result was the *Shentong* view of Middle Way Madhyamaka Yogachara Svatantrika (*Ch. V*). These two Madhyamaka schools—Prasangika and Yogachara—were to become the primary views of the dialectical Vajayana teaching vehicle—the Third Turning of Buddha's Dharma Wheel.

We've seen that Gautama Buddha viewed his teaching as a "middle path" or middle way between the ethical extremes of self-mortifying asceticism and sensory self-gratification. In Mahayana we see an epistemic enhancement of this middle way to include a centrist view between the metaphysical extremes of the eternalist, materialist substantial existence of phenomena, and the mentalist nihilistic nonexistence of phenomena.

Thus, this remarkable synthesis of the *ultimate* selfless emptiness of form—which abides in a relation of identity or sameness with the *relative*, conditional causal interdependent arising (*pratitya samutpada*) of appearing phenomenal form—is the final truth of the Buddha's Middle Way. "Form is empty; emptiness is form."

The Middle Way Prasangika Madhyamikas view the illusory reality (*avidya maya*) of nihilistic, mentalist Metaphysical Absolute Idealism as antithetical to the ethical dimension of any spiritual wisdom path, and perforce meaningless. So mentalist, Yogachara Metaphysical Idealism was suspect.

How then is it that Philosophical Idealism might preclude ethical conduct? Our karmic activity that *chooses* the practice that benefits beings is effectively negated. If all appearing reality is *ultimately* a mental illusion, the moral dimension of human action is effectively negated. Why bother to be compassionate? No spacetime reality, no ethical practice. For Prasangika the relative conventional, if nominal reality of the Middle Way bestows the great gift of a relatively real spacetime reality in which to practice the Buddha's karmic ethical path that ends human suffering, and that simultaneously bears the love-wisdom fruit of buddhahood.

In this way then does Buddhist metaphysics meet and merge with Buddhist ethics.

Karma and Free Will. Karma abides at the very heart of Buddhist ethics. It is discursively semiotically complex. Buddhist monks and nuns study its conceptual and non-conceptual subtlety for many years.

The Buddhist law of karma is cognitively situated within the natural scientific law of causality, cause and effect, that governs the physical and mental process of the boundless whole that is *kosmos*—all of the physical, mental, and other spiritual dimensions of reality being itself.

Karma means human ethical *action and result.* In the context of Buddhist morals it connotes ethical causal *consequences* of human action or conduct. Karma is moral causality—cause and effect. "That which we sow, thus do we also reap" (Jesus).

There are four kinds of human action that result in negative or positive karmic effects: 1) negative, non-virtuous actions that result in pain and suffering for living beings; 2) positive, virtuous actions that result in benefit for living beings; 3) karmically neutral actions that result in neither virtuous nor negative consequences; and 4) actions that include both negative and positive results. Actions may be of body (physical), speech (verbal), and mind (mental/emotional). (See the "Five Precepts" below).

Buddha's Four Noble Truths, and indeed all of the wisdom paths of our Great Wisdom Tradition, are dependent upon the metaphysical assumption that human beings have enough free will to *choose* some actions instead of other actions. Clearly, this is so.

Notwithstanding the modernist Laplacian/Newtonian "scientific" bias that all spacetime events are causally determined, human beings do have a bit of free will. And we are as well responsible for our unconscious motivation. Thus it is our *actions*—both conscious and unconscious—that determine our karma. Told Buddha, *"What you are is what you have been; what you will be is what you do now"*. As good a definition of karma as ever there was.

For example, we can, as a self-ego-I, at this moment *choose* altruistic compassionate thought, intention, and action to benefit others—the precious *bodhicitta*—that eases the suffering of sentient beings being here in time. We can *choose* to practice Buddha's Eightfold Path and the Six Perfections, however imperfectly, that are, in the fullness of time, the ultimate cessation of suffering of self and of others. We can *choose* such a life style over against harmful narcissistic egocentric conduct that is the primary cause of our suffering. We can *choose*, this very moment now, to connect, through "mindfulness of breathing" and mantra prayer, to primordial wisdom mind Buddha mind— our always already present indwelling Presence of That. Try it now for sixty seconds. Simply breathe mindfully for a minute or so. What do you feel?

From the seminal Buddhist Middle Way *Madhyamaka* metaphysical principle of causal interdependence—dependent origination or dependent arising (*pratitya samutpada*)—that is the very identity of emptiness/*shunyata* itself, it follows that any and all human action/conduct results in an ethical causal consequence that has karmic significance. The Buddhist view that pervades all the Buddhist vehicles is that human action is the inexorable karmic result of prior actions. Cause and effect. Karma is all pervasive in the causally interdependent dimension of human action.

Karma accrues both individually, and because we are all inherently, inter-subjectively interdependent and interconnected, karma accrues collectively or socioculturally. Again, on the accord of H.H. Dalai Lama, the law of karma is the ethical face of the scientific law of causality.

Karma inexorably functions in the causal chain of any action, namely, the *thought* or the *desire* (however brief) that causes the *intention* (conscious or not) to act, then the final execution of the act itself—*action*. Each link in the chain has its own karmic consequences.

The law of karma admits not of an ethical consequentialist, nor of a deontological calculus of excuses. The personal karma resulting from the suffering caused by an international arms dealer is not undone by his compensatory philanthropy. The karmic burden created by the abuse of a child is not mitigated by *bodhicitta* expressed elsewhere.

Once again, precious *bodhicitta*—compassionate thought, intention, and action for the benefit of living beings—is the open secret of human happiness. Altruistic *bodhicitta* is "good karma". So, arise upon the breath from the continuing drama of your habitual self-ego-I narrative, and do some good out there on the mean streets of reality. It will make you happy here and now.

The Five Buddhist Precepts. From the unity of the Two Truths, Relative form and Ultimate emptiness, naturally arise the Four Noble Truths and the Six Perfections (*Paramitas*); and from this the Buddha's Five Precepts or virtues, the practical moral injunctions of human ethical conduct for the lay practitioner who aspires to purify negative karma, and lead a happy, conscious life of mindful, skillful *bodhicitta*.

1) *Refrain from taking life.* Honor all life (*ahimsa*). Cause no harm to any living creature. This is an aspect of Right Conduct, the fourth injunction of the noble Eightfold Path. All life is utterly interconnected and interdependent—an integral ecology of mind. All sentient beings desire and deserve to live. Therefore, do no harm. Let your activity and your happiness be utterly harmless.

2) *Refrain from taking what is not freely given.* Greed is taking too much, more than our share, more than we really need. We

must learn to appreciate our interdependence with other beings, including our Mother Earth, and with the primal Life Current itself. As we cultivate generosity, the first of the Six Perfections, we learn to practice giving; to share, to *give wisely* of our time, energy, good will and money, to ourselves, then to others. Thus do we learn to practice an authentic, genuine integral ecology of body, mind and spirit.

3) *Refrain from false speech.* Right or authentic speech is the third injunction of the noble Eightfold Path to liberation from suffering, and ultimate happiness. Practice being a good listener. Listen with quiet, nonjudgmental and selfless compassion. Give up on trying to fix what you may think is broken—with yourself and with others. With great restraint encourage others to explore and perhaps reframe their difficult emotions and judgments. Help others to understand that thoughts and feelings—negative or positive—have no solid existence. They are merely thoughts and feelings, empty of any shred of intrinsic existence. Don't lecture on what you're sure others need, or should do. Don't criticize anyone.

When you speak, speak what is true, helpful and wise. Use your voice mindfully, carefully, kindly, encouragingly. In short, skillfully practice your precious *bodhicitta*. Please don't lie, cheat, gossip, bear false witness, or criticize others. Avoid harsh speech.

4) *Refrain from sexual misconduct.* Learn to be sexually mindful, kind, responsible, authentic, non-grasping/clinging, and non-manipulating. The regenerative energy is extremely powerful. Without mindfulness it can cause terrible harm to others, and thus to oneself. Cause no emotional-sexual harm. Learn to be sexually mindful, compassionate, and generous. "In the moment of love emptiness dawns nakedly" (Tulku Urgyen Rinpoche).

5) *Refrain from abusive use of intoxicant substances.* Food and negative thoughts—anger, hatred, lust, greed of self-ego-I—may also be abused. Be mindful and aware of all that

you allow to enter your precious body and mind stream. Practice mindful appreciation and restraint regarding the cognitive states of your body, speech and mind.

The Four Boundless States (*Brahma-vihara, the abodes of Brahma*). These Four Immeasurables (*apramana*) are the pre-Buddhist Hindu and early *Shravakayana*/Theravada Buddhist limitless mind states of 1) loving-kindness (*maitri*); 2) compassion (*karuna*); 3) empathetic joy (*mudita*); and 4) equanimity (*upeksha*), meditative and pragmatic. For a real emotional lift, learn the *tonglen* compassion meditation. Practice it to help heal the suffering of beings (*Appendix A*).

Practice these four boundless states that you are as a unity, for benefit of both self and others. The wondrous result of such practice is awakening to *bodhi* mind/wisdom mind Presence, expressed in kind loving conduct as the precious *bodhicitta*—unity of love and wisdom that is the very heart essence of all the Buddhist teaching vehicles.

Again, Mahayana *bodhicitta* is compassionate engaged action of the bodhisattvas, those beloved wisdom beings of the three times—past, present, future—who devote their lives in service to other beings. Most good people are bodhisattvas in training. *Bodhicitta* is the primary cause of "a mind in comfort and ease" (Longchenpa)—profound happiness for oneself, which profoundly benefits those in one's sphere of influence.

This great aspiration of *bodhicitta*, with engaged altruistic action is, through the inexorable law of cause and effect karma, the very cause of human *relative* happiness—human flourishing—and *ultimate* liberation from suffering—Happiness Itself, the harmless happiness that does only good; the happiness that cannot be lost.

Once again, Buddha told, *"What you are is what you have been; what you will be is what you do now."* Our past deeds are past, only a present memory. Our spacious empty future depends entirely upon what we *choose* to do in this present moment now, and then the next moment now, *ad infinitum*.

This transition from past to future through the eternal present requires that we accept, with gentle forgiveness of self-ego-I, full responsibility for our past negative deeds, and for our present ignorance/delusion (*avidya*). No blame. No excuses. Perfect practice is in the beginning, imperfect. Wisdom attainment rests in non-attainment. Selfless *Wu-wei*. Let it be as it is. Now act directly from your wisdom Buddha mind (*buddhajnana*).

It is selfless, mindful *shamatha*, with the surprising power of mantra prayer that rests, purifies, and stabilizes the "wild horse of the mind" from the nearly unbroken onslaught of thinking and worry of a narcissistic self-ego-I. Let it be as it is. Act from that.

The Five Hindrances. There is a part of us that does not want to be free; that fearfully resists proceeding too far along the Path to the ultimate happiness that is liberation, and enlightenment. That part of us is called self-ego-I. Ego sees the Path as dangerous. Sadly, ego prefers to remain in its uncomfortable comfort zones, maintaining a precarious status quo.

The ego's defense strategies for avoiding relationship are prodigious. They are extremely well defended by our practiced "ego defense mechanisms"—projection, denial, repression, and the rest. They are rooted in fear/anxiety and manifest as various forms of *doubt*. As one begins to recognize this discomfiting self-duplicity one gains a bit of control, step by mindful step.

Obstructions/obscurations to practice of the Path:

1) *Attachment*: habitual attraction and desire for sensory pleasure, greed, pride.
2) *Aversion*: fear/anxiety, anger, ill will, hostility, aggression, hatred.
3) *Laxity*: "sloth and torpor", dullness, drowsiness, laziness, endless excuses.
4) *Excitement*: restlessness, agitation, obsessive thought, rumination and speech.

5) *Paralyzing Doubt*: the usual litany of excuses, postpone-
ments, judgments, second guessing your knowing/feeling
confidence as to dharma, *sangha*, teacher's qualifications,
teaching style, guru devotion, deities, present adversity,
priority, timing, no time, ad nauseam. *Ego pride* is perhaps
the most destructive; and the hardest to see in oneself.

What to do? You already know. Yes, stay present upon
the mindful mantra breath to already present Presence of
your innermost love-wisdom Buddha mind (*Appendix A*).

The Three Pillars of Zen. 1) *Great Faith* in the process of
awakening; 2) *Great Doubt* in the process of awakening; 3) *Great
Determination* to continue in confidence, all the way to the end
of it. Great 20th century Zen Master Suzuki Roshi told it well:
"The only mistake you can make in your practice is to quit". Your
hindrances, your fear, your anger are but confusing and painful
apertures for love-wisdom mind Presence to enter in. Enjoy the
humor of the great process. Let it be as it is.

Buddhist Ethics and The Four Noble Truths. We've seen in
Chapter I that these four truths for one who would be noble of
body, mind and spirit provide the foundation of the wisdom unity
that is Buddhist ethics and philosophy. For Mahayana Middle Way
Madhyamaka, the Buddha's Four Noble Truths are founded upon
his Two Truths—Ultimate Truth (*paramartha satya*) and Relative
Truth (*samvriti satya*) arising therein. The Two Truths are the very
nature of the primordial ground itself, Buddha nature of mind.
Nagarjuna told in his justly renowned *Fundamental Wisdom of the
Middle Way*, in the chapter on the Buddha's Four Noble Truths
(Garfield 1995, Ch. *XXIV*, v. 8, 10, 14, 18, 19, 40):

The Buddha's teaching of the Dharma
Is based on two truths:
A truth of worldly convention
And an ultimate truth.

Without a foundation in the conventional truth,
The significance of the ultimate cannot be taught.
Without understanding the significance of the ultimate,
Liberation is not achieved.

For whom emptiness is clear,
Everything becomes clear.
For whom emptiness is not clear,
Nothing becomes clear.

Whatever is dependently co-arisen
that is explained to be emptiness.
That, being a dependent designation,
Is itself the middle way.

That which is not dependently arisen,
Such a thing does not exist.
Therefore a nonempty thing
Does not exist.

Whoever sees dependent arising
Also sees the truth of suffering
And its origin
And its cessation as the path.

Thus do the Buddha's Two Truths represent the profound prior unity of the two basic reality dimensions of arising and appearing physical and mental spacetime reality—1) relative, conventional, objective and subjective spacetime phenomena, and 2) ultimate, perfectly subjective nonlocal, nondual vast expanse of the intrinsically empty boundless whole itself that embraces and subsumes these relative conventional realities.

Both intellectual/conceptual and trans-conceptual/contemplative understanding are required to realize the primordial emptiness ground of reality itself—boundless nondual *dharmakaya*.

It is most important in the beginning to understand, by way of conceptual reasoning, that this seeming duality of the Two Truths understanding—conceptual and contemplative—is a false dichotomy. The Two Truths are an ontic prior, and always present phenomenal unity!

Thus it is, the Four Noble Truths and the Buddha's Eightfold Path to liberation from suffering cannot be auspiciously engaged without an understanding of the Two Truths (*Ch. VI*).

As we begin to understand the cause and effect nature of the Four Noble Truths, we are led to the Twelve *Nidanas* or Twelve Links of Buddha's Dependent Arising (*pratitya samutpada*). There are two classes of causal processes at work here—afflicted and enlightened, corresponding to our emotions and actions. The causal chain of afflicted emotion and action leads to demeritorious karma (action) and suffering in samsaric cyclic existence. The causal chain of enlightened emotion and action leads to meritorious karma and the gradual cessation of suffering that is liberation from cyclic existence (Dalai Lama 2007).

The first link in the causal chain of samsaric cyclic existence is the fundamental ignorance (*avidya, marigpa, ajnana*) that cloaks the emptiness nature of interdependently arising phenomenal reality, and the self that experiences it. Under delusional sway of ignorance we grasp at and cling to a seemingly solid, enduring self-ego-I, and a seemingly permanent, physical, intrinsically existent reality ground for it, namely, the "five aggregates" or *skandhas* of conditional existence. Thus do we traverse the twelve links of conditioned suffering that end in old age, death, and rebirth—again and again, for countless eons.

Therefore, there are in the Mahayana, two varieties of self-emptiness: 1) *emptiness of self,* an enduring psychological, conceptually unfindable self entity perceived as distinct from, and transcending the five *skandhas*—form, sensation, perception, mental activity, personal consciousness—and 2) *emptiness of (other) phenomena,* the absence or emptiness of intrinsic existence of the five *skandhas* of existence themselves that comprise the whole of spacetime reality.

Nagarjuna points out that the realization of *emptiness of self* (*Rangtong*) may free us from much suffering caused by the negative afflictive emotions; but it does not penetrate to the subtle root of primal fundamental ignorance (*avidya*) that reveals the inherent emptiness of all arising phenomena (*Shentong*). That root is *svabhava*, a very subtle grasping at our preconscious, deep cultural background conviction in the inherent *ultimate* existence of appearing physical and mental phenomenal form. We are very attached to our conceptual certainty that stuff ultimately exists. Nagarjuna, from his lovely *Precious Garland* (*Ratnavali*):

> As long as there is grasping at the aggregates,
> There is grasping at self.
> When there is grasping at self there is karma,
> And from that comes birth.

The first two noble truths, the Truth of Suffering and the Truth of the Cause of Suffering, describe the interdependent arising of the Twelve Links of Dependent Arising that are suffering. The third and fourth noble truths, the Truth of the Cessation of Suffering and the Truth of the Path that accomplishes cessation describe the gradual dissolution of the Twelve Links, and the resulting human happiness that is liberating awakening. On this freeing deconstruction of the causal process of cyclic existence, Nagarjuna teaches (quoted in H.H. Dalai 2005):

> When thoughts of 'I' and 'mine' are extinguished...
> Karma and afflictions cease and there is liberation.
> Karma and afflictions arise from conceptual elaboration;
> And cease through the realization of emptiness.

The destructive emotions—fear, anger, ill will, hatred, furious sense desire, greed, and pride that cause our suffering—arise from attachment to self and its presumed ownership of relative objects, including life, property, family, in-groups, ethnic identity, career, possessions, and the rest. Buddha told, "These things are not yours. What is not yours, give it up".

The urgent question now is, what, and who, and where is this strange and precious entity we call self-ego-I that is always the center of its self-created universe? And Who am I, ultimately? What is the origin, identity, and ultimate destiny of the actual human being, and of this awareness of it that I call "I", embodied here in the physical aggregates/*skandhas* of relative time and space? Who am I? That is the question. That is the ultimate question for the human conceptual enterprises of religion and philosophy. That is the question that the Buddha asks us to consider.

Most Eastern and Western religious philosophy assumes that the self that experiences appearing reality is unchanging, eternal, timeless, enduring, and *independent* of the physical and mental aggregates of form. Here, soul/self transcends spacetime being in form. We've seen that Gautama the Buddha denied the ultimate existence of such a permanent self entity. Self is not a changeless, eternal and independent soul or spirit, or "higher Atman Self". Rather, Buddha taught *anatman*, ultimate selfless-ness, or no-self. Yet, he affirmed the existence of a relatively real, conventional self who chooses what to engage, and what to avoid; and who chooses to engage or avoid the Eightfold Path to liberation from suffering in this hell of samsara.

As we have seen many times in these pages, while *relatively* and conventionally existent, self remains *ultimately avidya Maya*—an illusion borne of ignorance of who it is that we actually are—*vidya maya* remains present as our innate, indwelling Buddha nature/Buddha mind; luminous, trans-conceptual, nondual Presence of That, beyond name or concept (*namarupa*).

In short, the self *does* exist, not independently and absolutely, but relatively, nominally, in interdependent relationship with, and in dependence upon the five phenomenal aggregates of spacetime existence. Self is not a transcendent, enduring soul-like entity that transmigrates from one incarnation to the next. Both self (*atman*), and no-self (*anatman*) that is ultimately our selfless Buddha nature, are interdependently arisen, not some objective, independently real object, or objective spiritual essence.

So, both self and no-self Buddha nature are absent and empty of any conceptual, inherently real essential self-existence. Yet, because self and no-self co-exist in the realm of relative conventional truth, they are, ultimately, a prior and present indivisible unity, as we shall soon see. Again, Nagarjuna on the non-conceptual unity of relative self, and ultimate no-self (*Mulamadhyamakakarika* Ch. XVIII, v. 6, H.H. Dalai Lama/Thupten Jinpa translation):

> That there is self has been taught,
> That there is no self has been taught.
> But the buddhas have taught
> That neither self nor no-self exists.

The first two lines refer to a conceptually reified Hindu eternal Atman Self (*Samkhya, Upanishads, Charvaka*), or to materialist views that reduce self to physical embodied existence. The last two lines refer to the non-conceptual, unified, even nondual view of the Buddha. Conceptually, "neither self nor no-self exists". Self and no-self too are a conceptual false dichotomy.

H.H. Dalai Lama has pointed out that all four lines refer to the Buddha's view because the Buddha taught *both* self and no self in the sutras, depending on the cognitive capacity of his listeners. In either case, Buddha taught, in keeping with his Two Truths doctrine, the relative, conventional existence of a self in time who is able to make choices; but the ultimate nonexistence or emptiness of that self.

Moreover, Buddha rejected the ultimate intrinsic existence even of selflessness itself. Ultimately, everything is absent and empty of self-existence, including selflessness and emptiness. Conceptually imputing, reifying, then grasping at the intrinsic reality of emptiness, as if it were a great absolutely existing object or thing is, according to Nagarjuna, a deeply mistaken view. This is Chandrakirti's "emptiness of emptiness" (*shunyata shunyata*). Emptiness itself is empty of intrinsic self-existence. Form is empty; emptiness is form". No form, no emptiness. No emptiness, no form.

So again, self and no-self Buddha nature are utterly empty of "any shred" of intrinsic existence. We shall see in Chapter V in our discussion of Middle Way Prasangika *Rangtong* (empty of self), and Middle Way Yogachara *Shentong* (empty of other phenomena) that the "true" conceptual status of Buddha nature (*tathagatagarbha*) is far from settled in the heady wine of dualistic polemical Buddhist dialectics.

So, what precisely are these Four Noble Truths? As we saw in Chapter II, the first noble truth reveals *The Truth of Suffering*, that the suffering (*dukkha*) of living beings is omnipresent. Lord Buddha teaches that suffering has three faces: 1) the "suffering of suffering" that is physical and emotional pain, and our general dissatisfaction with the slings and arrows of outrageous spacetime existence; 2) the "suffering of change" that is the pain of being here in swiftly passing ultimately illusory time which brings only "sorrow, grief, and despair" as we and everything else decays and passes away; 3) "all pervasive suffering" is the very nature of this relative, conditional, inherently impermanent (*anitya*) existence of things in time, and the fundamental, unrelenting fear of the inexorable death of our embodied self-ego-I.

In the fullness of time all humans shall pass; then all earthly lifeforms; then our divine Mother Earth; our Solar System; galaxy; galaxy cluster; universe; *Kosmic* multiverse. All spacetime forms, whether physically or mentally embodied, in all planetary systems located anywhere in time, shall return again to the vast primordial emptiness whole, or ground in whom it always continuously endlessly, selflessly arises; and in whom it has never departed (*Appendix B*).

From the relative view, samsara is decidedly not a pretty picture.

The second noble truth is *The Truth of the Cause of Suffering*—that suffering has a cause or origin. The cause of human suffering? Attraction/attachment and aversion/ill will of a self-ego-I caused by ignorance (*avidya*) of the actual impermanent, selfless, interdependent nature of appearing reality as it is encountered by attention, perception and conceptuality of the human mind. This natural process causes thought, intention and action in service of self-ego-I. I, Me, Mine—the exact opposite of the causes of human happiness. The habitually "selfing" ego-I sees itself as the center of the world. It's dominant motif is self-cherishing of itself over all others, even family. Delusion indeed. Since all egos feel the same way, this biased habit of mind proves quite problematic for the well being, happiness, and continued existence of our species on this pretty little planet. What to do?

The good news? Suffering has a cure—the third noble truth—*The Truth of the Cessation of Suffering.* What then is this cessation of suffering? It is the forth noble truth, *The Truth of the Eightfold Path* that causes "the fading away and cessation of ignorance and sense craving".

The propitious result of this cessation of suffering is, for the Mahayana, *bodhicitta*—selfless altruistic cultivation of thought, intention, and action—arising upon the mindful breath, for the benefit of living beings. And that is, as we have so many times seen, the open secret of human happiness.

This superb no-self help advice from the Buddha begins with kind forgiveness of oneself. Beating yourself up for self-centered narcissism makes *bodhicitta* impossible. Manage your ego in the way a mother lovingly corrects her selfish child—with firm, wise loving kindness.

How shall we accomplish this wondrous mind state that is *bodhicitta*? Yes, we practice Buddha's Eightfold Path, and the love and wisdom of the bodhisattva Path as taught in the Mahayana *Six Paramitas* (Perfections).

Shantideva's great Middle Way *Madhyamaka* text, *Bodhich-aryavatara, The Bodhisattva's Guide to the Path of Awakening*, is perhaps the definitive guide to entering and accomplishing this prodigious Path of awakening to the ultimate happiness that is always "already accomplished from the very beginning", deep within us. (For more on the Buddha's Four Noble Truths please return to Chapter II.)

The Three Marks of Existence (*Trilakshana*, the Three Gates to Liberation). The *Trilakshana* is the Buddha's explication of the First Noble Truth, The Truth of Suffering. It is accepted by all Buddhist vehicles and schools.

These three qualities or characteristics of conditioned, de-pendently arisen spacetime existence are: 1) *suffering* (*dukkha*), the inherent adventitious adversity of being here in form; 2) *impermanence* (*anitya*), everything—the Five *Skandhas* of form—sensation, perception, mental activity, and personal consciousness changes and passes away. Trees, living species, sun and moon, stars, *kosmos* itself are transitory, arising and falling away endlessly; 3) *selflessness* (*anatman*), no-self, the inherently empty spacious insubstantiality of self and its experience of form.

Selflessness/emptiness of form obtains not only for relative phenomena but for all *dharmas*—the entire spacetime realm of conditional Relative Truth, and as well, the realm of nondual all embracing Ultimate Truth in whom it all arises and passes away. All *dharmas*, relative and ultimate, are empty of intrinsic existence, including ultimate emptiness/*shunyata* itself. H.H. Dalai Lama, after Chandrakirti, calls this absence of any substantial foundational ground for the stuff of time and space "the empti-ness of emptiness" (*shunyata shunyata*).

We must remember that these Three Marks of Existence, and the Buddhist Two Truths—relative and ultimate—are ut-terly interdependent, always an ontic prior, yet ever present phenomenal, non-conceptual, nondual unity. We separate them discursively, relatively, in order to reflexively recognize, then realize their ultimate inseparability. We reflexively critique the inherent limit of conceptual mind, through its own dualistic, binary, truth functional (true-false) logic—the limiting "Laws of Thought" that is the two-valued logic of Aristotle.

Our indwelling luminous wisdom faculty—both relative discriminating *prajna*, and ultimate *jnana, yeshe, gnosis*—directly, beyond our conceptual "web of belief" perceives, feels, and knows that everything, all interdependently arising, empty (*shunya*) physical and mental form is characterized by these three qualities of existence: *suffering, impermanence*, and *selflessness*. Such was the Buddha's enlightenment that has always been our own innermost intrinsic awareness Buddha mind (*buddhajnana*)—bright already present Presence (*vidya, rigpa*) of That.

It is *shamatha/sati* (quiescent mindfulness practice), and *vipashyana* (penetrating insight practice) that opens wide these Three Gates to Enlightenment. It is the assiduous practice of the Path of this teaching of the Buddha that bestows liberation from the ignorance (*avidya, marigpa*) that is the cause of suffering. It is this teaching that results in the relative happiness that is human flourishing (*eudaimonia, felicitas*), and ultimate Happiness Itself (*mahasuka, paramananda, beatitudo*), liberating happiness that cannot be lost (*Dhammapada* verses 277, 278, 279).

The *Trilakshana*, these Three Gates to ultimate happiness, is the Buddha's love-wisdom gift to us as to the way in which we, and everything else, truly exist as interdependent instantiations of the nonlocal, nondual unbounded whole of reality itself, in a word, *dharmakaya*, our "supreme source"—luminous always present Presence of That.

The Buddhist Refuge. Happiness and freedom from suffering? "It is already accomplished from the very beginning" (*Dzogchen* founder Garab Dorje). Once again, liberating Buddha love-wisdom mind Presence—our Buddha nature (*tathagatagarbha, tathata*)—is always already present, deep within us. It can never be lost. It has always been thus. It is That to which we awaken through identity shifting practice of the Buddha's Eightfold Path and the Six Paramitas. It is That in whom we take refuge.

Be that as it may, happiness is already the case. It is not elsewhere, in the relative world of things—in people, or in great personages, or in lofty holy concepts and beliefs. Hence, there is no need to seek it. Always present clear-light wisdom mind already knows this urgent radical truth. It is That to which we awaken—step by step—through the practice of the Path. Let it be so.

So, we open, connect to, and awaken to innermost secret Presence of our Buddha mind. We take refuge in That, "brief moments, many times", upon the mindful mantra breath. In Vajrayana this great primordial truth is understood as the "fruitional view". Ultimately, it seeks nothing, for that which we seek is already present. It is that secret to which we gradually, then suddenly awaken, upon each mindful breath, again and again. *Emaho!* Great joy!

Thus it is, the process of establishing an effective Buddhist practice that knows this great truth of love-wisdom Buddha mind Presence (*buddhajnana*) begins by taking refuge in the *three refuge sources* that are the precious *Three Jewels*. These Three Jewels are a one truth unity.

The Refuge Vow and Refuge Prayer are then: 1) "I take refuge in the Buddha" (the Buddha's love and wisdom); 2) "I take refuge in the dharma" (the dharma teaching of the Buddha through the guidance of a qualified *Lama,* or *Roshi,* or *Ajahn*); and 3) "I take refuge in the *sangha*" (the spiritual community which includes the luminous *rigzin sangha*, the *vidyadhara* lineage of all the buddhas and bodhisattvas of the "three times"—past, present, future). As we recite or chant this Refuge Prayer we are simultaneously immersed in the deeper strata of meaning of the perfectly subjective whole of Buddhist Refuge. We are taking refuge in the entire Buddhist View, Meditation/Path, and Conduct. How is this so?

Vajrayana Buddhist refuge has four voices or levels of subtlety of understanding that imperfectly map onto the ascending stages of the Path: 1) outer refuge: Buddha, dharma, *sangha*; 2) inner refuge: Guru, *yidam, dakini*; 3) secret refuge: channels, winds, drops (*nadis/tsa, lung/prana, bindu/thigle*); 4) "innermost secret" nondual refuge. Here the refuge sources are the three *kayas,* the three buddha bodies of existence—unbounded whole that is the *trikaya of the base* (*gzhi rigpa*)—the indivisible unity of the three *kayas,* or Buddha bodies of reality itself. These three are, in descending order of inclusiveness: *dharmakaya (OM), sambhogakaya (AH), nirmanakaya (HUM)*—thus the great mantra *OM AH HUM* (*Ch. IX*). Padmasambhava (Guru Rinpoche) perfectly expresses this nondual refuge thus:

> In the empty essence, *dharmakaya.*
> In the cognizant nature, *sambhogakaya.*
> In the manifold expression, *nirmanakaya.*
> I take refuge until full *bodhi* of enlightenment.
> Practice these three as a unity.

On the luminous accord of Tulku Urgyen Rinpoche,

> Dharmakaya is like space in that it accommodates the manifestations of the other two kayas. Space is all-encompassing...everything manifests and eventually disintegrates within infinite space...Samantabhadra, the primordial dharmakaya buddha is the equivalent of "God" or a supreme being in Buddhism. The sambhogakaya is like the sun, which appears in the sky and shines with unchanging brilliance. And the nirmanakaya is like the surface of water, which reflects the sun...Wherever there is water the reflection of the sun appears. Nirmanakaya manifests in many different ways...without ever leaving dharmakaya and sambhogakaya, and in accordance with

what is required to benefit beings...The three kayas...are in essence indivisible...sometimes called the essence-kaya, the fourth kaya, which is the essence of our mind...The three kayas...are merely symbols. What they refer to, the true meaning, is the nature of our own mind.

—Repeating the Words of the Buddha, (1996)

It is That basis or ground in whom we take refuge.

Taking refuge in the Three Jewels is not only the first formal step on "entering the stream" of the Buddhist Path, and the first engagement with the three *kayas* or Buddha bodies/dimensions of all existence, it is as well the precursor to entering the path of the bodhisattva, a being who lives life for the benefit of all living beings. Without discursive comment, *The Bodhisattva Vow*:

> Just as all the Buddhas have generated the
> mind of enlightenment, and accomplished
> the stages of the Bodhisattva Path, so will I,
> for the benefit of living beings, accomplish
> that same Path. Until the full bodhi of
> enlightenment I take refuge in the Buddha,
> the Dharma, and the Sangha.

We shall see in Chapter IX how it is that the three *kayas* and four refuges are already this essential prior and present "innermost secret" clear light love-wisdom mind unity. Refuge and our bodhisattva intention and action, with mantra prayer, is our always present love-wisdom touchstone. Thus do we voice the outer Refuge Prayer daily. Notice that all four refuges are accomplished simultaneously. Thus are the four refuges a prior and present unity.

Just so, to take refuge in the three precious refuge sources— the Three Jewels, Buddha, Dharma, Sangha—is to take refuge in one's own indwelling, always present clear light *bodh mind*— primordial love-wisdom mind itself, the very Buddha nature of mind—bright Presence of That. Herein abides great fearless confidence, far above, yet embracing our self-ego-I.

Taking refuge in the precious Three Jewels effortlessly generates the *la*-energy that nourishes, holds and protects the engaged practitioner, and the bodhisattva, on this joyous, difficult Path. The three refuge sources are always a singular unity.

It is the Lama, or Roshi, or Ajahn who gives formal refuge to the prepared student. The student practitioner then recites the Refuge Prayer as a part of his or her regular daily practice. Recite three, or seven, or twenty-one, or 108 times: *"I take refuge in the Lama/guru; I take refuge in the Buddha; I take refuge in the dharma; I take refuge in the sangha"*. Note that in this Vajrayana Refuge the Lama, seen as the Buddha, is also a refuge source. Use your 108 bead mala, of course.

Through the power of this Refuge Prayer, combined with quiescent mindfulness practice, the hyperactive "wild horse of the mind" begins to stabilize; and with that the *View*, which then motivates a commitment to the practice of the *Path*, resulting in relative happiness in the midst of our usual adversity. Then, in due course, and by grace arises the *Fruition/Result* that is liberation from adventitious suffering—enlightenment, Happiness Itself (*mahasuka, paramananda, beatitudo*)—ultimate happiness that does no harm, and so creates no karma; the happiness that cannot be lost (*Dhammapada* verses 277, 278, 279).

Such happiness lies not in the future, in some enlightened mind state. We cannot *become* happy later; but we can *be* happy now. Thus do we make our happiness/enlightenment goal our mundane *shamatha* and refuge practice, just as it is. "Make the goal the Path". For *Dzogchen* Master Adzom Rinpoche, "The fruit is no different at the pinnacle of enlightenment than it is at the primordial base".

The dynamic intrinsic awareness (*gzhi rigpa*) Presence (*vidya, rigpa*) of that primordial emptiness "groundless ground"—our always present Buddha mind (*buddhajnana*) already knows this great truth. Again, for Ad.zom Rinpoche, " All the limbs of the

Buddha's teaching have this one great purpose—to lead all beings to the nondual primordial wisdom". In That we take refuge.

The Four Mind Changes. "Make no mistake; these four reflections are the very basis and foundation for the path of enlightenment..." (Tulku Urgyen Rinpoche). After receiving and practicing refuge, and a bit of mindful *shamatha*, the student practitioner meditates upon "The Four Thoughts" that turn the mind from the suffering of *samsara* toward enlightenment. These are: 1) our precious human birth; 2) impermanence; 3) karma; 4) suffering—the hell of living in everyday *samsara*.

These four mind changes in one's culturally conditioned view bestow a basic heart-felt understanding of what is required to begin the foundational *ngöndro* practice of the Buddhist Vajrayana Path. It is this practice of the Four Thoughts that begins the transformation from our habitual, deep cultural background materialistic "global web of belief"—attentional, mental and emotional mind state imbalances of narcissistic self-ego-I that are the causes of human suffering—into natural, selfless, primordial wisdom of emptiness/*dharmakaya*.

All of the practice of the Buddhist Mahayana Path is embraced within this "primordially pure" state of open Presence (*vidya, rigpa*) of the *Dzogchen* fruitional View. Thus do we begin the process of accomplishing the certainty of realization already present in our inherent "undistracted ordinary mind", the natural clear light state of Presence of *Dzogchen* and Essence *Mahamudra*.

Now, as we have seen, from this primordial love-wisdom mind—bright Presence of That—spontaneously arises *bodhicitta*, engaged compassionate thought, intention, and action for the benefit of living beings being here in time and form. And that is the very cause of both relative and ultimate human happiness. Thus are Compassion and Wisdom the two limbs of the Buddhist Path.

Unless and until one frees oneself of the "two obscurations" that constitute primal ignorance (*avidya, marigpa*), there can be no liberation from suffering in samsaric existence. These two obscurations are: 1) the afflictive *emotional obscurations*—fear, anger, hatred, and the failure of *bodhicitta*; and 2) the *cognitive obscurations*—unsound distracted thinking that conceptualizes and reifies the separation of subject, object, and action/conduct.

Samsaric existence—surviving in a reality of emotionally afflicted, angry and narcissistic egos—is terribly painful. There comes a time when one realizes that one's own life is lived mostly in anxious uncertainty. Who is it then that knows, and is awake? Please consider this *koan*:

> Who is it that desires to know,
> and to be happy"?
> Who is it that is afraid and angry?
> Who is it that is born suffers and dies?
> Who is it that shines through the mind
> and abides at the heart of all beings
> already liberated and fully awake?
> —David Paul Boaz Dechen Wangdu

Good news! Who is it indeed? That wakeful Presence I Am! This dark cloud of unknowing that is the "wisdom of uncertainty" is the beginning of waking up; the beginning of the love-wisdom path to real happiness. The Four Mind changes, with an introduction to mindfulness meditation practice under the guidance of a qualified teacher—then, if you're lucky, a master—is a most auspicious first step. Lao Tzu, 5th century BCE founder of Taoism told it well: "The journey of a thousand miles begins with the first step".

Bodhicitta is for the Mahayana and the Vajrayana "awakened heart-mind", the mind of enlightenment. It has two faces, relative and ultimate. Relative *bodhicitta* is the sympathetic wish, the good will intention to benefit living beings. Ultimate *bodhicitta*, our great gift (*jinlob*) of being here in form spontaneously expresses itself as the engaged *bodhicitta* of action—beyond mere thought and intention—in the service of sentient beings. There is no time to lose. Now is the time.

Being Here Now: No Time, No Self, No Problem. Human happiness, both relative and ultimate, lies not in some blissful future mind state or condition. Happiness, both relative conventional, and ultimate, is always only here now; adversity and all. It's how we respond to the adversity that determines the depth of our peace and happiness. This ironic paradox (to concept mind, not to wisdom mind) is known to students of our Primordial Wisdom Tradition as "the paradox of seeking". Seeking already present happiness to allay suffering is a form of suffering.

As to the primordial emptiness of self, and of the phenomenal experience of such a self, it is often said of "the three times"—past, present, future—that only the present fully exists. But it is not so. Let's penetrate this curious notion of time and its relative tenses a bit more deeply.

The past is gone beyond, but a present memory. The future has not arisen, but a present anticipation of what is yet to be. Past and future continuously converge upon this present moment now. So only the present moment now is real, right? Not quite.

As we deconstruct the ephemeral process of relative time we see only past and future. Where or what is this "present moment"? Any event prior to a given micro-second X is past; and any event after it is future. Thus, there can be no present moment! Time is inherently non-objective and unfindable—relatively all too real; ultimately nonexistent.

So, not only are past and future *ultimately* illusory, but so is the present. Time is a relative conceptually useful semiotic/linguistic convention. Ultimately, it is illusory—*avidya maya*. Einstein's General Relativity reduced time to, in the master's words, "a very persistent illusion".

Just so, the self-ego-I is inherently, objectively unfindable—absent and empty of any intrinsic existence. Yet, and quite fortunately, here we are in all of our narcissistic, egocentric relative conventionally embodied raiment, in process of waking up to who we actually are.

As to the self in time, Nagarjuna told that the Buddha's view was this: there are two possible modes of the existence of appearing form—1) objectively, inherently, observer-independently real; and 2) nominally, conceptually imputed, linguistically designated, and observer-dependently real. The first is logically unsound, as we have just seen. The second is Buddha's view of emptiness/dependent arising—that self and all arising spacetime phenomena are absent and empty of intrinsic or ultimate existence, yet ontologically relative to our cultural, deep background semiotic, conceptual "global web of belief". In other words, self and phenomena exist not absolutely or ultimately, but only relatively, as linguistic conventions and conceptual names and constructs (*namarupa*).

Back to the present. Japan's greatest Zen Master Dōgen told, and Padmasambhava before him, this present moment now exists, not ultimately, but only relative to a past and a future. Being here in time—Dōgen's "*Ugi*/Being-Time"—is a moment "flashing into existence" from its vast open emptiness/*shunyata* Buddha ground. *Ugi* is a simultaneous array of the "three times", past, present, future. Our present life moment is so significant because it is adorned by our past and our future which are causally enfolded within it, while simultaneously unfolding in this ultimately nonexistent, relatively real present moment now. We can learn from our past, and learn not to fear our future. And all of this always embraced by nondual *turiya*, the timeless "fourth time" of the Hindu *Sanatanadharma*, and of *Dzogchen* (Ch. *VIII*).

Thus do we live in a single already vanishing instant now. But this precious moment now derives its meaning and significance for us from the context of a personal past and future.

Our egocentric, obsessive, discontented seeking of a perfectly contented "enlightened" future mind state is our primary obstruction to attaining the peace and happiness that is always only already present in this timeless, proto-existent eternal moment now. Moment to moment mindfulness of this process reveals ultimate happiness, Happiness Itself—not later, but now.

So again, we cannot *become* happy in the future. But we can *be* happy now. It is our already present Buddha mind love-wisdom mind Presence, always here now at the spiritual Heart (*hridyam*) that feels and knows this miraculous but conceptually paradoxical and ironic great truth of being here in relative time and form.

Wu-Wei. Yes, Buddha told it well, "Let it be as it is and rest your weary mind; all things are perfect exactly as they are....What you are is what you have been; what you will be is what you do now". These beautiful wisdom piths are known in the Taoist/Ch'an/ Zen wisdom tradition as *Wu Wei*, wise effortless action that arises through resting in quiescent non-action. From Lao Tzu's *Tao Te Ching*, (Chapter 48; author's translation):

> Pursuing wisdom
> I add something each day.
> As breath of formless Tao
> I drop something each day.
>
> I let it be as it is.
> Perfect as it is.
> Now I strive not for self.
> Care for others more and more.
>
> Wisdom non-attainment
> Is wisdom attainment.
> No I at all. No goal at all.
> All nothing at all.
>
> Only smile of Tao
> That I am now.

Hence, to be is to be impermanent, selfless, and interdependently arisen; yet to be is to be embodied in an ultimately illusory, presently real time, with a personal past and future. But, for the wise, such subject-object, self-other duality is dropped, almost moment to mindful moment. With practice the myriad afflictive conceptual and emotional distractions "self liberate" at, or near the very instant of their arising.

Here, now we can see, not some more real or greater reality ground beyond our spacetime being here, but the lovely great completion of all this relative conventional stuff arising within a thoroughly relative space and time; embraced by its prior primordial nonlocal, nondual sphere—the Perfect Sphere of *Dzogchen*; the great imprint of Definitive *Mahamudra* (*Ch. VIII*).

Yes, we live in this moment, but not only in this moment. To live only in the moment now, without awareness and memory of our personal past, and concern for our future is, for Dōgen Zenji, to "make our life meaningless". However, not to live in this moment now, is "to lose reality itself", which is always only happening in the present here and now. Cause and effect karma require a past and a future. Once again, *"What you are is what you have been; what you will be is what you do now"* (Gautama Buddha).

Moreover, Dōgen cautions that if we project or superimpose abstract conceptual imputation upon our immediately real direct perception (*kensho, satori, vipashyana*) of arising form, we shall fall into painful, alienated subject-object duality of a lonely, separate self-ego-I, and miss entirely the pristine and perfect selfless nature of being itself—*dharmakaya,* whose essence is emptiness—the very Buddha nature of mind that is nondual Presence of Dōgen's *Uji*/Being-Time.

As we penetrate our often afflicted human nature through the direct seeing (*kensho*) of mindful *shamatha* and *vipashyana* practice we begin to see clearly that there exists "no nature". Emptiness is the absence of any essential or *ultimate* self-nature of form in time. We discover that we are not *ultimately* perceiving subjects apprehending separate objects, but the interdependent primordial awareness wisdom unity of both cognitive poles at once.

Thus is the brutish duality of the subject-object split finally "dropped", and we abide relatively and imperfectly in the perfect selfless subjectivity of primordial wisdom Presence—nondual unity of bliss and emptiness. And when we forget? Mindful meditation upon the breath with the surprising surpassing power of mantra prayer connects us again, and again. *OM AH HUM* (*Ch. IX; Appendix A*).

No Time, No Self, No Problem. For Dōgen, when we "forget the self... body and mind drop away". There is no inherent *ultimate* nature at all. With the cessation of obsessive time-like conceptual imputation and reification of phenomenally pure direct perceptual experience we "drop body and mind" and see directly (*kensho, satori, vipashyana*) the "no nature" of self-ego-I and its realities. As Zen Master Suzuki Roshi told, "When we finally understand the nature of mind there is no problem whatsoever in this world".

But wait! Here we are! If there is no self, who is it that realizes this bliss of emptiness? What is the location of such nonlocal happiness? The relative-conventional embodied mind being here in time is the bodily location of the yogi's bliss. As if relative form and ultimate emptiness were ever separate at all. Our inherent ultimate already present Buddha mind does not transcend relative embodied being in time, but embraces and illumines it. Buddha gave us two truths: formless nondual ultimate, and relative spacetime form. We learn to "Practice these two as a unity".

Zen Master Dōgen Zenji sees no paradox here. The *ultimate* non-existence of form, and its *relative* real spacetime existence are a non-problematic out-picturing of the Two Truths. Abiding the cognitive duality of being here in Being-Time/*Ugi* is to "drop" our obsessive objectification of perceptual objects as separate from a perceiving subject. We must, through *shamatha/vipashyana* practice, cognize the prior ontic and present phenomenal unity of perceiving knowing subject with its intentional objects. We must drop our compulsive conceptuality. Ultimately we drop both dualistic *and* nondual cognition. Thus do we, as a self, open and embrace the selfless always already present Buddha wisdom mind Presence of *Ugi* being here in time. From that love-wisdom arises spontaneous *Wu-Wei bodhicitta* activity.

Therefore, it is the *relative* self-ego-I who *chooses* to establish the practice of the Path that results in *ultimate* Happiness Itself. No dilemma whatsoever. No problem at all.

We have seen that for the sage or *mahasiddha,* conception, judgment, and some of the afflictive emotions still arise from both immediate direct perception and conception, but such mind states "self liberate" at or near the instant of their arising. Thus, through assiduous practice are our afflictive emotional responses imperfectly self liberated. And thus do the Two Truths, relative and ultimate, remain always in their natural primordially pure condition of unity, just prior to the afflictive subject-object split. Skillful *bodhicitta* is the happy result.

For such a one, luminous clear-light awareness is the always already present nature of being here in time. Happiness Itself. Great joy! We human beings have this inherent Buddha mind capacity, deep within us. We recognize, then realize it through the two limbs of Buddha's teaching: wisdom and compassion. Thus do we engage Buddhist philosophy and ethics.

From the view of Relative Truth, time/change with its entropic, thermodynamic, asymmetric (future looking) one way arrow of time is, as physicists know, objectively real. Yet, beginning with Einstein's General Relativity Theory modern physics has come to deny the ultimate reality of time with its thermodynamic arrow. Likewise, from the view of Mahayana Ultimate Truth time is subjective and illusory, with no time arrow, while still displaying an all too real objective time (t) (Boaz 2021A). Again, for Einstein time (t) is but "a very persistent illusion".

Dōgen's Being-Time has then introduced a beautiful wisdom ballast to the Mahayana Two Truths view of the nature of our being here in time. How is this so?

Physics' thermodynamic arrow of time flows from past toward the future, but time is, as Dōgen pointed out, also arrayed simultaneously throughout the three times—past, present, and future. As both Dōgen and recent physics point out, there are more things in heaven and earth than are dreamt in our objective philosophies of time. Yes, the perfect sphere that is the timeless nonlocal (not dependent on time-like physical phenomena), nondual dimension of Ultimate Truth embraces and subsumes the dualistic dimension of temporal Relative Truth. Dōgen has helped us to deeply understand this great truth.

But how shall we balance these prodigious Two Truths—timeless nondual ultimate, and our all too real relative being here in time. How indeed. We engage the objective relative finite foreground while remaining present in the infinite perfect subjectivity of the timeless primordial background. Contemplative practice is the conscious cognitive finite portal into infinite basal awareness-consciousness itself in whom this whole wondrous reality process arises and is instantiated, and passes on.

Alas, all of this ostensible wisdom is little more than conceptual self stimulation before and until the wild horse of the mind opens wide as the sky and enters in already present quiescent Presence of timeless non-conceptual primordial love-wisdom mind.

Yes, Being-Time/*Ugi* Presence is a *choice*; the choice of fully engaging the practice of the Path. So, take refuge in the Three Jewels, practice mindfulness, "brief moments many times", and make your goal the Path itself. Still, this wondrous process begins with reading about and considering the View, as we are doing here; then finding a *sangha* and a qualified master to guide and support the practice.

Philosophers of physics and cosmology, if not always physicists and cosmologists, are discovering a post-eternalist (physics "block universe" orthodoxy is eternalist) *presentism* (only the present moment now really exists) in Dōgen's syncretic view of the unity of objective relative form in time, and perfectly subjective ultimate timeless emptiness. "Form is empty; emptiness is form". May I say it again? Buddha's Two Truths are always already a prior and present nondual unity.

Thus it is, our human happiness is always only present here and now; what you practice here and now. But, as Buddha told, "Don't believe what I teach out of respect for me. Come and see!". Establish your practice and see for yourself, step by mindful step.

Taoist Master Chuang Tzu: "You will not find happiness until you stop seeking it". *Dzogchen* founder Garab Dorje told, "To remain present without seeking is the meditation". Seeking future liberation from suffering is not a proper goal. The goal is a continuing moment to moment *process* of our *present* practice of the Path, such as it is. And all of our experience is the Path. So once again, "Make the goal the Path". The practice of the Path is both origin and aim of Buddhist ethics.

And who is it that enters in and practices the Buddhist Path? Relative self (*atman*) and ultimate no-self (*anatman*) are an already prior and always present unity. How is this so? Through realization of the identity of our already present "innermost secret" love-wisdom Buddha mind. Bright indwelling Presence of That. And yes, it is *relative* self-ego-I who *chooses* to inter in this *ultimate* happiness that cannot be lost. That is the beginning and the end of Buddhist ethics and *bodhicitta*—primary cause of human happiness. Thus it is. Let it be so.

This concludes our exploration of Buddhist ethics.

Buddhist Philosophy

The nature of mind is the unity of awareness and emptiness...
The nature of mind is clear light.

— Shakyamuni the Buddha

Buddha's Hinayana Eightfold Path, and the Mahayana Six Perfections teaches human ethical conduct for those who would be authentically and harmlessly happy—and who are willing to work wisely to help others do the same. Such a bodhisattva lifestyle is pervaded by the precious *bodhicitta*, the altruistic thought, intention and action for the benefit of living beings. It is the very secret of human happiness. What is the philosophical basis for this profound ethic of *bodhicitta*?

We've seen that this conduct is grounded in the wisdom of emptiness/*shunyata* with its three foundational metaphysical principles—impermanence/*anitya*; no-self/*anatman*, and dependent or interdependent arising/*pratitya samutpada*. Dependent arising shares a relationship of identity with emptiness, as we shall see.

In emptiness/*shunyata* Buddhist philosophy meets Buddhist ethics. The way in which these three core principles are interpreted by the Four Buddhist Tenet Systems (see below) constitute the View (*darshana*) which determines the ethical Conduct (*sila*), and actual practice of the Buddhist Path (*marga, Tib. lam*), whose Result or Fruition is Buddhahood.

The Buddhist promise of the ultimate happiness that is free-dom or liberation from suffering is dependent upon the full *bodhi* awakening of enlightenment, which in turn is dependent upon the knowing-feeling realization of the ultimate Buddha nature of mind (*tathagatagarbha, buddhajnana*) ultimate reality itself, and so of the complementary interdependent relational unity of the Buddhist Two Truths—Relative and Ultimate.

Broadly construed, Relative Truth (*samvriti satya, kunzog denpa*) is the dimension of form, conventional perceptually and concep-tually appearing phenomenal spacetime reality. Ultimate Truth (*paramartha satya, don dam den pa*) is emptiness/*shunyata*, timeless formless dimension of trans-conceptual, nondual primordial ground that is both origin and aim of our always present Buddha love-wisdom *bodhi* mind. It is this luminous *dharmakaya* dimen-sion in which, or in whom arises all of the appearing spacetime phenomena of Relative Truth (*Ch. VI*).

Here the ontic plot thickens. Buddhist Sutrayana and Tantrayana have not granted us a *unified* view of the Buddha's teaching. In Buddhism's rich philosophical history there have arisen several subtle and profound syncretic attempts to unify the primary Buddhist sutra and tantra tenet systems, and the various schools therein. For example, Tsongkhapa, founder of the Tibetan Gelug tradition emphasized the sameness of the wisdom streams of sutra and tantra. Conversely, Nyingma master Ju Mipham points out what he sees to be essential differences in both the View (*darshana*) and Path (*marga*) of basic sutra and tantra, as we shall discover in this chapter.

In any case, the evolution of Buddhist gnoseology has seeded several distinct offerings as to what correctly constitutes ultimate reality, and how.

Thus, not surprisingly, Buddhist metaphysical systems and what they mean for Buddhist soteriology (salvation) and practice have, over the past 25 centuries, evolved a notoriously vexing ar-ray of dialectical hermeneutical strategies. These are generally grouped into the *Four Buddhist Tenet Systems* which we shall briefly survey at the end of this chapter.

Please consider well these interpretations of the teaching of the Buddha. As one progresses through the yanas and the philosophical, ontological tenet systems one begins to decide upon one's own way to happiness. From the metaphysical ontology you choose, arises the phenomenal reality you deserve.

I have presented our exploration of Buddhist philosophy in this chapter in three sections: 1) A Note on Buddhist Hermeneutics; 2) Basic Principals of Buddhist Emptiness: Self, No-Self, and Buddha Nature; and 3) The Four Buddhist Tenet Systems: Variations on a Theme of Wholeness.

A Note On Buddhist Hermeneutics.

Hermeneutics is the art and science of provisional, fallible, usually polemical methodology and practice of the general and of the specific *interpretation* of poetic, religious, and philosophical texts. Our knowledge of the *meaning* of a text—whether relative, objective, literal, provisional; or definitive, subjective, ultimate— begins with a relative, conventional interpretation of its individual parts, and as well, to other related texts and ideas; and ultimately to the all embracing trans-textual wisdom whole itself. Ultimate meaning arises, in part, from relative interpretation of the core texts of any tradition.

Moreover, text translation necessarily requires interpretation. A text is interpreted through its translation so there is perforce, some hermeneutical space between a text and its translation. A translator necessarily, not always consciously, presumes some of the cultural and philosophical ideology of his or her prevailing cultural knowledge paradigm. Hermeneutical interpretation and translation evolve in sociocultural space and time. This adds even greater complexity when a translation spans centuries, traditions, and languages, as is the case with Buddhist texts.

Please consider, but don't believe, that *objective meaning*—the concepts, theories, beliefs, biases, and even intuitive "gut feelings" *about* the ultimate nature of phenomenal reality that constitutes a given cultures' individual and collective zeitgeist, its "global web of belief" (Quine 1969) as to what is real, significant, valuable and wise—is derived mainly from conceptual *interpretation*, with its many cognitive biases, of the texts that found and ground the philosophical, moral, aesthetic, and social principles of that culture. And the individual and collective-cultural deep background *subjective meaning* presuppositions are very much conditioned by that objective meaning. (For an unpleasant but edifying cognitive surprise, google "cognitive biases". Pick out your own special biases. Warning: this requires honesty and ego strength. Sadly, our human cognition is controlled by self-ego-I *pride* far more than we might wish to believe.)

For example, Western culture is conditioned by our deep background, mostly unconscious cognitive foundation in Greek (and Hebrew) Metaphysical Realism/Materialism, which has become hyper-objectivist, proto-religious, quasi-theistic Metaphysical Scientific Realism/Materialism—in a word, Physicalism—that has now colonized the Western mind.

By way of this omnipresent deep cultural background "confirmation bias"—interpreting new data as confirmation of present belief—our physical, mental, and spiritual realities have been reduced to mere "scientific" objective physical matter-energy ($E=mc^2$), in a word Physicalism. Subjective, trans-conceptual, even spiritual human cognition has, since the 17th century inception of the European Enlightenment (The Age of Reason), become more or less taboo. The unhappy result has been the dualistic calamitous split of knowing subject and its perceived intended object, and with that the misleading disjunction between science and religion/spirituality. Pernicious dualistic metaphysics indeed. The fruition of such ignorance (*avidya*) has been great suffering for living beings, including our Mother Earth.

Just so, our emotional and spiritual experience is reduced (scientific reductionism) to purely objective physical brain structure and function (metaphysical functionalism). Not much space here for love, nor for subjective emotional and spiritual intelligence. This one dimensional, lonely world view that is realistic Scientific Materialism/Scientism has left its true believers utterly outside in the *kosmic* cold! Dismal ontology indeed. From the metaphysical ontology you choose arises the phenomenal world you deserve.

Thus has Metaphysical Scientific Materialism—fundamentalist "Scientism" in its most extreme ideological cloak—become the prevailing mass cultural hermeneutical interpretation of appearing reality for the Western mind. "Science" is valorized and idealized as the solution for all problems. Its physicalist ontology is the unconscious culturally conditioned ultimate truth of all appearing reality for most of us. And most of us do not see that it is a multiform cognitive bias, merely a presumptive, unproven, unprovable metaphysical presupposition or interpretation; one of a plurality of possible metaphysical views.

For example, reality may instead be ultimately mental (Metaphysical Idealism). Metaphysical speculation, scientific or mythopoetic, *ipso facto* admits of no empirical inductive scientific, or formal deductive logical proof. Metaphysical ontology is grounded in hermeneutical, provisional, fallible, polemical confirmation bias of our preconscious global web of belief— in Western mind and culture—hyper-objectivist Metaphysical Scientific Materialism/Physicalism.

And what pray tell is the truth status of this post-skeptical theory of mine? Without a centrist post-metaphysical middle way alternative to the metaphysical extremes of Physicalism and Idealism, it is little more than philosophical self-stimulation. What to do?

Must we perforce choose *either* the substantialist absolute existence of Physicalism, *or* the absolute nonexistence of flaky Idealism? Are we destined to be forever encaged in this false dichotomy? Is there a centrist view between eternalist, materialist objective physical existence, and nihilistic subjective nonexistence? We shall son see that the Buddha's Middle Way fills the proverbial bill.

The task of philosophy—defined as the unity of love and wisdom (*philo-sophia*)—is to heal this false dichotomy, and restore the primordial unity of human scientific objectivity with its spiritual perfectly subjective ground. The restoration of the prior unity of Science and Spirit? No small matter is at stake. Human happiness depends upon it (Boaz 2021b, *The Noetic Revolution: Toward an Integral Science of Matter, Mind, and Spirit*, excerpted at *davidpaulboaz.org*).

I shall argue in these pages that the subtlest or highest Buddhist teaching—the Gelugpa *Rangtong* view of Tsongkhapa's Middle Way Prasangika Madhyamaka, completed in Nyingma nondual *Dzogchen* view and practice—accomplishes that noble aim (*Ch. VIII*).

Basic Principles of Buddhist Emptiness: Self, No-Self, and Buddha Nature

A Buddhist Middle Way. The propitious arrival and success of Mahayana Buddhism in the West in the last century has thickened this epistemic plot. Buddhist Mahayana Middle Way Madhyamaka liberation/enlightenment philosophy with its positive psychology and altruistic ethic of *bodhicitta* opens a profound, logical, and experiential path to human happiness that represents a centrist view between the absolute metaphysical extremes of solid monistic Western Materialism/Physicalism ("It's all just physical"), and diaphanous monistic Eastern and Western often nihilistic Idealism ("It's all just mental illusion"). That is to say, Madhyamaka, especially in its Prasangika raiment, has bestowed an ontic balance to the false dichotomy of *either* existence, *or* nonexistence. How is this so?

Middle Way Buddhism does not accept the absolute existence measured out by substantialist monistic Metaphysical Materialism;

nor does it accept the absolute nonexistence of nihilist monistic Metaphysical Idealism; nor does it endorse a problematic Cartesian Metaphysical Dualism, or other dualistic ontology.

Rather, the great Nalanda Middle Way Consequence School that is Prasangika Madhyamaka, founded by Nagarjuna and Aryadeva (2nd century), further developed by Buddhapalita (5th century), and more fully developed by Chandrakirti (8th century), and Tsongkhapa (14th century) is an empirical pluralism that avoids attaching to any single absolutist monistic metaphysical view—materialist or idealist.

In short, Buddhist Middle Way assumes the great invariant *one truth* of the prior and present complementary unity of the Buddha's Two Truths: 1) the phenomenal spacetime *relative* existence of form, and a conventional self which apprehends it; and 2) form's *ultimate* emptiness/*shunyata* or absence of intrinsic, absolute existence (*Ch. VI*). In the Buddha's immortal words, "Form is empty; emptiness is form. Form is not other than emptiness; emptiness is not other than form". Form is relatively, conventionally real but ultimately absent and empty of any whit of ultimate existence.

Indeed, Prasangika Madhyamaka—which is, on the accord of Chandrakirti and H.H. Dalai Lama, the very foundation of nondual *Dzogchen* view and praxis—avoids the conceptual imputation and reification of the substantial, inherent *ultimate* existence of anything at all. Well, that sounds like an idealist nihilist denial of material reality altogether—until one remembers that for Middle Way Prasangika physical and mental reality are indeed *relatively*, conventionally the all too "real world out there" (RWOT) that we have come to know and love, and firmly believe in.

Moreover, Buddhist Middle Way Prasangika Madhyamaka philosophy points a way toward an empirical, evidenced based rapprochement of hitherto incommensurable Science and Spirit. Therefore, "East is East, and West is West; and *ever* the twain shall meet". (Apologies to Kipling)

Viewed holistically or mereologically (part-whole relations), human understanding and knowledge may be seen as the discovery of the spirit and wisdom of the whole through analysis and interpretation of its particular parts in their interdependent relation with vast basic space (*ying*) of the implicate order of the boundless whole itself (*dharmadhatu*, Bön, *mahabindu*)—ground or basis of all explicate arising appearances.

Just so, in the context of our present hermeneutical discussion, an understanding of a particular textual idea refers us necessarily to other related texts and readings until a provisional, relative *interpretation* of its meaning emerges. And of course, interpretations differ. Hermeneutics understands this process as an epistemological, even ontological "hermeneutic circle".

It is important here to distinguish between *textual interpretation* as an activity directed toward discovering the intentional meaning of an author in a text, and *textual criticism* that is a provisional judgment of value as to the importance or significance of a text, or part of a text, with respect to a given set of cultural values.

Moreover, all texts have a *context*—authorial, intentional, historical, and cultural. In contradistinction to textual deconstruction, textual reconstruction considers texts in this larger hermeneutical context. We reconstruct this "nexus of meaning"—the epistemic and ontic aura of wisdom that surrounds and pervades the text—in order to arrive at a meaningful, relative-conventional, always provisional and fallible *textual interpretation*.

Clearly, the Buddha's *textual intention* was a solution to the ubiquitous problem of suffering of living beings, and especially of human beings. However, it is the provisional *textual criticism* of his myriad texts and their interpretive Buddhist Schools that is the hermeneutical rub. Buddhist practitioners must *choose* among this scintillating array of Relative Truth—dialogical, dialectical interpretations, both "provisional" and "definitive"—all the while knowing that this all is subsumed and embraced in the trans-textual dimension of the nondual primordial wisdom whole—Ultimate Truth itself.

Thus do we become disciplined—step by mindful step—in seeing our realities holistically rather than dualistically. The gradual result is sound *relative* reasoning, more or less free of destructive cognitive bias, and clear light *ultimate* primordial wisdom, Happiness Itself.

So, while hermeneutical relative interpretative truths as to Buddha's textual intention will differ (The Four Buddhist Tenet Systems below), Buddha's ultimate textual intention outshines (*abhasa*) through them all as our trans-conceptual, innate, nondual, indwelling Buddha nature/Buddha mind (*buddhajnana*) and its emergent spontaneously arising *bodhicitta* that is inherent therein.

What then shall we make of this seeming relativistic sea of hermeneutical intellectual self stimulation? To paraphrase Guru Rinpoche, Padmasambhava, we utilize the uncertainty of our ambulation through the hermeneutical space of the *relative* Path, knowing full well that the nondual *ultimate* certainty of the View is always already present as our innermost nondual *Bodhi* mind/ love-wisdom mind. In due course, and by grace (*jinlob*), it is that great truth—the prior and already present unity of the Buddha's Two Truths—to which we awaken each moment now.

That now said, let us, upon the way to nondual certainty of the View, further engage Buddhist interpretations—both provisional and definitive—of the Buddha's teaching for the ages.

***Principia Dharmata*: Basic Principles of Buddhist Emptiness.** The nondual unity of the three basic Buddhist metaphysical principles introduced above—the impermanence (*anitya*), selflessness (*anatman*), and causal interdependent arising (*pratitya samutpada*) of all appearing form—pervade all three vehicles of the Buddhist Path: 1) Shravakayana of the early Hinayana *Pali Canon* (the foundation of Southeast Asia Theravada); 2) Mahayana; and 3) the Vajrayana Tibetan Middle Way, namely Prasangika Madhyamaka and Yogachara Madhyamaka.

So once again, these three foundational metaphysical or philosophical principles of the Buddha's love-wisdom teaching on the emptiness of form of any essential, intrinsic, ultimate existence are: 1) impermanence (*anitya*) of form; 2) no-self or selflessness (*anatman*) of form; and 3) causal interdependence or "dependent arising" (*pratitya samutpada*) of form.

And we have seen that on the accord of the Buddha's Mahayana teaching vehicle the problem of primal human ignorance (*avidya, marigpa, ajnana*) is that we conceptually superimpose (*vikshepa, distraction*) permanence, a separate and independent self-ego-I, and an observer-independently real existence onto what is in truth of the ultimate view a causally *interdependent*, observer-dependent, selfless, and impermanent relative spacetime reality.

In other words, we conceptually impute, reify, and fabricate a substantial, independent, permanent "real world out there" (RWOT), including a solid substantially existing self-ego-I who experiences it. Under sway of ignorance (*marigpa*) and delusion (*moha*) we take ordinary direct perception of the naked, bare raw data of observer-dependent immediate sense perception, and conceptually construct, reify, and elaborate an observer-independently existing RWOT. The inauspicious result is centuries of terrible human suffering.

Please consider the following slightly spooky but revealing *vipashyana* thought experiment on the impermanence of self and its experienced phenomenal reality.

Imagine for a moment yourself, empty and absent your sense perceptions; absent your thoughts, feelings and memories about who and what you are; absent your sense of self-ego-I. What remains? Nothing remains! *Ultimately*, our realities are empty and absent "any shred" of intrinsic, ultimate self-existence. This then is the Ultimate Truth of relative-conventional, really real appearing form—these myriad forms of our perceptually and conceptually experienced spacetime realities—which after all bestows the freedom of the will to *choose* what to accept, and what to reject. Yet, this RWOT is ultimately nonexistent.

Still, the stuff of experience continues to arise as the conventional Relative Truth, Suzuki Roshi's Small Mind of appearing form. Because *ultimately* apparitional (*avidya maya*) physical and mental form is embraced and subsumed by Ultimate Truth—the boundless whole itself, *dharmakaya*, *kadag*, emptiness/*shunyata*—the Buddhist Two Truths are a metaphysical or ontological unity. The Two Truths that are Buddha's form and emptiness, *samsara* and nirvana, being here in time and its timeless primordial ground, are the in the ultimate view of Suzuki Roshi's Big Mind, one and the same (*samatajnana*).

In short, the ontological prior, and epistemological and phenomenological present unity of form and emptiness share an *ultimate* relation of identity. So, even as stuff appears and exists relatively, in the ultimate view of the wisdom of emptiness, "There is not the slightest difference between *samsara* and nirvana" (Nagarjuna).

Once again, from Buddha's lapidary *Heart of Wisdom Sutra*: "Form is empty; emptiness is form". The Buddhist Two Truths—relative form and its ultimate emptiness—share a metaphysical relation of identity. Selfless emptiness, *dharmadhatu*, *dharmakaya*, or Ultimate Truth, embraces and subsumes form or Relative Truth in whom it arises and participates, even as they arise and appear as two separate reality dimensions.

Therefore, in the nondual ultimate view this prior and present unity is nothing less than the whole *one truth*—invariant throughout all of our human cognitive awareness-consciousness processional—1) raw, pre-conceptual, attention-perception; 2) exoteric, objective, conceptual; 3) esoteric, subjective, contemplative; and 4) innermost, perfectly subjective nondual. Guru Rinpoche admonishes us to "Practice these as a unity".

If I may be permitted a bit of redundancy, in the transconceptual, "innermost secret" nondual ultimate view, the logical relation of this ancient atavistic duality of relative appearance and ultimate reality is one of sameness (*samatajnana*). The Ultimate Truth of emptiness is no more nor less than the Relative Truth of the "interdependent arising" of appearing reality whose putative existence is imputed and reified by our perception and conception. And all of that already subsumed by the all embracing dimension of Ultimate Truth—*shunyata, dharmakaya, kadag.*

Recall that the Buddha realized his full *bodhi* awakening/enlightenment under the proverbial *bodhi* tree (*Ficus religiosa*) when he finally understood this sublime unity of the Two Truths of reality—the astounding unity of the interdependent arising of relative form (*pratitya samutpada/tendrel*) that is not other than the ultimate emptiness/*shunyata* of form. All of the Buddha's teaching—from the Four Noble Truths to nondual *Dzogchen*—arise from and are founded in this momentous numinous Two Truths unity (*Ch. VI*)

This unified one truth peace of mind is present for each one of us, right here and now. It is, with precious *bodhicitta* conduct that spontaneously arises from it, the very secret of both relative and ultimate human happiness.

Thus do relative conventional "concealer truths" (*samvriti satya*) presume that which is greater and all inclusive, namely, Ultimate Truth (*paramartha satya*) in which they arise and are instantiated. But again, from the view of Ultimate Truth, relative reality as empty and absent "any shred" of *ultimate* existence. It is rather, observer-dependent, conditioned, impermanent, selfless, and causally interdependent.

And yet, we may enjoy the great gift (*jinlob, euengelion*) that is this really real relative-conventional spacetime world—precious form in relatively real but ultimately nonexistent time. Einstein told it well. "Time is an illusion, albeit a very persistent one". It is through this gift of time that we awaken to our own always present Buddha nature/Buddha mind. There is no time to lose.

We here conceptually separate the Two Truths only in order to holistically understand and realize the profundity of the whole singular, joyous mysterious process.

So, once again, Buddhist Mahayana metaphysics understands that there is no *essential* difference between the *relative* conventional stuff of appearing reality, and its selfless *ultimate* nature, the very Buddha nature of mind.

But wait! Recall the thorny Buddhist epistemic problem: if there is no self, just *who is it* that understands this vexing notion of selfless emptiness? Who is it that practices the Buddhist Path? Who is it that benefits from *bodhicitta*? Who is it that is liberated from suffering? *If such nouns are non-existent, who is it that acts out the verbs?* Conceptual dialectics necessarily ends in contradiction.

We've seen that our human cognition may be viewed as having four interdependent qualities or modes of awareness: 1) direct, unmediated sense perception; 2) indirect conceptual abstraction of the direct experience of sense perception; 3) subjective, trans-conceptual, contemplative cognition; and 4) nonlocal, nondual knowing-feeling wisdom unity of 1), 2), and 3).

It is 4)—this "innermost secret" primordial Buddha mind/ wisdom mind—clear-light Presence (*vidya, rigpa*) of That vast whole who understands the process. Who is it that I am? To resurrect an ancient Hindu Veda-Vedanta metaphor, *Tat Tvam Asi*. That I Am! That *buddic* Presence is our utterly selfless "supreme identity"—who we actually are, prior to any view, judgment, name, concept, or belief. It is that always present ultimate selfless *anatman* no-self who knows and loves this curious and unruly self-ego-I that so struggles to know its origin, identity, and aim. So, this is the "correct view" of the Buddha's *Heart of Wisdom Sutra* teaching on the Two Truths—"Form is empty; emptiness is form". Or is it?

Radical 2nd century Buddhist skeptic Nagarguna bespeaks the Buddhist Middle Way Madhyamaka doctrine of the View (*Mulamadhyamakakarika* XXVII v. 20, 29, 30, author's translation):

> If nothing is permanent,
> What could be impermanent?
> Permanence, impermanence,
> Both or neither?

Because all things are empty,
What view of permanence, self,
Dependent arising could there be,
And when, and to whom?

I bow down to Gautama Buddha,
whose great compassion revealed
the true dharma view,
that is free of all views.

In Nagarjuna's dialectic, because all things are empty of intrinsic existence, we are ever free of grasping at any conceptual metaphysical view, including the Buddhist view of emptiness itself. Buddha himself told in his *Heart of Wisdom Sutra*: "In emptiness there is no suffering, no end of suffering, no path, no wisdom, no attainment..." The wise avoid attaching to, asserting, or defending any conceptual view at all.

For Nagarjuna the Middle Way "is free of all views"—ultimately including the view that the Middle Way "is free of all views". Radical skepticism indeed. Nagarjuna is not skeptical of the Buddha's teaching. He is skeptical of textual conceptual elaborations of it. He is skeptical, as was the Buddha himself, of the capacity of inherently relative dualistic semiotic human concepts and beliefs to express the nondual Ultimate Truth of the deepest, subtlest teaching of all the Buddhas.

The Mahayana Madhyamaka Buddhist wisdom of emptiness—especially in its nondual *Dzogchen* raiment (*Ch. VIII*)—sees ordinary direct perception as displaying appearing phenomena to a sentient human consciousness in its momentary pre-conceptual purity as the raw, conceptually unelaborated, naked perceptual "bare attention" of "ordinary mind", just prior to any conceptually imputed and reified belief in the intrinsic existence of really real spacetime stuff; a RWOT; and as well, just prior to our attachment to any conceptual *view* or belief system about the whole metaphysical process of divining the origin (ontology), and the nature (epistemology) of appearing spacetime form.

In other words, almost immediately we contract from the freeing primordial purity of such luminous direct experience (*pratyaksa*) by habitually superimposing (*vikshepa*) or overlaying it with our tangled web of concept-mind's abstract dualistic, materialist views, concepts and beliefs *about* it—our imposing, reality constituting, deep cultural background "global web of belief" (Quine 1969) in inherently real stuff "out there"—a "real world out there" (RWOT).

We've seen that in the West this concept-belief system is founded in Greek Metaphysical Materialism, visited upon the Western monolithic monotheistic mind via four centuries of the modern and postmodern Cartesian obsessively thinking *cogito*—Descartes' "I think therefore I am"—our dualistic Modern European Enlightenment cultural paradigm.

Thus has the prodigious metaphysical ideology that is known to its critics as Scientific Materialism/Physicalism colonized the Western heart and mind. An odious split between perceiving subject and its objects of—I/me and everything else—is the fraught, unhappy result.

Our experience becomes henceforth a lonely duality of self and other—between self-ego-I as the center of the universe, with everything and everyone else outside. Thus arises human alienation, hostility, despotism, and war—in a word, suffering. The lonely, separate self then grasps at its narcissistic desire-mind seeking strategies for happiness in all manner of materialist compensating distractions, not the least of which is dualistic, separative, conceptual "spiritual materialism". Some of these distracting seeking strategies for happiness are quite destructive of self and others. Gautama Buddha understood this process of human ignorance (*avidya, marigpa*) well. He prescribed the Four Noble Truths of the Middle Way as the way out (or perhaps our way in).

Being Boundless Emptiness: Buddhist No-Self Help. How do we heal this sad, yet hopeful metaphysical, and emotional dilemma that is ignorance—our human condition? Suzuki Roshi, 20th century Zen master who founded Soto Zen in the United States teaches:

> The emptiness of mind is not a state of mind, but the original essence of mind, our original mind that includes everything within itself... When we forget ourselves, we actually are the true activity of reality itself. When we realize this fact, there is no problem whatsoever in this world (*Zen Mind, Beginner's Mind*, 1970, 2020).

Wu-Wei is the Taoist non-seeking way of Mahayana Zen mind/wisdom mind. Wu-Wei is an immediate, present moment non-reactive knowing-feeling response to appearing reality—objective or subjective, positive, negative, or neutral—that strikes an easy, concept-free balance between wise contemplative non-action, and gentle skillful spontaneous joy, speech, and action that arises directly from our compassionate love-wisdom Buddha mind—for the benefit of living beings. Herein abides our relative and ultimate human happiness. Our authentic Wu-Wei rests in That.

First, we spontaneously recognize, then, in due course, realize the "innermost secret" truth that the "supreme identity" of dualistic self-ego-I concept-mind is always already only our primordial wisdom Buddha nature/Buddha mind. Buddha told it thus: "Wonder of wonders, all beings are Buddha". Perhaps we're not yet fully realized buddhas, yet Buddha mind Presence is already present deep within us.

Buddha told it long ago: "Let it be as it is and rest your weary mind; all things are perfect exactly as they are". This is the view of Ultimate Truth. This is the Buddha's teaching for the ages.

So, we train, under the guidance of a qualified master, our unruly "wild horse of the mind". How? Through assiduous practice of the Path: Buddha's "mindfulness of breathing" and "penetrating insight" (*shamatha-vipashyana, Jap. shikantaza*). Through meditative mantra breath we remain present—moment to moment—to our all embracing love-wisdom Buddha mind (*buddhajnana*). *Wu-Wei* effortlessly arises from That. Even when we forget, it's right here to remember again. Imperfect, dualistic relative practices of the Path, and kind, skillful altruistic *bodhicitta* conduct make it so.

Thus do we skillfully utilize the self-ego-I of pragmatic dualistic Relative Truth to *connect* to innermost Presence of Ultimate Truth—our selfless love-wisdom Buddha mind—each moment now. And when we are distracted in forgetfulness, we remember again to return to the mindful mantra breath, again and again. Buddha mind rides the breath. Remain close to the breath (*Appendix A*).

Therefore, *Wu-Wei* is the effortless surrender of our obsessive goal directed seeking strategies after some suffering-free ultimate happiness that is already present within us.

Seeking our already present happiness to avoid suffering, is a form of suffering. Thus do we make, not future enlightenment, but the immediately present practice of the Path itself our goal—here and now, moment to moment, breath by mindful breath. As Chögyam Trungpa Rinpoche told it, "Make the goal the path".

Please recall, we cannot *become* happy in some perfect future mind state. We can only *be* happy here and now. How is this so? The future never shows up! It is always too busy becoming this present moment. Now is where everything happens. Past and future are elsewhere. The past is gone, but a present memory. The future has not yet arisen, but a present anticipation. Even the present moment is but the past that is already the future. Ultimately, time—the three times (past, present, future)—has no inherent existence! Yet, as Zen Master Dōgen reminds us, reality is still a simultaneous array of these three times. So, we must learn from the past, and learn not to fear the future. Contemplative mind training of the Path makes it so.

Therefore, the rigorous cognitive coupling of a relative self-ego-I with our nondual, selfless, ultimate *bodhi*/Buddha mind Presence is the profound contemplative awakening process (*Appendix A*, "Let It Be: Basic Mindfulness Meditation").

In due course, the great search falls away revealing the non-dual certainty of our already present love-wisdom mind pure Presence. *Mahasukaho!* Lama Wangdor Rinpoche:

> In this very act of seeking, the truth is revealed, just for a moment... Buddha is within you, clear and bright, and vast as space. This is the meditation. In this quiet, vast boundless emptiness there is nothing to construct, and nothing to do. In a carefree way, let it be as it is. Just relax into it. There is nothing other than this. Now then, rest in that peace. (*Santa Fe, NM retreat, 2003, author's translation*)

The great Ch'an Master Hui Neng (638-713), father of Ch'an/Zen Buddhism and author of the definitive *Platform Sutra* told well the nondual view: "Mind is Buddha from the beginning.... The only difference between a buddha and an ordinary person is that one recognizes it, the other does not".

For Huang Po, "You have always been one with the Buddha. So do not seek Buddhahood...Your seeking is doomed to failure".

Hakuin Ekaku (1689-1769), author of the justly famous Zen koan—"What is the sound of one hand clapping"—reformer and father of modern Renzai Zen speaks:

> From the beginning all beings are Buddha...Nirvana is right here now. As we turn inward and see our true nature, that true self now is no-self, our form now is no-form, our thought now no-thought...This earth where we now stand is the lotus pure land, and this very body the body of Buddha.
>
> —Hakuin Zenji

As to primordial buddhahood, the great 19th century Nyingma *Dzogchen* master Jamgön Mipham Rinpoche or Ju Mipham, (*White Lotus*, 2007) has told it well:

> Because the *sugatagarbha* (Buddha nature) consists in the qualities of enlightenment, which are spontaneously present from the very beginning, all the various paths that may be implemented serve only to render these qualities manifest...The paths simply render the primordial luminosity of the dharmakaya manifest. They do not create it...When the mandala of the profound ground—the authentic nature of primordial buddhahood—is realized, the mind becomes inseparable from the wisdom of all the Buddhas of the three times (past, present, future). The irreversible ground of realization is thereby accomplished. In that very instant supreme mastery is found—in which the ground and fruit are inseparably united.

In the clear words of great 20th century Buddhist *Dzogchen* master Adzom Rinpoche:

> When you fully realize this view and this practice, everything is the infinite display of Buddha bodies of light, and of primordial wisdom. These are the stainless and spontaneous displays of reality itself. Like the rays of the sun, they are utterly pure, for all impure appearances have vanished...May such practitioners become Buddhas for whom there is no bias, for whom all is of one taste so that infinite benefit arises.
>
> (Commentary on the *Longchen Nyingthig Foundational Practice*)

The profound nondual (no subject-object split) teaching of the Buddha is thus exemplified and expressed in the subtle cognitive pattern known as *Wu-Wei*, the wisdom of non-seeking. "To remain without seeking is the meditation" (*Dzogchen* founder Garab Dorje). The inherent paradox of all "spiritual" paths— the paradox of seeking that is the beguiling "paradox of the path"—must be understood and resolved, sooner or later, as we tread this joyous and difficult wisdom path. Such penetrating insight is a great blessing. Our relative and ultimate happiness is always already present, this precious moment now! Practice brings non-conceptual certainty of that. What a relief!

However, as it is fruitless to seek awakening/enlightenment, just so, the wise do not seek the practice or the wisdom of *Wu-Wei*. As Lao Tzu reminds us, "The *Wu-Wei* that does not aim at *Wu-Wei*, is truly *Wu-Wei*".

What shall we make of such a radical nondual wisdom empti-ness view? Please consider Dōgen Zenji's wisdom pith, "A teaching that does not arouse a defense of one's present beliefs is not a useful teaching". The love-wisdom Path is designed to shake us from our narcissistic uncomfortable comfort zones. As Dōgen told, "All that can shaken shall be shaken". In the insouciant gloss of Mark Twain,

It's not what you don't know that gets you in trouble.
It's what you know, that just ain't so.

The astute Buddhist practitioner refrains from mindless, specula-tive metaphysical conceptual conjecture, but rather, studies scrip-ture and commentarial literature of the Buddha dharma—even speculative Buddhist dialectics—toward a *practical* understanding that enhances skillful means (*upaya*), and compassionate *bodhicitta*. Thus does the yogi and yogini remain firm in trans-conceptual Zen mind/Buddha mind in whom arises the kind, skillful action of *Wu-Wei*. No dilemma. No problem at all.

Already being the wisdom of emptiness, we understand that mind has no solid form; and no self nature. Its thoughts and feel-ings are a will-o'-the-wisp, not to be taken too seriously. *But the actual nature of mind is selfless formless always present Buddha mind* (buddhajnana). There is nothing outside it. Nothing greater than it. So we rest our weary mind in luminous Presence of That.

Our already present love-wisdom Buddha mind is not a super upgrade "higher self" of our ego-I. It's not something we possess; not something we *have*, but the Presence that we actually *are*. So, it is useless to seek it, to strive for it in some future time or mind space. It's already here, indwelling at the Heart (*hridyam*) of each human being. It is that to which we awaken. That is the Buddha's highest nondual teaching.

OK. We human beings naturally and spontaneously abide in Buddha mind. Yet, we are not fully awakened Buddhas. Rather, we continuously awaken to our always already present indwelling Buddha nature. How? Of course, we listen to the injunctions of those who know. We take refuge in the precious Three Jewels (the Buddha, the dharma, and the *sangha*); establish our practice; and enter the relative gradual Path under guidance of a qualified master, and in loving presence of the *sangha* community. Without this Path, nothing new happens.

Mindfulness meditation practice (*smriti, sati, shamatha, bhavana*)—the intelligent, courageous *choice* to engage Buddha's original Eightfold Path, and the Six *Paramitas*/Perfections of the Mahayana—gradually heals the adventitious primal ignorance (*avidya*) of the invidious subject-object split, this obsessive objectification of the world with self-ego-I as the narcissistic center in opposition to all others. As we open to receive—step by mindful step—the efflorescence of our *bodhi*/love-wisdom mind Presence, this indwelling happiness is the wondrous result. Mind is always already Buddha—Happiness Itself. So we simply open heart and mind to receive it. *Emaho!*

We saw in Dōgen's *Ugi*/Being-Time that through *process* of practice of the Path we recover the great gift of *absolute bodhicitta*, freeing, liberating, effortless *Wu-Wei* spontaneity—delight of present moment direct perception (*yogi pratyaksa*) of being here as an honored guest of the phenomenal world, prior to habitually biased cognitive attachment to our ego-centric concepts and beliefs about it.

Through opening heart and mind to *absolute bodhicitta*, we spontaneously engage the *relative bodhicitta* that is at first but empathetic aspiration to benefit suffering beings; then the compassionate thought, intention, and *action* for the benefit of living beings. Thus are these three faces of *bodhicitta* the causes of our human happiness.

Quite remarkably, as we discover the absurd humor of this egocentric farce that is *samsaric* reality, we begin to reframe our mistaken view that we, as egos, are somehow special, enduring, substantial, permanent and independently existing self-entities. We begin to see that the seeming ambiguous dichotomy of the Buddha's Two Truths—Relative, conventional, dualistic, objective form; and Ultimate, nondual perfectly subjective emptiness—is a *false dichotomy*. How is this so?

The good news. Because, as we have seen, the absolute dimension of Ultimate Truth (*paramartha satya, don dam denpa*) embraces and subsumes the spacetime dimension of Relative Truth (*samvriti satya, kunzog denpa*) arising therein, we see clearly that the Two Truths of arising reality are quite naturally a prior and present *selfless* one truth unity. Through this wisdom yoga arises peace of mind, and a bit of bliss. Then, in due course and by grace, a lot of bliss—the wondrous unity of bliss and emptiness wherein we realize that knowing, feeling subject is already utterly unified with its luminous, numinous object of realization, even in the midst of these many conceptual and emotional distractions. It has always been thus. Yet, now we see it. Please rest, just for this moment now, in That. *Emaho!*

As we settle into and learn to actually rest in *bodhi* mind Presence—more or less beyond our concepts and beliefs *about* it—we gradually recognize, then suddenly realize that we're all in this reality thing together; that this banal old bromide is a great truth; that all this appearing stuff of reality, including all

of these experiencing ego-selves, is interdependent, interconnected, selfless, and impermanent—utterly absent and empty of any conceptually imputed permanent essence, or of any
observer-independent intrinsic ultimate existence—just as Buddha,
Nagarjuna, Padmasambhava, and Longchenpa told so long ago.

And all of this while being here in the all too real world of
relative time and form. So we still have to show up for work, pay
the bills, and be kind to one another, and to all beings, including our Mother Earth.

Gradually, step by step, we realize these three basic principles
of being here as Buddhist emptiness—the impermanence, selflessness, and interdependence of all this arising spacetime stuff.
And yes, we accomplish this through the practice of meditation—
shamatha (calm abiding upon the breath), and *vipashyana* (liberating penetrating insight). Such practice, in due course and by
grace, bestows the primordial wisdom-bliss (*jnana, yeshe, gnosis*)
of the inseparable "unity of appearance and emptiness"; of the
"unity of luminous clarity and emptiness"; and of "the unity of
bliss and emptiness"—primordial Buddha mind Presence of
emptiness that is liberation from human suffering. Then, if we're
lucky, dawns the full *bodhi* of ultimate enlightenment that was
present all along—Happiness Itself, the happiness that causes
no harm; the happiness that cannot be lost (*Appendix A*). This
then, is the lovely happy fruition of the practice of being here
now as boundless luminous emptiness. *Mahasukaho!*

Yet, we need not *believe* this. Examining the lives of the
Buddha, the Christ, the *mahasiddhas*, saints and sages of our
great Primordial Wisdom Tradition who have proven this truth
of awakening by the love and wisdom conduct of their lives, we
come to accept that that is who we actually are. Let this inspire
us to be here now in that boundless luminous emptiness—bright
Presence of That.

Let us then further engage these basic principles of the Buddhist
philosophy and the ethical practice of being here in the fullness

of emptiness—these three faces of Buddhist *shunyata*/emptiness: the ultimate impermanence, selflessness, and interdependence of arising relative form. First, impermanence.

1) **Impermananance** (*anitya*). There are two aspects: gross impermanence, and subtle impermanence.

B) *Gross impermanence* is constant *gradual* evolutionary change of the Relative Truth dimensional stuff of time and space. Seasons come and go. Our lovely bloom of youth all too quickly becomes the suffering of old age. Things and beings arise, abide for a while, and return again to their primordial emptiness. Nothing endures. Nation states, cultures, species, planets, stars, galaxies, even universes arise, and in due course, return to their basal primordial "groundless ground"—the emptiness of emptiness.

Modern cosmology knows this emptiness whence springs new form from nearly nothing as the "quantum zero point vacuum energy field" (ZPE), the "dark energy" of not so empty space that propulses the cosmos forever outward. Positively charged matter/mass and negatively charged gravity precisely cancel one another leaving a zero point nearly empty vacuum field (*Appendix B*).

Existence harbors the seed of non-existence. So, existence and nonexistence, life and death, are complementary opposites, each requiring the other. Yes, emptiness and form are a prior and present unity. That's the deal, like it or not, that we made at the beginning of the ride.

C) *Subtle impermanence* is the deeper truth of gross impermanence—that the very nature of relative spacetime reality being itself is profoundly, moment to moment impermanent. All of these physical and mental-psychological forms change in time on an *immediate* basis. You are a little bit older *now* than you were this morning. The contents of your visual field, and of your mind stream change from one moment to the next—an impermanent cognitive Heraclitian flux of here now present experience. Cause and effect micro-event moments and processes, our perception of them, are but a continuum of this constant change. No two causal form event moments are alike. "Change is the only constant". This is subtle impermanence.

2) **No-self/Selflessness** (*anatman*). Self-emptiness or absence of a separate self existence—is the great Buddhist truth that the stuff of reality—beings and their perceived objects by a separate, independently existing self-ego-I—possess no intrinsic, ultimate essence or existence. Stuff is, as Nagarjuna told, "utterly free of any shred of intrinsic (*sahaja*) ultimate existence". Though to be sure, in the Middle Way Madhyamaka, self and the phenomena arising to it have plenty of all too real relative-conventional existence.

In the *Dhammacakkappavattana Sutta,* and the *Kaccayanagotta Sutta* the Buddha presented his early Middle Way view that is free of the metaphysical extremes of 1) absolute existence, or eternalist, substantialist Metaphysical Materialism, and of absolute nonexistence, or nihilistic Metaphysical Idealism; and 2) the metaphysical extreme views of self, namely, a permanently existing soul self that endures after death of the physical body; and no continuation of soul self after death of the physical body.

Buddha's later "middle path" bespeaks a relative, conventional self that exists in relation to, or dependent upon an infinite matrix of multiple causes and conditions, not the least of which are the causes and conditions of human embodiment. And the *causes and conditions* that produce the actions/karma of such a relative conditional embodied self—positive, negative, or neutral—continue on into another rebirth. But no independent soul-self "transmigrates" into another body. Our self-ego-I is not itself reborn into a new bodymind. It is our karma/actions that continue.

So, the Buddha affirmed the reality of relative conventional spacetime existence—and of a relative, contingent self who experiences it. This conceptual dimension of Relative Truth is transcended yet embraced and included in the all pervading dimension of nondual Ultimate Truth.

In the Nyingma school of Tibetan Buddhism this seeming Two Truths duality of the Vajrayana is completed and perfected in the nondual (*advaya*, "not one, not two") one truth unity that is indwelling clear light awareness of the *Perfect Sphere of Dzogchen* (*Ch. VIII*). This perfectly subjective boundless whole, the very Buddha nature of mind, embraces and subsumes our entire human consciousness processional in whom it arises and abides. This human awareness is, as we shall see many times and many ways in these pages: 1) "bare" pre-conceptual ordinary direct perception; 2) outer, exoteric, conceptual, objective, material; 3) inner, esoteric, trans-conceptual, subjective, contemplative; and 4) innermost esoteric perfectly subjective nondual.

The nature of mind is the unity of awareness and emptiness...
The nature of mind is clear light.

—Shakyamuni the Buddha

Before we explore the third principle of *shunyata*/emptiness—dependent arising—let's probe a bit more deeply into the nature of Gautama the Buddha's teaching on *anatman* or no-self. (Non-Buddhists may safely skip this rather abstruse exploration of Buddhist dialectics.)

Apparitions of Self: Buddhist Madhyamaka Rangtong and Shentong. Emptiness/*shunyata* is the primary "object" of the

Middle Way Madhyamaka View, both Prasangika and Yogachara Svatantrika, while Buddha nature (*tathagatagarbha*) is the knowing subject. This subject and its object are ultimately indivisible and nondual.

Gautama Shakyamuni Buddha told that this empty absence of essence (*svabhava*), this selflessness, or no-self (*anatman*) aspect of the emptiness of phenomenal reality obtains for persons (*Rangtong*, "empty of self" or "intrinsic emptiness"), but as well to all "other" spacetime phenomenal existence appearing to a self (*Shentong*, "empty of other" or "extrinsic emptiness").

The *Rangtong-Shentong* dialectical distinction, though it has its antecedents in Sutrayana, is a Tibetan Buddhist invention. Both Gelugpa Je Tsongkhapa, and Nyingmapa Ju Mipham criticize the extrinsic emptiness of the *Shentong* view for its inability to grasp the trans-conceptual nondual ultimate nature of the Buddha's *shunyata*/emptiness. Mipham's lucent *Beacon of Certainty* is such a critique. Nonetheless, in his *Lion's Roar Proclaiming Extrinsic Emptiness* Mipham defends the *Shentong* view.

Yet, Mipham is equally critical of the *Rangtong* intrinsic emptiness view of the Prasangika Madhyamika's absolute negation of the ultimate dimension of reality. If too much is negated how are form and emptiness to be Buddha's prior ontological unity? How are Buddha's Two Truths—"Form is empty; emptiness is form" to be unified, and realized? Nor is such an absolute negation of form compatible with the nondual *Dzogchen* View. Mipham was after all a *Dzogchen* master. So, we find Mipham correcting both the *Shentongpas* and the *Rangtongpas*—toward a higher synthesis.

Ju Mipham was acutely aware that the Buddha's teaching vehicles and their schools must be established through contemplative meditative equipoise by skilled yogis and yoginis, and by meditation masters—not by the conceptual dialectics of lesser minds. Thus is Mipham an advocate for post-dialectical, nondual primordial wisdom (*jnana, yeshe*)—to wit, our ultimate Buddha nature (*tathagatagarbha*). *Rangtong* and *Shentong*. Mipham understood that we need them both.

Well, was the great 19th century *rimé* master Ju Mipham (1846-1912) a Yogachara *Shentongpa*, a Prasangika *Rangtongpa,* or of a view that lies beyond, or prior to either one? Scholars disagree. What is clear is that Mipham was a lucent syncretic thinker who perfectly balanced the human cognitive dimensions that are relative conceptual, and contemplative nondual.

Nyingmapa Mipham's esteemed Nyingma predecessor Longchenpa states, 500 years earlier, that Prasangika is the highest view of the Middle Way Madhyamaka, which itself is the supreme view of the Four Buddhist Tenet Systems—the very foundation of the pinnacle of Buddha's teaching—nondual *Dzogchen* view and practice, though the Buddha could not have known the Tibetan term *Dzogchen*. As Mipham unified his mind with the "omniscient" mindstream of Longchenpa he was surely effected by this post-dialectical view.

John W. Pettit, in his *Mipham's Beacon of Certainty*—a work of the highest possible excellence—argues that Mipham, while appreciating the extrinsic emptiness of *Shentong*, was finally a Prasangika *Rangtongpa*. Mipham's great ecumenical *rimé* text, and his many Madhyamaka commentaries reveal his affinity for the Prasangika *Rangtong* view. Notwithstanding his exposition and tepid defense of *Shentong* in the *Lion's Roar,* which may well have been composed at the behest of his *Shentong* teacher Khyentse Bangpo, nowhere does Mipham argue for *Shentong* extrinsic emptiness. Acolytes of *Shentong* extrinsic emptiness generally argue their point most assertively. Mipham does not (Pettit 1999).

We shall see that Ju Mipham's sublime syncretic understanding has contributed to a propitious synthesis of the centuries old *Rangtong-Shentong* dialectic. Perhaps the great master realized that the highest view of any dualistic conceptual dialectical process rests ultimately, as Nagarjuna told, in no need for a view at all. The post-conceptual and nondual *direct* experience (*yogi pratyaksa*) of Buddha's Ultimate Truth rests beyond all names, concepts, beliefs, and formal cognitive processing. Therefore, let dialecticians of all stripes lay down their "negation of negations" long enough to rest in that post-dialectal, quiescent nondual ultimate non-synthesis.

Well, how shall we understand this heady dialectical cognitive process that is *Rangtong* and *Shentong?* According to the extrinsic emptiness of the *Shentong* view, all relative-conventional appearing reality, the spacetime dimension of Relative Truth (*samvriti satya*) are inherently absent and empty of *svabhava*—any intrinsic objective existence. Prasangika *Rangtongpas* agree.

However, argue *Shentongpas*, the dimension of all-embracing Ultimate Truth (*paramartha satya*) is not empty of its own primordial nature, its Buddha essence or *tathagatagarbha*. Indeed, this *mahashunyata* or *ultimate* great emptiness is brimming with the supreme qualities of not only its inherent Buddha nature, but primordial wisdom (*jnana, yeshe, sahajajnana, gnosis*), and as well the Trikaya of the Base (*gzhi rigpa*) that are the three buddha bodies of the boundless whole of reality itself. For *Shentongpas* these "perfect buddha qualities" are *ultimately* real and existent, even as the qualities of relative appearing phenomena are empty of any such existence.

The intrinsic emptiness of the *Rangtong* view of Middle Way Prasangika Madhyamaka, and the extrinsic emptiness of the *Shentong* view of Madhyamaka Yogachara Svatantrika are then different views on the Buddha's *shunyata*/emptiness. According to both *Rangtongpas* and *Shentongpas* relative conventional appearing phenomena are always deceptive. Things are not as they appear. Rather, they are deluded perceptual and conceptual elaborations of a self, empty of any iota of inherent essential nature or existence. So far, everyone agrees.

But for *Rangtongpas*, that's not empty enough. *Rangtongpas* further insist that the ultimate existence of Buddha nature (*tathagatagarbha*), Buddha bodies (*kayas*) of reality, and primordial wisdom (*jnana, yeshe, gnosis*) are as well, *ultimately* delusional conceptual Relative Truth entities.

On the accord of *Shentongpas*, this *Rangtong* view misses the point that the ultimate wisdom that is Buddha nature/Buddha mind (*buddhajnana*) cannot be deceived. Thus does *Shentong* hold that the Mahayana emptiness of the Second Turning of the Wheel of Dharma is a "provisional" teaching, while the Buddha nature/*tathagatagarbha* of the Vajrayana Third Turning is a "definitive" teaching of the Buddha.

So, Yogachara *Shentong* affirms the Prasangika *Rangtong* view as to the emptiness of relative-conventional appearing reality, but not of the ultimate emptiness of primordially enlightened Buddha mind.

In other words, *Shentong* extrinsic emptiness sees the precious qualities of enlightened Buddha nature, the full *bodhi* of primordial Buddha wisdom mind, and the *kayas* as empty of conceptual essence, but not empty of their own Buddha essence. In this way these trans-conceptual, nondual enlightened "qualities" ultimately exist—while the apparitional realities of our spacetime relative being here are ultimately non-existent.

The *Rangtong* Gelug tradition, following its founder Tsongkhapa, most Sakya Lamas, and some Kagyu and Nyingma scholars, including Ju Mipham in his lustrous *Beacon of Certainty*, criticized the Yogachara Madhyamaka *Shentong* view as a conceptual reification and imputation of the Buddha's dimension of Ultimate Truth, and a denial of even the relative-conventional reality of the stuff of the dimension of Relative Truth. Conversely, so it is argued by *Rangtongpas*, Prasangika Madhyamaka sees an identity and *ultimate* unity of the Buddha's Two Truths, with the nondual ultimate sphere subsuming and embracing the domain of the relative-conventional. But even this ultimate sphere is subject to the Prasangika *Rangtong* negation.

Remarkably, esteemed Nyingmapa Dudjom Rinpoche, in contradistinction to Gelug *Rangtong* Prasangika orthodoxy, has stated that the *Shentong* extrinsic emptiness view, in contradistinction to Longchenpa, is the highest view of the Mahayana vehicle. (*The Nyingma School of Tibetan Buddhism*, Vol. I, 1991, p. 205 ff)

Buddha taught that all appearing stuff, all phenomenal *dharmas*—trees, stars, living beings—are always already Buddha nature (*tathagatagarbha*). Emptiness/*shunyata*, and Buddha nature: are these two different; or somehow the same? 1) Are all appearing phenonenal dharmas, including emptiness itself, empty of intrinsic ultimate existence? 2) Are all phenomenal dharmas, including Buddha nature itself empty of intrinsic ultimate existence?

Clearly, it depends on the view (*darshana, lta ba*). Broadly construed, Je Tsongkhapa and his Gelugpas answer yes to both of these questions. Roughly, this is the *Rangtong* view. Longchenpa, Mipham and their Nyingmapas answer yes to the first of these questions; a qualified no to the second. Is this a *Shentong* view, or not?

For *Shentongpas* Buddha nature—that all things and beings are inherently Buddha nature—survives the radical *Rangtong* Prasangika emptiness phenomenological reduction/negation or transcendental *epoche*. That is to say, for Prasangika everything arising to or in human cognition is, in the ultimate analysis, absent and empty of "any shred" of independent intrinsic (*sahaja*) or ultimate existence—just as 2nd century Madhyamaka founder Nagarjuna told. Although, to be sure, all of it exists nominally, as relative-conventional stuff.

In the Tibetan Vajrayana fourth tenet system, philosophical view and contemplative and ethical practice—the View and the Conduct that are the platforms for realization or fruition of our innate intrinsic awareness Buddha nature/Buddha mind—are dependent upon the *conceptual* understanding of 1) the relative provisional meaning; and 2) the definitive ultimate meaning of the true nature of ultimate reality itself ("The Four Buddhist Tenet Systems" below).

In other words, the Vajrayana Path functions as the relative view of the ultimate nature—Ultimate Truth—of the object of emptiness, and of the subject, Buddha nature who realizes it.

So, both Tibetan Buddhist Gelugpa school founder Je Tsongkhapa, and Nyingma school luminary Ju Mipham were concerned to offer a logically consistent, integral and syncretic interpretive system that embraced both the exoteric objective metaphysical dialectics on primordial emptiness in Sutrayana tradition, and the esoteric subjective primordial wisdom (*jnana, yeshe, gnosis*) that is Buddha nature/Buddha mind of Tibetan Tantrayana/Vajrayana that is completed in the nondual teaching pinnacle *Dzogchen,* the Great Completion (Great Perfection). These two great masters reached different syncretic conclusions, reflected in their views on *Rangtong* (Tsongkhapa), and the union of *Rangtong* and *Shentong* (Mipham). More on this below.

Tibetan Buddhism has for centuries struggled with the admittedly abstruse conceptual problem of reconciling the view of utter "emptiness of essence" of a *relative* self—Buddha's "*Sabbe dharma anatta*", ("All phenomena are no-self")—with the view of an ostensibly eternally real *ultimately* existent Buddha nature or Buddha essence within the person, and indeed in all phenomena. Is "All phenomena are no-self" (*anatman*) a pithy platitude, or the Ultimate Truth of appearing reality itself?

In short, does Buddha nature *ultimately* exist at the heart of human and other beings, and as well of "other" phenomena, or is it a mere *relative* truth, established, imputed and reified by conceptual minds? "For no small matter is at stake. The question concerns the very way that human life is to be lived" (Plato, *The Republic*, Book I).

No Edges. The nondual truth of the matter, or of any apparent conceptual dilemma, abides somewhere in a prior ontic and present complementary phenomenal unity. Ontology, phenomenology, and conduct may always be unified. How do we accomplish this? As Guru Padmasambhava told, "Keep your view as high as the sky, and your deeds as fine as barley flour...Practice these two as a unity".

Buddhist dialectical hermeneutics may be seen as a relatively constrained, conventional means or method to discover and clarify such a unity; to unify that which has been torn asunder by the discursive semiotics of language—all the while remembering that all such relative objective conceptual truth is inherently provisional and fallible—referring always to the contemplatively established, perfectly subjective boundless whole in whom this all arises and participates.

For Buddhist Vajrayana, all form is a relative and ultimate instantiation of that shunyata/emptiness "groundless ground". As Buddha told so long ago in his Fourfold Profundity": "Form is empty; emptiness is form. Form is not other than emptiness; emptiness is not other than form" (from his *Heart of Wisdom Sutra*).

Please consider this. The buddhas, *mahasiddhas,* sages and saints of the great Primordial Wisdom Tradition of our species, throughout the three times—past, present and future—have told it well: there is a diaphanous, post-dialectical, trans-rational, inter-dimensional nondual unity that transcends yet embraces the dualistic conceptual dialectical limit of relative thinking mind.

As to the Buddhist tradition, for Buddhists of all stripes that nondual unity is known by the name of Ultimate Truth Buddha nature (*tathagatagarbha*), or Buddha wisdom mind (*buddhajnana*). It quite transcends our all too human conceptual mind. This then represents the subtlest or highest dialectical synthesis; "gone utterly beyond (*parasamgate*)" common conceptual dialectical cognition. And "wonder of wonders", that unifying all-embracing love-wisdom mind is always already present and awake at the very Heart (*hridyam*) of the human being. Bright Presence of That. Who Am I? That I Am! Without a single exception.

This deep, noetic (body, mind, spirit unity) cognitive coupling of our dualistic, objective conceptual mind with our nondual, perfectly subjective love-wisdom Buddha mind has great constitutive power that extends our human cognitive capacity and reach beyond the self imposed finite edges of mere thinking, to infinity, and back. Please don't *believe* this, but consider it a noetic possibility as we further engage the heady dualistic hermeneutical dialectics of Middle Way Buddhist philosophy.

Moreover, given our human propensity to perceive and construct physical and mental edges and geometrical and cognitive boundary limits, it is useful to be present to another consideration.

Buddhism is founded upon the Buddha's oft stated Two Truths premise that there is, to borrow a term from postmodern physical cosmology, no cognitive "domain boundary wall"—no edge separating what appears from what ultimately is; no boundary between conventional Relative Truth and all-inclusive Ultimate Truth. Try as we may, there exists, *ipso facto*, no inherent conceptual or physical boundary limit to all embracing *Kosmos*—the vast unbounded whole that is nondual infinite reality itself—the "many mansions" of our physical, mental, spiritual *Kosmic* home. Holistic cognition indeed.

Just so, for Prasangika Madhyamaka *Rangtongpas* (intrinsic emptiness) the Ultimate Truth nature of all arising phenomena, both "self and other", transcends and includes any and all objective, discursive, conceptual elaboration or complexity. But independent spacetime stuff does not *ultimately* exist! That's the bad news.

The good news? In the *Rangtong* Prasangika view, in the phenomenal dimension of Relative Truth interdependently arising phenomena do indeed possess a relatively, conditionally real existence. Our appearing realities—our conventional self in a relatively real "real world out there" (RWOT)—may be "absent and empty" of ultimate existence, but here we are! So we still have to show up for work, and be kind to "other" beings. So, stuff is real! The dialectical burden of rejoinder for any idealist ontology that presumes to deny this tangible fleshy existence of ours is heavy indeed.

Better news yet, if we choose to see it. Being here in space and time is the great gift (*jinlob*), absolute *bodhicitta, euengelion*) that bestows the cause and effect reality in which we have a bit of relative time, and free will, to *choose* to awaken to our "supreme identity" that is nothing less than liberation from the ignorance (*avidya, marigpa*) that causes our suffering. That blissful, luminous clear light mindstate is Happiness Itself.

In short, as we have so often seen in these pages, appearing spacetime stuff is relatively existent, just not ultimately existent.

Like the gossamer reflection of the moon in a pool of water, the "real" physical moon is absent, yet there exists something real here, namely, the moon's *reflection*. Thus does Middle Way Prasangika avoid the two metaphysical extremes of nihilistic nonexistence (Metaphysical Idealism), and of permanent ultimately real material existence (Metaphysical Materialism/Physicalism, eternalism).

We've seen that for Madhyamaka Yogachara *Shentongpas* (extrinsic emptiness; Metaphysical Idealism based in the "mind only" Chittamatra school of Asanga and Vasubandu) Buddha nature (*tathagatagarbha*) is the Ultimate Truth of all appearing reality, uncaused and unchanging ultimate nature of mind and all of its experience. Thus, the metaphysical extreme of nihilistic nonexistence is ostensibly avoided because Buddha nature truly exists ultimately and eternally. How does it exist? It exists as its own intrinsic essence, beyond our concepts *about* it.

Yogachara Middle Way Idealism has for centuries been vigorously criticized by the Middle Way Prasangikas as eternalist/substanialist. For Madhyamaka Prasangika *Rangtongpas* not even Buddha nature exists ultimately. It too is ultimately a relative truth, albeit a very substantial one.

As you can see, the dialectical party is getting rough. However, when the dualistic conceptual going gets tough, the wise rest in nondual Buddha wisdom mind.

For Yogachara extrinsic emptiness, *Shentong*, "emptiness of other" means that in the spacetime dimension of Relative Truth appearing stuff is interdependently arisen (*pratitya samutpada*). From the very beginning, spacetime reality does not *ultimately* exist—just like the Prasangika view. Thus is the metaphysical extreme of eternal, permanent, substantial, material existence avoided.

Therefore, for *Shentong*, (*shen* = other; *tong* = empty) "emptiness of self" means that relative conventional phenomena interdependently arising in mind is always only the selfless Ultimate Truth of eternal, definitively and ultimately existent Buddha nature (*tathagatagarbha*). Relatively viewed, all appearing *dharmas* are emptiness/*shunyata*—Buddha's Interdependent Arising (*pratitya samutpada*). Ultimately viewed, this all is not but concept-free primordial *dharmadhatu*—unborn, unceasing, uncreated luminous basic space (*cho ying*) of phenomenal reality—the indivisible unity of clarity and emptiness.

This then is in the Yogachara view of the "Threefold Nature": 1) the "perfectly existent nature", namely, ultimately existent Buddha nature which transcends and embraces 2) the relative, false "imputed/conceptual nature", and 3) the equally false "dependent nature" which arises in relative dependence upon merely external factors.

The Yogachara *Shentongpas* wish to deracinate and negate, on the ground of the perfectly existent Buddha nature of mind, the false "concealer truths" of the dimension of Relative Truth (*samvriti satya*)—relative conceptually elaborated "imputed nature", and the "dependent nature".

However, Buddha mind wisdom (*buddhajnana*) is the dimension of Ultimate Truth (*paramartha satya*), the "perfectly existent nature", wholly absent and free of such superimposed (*vikshepa*) semiotic constructs as existence and nonexistence, subject and object, true and false, and the rest; utterly untainted by our relative, pre-conceptual, deep cultural background "global web of belief" (Quine 1969). Ultimate Buddha nature/Buddha mind has been empty of such samsaric defects "from the very beginning". It has always been thus.

For Prasangika *Rangtongpas*, Buddha nature is said to be *ultimately* empty of all *conceptual* attributes, both "self" and "other". But this must include even the uncaused, unceasing spontaneously present "pure and perfect qualities"—the *Shentongpas buddic* qualities of the *kayas*, and of primordial wisdom (*jnana, yeshe, gnosis*).

And that is the rub for the Shentongpas who argue that Buddha nature is not empty of dharmakaya for in the ultimate view it is dharmakaya. Buddha nature is primordial purity (kadag) that is not empty of its own spontaneous presence (lhundrup). Buddha nature cannot be negated and reduced to ultimate nonexistence via Nagarjuna's radical

Prasangika shunyata/emptiness epoche. However, for both Shentong and Rangtong, Buddha nature is empty and absent the adventitious stains of relative samsaric existence.

In the *Dzogchen* view, the Buddha nature of mind is "no different at the pinnacle of enlightenment than it is at the primordial base" (*Dzogchen* Master Adzom Rinpoche). Buddha nature/ Buddha mind—beyond our concepts about it—embraces, pervades, and is not other than the primordial ground or base (*gzhi*), and the freeing, feeling knowing awareness of That (*gzhi rigpa*); the Path (*lam*) which reveals That; and the enlightened Result or Fruition which is That. That is the subtlest or "highest" nondual teaching: *Dzogchen;* Essence *Mahamudra; Madhyamaka* of the Definitive Meaning; *Saijojo* Zen (*mujodo no taigen*), which are the same, on the accord of H.H. Dalai Lama, with respect to this Result—Buddhahood.

The seventy-five dharmas of the *Pali Canon* that become the Mahayana eighteen *dhatus*, twelve *ayatanas*, and five *skandhas* of arising and appearing spacetime existence—animate and inanimate, self and other—are the vast, infinite expanse of this ultimate primordial Buddha nature of mind—numinous Presence of That that we are now.

We have seen that in the Buddhist teaching vehicles and their various schools Buddha nature is generally seen as a nonconceptual, innate, unborn, unceasing, uncaused, and timeless-changeless continuity of primordial awareness wisdom arising throughout the whole of our human awareness-consciousness processional: 1) naked, bare attention/perception; 2) objective concept and belief; 3) subjective trans-conceptual contemplative; and 4) perfectly subjective nondual. This bright spontaneous always present Buddha Presence (*vidya, rigpa*) of that primordial groundless ground (*jnana, yeshe*) is the "supreme identity" of human being here in time and form. And we are That. *Emaho!*

Rangtong Emptiness and Shentong Buddha Nature. Thus arose in the lustrous history of the Buddha's Mahayana vehicle, the fourth and "highest" tenet system ("The Four Buddhist Tenet Systems" below), the Middle Way Tibetan Vajrayana Madhyamaka with its two distinct views—Prasangika Madhyamaka (*Rangtong intrinsic emptiness*) and Yogachara Madhyamaka (*Shentong extrinsic emptiness*)—on the true and *ultimate* nature of reality itself : 1) *shunyata*/emptiness; and 2) Buddha nature/Buddha essence. Each of these is as well concerned to establish the unity of the Buddha's Two Truths, Relative and Ultimate. The often contentious, 1500 year old dialectic between these two Madhyamaka schools continues still. Is there a reasonable synthesis?

So let us now, while dodging the really scholarly stuff, probe just a little more deeply into the pragmatic profundity of this centrist Middle Way teaching of the Buddha. How do *Rangtong* and *Shentong* differ, and how is it that they are unified?

We've seen that *Rangtong* is the Tibetan Buddhist mainstream view of the Middle Way Madhyamaka Prasangika philosophy of H.H. Dalai Lama's Gelug school. Gelug founder Je Tsongkhapa (1357-1419) criticized *Shentong* from his Nagarjunian view of *mahashunyata* that claims all phenomena—*including Buddha nature itself*—are *ultimately* empty of self-existence, both in the dualistic domain of veiled conceptual Relative Truth, and in the nondual open clear light of Ultimate Truth. And even emptiness itself is empty of intrinsic ultimate existence. It too is a conceptually imputed relative truth and is established by a conventional conceptual mind. This cardinal view is known since Chandrakirti as "the emptiness of emptiness" (*shunyata shunyata*).

So, for *Rangtongpas* both emptiness and Buddha nature are reduced to the "concealer truth" reality dimension of Relative Truth (*samvriti satya*). Buddha nature too, with its wondrous "pure and perfect qualities", and its primordial wisdom is merely relative and conventional. It does not exist *ultimately*. *Shentongpas* vigorously disagree.

Rangtong, "intrinsic emptiness", over against *Shengtong* "extrinsic emptiness", is the orthodox view of the "new translation"

Tibetan Buddhist Gelug and Kagyu schools—but not always of the "Ancient Ones", the Nyingma school—and of much of the 19th century Buddhist ecumenical *Rimé* movement, with the (probable) notable exception of Nyingmapa Ju Mipham Rinpoche, as we shall see.

Yogachara. In contradistinction to the relative Realism (the reality of the phenomena of Relative Truth) of the *Rangtong* of Nagarjuna (2nd century), and Chandrakirti (8th century), the *Shentong* Yogachara chittamatra/mind only of Asanga and Vasabandu (4th century), and Bhavavivika (6th century) is an ontic Metaphysical Absolute Idealism, further established at the great Nalanda University in the 6th century by Dharmapala with his doctrine of "nothing but concepts". Gunamati and Sthiramati later established a modified Idealism in an attempt to synthesize Yogachara with what was to become the Prasangika view of Nagarjuna. The Prasangikas were unimpressed. From that syncretic effort evolved the logic of Dignaga and his heart son Dharmakirti.

The "yoga" of Yogachara derives from its emphasis on non-conceptual contemplative meditation practice. Etymologically, the Sanskrit word "yoga" means "yoking" or union of the relative dimension with the ultimate dimension—the realization of the prior and always present ontic and phenomenal unity of the Buddha's Two Truths. Yogic practice is, for Yogachara, the only path to realization of the three buddha bodies (*trikaya*), and the "pure and perfect" qualities of our inherent, ultimately existing Buddha nature (*tathagatagarbha*), or Buddha mind (*buddhajnana*). The conceptual reason and analysis (*kalpana, anumana-pramana*) of the Prasangikas, it is argued, is not adequate to this yogic realization (*yogi pratyaksa*) task.

Yes, on the mentalist idealist view of Yogachara, all experience of dependently arising reality is "mind only", or *chittamatra*. The stuff of appearing form has neither relative nor ultimate reality. There are no real objects or things, only the experiential *process* of false, conceptually imagined, dependent phenomena. Our seemingly solid universe of appearances is *chittamatra*, nothing but mind. Absolute Metaphysical Idealism indeed.

We have seen that from this idealist doctrine naturally arises the seminal "threefold nature" of the Yogachara view. All relative, appearing phenomena are: 1) conceptually imagined and imputed (*parikalpita*); 2) dependent (*paratantra*); and 3) ultimately perfect (*parinishpanna*). All human cognition, all that can be apprehended and known by the mind—self, perception, conception, yogic-contemplative experience, Buddha nature—all phenomena are *chittamatra* or mind only. And yet, "perfect" Buddha nature exists ultimately. How shall we understand this?

Phenomena are mere imagined false cognition. And this concept-mind that indulges it is dependent upon a vast matrix of interdependent causes and conditions beyond itself; in a word, Buddha's Dependent Arising (*pratitya samutpada*). Further, all of this arising spacetime experience is, in its ultimate nature, "perfect just as it is" (Gautama the Buddha).

What is this ultimate perfect nature? It is nothing less than boundless emptiness/*shunyata*—trans-conceptual, selfless, uncaused, immutable, formless, nondual, *tathata*—"suchness" or "thatness". *Tathata* is a *tathagata* (perfect buddha) manifesting in relative spacetime *nirmanakaya* form. In its ultimate meaning *tathagata* is *tathagatagarbha* our indwelling, inherent Buddha nature—*shunyata, dharmata, dharmakaya*, primordial wisdom (*jnana/yeshe*). "All That I Am!" As Buddha told, "Wonder of wonders, all beings are Buddha".

Thus it is, for Yogachara, all arising relative form is not but ultimate perfectly subjective emptiness. As Buddha told so long ago, "Form is empty; emptiness is form".

The ultimate Buddha nature of Yogachara, sometimes known as a "Buddha Self", is construed by their Prasangika interlocutors as a metaphysical commitment to an ultimately existing Atman Self. Such a view ostensibly breeches the Madhyamaka sacrosanct *anatman* no-self doctrine—"emptiness of self"—which *ipso facto* precludes an intrinsically existing ultimate, Atman Buddha

Self. This apostate lapse into an eternalistic substantialist meta-physic was anathema to the *anatman* doctrine of Middle Way Madhyamaka—whether Yogachara or Prasangika.

So, does Buddha nature ultimately exist, or not? Are we even asking the right question?

The *Shentong* view was probably first articulated by Sakya school Lama Dolpopa Sherab Gyaltsen (1292-1361). Dolpopa Rinpoche later joined the Jonang School. He may have been the first lama to distinguish between scriptural "provisional truths" which require interpretation, and "definitive truths", which stand alone as expressed in scripture.

In any case, the *Shentong* view, that Buddha nature (*tatha-gatagarha*) is much more than a Relative Truth phenomenon—and indeed *is* the all inclusive Ultimate Truth—was argued by Yogachara Madhyamaka school Indian Nalanda University Abbot Shantarakshita (725-788) in his lapidary *Madhyamakalamkara* text. However, he accomplished in this text a remarkable synthesis of the *Rangtong* and *Shentong* views, as we shall soon see.

So, the view of Yogachara Svatantrika Madhyamaka is a *Shentong* view. Broadly construed, it is as we have seen, the view that, while in agreement with *Rangtong* that *relative* reality is utterly empty of any self-nature (*svabhava*), still, *ultimate* real-ity or Ultimate Truth is intrinsic Buddha gnosis, *buddhajnana* itself—all embracing Buddha nature, primordial wisdom mind (*jnana, yeshe, gnosis*)—and so empty of all phenomena appearing "other" than self; that is to say, empty of relative, convention-ally appearing phenomenal reality. So, in contradistinction to the Prasangika *Rangtongpas*, *Shentong* Buddha nature is not empty of its own intrinsic ultimate existence, but is itself that ultimate existence.

In other words, for the *Rangtong* view the great whole of continuously appearing phenomenal reality, *both* self and other, is *shunyata*, absent and empty of self-nature in *both* the view of Relative Truth, and of Ultimate Truth. However, for *Shentong* the Ultimate Truth of our primordial clear light Buddha nature is not empty of the three buddha bodies of reality—the *Trikaya* of the Base—and of primordial wisdom as these *are* ultimate intrinsic existence itself.

Once again, Ultimate Truth, nondual Buddha nature/ Buddha mind is seen in this Yogachara Madhyamaka *Shentong* view of emptiness as the luminous basic space of *dharmadhatu,* truly intrinsically, ultimately existent—in contradistinction to the Madhyamaka Prasangika *Rangtong* view of Nagarjuna and Chandrakirti, which sees even Buddha nature as a mere relative truth, established by a conceptual mind. All such relative truths are, in the Prasangika view, utterly absent and empty of "any shred" of intrinsic ultimate existence, even though they really do exist nominally, relatively in the dimension of spacetime Relative Truth (*samvriti satya*).

For *Shentong* then, broadly construed, the absolute dimension that is Ultimate Truth (*paramartha satya*) is nondual Buddha nature, numinous primordial emptiness ground and very nature of mind in which, or in whom all these arising relative-conventional "concealer truths" of the spacetime dimension of Relative Truth arise, participate, and are instantiated. Buddha nature that *is* Ultimate Truth, for *Shentongpas,* is not negated or reduced to a relative truth via the Prasangika emptiness *shunyata reduction/ epoche.* For *Shentong,* Ultimate Truth Buddha nature survives the *Rangtong* emptiness phenomenological reduction as a truly existent ultimate reality, as we have seen above. And of course, that is the rub for Madhamaka Prasangika *Rangtongpas.*

Please recall that, because for all Madhyamikas the world of relative truth, and the self that animates it, is not *ultimately* real, it is abundantly clear that it still has profound *relative* value. Who is it after all that acts out all of these ultimately empty and nonexistent nouns? Who is it that devotes one's life to the benefit of ultimately nonexistent beings?

So, centrist Madhyamaka does not, must not engage in off-putting nihilistic denial or denigration of our problematic relative self-ego-I; although too much recent Tibetan Buddhist Vajrayana popular interpretation makes it seem so. Well, what *did* Buddha say about the self?

We've seen in Chapter II that Gautama Shakyamuni the Buddha declined to discuss the metaphysics of the self, nor of the *Kosmos.* "I teach only suffering and its cessation." *Pali Canon* scripture has him teaching that there is no self; and also that we must work to lift and illumine a relatively real self. It is self after all that more or less freely chooses what conduct to adopt, and to avoid. It is relative self-ego-I that realizes ultimate no-self or *anatman.* I have said above that self and no-self is a false dichotomy. *Atman* and *anatman* are a non-conceptual complementary unity. So, is there a Buddhist self or not? It still depends on the view—relative of ultimate.

Our understandably irritating cognitive dissonance is here assuaged by the Madhyamikas thusly: Middle Way Madhyamaka Prasangika is a centrist view of Buddha's nondual no-self *anatman* teaching, to wit: ultimately empty and nonexistent selfless *anatman*—always pervaded by already present Presence of nondual Buddha mind (*buddhajnana*)—acts as a self in this relatively real world of spacetime existence to lessen the suffering of living beings. Both *Rangtongpas* and *Shentongpas* should be happy here.

Nyingmapa Ju Mipham, always sympathetic to *Shentong* without fully endorsing the *Shentong* Yogachara view of Shantirakshita, and following Nyingma Longchenpa's lead, suggests a centrist view that nearly completes the propitious unification of the hitherto fractious *Rangtong-Shentong* dialectic. Just so, in both the state of non-conceptual meditation, and in the midst of dialectical debate, Prasangika assumes and asserts no *ultimate* philosophical view whatsoever. But in the post-meditation state of relative, conventionally real commonplace reality both existence and non-existence obtain. How else could we "hue wood and carry water", keep our jobs, and remain free of incarceration in an asylum?

Mipham definitively expresses his answer to the thorny, perennial question as to "whether Madhyamikas have a position or not". From his *Beacon of Certainty* (Topic I; author's translation):

What is the Nyingma view?
In the state of the great primordial wisdom of unity...
Both existence and nonexistence are conceptual imputations.
In the ultimate view, neither can be accepted.
Thus is the aboriginal dharmata beyond all concept and belief;
Beyond both negation and assertion;
Utterly free of all views.

"Utterly free of all views". Precisely Nagarjuna's proto-Prasangika/*Rangtong* teaching! Thus does nondual Ultimate Truth that is primordial empty/*shunya* reality itself (*dharmakaya*) transcend yet embrace the *false dichotomy* of 1) relatively existent form (and a self to experience it), and 2) ultimate emptiness ground (*gzhi rigpa*) of form—innate Buddha gnosis (*sahajajnana*), Buddha mind (*buddhajnana*). After all, these dimensional worlds are established by the relative, conventional concept mind of an observer self in conceptually relative time and space. Do we have here an incipient rapprochement of Prasangika *Rangtong*, and Yogachara *Shentong*? Let's see. (John Pettit 1999, is highly recommended reading on Mipham's proto-*Shentong Dzogchen* view.)

We must remember that, whereas Prasangika *Rangtong* sees ultimate emptiness as a negation of a *conceptual* absolute, namely, Buddha nature, for Mipham the correct view is "beyond all concept and belief", abiding in *buddic* nonlocal, nondual primordial awareness wisdom (*jnana, yeshe, gnosis*) itself. It is that innermost wisdom *Perfect Sphere of Dzogchen* Presence that is trans-conceptually realized by our Buddha nature/Buddha mind, which in its relation to emptiness/*shunyata is* Buddha mind, the utter absence of conceptual elaboration and fabrication of entities—relative or ultimate. "Aboriginal *dharmata* is beyond all concept and belief" (Mipham).

Thus does Ju Mipham, in his prodigious *Beacon of Certainty*, address the contentious notion of Buddha essence (*tathagatagarbha, sugatagarbha*) that is the root of the *Rangtong-Shentong* deliberation. He sees Buddha nature as beyond the metaphysical extreme of monistic materialist eternalism. It is not a substantialist "Buddha Self", as some of Yogachara's more anxious Prasangika critics allege. Indeed, our primordial, always already present Presence of *buddhajnana* is utterly "empty of conceptual attributes". The wise "Leave it alone, and let it be as it is" (Buddha).

In accordance with the nondual *Dzogchen* view of the indwelling intrinsically perfect spontaneous presence (*lhundrub*) of *buddic* awareness, ultimate Buddha nature is always already perfectly complete and present without the conceptual baggage of *Shentongpa* assertions about enlightened awareness "pure and perfect qualities". Perhaps our inherent *bodhi* mind/Buddha nature is in no way dependent upon our concepts and beliefs *about* it. Perhaps it just *is*. Perhaps one should, to use the Buddha's pith: "Rest your weary mind and let it be as it is; all things are perfect exactly as they are".

We've seen that Gelug intrinsic emptiness *Rangtongpas* consider Buddha wisdom mind (*jnana, yeshe*) not a definitive ultimate teaching, but a provisional teaching. *Ultimate* Buddha nature is surrendered, along with everything else, including emptiness itself, to the *shunyata eidetic* reduction. Conversely, Mipham, with the extrinsic emptiness of the *Shentongpas* do see Buddha gnosis as a definitive ultimate teaching. Drop the dialectical concepts, and where is the problem? Buddha is already present in everything!

Gelug founder Je Tsongkhapa, and Nyingma master Ju Mipham are in agreement on most of the key Madhyamaka points. In short, Ju Mipham's enhancement of Shantirakshita's *Rangtong-Shentong* synthesis (below)—that "dharmata is beyond all concept and belief"—if not definitive, represents perhaps the best posit on offer.

As to our enduring question: do we have, does reality have, an ultimate Buddha nature, or not? Conceptually considered, it depends on the View—conceptual relative, or nondual ultimate. Or does it? As this false conceptual dichotomy is, as great Zen

Master Dōgen told, "dropped" into the dialectical dust bin of history, the pernicious cognitive duality that relentlessly splits these Two Truths outshines as their prior, nondual ontic unity. What most certainly remains in this rarified state is clear light luminosity of all-pervading primordial whole, by whatever name, quite beyond the semiotic "web of belief" (Quine 1969) of discursive human cognition. "A rose by any other name would smell as sweet" (Juliet Capulet). Feeling-knowing love-wisdom mind unity of the Buddha's Two Truths? Direct numinous heartmind experience of That? Human happiness itself.

Be That as it may, the earnest Yogachara *Shentong* view has, with the rising hegemony of orthodox Gelug Prasangika, fallen on hard times. We've seen that the main Tibetan Buddhist schools, especially Gelug, criticize *Shentong* as violating the sacrosanct view of the Mahayana that the venerated doctrine of *shunyata*-emptiness must not conceptually posit or permit *any* ultimately existing entity, or mind state, not even ultimate Buddha nature (*tathagatagarbha*), or Buddha mind (*buddhajnana*). We've also seen that this sticky dichotomy vanishes upon resting the busy mind in the nondual primordial Buddha nature of mind. It's like coming home.

Shentong Yogachara Madhyamaka has been branded by many *Rangtongpas* as "eternalistic *Madhyamaka*"—that *Shentong* violates the Middle Way principle of avoiding the metaphysical extreme of eternalism by positing the ultimate reality of eternal Buddha nature. Recall, that centrist Madhyamaka Middle Way, whether Yogachara or Prasangika, presumes to avoid the metaphysical extremes of the nihilism of nonexistence, and of the eternalism, substantialism, and materialism of observer-independent existence; so this charge constitutes a serious criticism in the relative domain of Buddhist dialectics. I have here and elsewhere argued that Ju Mipham's iconoclastic, antinomian trans-conceptual view substantially reduces, if not altogether negates this charge of substantialism (cf. Mipham quote above).

Nyingma *Dzogchen* master Ju Mipham Rinpoche (1846-1912), his master Patrul Rinpoche, and most of the 19th century ecumenical

Rimé movement, with the notable exception of *Shentongpa* Jamgon Kongtrul, have more or less arrived at a syncretic *Shentong-Rangtong* understanding after 10 centuries of Buddhist dialectics. This ecumenical epistemic turn is grounded in *Shentongpa* Shantirakshita's paradigm shifting synthesis, as we shall see. Yet, the Gelugpa *Rangtong* view remains in the majority among academic Buddhologists.

Neither the great omniscient 14th century Nyingma school Longchenpa, nor 19th century Nyingmapa Ju Mipham use the *Shentong* epithet to describe their Middle Way Madhyamaka views. Are they then *Rangtongpas*? No. Neither of these masters has become mired in the false dichotomy of *either Rangtong, or Shentong*.

Nyingma *Dzogchen*, The Great Perfection, its view and praxis, is grounded in Buddha nature, the nature of nondual primordial wisdom (*jnana, yeshe, gnosis*). We saw above with Mipham's *Dzogchen* view, that such post-rational, non-conceptual, nondual Buddha gnosis *ipso facto* transcends yet embraces all conceptual dichotomies—knowing subject and object known; affirmation and negation; existence and nonexistence; correct and incorrect view; *Rangtong* and *Shentong* view. *Parasamgate*: "gone utterly beyond" dialectical thinking mind. And none too soon!

Thus, for Gelug Prasangika, are such noble ideas in the mind, along with our less noble notions, all subject to negation via the *shunyata transcendental epoche*? Are our appearing realities, objective and subjective, ultimately non-existent? That is the question. If this ultimate empty Buddha nature of mind transcends even the intellectual virtuosity of our greatest conceptual minds, with all their wondrous ideas, then the noble relative conceptual *idea* of Buddha nature must be committed, as Victorian polymath and skeptic David Hume might have said, to the all consuming purifying flames of ultimate nonexistence (*Vidya Maya*).

In other words, it seems that for Prasangika our noble notions of Buddha nature/Buddha mind must be committed to a non-realm of ultimate nonexistence. Does such a conceptual deconstruction of a noble idea in conventional mind—Suzuki

Roshi's relative conceptual Small Mind—negate that ultimate Big Mind Buddha mind in which, or in whom this all arises? Is such a radical phenomenological reduction nihilistic? We have briefly surveyed the two prevailing views: the intrinsic emptiness of Prasangika *Rangtong*, and the extrinsic emptiness of Yogachara *Shentong*. Let us then continue our holistic approach, that we may discover a unifying cognitive transept.

Mereology is the study of the logical relation of parts—microscopic to macroscopic—to their greater more inclusive wholes—and ultimately, to the vast boundless whole (*dharmad-hatu*, Bön, *mahabindu*) in whom all physical and mental *Kosmos* arises. Does not this *relative* multiplicity of arising and appearing spacetime parts bespeak a more subtle nondual ontologically prior, yet phenomenally present all embracing *ultimate* whole, by whatever relative name or concept?

All of our noble Buddhist interlocutors—*Rangtongpas* and *Shentongpas* alike—agree that the *shunyata* phenomenological reduction denies "any shred" of ultimate existence to our *relative* concepts and beliefs *about* appearing reality, and as well, to our concepts and beliefs *about* the ultimate ground of that reality, by whatever name—*shunyata*, Buddha nature, *kadag*, Tao, Atman/ Nirguna Brahman, and the rest.

Is the subtle ontological referent of that trans-conceptual, nonlocal, nondual ultimate reality ground itself thereby reduced to ontic oblivion? Buddhist dialectics asks, is there an ultimate reality ground, or even a non-conceptual Madhyamaka "ground-less ground" ontologically prior to our concepts and beliefs *about* it? That is our present metaphysical grail quest.

Cognitive caveat: From the metaphysical ontology you choose, arises the phenomenal reality you deserve.

What did Gautama the Buddha teach us in this regard? The bad news, Buddha declined to participate in philosophi-cal dialectics as to the ultimate nature of self, and of the vast *Kosmos*. The good news: "It is only suffering and its cessation that I teach...because this is the cause of awakening" (p. 3 above).

Buddha declined to engage conceptual metaphysical conjecture. Worth remembering as we engage the heady wine of conceptual Buddhist dialectics.

The beloved Nyingmapas Longchenpa and Mipham, with the *Shentongpas,* have replied to our question as to *Rangtong* ultimate *nonexistence* of even primordial Buddha nature, in the negative. Buddha nature and its pure and perfect qualities—wisdom and the *kayas* or buddha bodies of reality (*dharmakaya, sambhogakaya, nirmanakaya*), and the ten powers—ultimately exist! Does this make these two great masters *Shentongpas?* I have argued herein that the simplistic dichotomy of *either Shentong or Rangtong* is a false dichotomy. With the Buddha, the wise will avoid dualistic metaphysical speculation. If we are to persist, we must continue our grail quest for a syncretic middle way view between these two Middle Way views. And persist we will.

Before we turn to Shantirakshita's great *Rangtong-Shentong* synthesis, which Mipham used in his own synthesis, let us quickly conclude our "no edges" dialectical consideration.

It is the nature of dialectical discourse to seek, after thesis and its antithesis are established, a more complete or higher synthesis which evolves from the first two phases of the process. The history of Buddhist dialectics out-pictures this Hegelian interpretive hermeneutical process.

Each of the Three (or four) Turnings of the Wheel of the Buddha's dharma, and each of the noble Four Buddhist Tenet systems, transcends yet embraces, includes and completes the previous system. The ultimate result of this dialectic is said by the Gelugpas to be the *Rangtong* Prasangika Madhyamaka view of Nagarjuna, Chandrakirti, and Tsongkhapa. On the accord of H.H. Dalai Lama, this view constitutes the epistemic foundation of the post-dialectical view of nondual *Dzogchen,* the Great Completion, with its supreme ninth vehicle *Ati Yoga* practice (*Ch. VIII*).

In this way have 20 centuries of Buddhist dialectics culminated in an imperfect synthesis of *Rangtong* and *Shentong,* as we shall hopefully see in our very brief survey of Shantirakshita's *Shentong* syncretic view—the holistic precursor to Mipham's ecumenical *rimé* view.

East or West, in philosophy, in science, mathematics and logic, and in philosophy of science this process of seeking that next more inclusive syncretic theory is never ending. Ultimately there are no edges, only nondual infinity. The dominion of Relative Truth—science, metaphysics, philosophical dialectics—remains, for as long as space and time endure—provisional, fallible, and objectively uncertain. For definitive certainty we shall have to go wholly beyond our dualistic "Small Mind" relative, conventional "global web of belief" (Quine 1969), and enter in contemplative nondual ultimate primordial wisdom gnosis (*jnana, yeshe*).

Therefore, relative-conventional knowledge discourse is inherently dialectical. Present synthesis is incomplete and leads to an antithesis, which yields a new more inclusive synthesis—until that is, interlocutors remember to relax the busy uncertainty of provisional dualistic mind into its "supreme source"—the *no edge*, no boundary condition definitive certainty of always already present nondual Buddha mind, beyond any concept of it. Ah, the cognitive consummation devoutly to be wished.

Once again, as Buddha told, "Let it be as it is and rest your weary mind; all things are perfect exactly as they are." We must perforce move beyond mere dualistic conceptual dialectics toward nondual contemplative unity. I have elsewhere termed this integral wisdom imperative the Noetic Imperative (Boaz 2021b).

Shantirakshita's Great Rangtong-Shentong Synthesis. In the 8th century *Shentongpa* Shantirakshita (725-788) in his profoundly syncretic *Madhyamakalamkara* treatise on the Buddhist Two Truths doctrine famously synthesized the Middle Way relatively realist Prasangika Madhyamaka *Rangtong* ontology of Nagarjuna with the Metaphysical Idealism of the Svatantrika Madhyamaka *Shentong*—the *chittamatra* ("mind only") phenomenology of the Yogachara school of Asanga and his half brother Vasabandu.

Shantirakshita's centrist version of *Shentong* prevailed until it was largely replaced by Tsongkhapa's return to classical Prasangika Madhyamaka *Rangtong* in the 15th century. Ju Mipham utilized Shantirakshita's argument in what many Nyingmapas consider a decisive critique of Tsongkhapa's Prasangika view (Pettit 1999).

Vajrayana Madhyamaka Prasangika and Yogachara Svatantrika Madhyamaka Middle Way doctrines comprise the two main philosophical schools of the Buddhist Mahayana teaching vehicle. Longchenpa: "The Madhyamaka is the most sublimely profound secret found in the teaching of the Sage". We have seen that this great *Dzogchen* master, systematizer of Garab Dorje's *Dzogchen* teaching, was sympathetic to the *Shentong* view, although he did not use the term *Shentong*.

Tibetan doxographers now use the unwieldy epithet Yogachara-Svatantrika-Madhyamaka to refer to Shantirakshita's great synthesis (Four Buddhist Tenet Systems below). His *Madhymakalamkara* has had a unifying effect, however imperfectly, on the continuing drama of the 12th through 19th century Two Truths doctrinal dispute between *Rangtong* relative "intrinsic emptiness", and *Shentong* ultimate Buddha nature.

Building upon Shantirakshita's seminal text (composed with his heart son Kamalashila) H.H. Dalai Lama has offered what some have seen as an imperative rendering of this unifying view: Prasangika Madhyamaka Rangtong emptiness is the correct view of Ultimate Truth, while Yogachara Madhyamaka Shentong Buddha nature is the correct view of Relative Truth. Thus does Vasubandu's Shentong Yogachara phenomenology give us the best account of an objective, relative, conventionally appearing spacetime reality; and Tsongkhapa's Rangtong Prasangika ontology the best account of nondual ultimate reality. After all, Yogachara is a metaphysical presupposition about the existential status of relative phenomenal appearance; while Prasangika is a metaphysical presupposition about the ultimate nature of that appearing reality.

Both Prasangika Madhyamaka *Rangtong* and Yogachara Svatantrika Madhyamaka *Shentong* aim to establish the Buddha's *anatman* or selflessness; and both wish to demonstrate the nondual Buddha nature of mind—that self-ego-I (*atman*) and its objective "real world out there" (RWOT) is but a nominal, *relative* conceptual imputation and reification, with no *ultimate* intrinsic observer-independent existence at all. But again, these two Middle Way sub-schools differ on the existential status of Buddha nature with its "pure and perfect qualities" of nondual wisdom (*jnana, yeshe*), and the *kayas*. For Yogachara, Buddha essence (*buddhajnana*) or Buddha nature (*sugatagarbha, tatha-gatagarbha*) remain, not relative and conventional, but eternal and ultimate.

So, Yogachara's phenomenology of mind gives us pause as to our reifying fabrications (*prapanca*) of dualistic, relative, objective concept mind; that the view that inherently real objects exist and present to a subject just as they appear, is false. Yogachara is thus a step toward Prasangika's ultimate view of the "emptiness of emptiness"—perfectly subjective nondual reality is itself empty of intrinsic existence, just as Nagarjuna told in his great definitive 2nd century Fundamental Wisdom of the Middle Way (*Mulamadhyamakakarika*).

Indeed, Prasangika *Rangtongpas* have sometimes derisively told that Yogachara *Shentong* is for those without the capacity to understand the ultimate emptiness of emptiness. Shantirakshita, and later, Mipham have insisted upon a creative synthesis of the Ultimate Truth that abides in and pervades both views.

However, this ontic step function from relative phenomenology to an ultimate ontology in no way detracts from the Yogachara *Shentong* ultimate analysis. Rather, it explicates and completes it. This is so because to assert that relatively arising appearances are wholly absent and empty of any whit of intrinsic *ultimate* nature is, *ipso facto* to affirm their *relative*, conventional existence! After all, the relative existence of something is required to deny its ultimate existence. Relative conceptually imputed and reified reality, and its ultimate emptiness are thus complementary and interdependent—like existence and nonexistence; life and death, knowing subject and separate object; truth and falsity; ignorance and wisdom; quantum wave and particle; emptiness and Buddha nature—you can't have one without the other.

Deep relative ontic and epistemic/phenomenal reflection (*pramana, tshad ma*) while resting simultaneously in the Buddha mind Presence (*vidya, rigpa*) of ultimate non-conceptual, nondual luminous clarity—clear light wisdom mind nature (*jnana, yeshe, gnosis*)—reveals that there is, ultimately, no such relative, nor even ultimate nature at all. One comes to realize that phenomenal objects appearing to a perceiving subject are absent and empty of any iota of objective substantive conceptual existence, nor of conceptual subjective nonexistence. Yet relatively, here we are!

Thus is the inherent limit of language, of semiotic logical syntax reflexively ascertained. We utilize *Rangtong* logic to reflexively deracinate and critique itself; to point out its natural implicit limit in any merely explicit conceptual description of ultimate reality. Does this conceptual limit not include all dualistic, inherently *Kosmically* ironic dialectical cognition—Buddhist, or otherwise?

What remains after such a radical phenomenological reduction/*epoche*? *Shentong* Buddha nature remains! *The concept of Buddha nature is just a concept, albeit a substantial one. Yet Buddha nature* itself *abides at the heart of all living beings, and indeed at the Kosmic heart of all appearing reality—animate or inanimate.* It is the luminous, bright indwelling *buddic* Presence of That that we feel at the spiritual heartmind (*hridyam*). We are by now clear that this Presence is beyond the reach of any concept or belief *about* it. That is the teaching of the Sage of the Shakya Clan.

That primordial Buddha nature/essence is *ultimately* already present in form, beyond belief, seems to be the *conceptual* open question of Buddhist dialectics. However, as to trans-conceptual direct yogic experience (*yogi pratyaksa*) there is no question whatever as to its true, post-dialectical reality. Too many Buddhist scholars notwithstanding, no no-self respecting Buddhist yogi or yogini would negate the contemplative meditative certainty of Buddha mind (*buddhajnana*) Presence, conceptually classify it what you will.

We must remember this great pragmatic experiential truth in our heady exploration of Buddhist Two Truth dialectics, which indeed often strays far afield from our always already present Presence of the Buddha mind essence that we are now—however we may choose to name and conceive of it.

Thus is the atavistic myth that is subject-object duality—in all of its myriad conceptual cloaks, and with all of its attendant suffering—brought to cessation. Deeply understanding this intimate relationship with our own human subjectivity—conceptual or gnosimic—is forever changed. And that, after all, is the aim of all Buddhist wisdom. (For excellent historical context on this post-dialectical nondual view see Garfield 2015, Ch. 6.)

What remains in the apparitional wake of this nondual alchemy of Buddha wisdom mind? Just enough: Cognizant Presence; Love; Poetry and Song; and *Samadhi.*

Thus it is, Shantirakshita's beautiful syncretic view, and Ju Mipham's enhancement of it, unifies hitherto incommensurate, but now complementary Yogachara relative phenomenology of mind with Prasangika ultimate ontology of the very nature of mind (buddhajnana)—these two abiding always in the nondual buddic embrace of primordial sameness (samatajnana).

Khenpo Tsultrim Gyamtso (2001) suggests that Prasangika *Rangtong* is the "highest view in terms of analysis", and Yogachara *Shentong* is "the most profound view in terms of explaining meditation". The former is grounded in exoteric logical reasoning, the latter is grounded in esoteric contemplative practice. Do we not require both?

Rangtong intrinsic emptiness or "emptiness of self" conceptually deracinates all possible reference points for any intrinsic existence of appearing phenomena to which we, as ego-selves, may cling. It utterly consumes our "common sense" desire-mind belief in an essential self-ego-I abiding in a material "real world out there" (RWOT). This serves our human rational, objective intelligence. Yet Prasangika *Rangtong* does not wholly depart the dimension of conceptual Relative Truth to discover That that lies beyond. For *Shentongpas, Rangtong* does not rest in trans-conceptual, perfectly subjective nondual clear light Buddha nature of mind. On the *Shentong* view, *Rangtong* bespeaks, correctly, what reality is not, but is not so clear as to how human beings contemplatively realize this great liberating truth.

Shentong extrinsic emptiness points the way to our already present, indwelling clear light Buddha nature of mind through instruction in perfectly subjective nondual contemplative cognition. This serves well our human trans-rational, subjective intelligence.

There are many ways to conceptually slice the cognitive epistemic pie of human awareness. We have seen that broadly construed, the mind has perhaps four voices, four intelligence potentials: 1) pre-conceptual naked attention/perception; 2) exoteric, conceptual, objective cognition; 3) esoteric subjective, contemplative cognition; and 4) greater esoteric, perfectly subjective "innermost secret" nondual awareness potentials.

Now the conceptual process of dialectical thinking is inherently dualistic. It tends to polarize and compartmentalize our cognitive activity into mere discursive intelligence. Therefore, we are well advised to remain in a balanced, centrist state of mindfulness when engaging such activity, or any activity. In any case, it seems that human awareness requires both *Rangtong* and *Shentong* cognitive modalities.

It has been said that the subtlest, "highest" teaching pinnacles of the Buddha's teaching—nondual *Dzogchen* and Essence *Mahamudra*—transcend dualistic Buddhist dialectics of *Rangtong* Middle Way Prasangika Madhyamaka, and *Shentong* Yogachara Madhyamaka. How shall we understand this?

The non-conceptual, nondual Nyingma *Dzogchen* and Kagyu Essence *Mahamudra* Views—which are said to be metaphysically identical—are *ipso facto* (by definition) transcendent of, yet inclusive of the conceptual dualistic dialectics of the *Rangtong-Shentong* deliberation. This "highest" trans-conceptual, non-deceptive definitive teaching is free of thinking, concept, and belief. It admits of no logical proof, and so is not subject to rational refutation.

This highest nondual *View* with its direct yogic *Meditation* is enfolded in and participates in the reality dimension of Ultimate Truth (*paramartha satya*); whereas the Buddhist dialectical vehicle unfolds in the dualistic spacetime dimension of Relative Truth (*samvriti satya*). *Dzogchen* and Highest *Mahamudra* have the great potential for the Result or Fruition that is perfect Buddhahood. The lesser dualistic conceptual paths serve only as preparation for such a fruitional view.

In the direct nondual meditation nothing is added; nothing is removed. So, we "let it be as it is" and rest—free of conceptual contrivance—in *buddic* clear light nature of mind. Seeing that great truth we understand that we are always already free of any separation from That. Our inherent Buddha nature—the very nature of mind—is empty and free of the adventitious defects of relative spacetime samsaric existence. Yet, it is not absent or empty of its own innate clear light Ultimate Truth qualities—primordial wisdom Buddha mind, and the *kayas* which arise and manifest through it.

So, runaway dualistic conceptual dialectics in no way conditions our nondual, always already present Buddha nature/Buddha mind, by whatever name, concept or belief. Yet, dualistic dialectical study may well serve the realization of it—immediate, direct bright Presence of That! Good to know.

For those of us who choose to engage Buddhist dialectics this proto-unified view of Shantirakshita and Ju Mipham may or may not suffice to yield a satisfying synthesis that rests this otherwise endless dialectal conundrum. Ultimately, there is no edge, no boundary, no limit to nondual infinite reality itself, already being here for our relative and ultimate experience—now upon each mindful mantra breath. Dualistic and nondual practice (*samadhi*) make it so.

Self, No-Self and Buddhist Dialectics: Why Bother? Yes, Buddhism requires, for those who would make effort to understand it, a difficult but joyous balanced collaboration between 1) contemplative direct nondual yogic experience (*yogi pratyaksa*), and 2) the dualistic, conceptual but still authoritative cognition of enlightened study (*pramana*) of Buddhist texts and commentaries.

So, who needs the heady wine of buddhist dialectics? What is the big deal about no-self? My meditation practice is doing just fine without a bunch of intellectual self-stimulation.

I have yet to encounter, through study or in person, a Lama, Roshi, or Ajhan who did not emphasize a firm conceptual understanding of Buddhist sutra and tantra scripture—philosophy and the ethical conduct that arises from it. But we need to know when to let it go, and rest in the nondual nature of mind.

A well established Buddhist practice requires that one actually understand what it is that one is practicing. To paraphrase Je Tsongkhapa: one cannot accomplish much of anything in meditation practice unless one knows what it is, and how to do it. Practice must include both voices of our human cognition—objective, conceptual knowing; and subjective contemplative feeling-knowing direct experience (*yogi pratyaksa*). Therefore, we research, study and practice the injunctions of those who know, all the way back to Gautama the Buddha. We need to know what the Buddha actually taught, and how to integrate it into our lifeworld practice.

The philosophical dialectics of relative reflective thinking (*kalpana, anumana pramana*) are indeed an authentic, if dualistic way of knowing the inexpressible nondual ultimate. Padmasambhava told it well, "It is only through relative truth that ultimate truth is realized. Practice these two as a unity". This penultimate wisdom process is further advanced in direct, conceptually ineffable, trans-conceptual, meditative, even nondual mystical yogic cognition (*yogi-pratyaksa*). It is completed ultimately in nondual *Dzogchen*, and in Essence *Mahamudra*, and in Saijojo Zen—under the guidance of a qualified Lama or Roshi.

There is no cognitive "domain boundary wall" or limit at all between these seemingly separate worlds—relative and ultimate. They are always a prior, yet present complementary love-wisdom unity. Real practice of the injunctions of the Path makes it so. Once again, no need to *believe* all of this. Only consider it as you tread your own joyous and difficult path. We must discover our own balance.

It is said that for Middle Way Prasangika and Yogachara Svatantrika this marvelous direct yogic cognition is still not *ultimate* knowledge that is the nondual Buddha mind wisdom of emptiness of appearing phenomena. How is this so?

Even *yogi-pratyaksa*—subtlest of the four types of Sutrayana (Sautrantika) direct perception (sensory, mental, self-awareness, yogic)—while it perceives "selfing" *atman* and selfless *anatman*, remains tainted by much sensory data from the side of the subject, so it remains very subtly corrupted and encaged in basic dualistic ignorance (*avidya*), the odious atavistic semiotic subject-object split. For healing and completion of this most basic relative separation—ultimate unification of the subject or mind, and the object that is the wisdom of emptiness/*shunyata*—we must defer to the *Dzogchen* view, the ultimate nondual view and practice wherein we discover that subject and object have never been separated at all (*Ch. VIII*).

Meanwhile, the *buddic* nondual wisdom of emptiness, far from denigrating the obsessive discursive mind of self-ego-I, is facilitated by a correct dualistic conceptual understanding, as we have seen. Again, we need both aspects of human cognition—objective and subjective—to be free of the ignorance of self-ego-I, and its attendant suffering. We do, after all, abide in these two worlds at once—relative conventional, and nondual ultimate. Unifying these two—however imperfectly—in our everyday lifeworld is our engaging and amusing human condition.

Just so, during and following selfless nondual yogic mystical cognition, dualistic dialectical cognition then naturally proceeds to quite imperfectly semiotically unpack and express this hitherto inexpressible nondual ultimate. In this "two ways at once" does dualistic relative conceptual understanding enhance the realization of selfless nondual ultimate primordial Buddha love-wisdom mind, and its relative practice in this precarious phenomenal domain of self-ego-I.

Therefore, it is not wise to deny or denigrate our unruly ego-I. This was not Buddha's intention. It is our not entirely reliable dualistic concept mind that models, articulates and serves as a contemplative awareness *portal* into our always present nondual innermost love-wisdom Buddha mind, the very clear light nature of mind whose always present numinous Presence already embraces it.

Understanding the No-Self Knowing Process. To be clear, we are told by those who know that relative dualistic conceptual mind does not "expand" or "dissolve" into ultimate nondual Buddha mind, or into anything at all. Why? Because all embracing mind is already everything. These two domains—relative and ultimate—are indivisible. We first understand this conceptually; then more profoundly.

In the clear words of Lama Professor Ann C. Klein Rigzin Drolma (Klein 1998):

> Starting roughly with Dignaga (d. 540 A.C.E.), Buddhist philosophers began to discuss perceptual errors—sources of suffering—in terms of direct and conceptual perception (*pratyaksa* and *kalpana*) and their objects. According to these philosophers, there are only two types of valid cognition, direct perception (*pratyaksa-pramana*) and inference (*anumana-pramana*). Since ordinary direct perception is insufficient to a conscious ascertainment of subtle impermanence or selflessness, the only type of valid perception by which ordinary beings can at first know such phenomena is conceptual.

The conceptual activity of the busy, seeking mind is thus an auspicious beginning. We begin by asking the right questions! Contemplative cultivation of such inferential knowing then enables yogic direct perception (*yogi-pratyaksa*), the gradual practice of which liberates the practitioner from the surly bonds of suffering caused by ignorance (*avidya, marigpa, ajnana*) of the Buddha's basic principles of emptiness: *anitya*-impermanence, *anatman*-selflessness, and *pratitya samutpada*-interdependent arising of form in time.

From the early pre-Mahayana wisdom of the *Pali Canon*, a caveat in this regard:

> For bodhisattva mahasattvas who are beginners one must explain the Six Perfections (inferential valid cognition) with a reference point, with the notion that suchness (*tathata, dharmata*) is expressible. That is to say, they must understand the nature of the elements to be arising and perishing. Only then should they familiarize with the idea that all phenomena are in essence inexpressible, non-arising, non-ceasing, not perceptible, and not ultimately existing.
>
> —Akashagarbha Sutra 1.15

These two canonical views—conceptual understanding and direct yogic experience—seem to agree on the relative inferential and conceptual expressibility (*kalpana*) of *tathata*, impermanent, selfless *dharmata*. Do they agree on the expressibility of its ultimate direct experience or perception (*pratyaksa-pramana*)?

Professor Klein continues (Klein 1998):

> Conceptual thought is not transformed of its own force into direct experience...Most significant is the gradual union of conceptual understanding with increasingly stabilized periods of concentration. The practitioner alternates between

analytical meditation (*dpyad sgom*) and stabilizing meditation (*'jog sgom*). Finally, one reaches the point where instead of analysis acting as an interference to stabilization, or stabilization weakening analytical understanding, each enhances the other. This union of analytical or insight practice with a concentration developed to the point of calm abiding (*samatha, zhi gnas*) is called special insight (*vipasyana, lhag mthong*). Attainment of this union of insight and concentration marks the beginning of the second of five paths or stages of practice, the path of preparation (*prayoga-marga*).

It is the attainment of such a preparatory union of *shamatha* and *vipashyana*—direct yogic feeling-knowing perception (*yogi pratyaksa*)—that is hard to come by in the earlier stages of the Buddhist Path. In the beginning our innermost secret Buddha nature/Buddha mind—bright Presence of That—remains more or less captive to our concepts *about* it. The meditation master will help to point out directly this luminous clear light nature of mind. Nagarjuna told it well 2000 years ago (Garfield 1995):

> Fools and reificationists who perceive
> The existence and nonexistence
> Of objects
> Do not see the pacification of objectification.

What has gradually become clear from 2000 years of such dialectics is that the product of dualistic relative discursive human concept mind—even at its interpretive pinnacle in the later stages of the Path—still remains largely unpacified, provisional and uncertain. The deep selfless wisdom certainty of the nondual ultimate nature of mind remains the province of the nondual ultimate. Knowing this (*gnosis, jnana, yeshe*)—now gone utterly beyond the domain of the reified subjects and objects of objective cognition—the obsessively busy objective mind is finally pacified. And yes, it requires a bit of practice.

Together unified these two cognitive dimensions—these "two types of valid cognition"—bestow great constitutive power for the devoted practitioner of the primordial wisdom Path. This power is spontaneously expressed through selfless, skillful, compassionate action in the service of living beings. Such thought, intention and action for the benefit of beings is known, as we have seen, as skillful *bodhicitta*—enlightened heart-mind—the very secret of human happiness.

That said, the Hinayana *Pali Canon* view—Vaibhasika (Sarvastivada) and Theravada, the first of the Four Buddhist Tenet Systems—does not well lend itself to a perspicuous conceptual understanding and expression of the veiled dimension of nondual Ultimate Truth, if indeed that is even possible at all. The Tibetan Vajrayana Gelug school perhaps comes closest to doing so. In any case, that is the prevailing view of current Middle Way Madhyamaka scholarship—both Prasangika and Yogachara. Theravada Buddhists do not agree (Thanissaro 2015).

Lama Professor Klein: "The Dalai Lama once remarked, having cited the importance this textual material has for realizing the inexpressible ultimate, 'after all, it is not *that* inexpressible' ".

Be that as it may, we have seen that human awareness-consciousness includes these three "luminous and knowing" cognitive voices—1) outer, exoteric, objective, conceptual (*anumana pramana, kalpana*); 2) inner, esoteric, directly subjective, contemplative (*shamatha, vipashana*); and 3) perfectly subjective nondual (direct *yogi pratyaksa*), "utterly gone beyond" (*parasamgate*) subject-object duality. Our indwelling love-wisdom Buddha mind knows, feels and utilizes all three at once. Practice and devotion make it so.

Thus do we tame, even liberate the mind from the adventitious cage of ignorance (*avidya, marigpa, hamartia-sin*) that causes terrible suffering for living beings. The resulting awakened, gentle, happy mind state spontaneously expresses itself as selfless, altruistic, compassionate *bodhicitta*—the thought, intention, and action for the benefit of living beings. And this, after all, is both origin and aim of dualistic conceptual Buddhist dialectics. Indeed, on the accord of all the Buddhas and *mahasiddhas* of the three times, *bodhicitta* (*mahakaruna*), is the primary cause of human happiness. As to our urgent question, Why bother? That is why we bother to study Buddhism.

(For a definitive doctrinal history of the Indo-Tibetan philosophical schools—both Buddhist and Hindu; both Hinayana and Mahayana—see the Tibetan Gelug *Siddhanta*. See also John Pettit's *Mipham's Beacon of Certainty*, 1999; Jay Garfield's *Engaging Buddhism* 2015; Jeffrey Hopkins' *Mountain Doctrine*, 2017; Ann Klein's *Unbounded Wholeness*, 2006.)

Brief Wisdom Excursus. Perhaps we might altogether shift our cognitive universe of discourse from semiotic (logical syntax, meaning/semantics; pragmatics/speech acts) conceptual knowing to post-conceptual nondual knowing. Please consider the following thought experiment.

In such instances of problematic Buddhist hermeneutical dialectics, or any other dialectical process, it is perhaps wise to simply surrender the whole conceptual shebang, however imperfectly, into the already present conceptually quiescent peace of the unborn, unceasing primordial space of *dharmadhatu* (the basic space/*ying* of nondual reality itself). Thus do we reenter concept-mind refreshed, and awake.

In the Buddha's teaching we all arise and participate in this vast aboriginal, uncreated "basic space" of *dharmadhatu*. We are, necessarily, never separate from That. Our vast *bodhi* mind knows this. Opening to receive always present numinous Presence of That is Happiness Itself, the ultimate happiness that cannot be lost. But don't believe it! As Buddha told, "Come and see".

After all, *conceptual certainty* as to primordial emptiness of the Buddha's teaching, or of a Theory of Quantum Gravity, or of the foundational axioms of mathematics and formal logic, is *ipso facto* precluded within the cognitive sphere of relative-conventional truth (*samvriti satya*). How shall we understand this?

We have been led to believe by our Western (Greek) deep cultural background prevailing metaphysic of Modern Scientific Materialism/Physicalism that all of appearing reality—physical, mental, emotional, even spiritual—may be explained by, or reduced to, our "global web of belief" (Quine 1969) of purely physical Science; proto-religious "Scientism" in its fundamentalist robes. But it is not so.

To attain the subtler, deeper multi-dimensional truth of the matter we must, in certain timeless moments, actually cognitively suspend or "bracket" four centuries of European Modernity— the conceptual, objectivist-materialist cognitive bias that is the infernal machine of the obsessively thinking Cartesian *Cogito*, our impossible atavistic π in the sky desideratum for perfectly objective conceptual certainty. Mindful *shamatha* serves this deeper wisdom purpose.

Thus do we contemplatively shift our immediate attentional awareness from heady, "selfing" *objective* concept-mind to that selfless trans-conceptual (*yogi pratyaksa*) nondual realm that does indeed admit of perfectly *subjective* certainty. Here, now there is no dilemma. No problem at all. We have a choice. We may *choose* this practice of the love-wisdom Path. It is our courageous self-ego-I that, sooner or later, must make this "choiceless choice".

Well, what remains after this post-empirical, post-skeptical wisdom of emptiness "transcendental *epoche*"? What is the result of this gradual, step by step choice to shift our awareness from the proverbial "wild horse of the mind" to a deeper strata of awareness-consciousness? What remains is only this selfless, empty, luminous clear light of primordial wisdom Buddha mind—bright Presence of That. Happiness itself.

Yes, the desideratum devoutly to be wished. Such wishful, then engaged devotion to the Path makes it so. *Emaho!* Lao Tzu told it well: "A journey of a thousand miles begins with the first step". Then, after we enter in and establish our practice of the Path, we take that next step—all the way to the end of it.

The buddhas, *mahasiddhas*, and great avatars of the three times—past, present, future—who have come to earth for our benefit have demonstrated through their lives this love-wisdom potential that already abides at the Heartmind (*hridyam*) of each human being. This happiness is already the case; always present. But it requires a bit of discipline, and yes, courage to open and receive it. Awakening to our indwelling happiness requires a bit of practice, and then more practice, all in the loving context of the "Three Jewels"—the Buddha seen in the living master, the dharma teaching, and the precious *sangha* community.

Then, if we're lucky, we arise from such post-formal bliss and do some good for somebody. It is this great truth of the selfless *bodhicitta* of engaged compassionate thought, intention, and skillful action that pervades all of Buddha's teaching.

Human happiness and freedom from suffering is dependent upon this compassionate cognitive shift from benefiting self, to benefiting all living beings, including our precious Mother Earth. This prodigious heartmind change begins with kind, compassionate thought, intention and action toward oneself. So, just for this precious moment, breathe mindfully and love and accept yourself exactly as you are now. Feel gratitude to God and Guru for your precious life, just as it is now. Feel your connection to everyone and everything. Self-ego-I may resist such selfless cognition. "Innermost secret" love-wisdom mind finds it natural and joyous.

Bodhicitta has the additional benefit of grounding most of the adventitious, ornamental dialectics to which I have herein subjected you, my dear Reader, in this often heady and difficult explication of the Buddha's teaching. Not to mention, *bodhicitta* is the very secret of opening to receive both the relative and ultimate human happiness that are already present within us.

Always Already Anatman. Therefore, as to Buddha's teaching on *anatman*/selflessness, the centrist Middle Way Madhyamaka teaching is that there is no absolute *essential* self-identity, not even a Hindu personal "supreme identity" Atman Self that is one with Brahman; not even our precious Buddha Self concept. The nondual reality of such beautiful conceptual self ornaments is perhaps greater than we think.

Thus it is, the self-existence of the beings and things of form are forever relegated to the dimensional realm of Relative Truth. That at least is the prevailing view of Middle Way *Madhyamaka Prasangika*, which H.H. Dalai Lama reminds us is the Mahayana Middle Way Prasangika *provisional* foundation of *definitive Dzogchen* view and praxis.

May I say it again? "Spacetime reality is not as it appears; nor is it otherwise" (Patrul Rinpoche). In the Mahayana Middle Way view all appearing reality—persons and things—even ultimate reality's very emptiness ground—primordial Buddha nature itself—is empty of "any shred" of intrinsic, absolute or ultimate self-existence, wholly impermanent, selfless, and interdependently interconnected. Yet, relatively and conventionally, here we are, brimming with nondual Buddha nature!

This view, as H.H. Dalai Lama, following the syncretic teaching of Shantirakshita, has told, is the correct relative view of *shunyata/* emptiness. That primordial Buddha nature is always present as/ to this process, is the correct ultimate view of emptiness. We have seen that it is useful to understand these Two Truths—Relative and Ultimate—as complementary faces of a prior unity.

Yet, there is always this indwelling trans-conceptual numinous cognizance, this "innermost secret" Presence (*vidya, rigpa*) of Buddha mind—by whatever name or concept—that knows and feels the quiescent nondual truth of it. *Mahasukaho!* Happiness Itself! That is the Buddhist View. That is the luminous teaching of the Buddha.

In Summary of Buddhist *Anatman*/Selflessness. Most, but certainly not all of the Buddhist world views the fecund fullness of emptiness—both void negative "objective emptiness", and luminous *buddic* "subjective emptiness"—in whom this all arises and participates is itself absent and empty any trace of essential intrinsic or ultimate self-existence.

We've seen that this *Rangtong* Madhyamaka Prasangika negation of the absolute or ultimate existence of emptiness itself is called the "emptiness of emptiness" (*shunyata shunyata*). Self-ego-I and its experience—self and other—possess not a whit of intrinsic, ultimate existence.

Yet, relatively, here we are; real sentient beings in a phenomenally "real world out there" (RWOT), with the real perfectly subjective Presence of our innermost Buddha nature/Buddha mind. This relative-conventional, really real, if not ultimately real spacetime existence is the great reality gift from the Buddha to us via his teaching of the Two Truths—relative and ultimate (*Ch. VI*). Beings and stuff really exist. So our thoughts, intentions, and actions have real karmic consequences. If spacetime existence were ultimately illusory this could not be so.

We need to really be here in objective relative time and space, and to skillfully utilize our objective relative real minds in order to awaken to this miracle that is perfectly subjective ultimate reality itself in whom this all arises and participates. And we have only a few short years in which to do so! This is perhaps as good a definition of the human condition as any.

Both Buddhists and physicists agree that self in time, in the trans-material ultimate view, is illusory and unreal. Yes, Einstein referred to time (t) as "an illusion; albeit a very persistent one". In this dimension of Relative Truth time flies at light speed. As to awakening, there is no time to lose.

OK. Emptiness/*shunyata* is empty and absent of ultimate existence. How then *does* emptiness exist? Emptiness exists only via our conceptual imputation and reification. H.H. Dalai Lama tells us that "Emptiness is established by conventional minds". It is not a preexisting primordial ground of everything, though it is too often conceptualized to be that.

For Middle Way Buddhists there is no *ultimately* existing ground. Ultimate selfless *shunyata*/emptiness, *dharmakaya*, *kadag* is thus a paradoxical "groundless ground" of all that arises and appears therein as form. Yet, real, non-illusory *relative* form continues to arise from its *ultimate* base (*gzhi rigpa*). "Form is empty (*shunya*, Tib. *stongpa*); emptiness (*shunyata, stongpa nyi*) is form". Human instantiations of this relative form have given us, by design and by grace, a *choice* to consciously realize luminous numinous emptiness—nondual Buddha mind wisdom of emptiness, our "supreme identity".

We recognize, then realize this great truth through surrender of our concepts and beliefs about it. How? As many of my readers know, it happens in deep, peaceful contemplative connection to our selfless always present Buddha love-wisdom mind—bright indwelling Presence of That—mirrored always by the Master, and continuously arising through dharma teaching and mantra prayer, and through loving presence of the *sangha*, the spiritual family (*Appendix A*: "Let It Be: Basic Meditation Practice").

In any case, as to the absence of an ultimately existing primordial ground, 20th century Tibetan Buddhist master Chögyam Trungpa insouciantly advises:

> The bad news is that we are all falling through space with no parachute, and nothing to hold on to. The good news is that there is no ground.

This concludes our exploration of *anatman* or no-self/selflessness, the second of the Buddha's three foundational principles of *shunyata*/emptiness that is our Buddha nature of mind.

3) **Interdependence/Dependent Arising.** The *Sagaramiti Sutra* teaches that the intrinsic existence of all appearing phenomenal reality is refuted by the Buddha's logic

of Dependent Arising (*pratitya samutpada*). "That which arises dependently (interdependently) is free of inherent existence". How shall we understand this?

We've seen that the three faces of Buddhist emptiness/*shunyata* are impermanence (*anitya*), selflessness/no-self (*anatman*), and interdependent arising (*pratitya samut-pada*). These three are already unified, beyond concept and belief, in our nondual primordial wisdom Buddha nature of mind—*dharmakaya* itself—personified as archetypal Primordial *Adi Buddha* Samantabhadra (Tib. Kuntazangpo), Buddha of all-embracing *dharmakaya* dimension (*Ch. IX*). We realize it through the two faces of human cognition—conceptual valid cognition (*pramana*), and yogic direct perception (*yogi pratyaksa*).

Dependent arising or dependent origination is the Buddha's premodern presentation to us of the modern scientific truth of causality, cause and effect. All of the physical, mental and social phenomena of the vast causal matrix that is David Bohm's "implicate order of the unbounded whole"—luminous infinite basic space of *dharmadhatu*, all embracing nondual *Kosmos* itself that continuously arises to the sensory perception of any present sentient beings—is wholly interdependent, and causally interconnected. No instance of form is independent and unrelated to this vast, empty, unborn, uncreated, uncaused whole. All instantiations of form participate in that vast expanse—spiritual sun of all illuminating *dharmakaya*, whose very essence is *shunyata*/emptiness (*Ch. IX*). Our vast Buddha love-wisdom mind—luminous Presence (*vidya, rigpa*) of That—is the knowing-feeling of it.

It is this seminal principle of interconnectedness that the Buddha auspiciously termed "interdependent arising", or "dependent origination", or "interbeing" (*pratitya samutpada*).

Moreover, this dependent arising of form is metaphysically equivalent to the impermanent, selfless innate luminous clear light emptiness (*shunyata*) of all appearing phenomena. They are the same, pristine cognition of sameness (*samatajnana*). The "fourfold profundity" of form and emptiness of Buddha's luminous *Heart of Wisdom Sutra*" (*Maha prajnaparamita mitahridaya sutra*):

Form is empty; emptiness is form.
Form is not other than emptiness;
Emptiness is not other than form.

Buddha's Two Truths are thus appearing *relative* form and its inherent *ultimate* emptiness.

Nineteenth century Nyingma master Ju Mipham interprets, in the clear words of H.H. Dalai Lama, the Buddha's Fourfold Profundity thusly (H.H. Dalai Lama 2005):

'Form is empty' presents the emptiness of the phenomenal world thereby countering the extreme of existential absolutism, the mistaken belief that all phenomena have absolute reality. The second statement, 'emptiness is form' presents emptiness as arising as dependent origination, thereby countering the extreme of nihilism, the mistaken belief that nothing exists. The third statement, 'emptiness is not other than form' presents the union of appearance and emptiness, or the union of emptiness and dependent origination, countering both extremes, nihilism and existential absolutism, at once. The fourth statement, 'form too is not other than emptiness', indicates that appearance and emptiness are not incompatible, abiding instead in a state of total unanimity. Thus, these four aspects (of emptiness) are understood as presenting total transcendence of all conceptual elaborations.

Therefore, 1) arising, appearing form is empty of intrinsic existence (*shunyata*); 2) this inherent emptiness of form is affirmed as identical to the interdependent arising of form (*pratitya samutpada*); 3) emptiness and appearing reality are viewed as a prior and present nondual unity; and 4) this nondual unity of form and emptiness transcends yet embraces the natural dimensional limit of relative conventional language and conceptual thinking (*kalpana*), or valid cognition (*pramana*)—the first of our two cognitive modalities—the second being yogic direct perception (*yogi pratyaksa*). His Holiness refers to these two levels of our human understanding as "conceptual experience, and feeling experience".

Buddha's *Heart of Wisdom Sutra*, after addressing the wisdom of the emptiness of form, then affirms that this wisdom be also applied to the remaining four aggregates (*skandhas*) of conditional existence—feeling, perception, mental formation/construction, and personal consciousness. As Buddha wisdom mind rises, obstructed *kleisha* mind falls away. When the mind is liberated from these five *shandhas*, in complete absence of, and freedom from any independent reality formation whatever, it awakens to its always already love-wisdom Buddha nature/Buddha mind. Bright Presence of That. *Emaho!*

This Fourfold Profundity is then a centrist or middle way of avoiding the two metaphysical extremes of "eternalist" absolute existence, and "nihilist" absolute nonexistence (Metaphysical Materialism/Physicalism and Metaphysical Idealism) as to the nature of appearing spacetime phenomenal reality. This Middle Way Madhyamaka view is shared by all four Tibetan Buddhist schools—Nyingma, Gelug, Kagyu, and Sakya.

The "highest" or subtlest teaching of these four schools, and indeed of the Four Buddhist Tenet Systems (see below) is, on the accord of His Holiness, the middle way teaching known as the Madhyamaka Prasangika of Nagarjuna, Chandrakirti, and Tsongkhapa.

So, once again, the Buddha's Two Truths are relative form, and its ultimate emptiness. Two thousand years ago Indian Buddhist sage and Mahyana Madhyamaka Middle Way founder Nagarjuna (d. 55 C.E.) told it this way *(Fundamental Wisdom of the Middle Way, Garfield 1995):*

> The Buddha's teaching of the Dharma
> Is based on two truths:
> A truth of worldly convention
> And an ultimate truth.

We perceive and conceive the everyday reality of Relative Truth via our sense perception and conceptual mind. And we *directly* experience, beyond our senses and our beliefs, the suchness or thatness *(tathata)* of Ultimate Truth through mindful *shamatha,* and the penetrating analytic insight of *(vipashyana),* which is none other than direct yogic knowing-feeling perception *(yogi pratyaksa).* The Two Truths are not separate independent realities but two voices of an all-pervading *one truth,* invariant throughout our awareness-consciousness processional that includes all human cognitive processing: immediate perceptual, objective conceptual, subjective contemplative, and perfectly subjective nondual.

In the Dedicatory Verses to his eminent *Fundamental Wisdom of the Middle Way (Mulamadhyamakakarika,* Garfield 1995) Nagarjuna reveals:

> Whatever is dependently arisen is
> Unceasing, unborn,
> Unannihilated, not permanent,
> Not coming, not going,
> Without distinction, without identity,
> And free from conceptual construction.

Nagarjuna asserts here the fundamental unity of emptiness or Ultimate Truth, and dependent arising or Relative Truth. In the final chapters he confirms the identity of nirvana and buddhahood with Ultimate Truth.

This innate metaphysical unity of the Buddha's Two Truths is nothing less than the root Middle Way view of Chandrakirti's 8th century Madhyamaka Prasangika whose restatement in his *Prasannapada* of Najarjuna's "emptiness of emptiness" completed the dialectical stream that continues through Gelug School founder Tsongkhapa (15th century), and on to H.H. Dalai Lama.

It is the interpretation of Nagarjuna's foundational Mahayana Treatise in *Ch. XVIII, Verse 18* that has fueled centuries of Buddhist dialectics between the *Rangtong* Prasangika and the *Shentong* Yogachara Svatantrika Middle Way Madhyamaka sub-schools (Garfield 1995):

> Whatever is dependently co-arisen
> That is explained to be emptiness.
> That, being a dependent designation
> Is itself the middle way.

> Neither from itself nor from another,
> Nor from both,
> Nor without a cause,
> Does anything whatever, anywhere arise.
> (Chapter I, v. 1).

> Appearing things are both real and not real.
> Things are both existent and nonexistent.
> And things are neither real nor not real.
> That is Buddha's teaching.
> (*Chapter XVIII, v. 9*, author's translation)

> The existence of self has been taught.
> The Buddhas have taught the doctrine of

No-self. And the Buddhas have taught the
Doctrine of neither self nor no-self.
(*Chapter XVIII, v. 6*, author's translation)

Ultimately, self and all arising phenomena appearing to a self, do not *ultimately* exist. And that includes our concepts and beliefs *about* Buddha nature, primordial wisdom, and the three *kayas*. "Without distinction, without identity and free of conceptual construction" applies to all appearing physical and mental phenomena.

Well, what is it that rescues this rather abstruse, highly skeptical Middle Way view from the nihilist jaws of monistic Metaphysical Absolute Idealism—whether East or West? Not surprisingly, it is the centrist "middle path" between the metaphysical extremes of monistic eternalist/materialist absolute existence, and monistic nihilist/idealist absolute nonexistence.

In short, as we have seen many times before, Nagarjuna's Middle Way Madhyamaka view of the Buddha's Two Truths—Relative Truth and Ultimate Truth—asserts that yes, all of this relative phenomenal spacetime stuff is absent and empty any whit of independent intrinsic Ultimate Truth existence. The inherent absence or emptiness of interdependently arising phenomena *is* its absence of intrinsic, ultimate existence. *Shunyata*/emptiness just *is* the Buddha's dependent arising (*pratitya samutpada*). His Holiness adds, paraphrasing Nagarjuna, "There is nothing that is not dependently arisen, so there is nothing that is not emptiness".

However, and most fortunately for all of us, our everyday lifeworld still really exists as the relative, conventional dimension of interdependently arising Relative Truth. Spacetime stuff does not inherently exist as we perceive and conceive it; but such phenomena are not entirely nonexistent. They are nominally real, and established by way of the conceptual imputation and reification of relatively, conventionally existing human minds. (*Ch. VI*, "The Fundamental Two Truths" further explores the Buddha's *Heart of Wisdom* sutra, and Nagarjuna's "middle path".)

That things truly exist substantially, just as we apprehend them, is the primal ignorance (*avidya, marigpa*) that the Buddha told is the root and primary cause of human suffering. Things are not as they appear! How shall we understand this strange and counter intuitive ontology?

The Three Faces of Interdependent Arising. Buddha spoke of three aspects of the interconnected, interdependent arising of form from its "primordially pure", empty clear light *dharmakaya* "groundless ground".

A) *Causal Interdependence*: all arising form is the result of the vast matrix boundless whole (*dharmadhatu*) of prior and present utterly interconnected causes and conditions. Causality: cause and effect, is the causal foundation of modern science.

B) *Mereological Interdependence*: Mereology is the study of part-whole relationships. As to Buddhist mereology, the arising physical and mental parts of reality depend upon the vast whole in whom they arise and participate. Conversely, the great whole depends upon the participating parts that constitute it. Just so, the many parts of your body depend upon the whole body; and the body depends upon its parts. Wholes and parts are necessarily complementary. But wholes are not always reducible to their parts, as the principle of "scientific reductionism" insists. The ultimate *Kosmic* whole, *dharmakaya* "groundless ground"—Samantabhadra—in whom this all arises and is instantiated is greater than the sum of its parts, and utterly embraces and subsumes its parts. No parts, no whole. No whole, no parts.

C) *Conceptual Imputation*: All interdependent arising of our appearing phenomenal realities are a function of human conceptual reification, imputation, attribution, and designation. We fabricate, then elaborate our realities via our conceptual, *ontologically relative* "global web of belief" (Quine 1969)—Kant's relative conventional conceptual categories of existence.

In other words, arising physical and mental forms are the cognitive products and biases of our social inter-objective, and cultural inter-subjective deep background (unconscious) cognitive categories of understanding; our unexamined metaphysical assumptions about our appearing spacetime realities. For the Western mind this belief system is Scientific Materialism/Physicalism. Our ontological categories of being here in space and time are relative to our conventional linguistic, semiotic web of concept and belief. *Ontological relativity indeed.*

H.H. Dalai Lama on these three voices of Buddhist interdependent arising:

First, all conditional things and events in the world come into being only as a result of the interactions of causes and conditions. They don't just arise from nowhere, fully formed. Second, there is mutual dependence between parts and the whole: without parts there can be no whole, without a whole it makes no sense to speak of parts... Third, anything that exists and has an identity does so only within the total network of everything that has a possible or potential relation to it. No phenomena exists with an independent or intrinsic identity.

—H.H. Dalai Lama, 2005, p. 64

His Holiness further distinguishes between "objective empti-ness" and "subjective emptiness". Objective emptiness or "ob-jective luminosity" is a "non-affirming negative phenomenon" (*prasajya*), the absence or negation of any independent intrinsic existence, or self to experience it. Both self and its perceived "other phenomena" are empty of any whit of inherent, ultimate existence.

But the Buddha's great emptiness—*mahashunyata*—is not, in the ultimate view, merely a *non-affirming* negative. In the subtlest or highest view of the nondual Tibetan tantras—the view of *Dzogchen*, Highest Yoga Tantra (*Anuttara yoga tantra*), and Definitive Essence Mahamudra—negated phenomena appearing to a self as relative conventional reality are replaced by "subjective emptiness" (*nay lug*), the *affirming* clarity and luminosity of the clear light (*'od gsal*, Skt. *prabhasa*).

So, *mahashunyata*, the great emptiness is not merely the negative absence of form. This is not the whole story. Emptiness is equally the *luminous clarity of the primordial clear light Buddha nature of mind*. The nondual, non-conceptual, naked ordinary direct yogic perception (*yogi pratyaksa*, Jap. *satori*, *kensho*) of unmediated experience is "wisdom realizing emptiness", wholly uncontaminated by conceptual cognition. Yet, we must conceptually, dualistically unpack this whole shebang after the nondual fact of the matter, as we are doing here.

Such an understanding is most important to the view and practice of the wisdom of emptiness. Je Tsongkhapa (1357-1419), founder of H.H. Dalai Lama's Gelug school of Tibetan Buddhism, reminds us that we must correctly identify the *negandum*, that which is to be negated, in this process of realizing *shunyata/ emptiness*, lest we negate too much, or too little. We must find the middle way between totality of negation of absolute existence, or of absolute nonexistence. If we negate too much of this arising form we depart the Madhyamaka Middle Way view and fall into dark nihilism, the extreme view of monistic Absolute Metaphysical Idealism that altogether denies the existence even of relative form.

The history of philosophy and religion has had a difficult time indeed denying that there is something real here that appears to our senses and our mind. Whatever its nature, something somehow exists! Just pinch yourself. Moreover, if nothing exists, not even moral agents, our choices don't much matter. Why bother to practice ethical precepts; to be kind to one another?

Conversely, if we negate too little of this continuously arising relative form from its nondual ultimate emptiness ground, we fall into the extreme of monistic absolute materialist eternalism—Metaphysical Materialism/Physicalism, or worse, fundamentalist proto-religious "Scientism". This extreme realist-materialist view encourages the reification and conceptual imputation of an intrinsically existing "real world out there" (RWOT); and all its grasping and clinging to a permanent self-ego-I with its afflictive emotion—Aversion: fear, anger, hatred; and Attachment: furious sense desire, greed, pride—the very causes of human suffering and unhappiness.

Thus it is, the Buddhist Middle Way sub-school that is Madhyamaka Prasangika, the very foundation of the *Dzogchen* view according to Chandrakirti and His Holiness Dalai Lama, bestrides the path that negates the intrinsic *ultimate* existence of appearing form, while acknowledging this great gift of its conventional, *relative* existence. Our beloved spacetime stuff is really real; just not absolutely, ultimately real. So, we still have to show up for work, and be kind to living beings.

In the nondual *Dzogchen* view of the Great Perfection (*Ch. VIII*), on the wisdom accord of ecumenical *Rimé* Nyingma master Ju Mipham Rinpoche,

> Within the essence, original wakefulness which is primordi-
> ally pure (*kadag*) manifests the nature, a luminosity which
> is spontaneously present (*lhundrub*).

Form is empty; emptiness is form. Nice holistic concept, or unifying nondual truth?

Great Neo-Vedanta master Ramana Maharshi told it well, "The problem for human beings is that most spiritual experience is just concepts; nothing but concepts". Even primordial Presence of our indwelling, innermost *bodhi* mind wisdom mind/Buddha nature is, at the beginning of the Path, mostly concept and belief. When we learn that Buddha nature and *dharmakaya* do not ultimately exist, we are confused, or worse. Then, through practice of the Path we begin to understand that these precious non-entities are non-existent as *concepts*, but abide always at the spiritual Heart (*hridaym*) through our non-conceptual yogic *direct* experience of them. As we free our mindstream from near total dependence upon concepts to construct our solid external realities, now may we enter in the nondual love-wisdom mind Presence of our actual Buddha nature, above and beyond and free of mere discursive concept and belief. It's a whole new wonderful world! Assiduous practice makes it so.

With the patience and diligence of practice of the Path, and devotion to our spiritual master, such adventitious concepts and beliefs open wide into direct *feeling experience*—bright knowing Presence (*vidya, rigpa*) of That. As one's practice begins to stabilize, knowing and feeling gradually come together as a total practice unity. As if they were ever be separate at all. Good to remember when engaging the conceptual heady wine of Buddhist dialectical philosophy.

Yet, our intellectual, conceptual understanding is a most auspicious beginning. And it continues—should we be so lucky—all the way to the fourth "stage of no more learning". Conceptual relative understanding aids in establishing the View, which motivates the establishment and continuation of the Meditation, under guidance of the master, that is the authentic practice of the Path.

As we begin to understand that we reify and thus reduce our precious selfless wisdom mind Presence of the basal primordial ground to mere concepts and beliefs of an ultimately apparitional self-ego-I, sooner or later the existential shock opens us into the "wisdom deep"—the actual subtle reality of nonlocal, nondual Ultimate Truth. And we know it through our non-conceptual, trans-rational, innermost Buddha mind (*buddhajnana*), *vidya*, *rigpa* Presence—direct *knowing-feeling experience* of That. And That is a certainty that cannot be accomplished by self-stimulating ornamental Buddhist metaphysical abstractions, no matter how sublime.

Be That as it may, step by step we utilize the relative Path to awaken to our ultimate Buddha love-wisdom nature of mind. We learn to "Practice these two as a unity" (Padmasambhava).

No Self, No Problem. *"All the evil, fear and suffering of the world is caused by serving the self. All the happiness of the world is caused by serving others* (Shantideva).

Due to impermanence/change (*anitya*) of all causally interdependently arising phenomena, nothing has an *intrinsic* self-nature. The consciousness of persons, and of all "other" phenomena appearing to such a self-ego-I in this implicate unbroken whole, arise into an explicate, selfless (*anatman*), constantly changing continuum of causes and conditions, with no logocentric, absolute permanent self-identity at all.

Old Zen *koan*: "Who are you in the space between two thoughts?" Indeed, it is this profound spaciousness (*dharmadhatu, cho ying*) through which, or in whom everything—physical mental, societal, spiritual—arises and participates. *Well, if self is illusory, who is it that knows/realizes this selfless wisdom?*

We've seen that Vajrayana bespeaks the "two selflessnesses"; the selflessness of the person (*Rangtong*), and the selflessness of experienced phenomena (*Shentong*). For the contemplatively stabilized mind (*samadhi, dhyana*) realizing emptiness—the unity of *shamatha/* mindfulness (settling the "wild horse of the mind" into its natural quiescent state), and *vipashyanā* (analytic penetrating insight)—the *absence* of self-nature in all arising form, both "self" and "other", is a *relative* view. In the *ultimate* view, the false conceptual dichotomy of "self" and "no-self" are a nondual, post-dialectical unity.

So, who is it that knows? Indwelling always already present Buddha mind/wisdom mind knows. *Lama Khen, Lama Khen.* Inner Lama mirrored by outer Lama knows (*Lama khen*). Numinous luminous perfectly subjective Presence (*vidya, rigpa*) of That knows. Who am I? The Hindus have told it for 6000 years: *Tat Tvam Asi. That I Am!* (That thou art.)

So we have here an authentic, auto-noetic reflexively aware (*rang rig yeshe*) liberating realization of nondual (interdependent trans-conceptual subject/object unity) "primordial wisdom of emptiness". Such "basic wisdom" is the prior epistemic unity of ignorant (*avidya, marigpa*), *relative* mind brimming with self-ego-I, and the innate selfless "luminous clear light mind" or Buddha wisdom mind that gently embraces ego/self—like the mother loves the child—in *ultimate* emptiness ground itself. This boundless, interdependently arising whole is our all-pervading inherent "supreme source" (*kunjed gyalpo*, basic space/*ying* of *dharmadhatu*, *cittadhatu*). No dilemma. No problem at all.

This concludes our discussion of the three principles of the Buddha's *shunyata*/emptiness: impermanence (*anitya*), selflessness (*anatman*), and interdependent arising (*pratitya samutpada*).

The Four Buddhist Tenet Systems: Variations on a Theme of Wholeness.

First, a brief prelude. The roughly 6000 year old philosophical, religious, and spiritual history of our species—in both the East, and much later in the West—has been concerned with understanding the apparent, usually obvious truth that things are not as they appear. Physicists, neurobiologists, social scientists, and psychologists all agree, physical and mental spacetime reality arising to human sensory perception and mental conception are in one way or another deceptive. Twentieth and 21st century physics and cosmology further thickens this quantum entangled plot. We need a skillful means for handling the cognitive confusion that here arises—for both Science and Spirit.

We urgently require both objective conceptual, and subjective non-conceptual, contemplative cognitive strategies for ascertaining what is apparently, relatively, conventionally real and existent; and what exists ultimately, even spiritually, beyond our obvious apparent realities. Viewed holistically, the question becomes: what is our human relationship to the vast ultimate boundless whole in which, or in whom this all arises. Are we separate from That; or somehow unified in it? Or something in between? And in any case, how is it so?

In the East, pre-Vedic contemplative religious-philosophical practice arose in the Indus Valley at least 6000 years ago; although the earliest traces of proto-Hindu deities are found in Bhimbetka rock paintings and carvings dating to 30,000 BCE, or older!

Gautama Shakyamuni the Buddha, the Buddha of this present age, arose in Northeastern India at the end the Vedic period, in the 5th century. He studied with at least three Hindu Vedic masters, and became an adept of Vedic and Upanishadic contemplative praxis. Upon his full *bodhi* awakening Buddha became clear as to the ultimate ontological unity of the Two Truths—relative spacetime form, and its ultimate emptiness. He then formulated his early teaching in response to his Hindu Sanatana Dharma previous teaching. He adopted many Vedic terms and some of its teaching, including cause and effect human action or karma, and *ahimsa* (do no harm to living beings), both of which he adapted to his own Buddhadharma teaching.

The epithet "Buddha" (awake) appeared in early Hindu scripture to refer to Vedic deities. Other Buddhist symbols and terms that began in the Hindu Sanatana Dharma include the *dharma chakra* (which appears on the state flag of India), *mudra, rudraksha* or mala prayer beads, mantra, yoga, *dukkha* or suffering, *dhyana* or meditation, *nirvana, moksha, nirodha, klesha, prajna, maitri, chakras, nadis* or energy channels, *tummo* prana energy or *kundalini*, and many more. Buddha's Noble Eightfold Path shares several practice ideals with the Hindu Yoga tradition, and valorizes many Hindu saints who appear in Mahayana and Vajrayana *sadhanas*.

What the Buddha did not accept from the Sanatana dharma was the Hindu theistic Absolute Nirguna Brahman/Parabrahman creator God, nor its permanent, eternal Atman Soul Self as liberators of human suffering. Indeed, as we have seen, utter selflessness or *anatman* was to become, with *shunyata*/emptiness, and dependent arising, his three primary philosophical teaching principles. As to the Buddha's ethics, altruistic *bodhicitta*—the thought, intention, and action for the benefit of living beings—was his primary ethical principal.

The teaching of the Buddha is thoroughly non-theistic. The Vajrayana's Primordial *Adi* Buddha Samantabhadra, Buddha of formless ultimate *dharmakaya* dimension, is according to recent Tibetan *Dzogchen* master Tulku Urygen Rinpoche, a Buddhist *non-theistic, quasi-creator* God.

Buddha frequently references in the sutra texts, Vedic deities and the great Hindu *rishi* masters as buddhadharma protectors. Buddha also repudiated the Hindu caste system, and the denigration of women. Buddha emphasized not belief and faith in his dharma teaching, but the attitude of *ehi-passika*, "come and see". "O monks (and nuns), do not believe what I teach out of respect for me. Come and see for yourselves". Direct knowledge and wisdom (*yogi pratyaksa*), and compassionate *bodhicitta* aspiration and action is emphasized over concept, faith, and belief in the Buddha's teaching.

Although the early Upanishads were extant in the Buddhas time, Hinayana *Pali Canon* texts do not mention them. However, early Buddhist texts do refer to the Brahma deities, and entry into the ultimate dimension of Brahma may result from Buddhist meditation practice. In the *Digha Nikaya* of the *Pali Canon* "union with Brahma" is seen as liberation. Buddha states that a true Hindu Brahmin is not merely defined as one of the highest caste, but a Buddhist *Arhat*, the result of meditation accomplishment.

Still, the Buddha is critical of the notion of Brahman the Absolute as "permanent and eternal". Told the Buddha, "Truly the Baka Brahma is steeped in non-wisdom". The eternal Atman Self that is one with Brahman is replaced by Buddha's *anatman* or no-self, and *anitya*, or impermanence.

In the *Khandha Samyutta* (47) (*Pali Canon*), all concepts, beliefs, and assumptions—conscious or unconscious regarding self (*atman*), and an ego (*ahamkara*)—are reducible to one or more of the five aggregates/*skandhas,* and are thus impermanent (*anitya*), and absent and empty (*shunya*) of any whit of intrinsic ultimate existence (*svabhava*). Indeed, it is persistent ego desire with its deep cultural background assumption of a real permanent self-ego-I that dooms human being to near endless *kalpas* of cyclic existence, precluding awakening/liberation during those intervals of being.

Finally, the Buddha did not accept the overall absolutist philosophical position of the Vedas and the Upanishads ("the end of the Vedas"). That said, nondual Advaita Vedanta of Adi Shankara (8th century CE), who argued against Buddha's *anatman* no-self in favor of the Atman Self, parallels later nondual Buddhist *Dzogchen* teaching to a surprising degree (*Ch. VIII*).

A word on Buddhist hermeneutics or conceptual interpretation, vis-à-vis deeper trans-conceptual, contemplative understanding is here in order. Let's use a pithy example. The justly famous Upanishadic pith, "*Tat Tvam Asi*" (That Thou Art, or That I Am) is refuted in several early Buddhist sutras as affirming a kind of permanent Vedic *Kosmic* Soul Self or Atman "higher self" essence. In the Judaic Christian tradition Jesus the Christ speaks of himself as the "I Am That I Am" Presence of Moses and the Prophets—a parallel view.

However, as we have so often seen in these pages, the truth of the matter so often depends upon the view—exoteric, conceptual, relative; or esoteric, contemplative, ultimate—or perhaps even a middle way. The Buddha's early *Pali Canon* critique of Vedic/Upanishadic ontology and praxis seems generally directed toward a conceptual, relative view of external, exoteric and internal esoteric self-existence—in short, an eternal Atman Self, in one of its deceptive metaphysical cloaks.

Just so, from the innermost esoteric or "innermost secret" nondual view of Buddha's much later subtlest or "highest" teaching—*Dzogchen Ati Yoga*—*Tat Tvam Asi* does not intend a *relative* eternally existing Atman Self at all. Rather, it intends or points to the nondual luminous clear light state of selfless Samantabhadra, *ultimate* Supreme Source (*Kunjed gyalpo*) that is not other than our *buddic* "supreme identity"—bright Presence of That.

Therefore, on the nondual Buddhist view, the subtle referent of "*Tat*-That" in *Tat Tvam Asi* is not a self but the utterly selfless (*anatman*) nondual Buddha nature of mind—*tathata, tathagatagarbha*—perfectly subjective Buddha mind (*buddhajnana*) Presence (*vidya, rigpa*) of the vast expanse of boundless whole itself, primordial emptiness ground of *Perfect Sphere of Dzogchen*, wholly beyond our conceptually imputed ideas *about* any of it. This of course is the contemplative, trans-conceptual, nonlocal, nondual ultimate view—"gone utterly beyond" (*parasamgate*) our concepts and beliefs *about* self and phenomena. This selfless "I Am" Presence is experienced directly (*yogi pratyaksa*), just as it is, prior to conceptualizing it. (*Dzogchen Ch. VIII*)

It's wise and good to remain closely connected and cognitively present to our all-embracing, always already present nondual primordial wisdom mind (*jnana, yeshe*) as we presume to critique non-Buddhist views; and as we conceptually elaborate the Buddha's prodigious teaching, both relative and ultimate.

We are so habituated to common conceptual thinking about our appearing realities that we tend to conflate discursive thoughts with subtler, trans-conceptual, contemplative, even nondual modes of human cognition, unwittingly reducing such clarity to less inclusive perceiving and thinking cognitive modes. This higher human functioning remains an "undiscovered land", until we come to know it through non-conceptual contemplative practice, and selfless *bodhicitta*—the open secret of human happiness. That was Gautama the Buddha's great gift to all of us.

From the *Majjhima Nikaya sutta*: "The wise do not come to the conclusion: This alone is Truth, and everything else is false". Elsewhere Buddha says, "To attach to one view, and belittle other views as inferior is not wisdom". Good to know when deciding which views are "definitive", and which views we find inferior.

Thus did Gautama the Buddha teach in these "two ways at once"—exoteric relative, and esoteric ultimate—depending upon the capacity of his listener. We are well advised to consider this pragmatic relative truth when engaging the greater, subtler dimensions of his teaching.

As to meditation and liberation, Buddha enhanced the centuries old practices of the Upanishads and Vedas with the practice of mindful *shamatha* (*sati*), calm abiding. In the Vedic tradition the Hindu sage is finally liberated, after a life of meditation, at death. In Buddhism the sage is liberated through the contemplative, compassionate life that he or she lives well. The Hindu Brahminic sage enters nondual *moksha/nirvana*/liberation at death. The Buddhist sage enters nondual *nirvanic* liberation during life. That said, let's engage the Buddhist philosophical systems.

The Four Buddhist Tenet Systems. Khenpo Tsultrim Gyamtso Rinpoche (2001) teaches that Gautama the Buddha's foundational Two Truths—relative and ultimate—are best understood through the Three Teaching Vehicles (*yanas*), in the context of the Four Tenet Systems.

In brief, the three vehicles include the foundational Hinayana (Indian *Pali Canon*), the Indian Mahayana, and the Tibetan Vajrayana (Secret Mantra or Mantrayana) teaching vehicles. The Hinayana is the very Buddhist *teaching foundation* of all that was to come. It is decidedly not a "lesser vehicle".

Longchen Rabjam (Longchenpa), in his *Precious Treasury of Philosophical Systems*, most authoritatively articulates and critiques in great detail all four of the Buddhist tenet systems, and as well the five pre-Buddhist, and non-Buddhist Indian "spiritual approaches" that are founded in the Vedic Hindu Samkhya system. These include the Metaphysical Realism of Samkhya, Shaivite, Vishnavite, and Jain, and the Metaphysical Nihilism of Barhaspatya.

The main difference between non-Buddhist views and Buddhist views is the former's assertion of a truly existing individual self-ego-I. Buddhists posit the *relative* existence of a relative self acting in the world to benefit living beings, but deny that this self possesses any intrinsic *ultimate* existence. All four Buddhist philosophical systems share this view of *anatman,* the no-self of the individual. For 14th century *Dzogchen* Master Longchenpa:

> A Buddhist is someone who holds the Three Jewels as sacred sources of refuge (both causal and fruitional refuge), and accepts the four axioms that define Buddhist doctrine... (these are) Everything compounded is impermanent; everything that is corruptible produces suffering; all phenomena are empty (selfless) and have no independent nature; and nirvana is the state of peace...My extensive analysis of (Buddhist) approaches has two parts: the cause-based dialectical (Mahayana) approaches, and the fruition-based secret mantra (Vajrayana) approach.
>
> (*Precious Treasury of Philosophical Systems*, trans. Richard Barron, Padma Publishing, 2007, p. 66)

The Four Buddhist Tenet Systems include 1) Indian Vaibhasika; 2) Sautrantika (Sutra), both included in the Hinayana teaching vehicle; 3) Indian Mahayana Chittamatra (Mind Only); and 4) Tibetan Middle Way Madhyamaka with its *Rangtong* and *Shentong* dialectics. So, tenet three belongs to the Mahayana teaching vehicle; tenet four to the Tibetan Vajrayana teaching vehicle.

All Four Buddhist Tenet systems share the foundational teaching of the Buddha as to *anatman* or selflessness/no-self; and the Four Noble Truths. Differences in interpretation arise as to the nature of *shunyata*/emptiness, and of our luminous clear light Buddha nature. What is the relationship of emptiness and Buddha nature? How does appearing reality *ultimately* exist? How does *shunyata*/emptiness itself exist? For Hinayana, Tenet 1)—Vaibhasika, and tenet 2) Sautrantika/Sutra—external objective reality truly exists. Spacetime stuff is ultimately real.

For Mahayana, Tenet 3)—Chittamatra, and Tibetan tenet 4) Middle Way Madhyamaka—appearing objective reality is utterly absent and empty of any whit of *ultimate* existence, though it does exist *relatively*, nominally, and conventionally. So we still have to show up for work, and be kind to living beings.

It is generally agreed among the Three Vehicles that the Hinayana represents the First Turning of Buddha's Dharma Wheel (*dharmachakra*), at the Deer Park in Sarnath; the Mahayana the Second Turning, at Vulture Peak; and the Tibetan Vajrayana with its Buddha nature, the Third Turning (*Ch. II*).

Now, each of these Four Tenet Systems has important sub-schools. A bit more detail shall aid our relative conceptual, and even our ultimate understanding.

1. **Vaibhashika.** The first of the Four Buddhist Tenet Systems, Vaibhasika (Sarvastivada), known as the Great Exposition or the Particularist school, includes the Hinayana Shravakayana, the Vehicle of the Listeners/Hearers and the Hinayana Pretyekabuddhayana, the Vehicle of the Solitary Buddhas who accomplish their Buddha gnosis "outside" the formal Shravakayana context.

Historically, Hinayana Vaibhashika had 18 sub-schools. The only one now extant is Theravada, active throughout Southeast Asia; and alive and well in the United States as the Thai Forest Tradition, located in Escondido California. Theravada is Buddha's oldest teaching vehicle. Theravadins have preserved their great tradition in the ancient 1st century Indian *Pali Canon*.

Vaibhashika follows Vasubandu's *Abidharmakosha*. Their understanding of the Buddha's Two Truths is this: because both arising physical phenomena and the mental phenomena of mind are reducible to their constituent parts, they are relatively existent, but not ultimately existent. Well, what *is* ultimately existent? It is the fundamental atomic "partless particles" of matter that cannot be further divided.

As for mind, the real consists of the most minute indivisible *present* moment of mind, prior even to attentional/perceptual cognition. Past and future don't exist. The past is gone, but a present memory. The future has not yet arisen, but a present anticipation. Even this present instant is to brief to grasp, already "gone beyond". So, in Vaibhashika, and in *Dzogchen* we abide in the spacious emptiness of the Buddha nature of mind, "gone utterly beyond" (*parasamgate*) our relative names, concepts, and beliefs about it. We rest in the selfless, nameless, formless (*namarupa*) cognizant bright Buddha Presence of That. That is the nonlocal, nondual moment to moment non-meditation that pervades the Buddha's teaching tenet systems, from Vaibhashika to *Dzogchen*.

Vaibhashika reductionist "partless particles" maps nicely, if imperfectly, onto the 20th century scientific materialist view that is "scientific reductionism"—eternal subatomic quarks and leptons (*Appendix B*). With the advent and growth of non-objectivist quantum mechanics this old orthodoxy has evolved, and our Western physics and cosmology have matured. Yet, this waning reductionist, materialist view of Scientific Materialism still colonizes Western mind and culture.

Just so, the first three Buddhist Tenet Systems have evolved, over the course of 25 centuries, into Middle Way Madhyamaka—the Tibetan Vajrayana foundation of the teaching pinnacle that is *Dzogchen* and Essence *Mahamudra*.

Longchenpa's "Refutation of the Vaibhashika Position":

> Vaibhashika "cannot be defended as correct for three reasons: the assertion that minute particles are ultimately real entities is untenable; the assertion that mind and mental states do not involve reflexive consciousness is untenable; and this system's position on distinct formative factors is untenable. (Longchenpa *Ibid.* 73)

2. **Sutra/Sautrantika.** There are two Hinayana sutra sub-schools—Followers of Scripture (Vasubandu's *Abhidharmakosha*), and Followers of Reasoning (Dharmakirti's *Seven*

Treatises on Valid Cognition). Sutra school views Buddha's Two Truths as constituting the conventional reality of Relative Truth (*samvriti satya, kunzog denpa*), and the authentic reality of Ultimate Truth (*paramartha satya, don dam denpa*). Roughly, conceptual abstractions are mere relative truths absent and empty of true or ultimate existence. So, only appearing unique and independent *particular* objects that actually "perform a function" truly, ultimately exist.

For example, recall for a moment the beautiful bouquet of red roses that sits now on your dining room table. Then walk to the dining room and see, touch and smell the bouquet. What is the difference? Your memory of the bouquet is an example of an abstract universal. A "universal" is what "particular" things have in common, their qualities or characteristics. Universals are conceptual abstractions or abstract entities that may be exemplified and instantiated by an indefinite number of particular concrete things. Our memory of the roses on the dining room table, and all the roses of the three times share the *universal* that is "roseness". But only the *particular* roses on the dining room table perform the particular rose functions of aroma, redness, and being here now as *this* lovely bouquet of red roses.

So for Sutra/Sautrantika, abstract universals have no *ultimate* existence. It is only the present concrete functioning particulars that really exist. Thus, for Sutra, appearing particular objective spacetime phenomena ultimately exist! Universals are abstract conceptually reified imputations that are empty of any ultimate existence. Nonetheless, on the accord of Sautrantika, the primordially existent basis or ground in which, or in whom all this imputed spacetime stuff arises is, by its very nondual nature inherently free of them. So, paradoxically it ultimately exists. (This is paradoxical to concept mind, but not to Buddha mind.)

And this apparent inconsistency introduces the ancient atavistic, inherently vexing philosophical "problem of universals". Any relative deliberation about universals and particulars must confront this thorny problem. For example, what is the ontic status of such Buddhist universals as Buddha nature, *dharmakaya, dharmadhatu,* primordial *Adi Buddha* Samantabhadra, and the rest? In Buddhist ontology the resolution arises in the context and interpretation of the Two Truths—relative and ultimate—dominant trope.

Longchenpa's "Refutation of the Sautrantika Position". He lists six reasons for Sautrantika's untenability. These six refute the main assertions that:

> external objects are ultimately real...that obvious forms of matter that manifest have the same nature as consciousness...it cannot be proved that there are objects that present sense data. (*Ibid.* 77)

This Sutra/Sautrantika view will evolve to ever greater clarity and acuity as we progress through the next two tenet systems, namely 3) Chittamatra (Mind Only), and 4) the centrist Madhyamaka or Middle Way of Yogachara Madhyamaka, and of Prasangika Madhyamaka ontologies and epistemologies. (Ontology is concepts about the ultimate nature of *being/ontos*); and epistemology is concepts about how we arrive at this ultimate *knowledge/episteme*).

3. **Chittamatra.** The Mahayana Chittamatra or Mind Only Buddhist tenet system also has two important sub-schools: Followers of Scripture, following Asanga's *Five Treatises on the Grounds*; and the Followers of Reasoning, who follow Dharmakirti's *Seven Treatises on Valid Cognition*.

Broadly construed, as to the Buddha's Two Truths, our first two Buddhist tenet systems, Hinayana Vaibhasika and Sutra/ Sautrantika affirm the objective existence of appearing external objects, as we have seen. Spacetime stuff is inherently (*sahaja*) real and existent. For our third and fourth tenet systems— Chittamatra and Madhyamaka—such phenomena are inherently illusory and ultimately non-existent, wholly absent and empty (*shunya*) of ultimate existence, while still displaying to mind as a relatively and conventionally real self-ego-I, with its myriad interdependent phenomenal arising. Twenty-five centuries of Buddhist dialectical philosophy has proven to be relentlessly dynamical, to say the least.

All four of the Buddhist tenet systems agree on The Conduct—compassionate *bodhicitta*. But with the advent of the Mahayana tenet systems—Chittamatra and Middle Way Madhyamaka (Yogachara and Prasangika)—extreme differences began to arise as to the philosophical View of the Buddha's Two Truths.

"Chittamatrins hold that all that is knowable is subsumed under three headings: imputation, dependence, and the absolute" (Longchenpa). These constitute the Chittamatra Fourfold Nature of reality itself. There are five bases of knowledge: the bases of form, mind, mental states, situational "paradigms" which are variations on these three, and uncompounded phenomena. These five are expressed differently by the two Chittamatra sub-schools: those who consider consciousness to entail sense data (*hyle*), and those who deny sense data (*Ibid.* 87).

The mentalist, metaphysical idealist Chittamatra view, founded in the 4th century by Asanga and Vasubandu, is philosophically a Metaphysical Absolute Idealism. What is this extreme counter-intuitive view? From Jamgon Kongtrul Lodro Thaye, (*Treasury of Knowledge*):

> Perceived objects and perceiving subjects are mere appearance. Consciousness that is self-aware and empty of duality is genuine. This is the presentation of the Mind Only school.

Appearances are always deceptive, arising through the *process* of our habitual perceiving and thinking patterns. Through such valid reasoning cognition (*anumana pramana*) Chittamatra has established that the objects of objective reality do not ultimately exist; therefore perceiving subjects cannot ultimately exist.

Reality—perceived object and perceiving subject—is absent and empty of either objective or subjective inherent existence. While the pernicious subject-object split is alive and well in the real world of Relative Truth, in the purity of the ultimate view it is illusory. So, we are well advised to stay present to the nondual view of Ultimate Truth and live in the prior perfectly subjective unity of all these diaphanous objects of our appearing, not so real RWOT (real world out there).

Therefore, for Chittamatra, only "self-aware", subject-object empty, nondual mind exists. All relative, dualistically appearing perceiving subjects, and their perceived objects, are but appearances in/of mind, with no genuine inherent or ultimate existence at all. Only "mind consciousness" itself that is self-aware and empty of the duality of perceiving subject and its perceived object is ultimately existent and genuinely real.

We shall see in a moment that for Tibetan Middle Way Madhyamaka Prasangika "self aware mind consciousness" may not be so easily established by relative conceptual cognition.

In Chittamatra appearing reality exists relatively, but as mind only. Mind Only ultimately exists. Things and their perceiving subjects/selves exist not as subjects and their objects, but as a singular mental knowing *process*. Beyond this "self aware" Mind there exists no other reality.

Furthermore, illusory appearing reality arises and manifests from the formless dimension of the *alaya-vijnana*, the all-ground or "storehouse consciousness" (*akasha*) in which Chittamatra's Eight Consciousnesses are collected.

Whereas Sutra/Sautrantika sees arising phenomena of the Eight Consciousnesses as perceptual valid cognition (*pramana*), Chittamatra sees nothing outside the mind. Common sense naive realism, derived as it is from the sense consciousnesses, is deceived, invalid cognition.

Thus does Chittamatra divide all phenomena into the *Threefold Nature* or the *Three Natures*: *conceptual-imputed*, *dependent*, and absolute or *perfect-ultimate*. The conceptually imputed nature, and the dependent nature comprise the deceptive dimension of Buddha's Relative Truth whose essential nature is nothing less than the naturally luminous and perfectly established "perfect-ultimate nature"—*shunyata*/emptiness, the Buddha's Ultimate Truth, nondual Buddha nature (*tathagatagarbha*, *tathata*/thatness/suchness). Contemplative realization of the Mind Only perfect-ultimate nature is the full *bodhi* wisdom mind of liberation and enlightenment.

We shall see next that Chittamatra or Mind Only is the foundational metaphysical tenet for the Metaphysical Idealism of the Yogachara Madhyamaka third tenet system.

Longchenpa's "Refutation of the Chittamatra Position" (Longchenpa *op. cit.* 98). Both Chittamatra schools affirm 1) nondual consciousness is ultimately existent—there is no perception of a split between an object perceived and a perceiving subject; and 2) the appearance of raw sense data is either authentic, or it is false. However, both of these views demonstrate invalid cognition:

> There is a fundamental contradiction in there being two factors—something to be conscious of and something conscious of it—in a single moment of a single cognitive act; it is also impossible for consciousness to be reflexive... just as a sword is unable to cut itself... consciousness is unable...to be conscious of itself. (Longchenpa *op.cit.* 98)

Mahayana meditation (Chittamatra, Madhyamaka) begins with taking refuge in the Three Jewels, and arousing the wondrous altruistic *bodhicitta*—thought, intention, and action/conduct for the benefit of living beings.

So here and now, settle in to your mindful breath. Become pre-dialectally aware, just prior to any "single moment of a single cognitive act", non-conceptually, *directly*, meta-cognitively, reflexively aware of your present awareness—whatever arises from the outside, and from the inside. Notice that none of it has any solid existence. Observe the fluent, spacious emptiness of the whole shebang. Without thinking about it, open your heart and mind to the potential understanding that this absence or emptiness of the ultimate existence of the stuff of reality is the actual truth of the matter. Rest in That. Let it be as it is, without thinking about it. Feel That.

As conceptual thinking or feeling distractions naturally arise, label it all "distraction" and release it on the out breath; or let it drift by on the vast empty sky, like a cloud, leaving no trace. Return to the breath, again and again. Now, observe that your outer world and your inner world are only luminous empty mind. Directly experience That.

Stop reading and thinking and go ahead and do it now for two or three minutes, or more. Thus will you understand, and feel the still peace of Mahayana nondual luminous emptiness that is your actual Buddha nature, the very nature of mind, mostly beyond awareness of a perceiving subject observing a carnival-like display of separate objects.

That is nondual, perfectly subjective primordial awareness-consciousness itself that pervades all four of the Buddhist tenet systems. Bright *buddic* Presence of That (*tathata*). Such nondual *direct* yogic perception (*yogi pratyaksa*) abides beyond, or cognitively prior to Buddhist conceptual dialectics, or any other conceptual processing (*Appendix A*). What a relief it is. *Emaho!*

4. **Madhyamaka.** "The second major Mahayana tradition, the Madhyamaka, is the most sublimely profound secret found in the teaching of the Sage" (Longchenpa *Ibid.* 99).

This system acknowledges the five bases of the knowable, but these are subsumed within the two levels of truth (Buddha's Two Truths); therefore, the Madhyamikas say that all phenomena inherently lack any finite essence (*Ibid.* 99).

The Mahayana/Vajrayana Middle Way Madhyamaka's ontological reach extends even beyond that of mentalist Chittamatra, who have established that only "self-aware" consciousness—Mind Only—ultimately exists. For Madhyamaka, especially the *Rangtong* of Prasangika Madhyamaka, not even the entity, or process of a personal, or even a universal self-aware mind consciousness ultimately exists. Lustrous exemplars of this view are Rangtongpas Chandrakirti (*Madhyamakavatara*) and Shantideva (*Bodhicharyavatara*). For nondual self-aware, self-arising ultimate primordial wisdom (*yeshe*) of the luminous awareness-consciousness base or "groundless ground" (*gzhi rigpa*) we must refer to the nondual view of *Dzogchen*, or to the view of Essence *Mahamudra* (*Ch. VIII*).

Thus it is, all phenomena, outer objective, and inner subjective are essenceless, absent and empty of intrinsic or ultimate existence—nothing more nor less than the adventitious coalescence of utterly impermanent, interdependent relative-conventional causes and conditions (the effects of prior causes). This process is the Buddha's interdependent arising (*pratitya samutpada*), wholly free of, and transcendent to any Hindu or Judaic-Christian theistic First Cause, or Creator God.

The Buddha's Two Truths in Middle Way Madhyamaka. Nagarjuna (d. 55 AD) teaches that:

> The Dharma taught by the buddhas
> Depends entirely on two levels of truth:
> The relative truth of the world,
> And the truth that has ultimate meaning.

Longchenpa: "The knowable that manifests in myriad ways to a confused mind constitutes what is relative, whereas that which abides beyond any description, imagination, or expression whatsoever is classified as what is ultimate". Moreover, Relative Truth is twofold: "objects of flawed faculties, and objects of flawless faculties". The flawless faculties of all the buddhas do indeed experience relative spacetime reality flawlessly, as empty of any inherent existence.

> The Prasangikas hold that the nature of the levels themselves, being emptiness, is beyond analysis. Emptiness is the basic space in which things manifest... If analysis were to conclude that these 'two levels of truth' are separate from one another, it would be mistaken. (Longchenpa *op. cit.* 116-117)

Thus are the Two Truths of the Buddha's teaching a prior and present perfect nondual unity, *one truth,* invariant through all human cognitive states—direct attention-perception; objective concept-belief; subjective meditation; and perfectly subjective nondual *buddic* luminosity.

> These two levels of truth can be validated by logic. It is logical that *dharmadhatu,* the basic space of phenomena, the ultimate level of truth is freedom from conceptual elaboration, because it is not the province of ordinary consciousness, which entails conceptual frameworks. (Ultimate Truth) is realized through nondual timeless awareness, in a way that involves no such elaboration (*Ibid.*)

How do we "put this understanding into practice"? While recognizing the wisdom of *shunyata*/emptiness, and arousing *bodhicitta,* the heartmind of enlightenment, the bodhisattva arises from nondual meditation and engages thought, intention, and action for the benefit of living beings in "post-meditation" relative conventional conduct. Thus are the Buddha's sublime philosophy, and the skillful means of ethical practice that arise there from, a lifeworld unity. Thus "one will finally attain the two sacred kayas of buddhahood: dharmakaya and rupakaya". This prior unity of primordial wisdom and compassion are the two limbs of the Buddha's sublime nondual teaching.

So here, "The ground aspect of Madhyamaka is subsumed within the two levels of truth; the path aspect, within twofold spiritual development; and the fruition aspect, within the two kayas" (*ibid.* 120). And this is the open secret of human happiness. *Mahasukaho!* Therefore, arise from your meditation and do some good. It will make you happy.

The Buddha's Two Truths in Middle Way Madhyamaka "are assigned on the basis of the mind of an ordinary person in the world". As our ordinary mind begins to understand the prodigious logic of the non-conceptual dimension—the absence of any independent nature or self-existence—this understanding becomes the "basis for the classification" of the Two Truths, relative (*samvriti satya*), and ultimate (*paramartha satya*). From Chandrakirti's *The Entrance to the Middle Way*:

> Because neither of the two levels of truth has an independent nature, they are neither permanent entities nor nihilistic voids.

For Longchenpa, Relative Truth (*kunzog denpa*) may be characterized as the relative experiential data of the "six consciousnesses" and their *skandhas* as they perceive, impute, conceive, and reify their inherently illusory objects. Ultimate Truth (*don dampa*) is characterized on the basis of *dharmadhatu*, the ultimate unbounded whole of the basic space (*ying*) of all appearing relative, conventional phenomena that arise within it, and are instantiated in time and space through it. The vast expanse of this nameless, selfless, timeless boundless nondual ultimate whole embraces and subsumes its relative parts in a perfectly subjective unity—beyond name, concept, and belief.

So yes, Relative Truth manifests as the deceptive, dualistic "concealer truths" of conceptual imputation, elaboration, and reification of the raw data of the six consciousnesses. "All the phenomena of samsara (ordinary mind and mental states...) are relative" (Longchenpa). In the clear words of Chandrakirti:

Ignorance obscures the true nature of phenomena and therefore falsifies everything. Any of its fabrications, which seem to be true, were said by the Sage to be (only) "relatively true". (Chandrakirti *Ibid.*)

Longchenpa on Ultimate Truth:

As to what characterizes ultimate truth, it is in essence a freedom from dualistic elaboration...In that it cannot be realized by means of verbal descriptions and the like, it cannot be understood by means of anything other that itself. It is beyond concepts, for the sullying factors of ordinary mind and mental states subside within the basic space of phenomena. It is free of all conceptual elaboration, and it is impervious to any system of tenets...Even the middle way, free of conceptual elaboration, cannot be established... In brief, nirvana is a state of profundity and peace; it is basic space, completely pure by nature, and it is the mind, free of all obscuration, that realizes this space—the timeless awareness of buddhahood, to which this completely pure field manifests without change...the state of meditative equipoise, as well as those post-meditation experiences of profound insight that are essentially identical to that state. All of these constitute what is ultimately true (Longchenpa *op.cit.* 117).

As you may have suspected, Madhyamaka has two main sub-schools; "two major branches". These are the Yogachara Svatantrika (Yogic Autonomy school; *Shentong*), and the Prasangika (Middle Way Consequence school; *Rangtong*). Of these two "highest" Madhyamaka branches, "The Prasangika system expounds the very highest view of all the cause-based dialectical approaches" (*ibid.* p.126). (Madhyamaka is the Buddhist Middle Way teaching of the Madhyamikas who follow it.)

Recall from our "*Rangtong* and *Shentong*" discussion in this chapter, *Rangtong* is "emptiness of self", or intrinsic emptiness, and *Shentong* is "emptiness of other", or extrinsic emptiness.

Prasangika *Rangtong* explains *shunyata*/emptiness as a "non-affirming negative"; the negation of self, and of "other" phenomena perceived by a self. This apparitional face of phenomenal reality is *dharmin* (Tib. *cho can*).

Yogachara *Shentong* utilizes an *affirming* negation; emptiness is more than a negative void. Indeed, emptiness is—after the radical *Rangtong* Prasangika transcendental emptiness reduction—the remaining clear light luminosity of nondual primordial wisdom (*jnana, yeshe*) that is none other than our Buddha nature/Buddha mind (*buddhajnana*) itself; innate Buddha gnosis of pristine *buddic* cognition of sameness (*samatajnana, nyam nyid yeshe*). So many words and concepts for That that is empty of words and concepts!

We discovered in the *Shentong* view that the seed of *Dzogchen*, ultimate primordial wisdom (*jnana,yeshe*) "primordial purity" (*kadag*) of the *dharmakaya* base/ground (*gzhi rigpa*) is empty of any *relative* appearing reality—empty of anything "other" than itself—but not empty of its own "spontaneous presence" (*lhundrub*)—the very Buddha nature/Buddha essence of mind. Primordial *Adi Buddha* Samantabhadra/Vajradhara—selfless innermost bright Presence of That.

In *Rangtong*, "intrinsic emptiness of self", we meditate upon the utter absence of self-ego-I— on *dharmadhatu*, selfless, boundless primordial whole, free of conceptual fabrication. In *Shentong*, "extrinsic emptiness of other", we meditate on what is "other" than oneself, *all* phenomena—emptiness of self and emptiness of a self appearing through the matrix of all arising spacetime phenomenal reality. For *Shentong*, the Buddha's *shunyata*/emptiness is pervaded by ultimate *tathagatagarbha/sugatagarbha*—Buddha nature—the unity of luminous clarity and emptiness. These two share a metaphysical relation of identity—two faces of one nonlocal, nondual *buddic* principle.

In both *Rangtong* and *Shentong* contemplative depth of understanding of nondual emptiness evolves through dualistic and nondual practice until even the subtlest concepts of emptiness and Buddha nature Presence are surrendered to the formless ultimate—direct, nondual (*advaya*, "not one, not two") clear light luminosity—the union of luminosity and emptiness.

From the view of Ultimate Truth, in the Hinayana or First Turning of Buddha's Wheel of Dharma, the ultimate is selfless *shunyata*/emptiness. In the Mahayana Second Turning it is emptiness of both self and all "other" phenomena appearing to a self that is entirely free of compounded complexity and conceptual fabrication and elaboration. In the Vajrayana/Secret Mantra Third Turning of the Wheel the nondual ultimate nature of mind is the clear light luminosity of Buddha Nature (*tathagatagarbha*)—in the *Ati Yoga* of the Great Perfection— the *Perfect Sphere of Dzogchen*.

That said, nondual *Dzogchen* transcends, yet embraces all philosophical views, semiotics, concepts, and beliefs. Just so, *Dzogchen* may express and manifest through *Shentong* or *Rangtong*; or through any tenet system view, or path, or bodhisattva conduct (*Ch. VIII*).

Since the advent of the 19th century Vajrayana ecumenical *Rimé* movement, many lamas have told that we require *both* the *Rangtong* and the *Shentong* views. We come to understand the emptiness of intrinsic existence of appearing reality through *Rangtong*; and the luminosity of our indwelling Buddha nature through *Shentong*. The radiant cognizance of the appearing phenomenal world, with the bright luminous clarity of its perfect emptiness—always already a present unity.

Shentong lamas sometimes view *Rangtong* as a practice bridge to *Shentong*. We begin by understanding *Rangtong* selflessness (*anatman*), the no-self of all phenomena; then may we fully understand and realize the *Shentong* luminous Buddha nature of mind.

We shall now very briefly review the two seminal Buddhist Middle Way Madhyamaka tenet systems, Yogachara and Prasangika, in terms of their ontology—what *ultimately* exists.

The three approaches to the Buddha's *Path*—Hinayana Shravaka, Pretyekabuddha, and Mahayana Bodhisattva—as practiced within the four tenet systems exceeds the scope of our present exploration of Buddhist philosophy. We obliquely engaged the Path under the rubric "Buddhist Ethics" in Chapter IV. However, the Path is definitively presented by *Dzogchen* master Longchenpa in Richard Barron's excellent translation (*Op. Cit.* Longchenpa 2007).

This next bit of Buddhist dialectics is wondrously intriguing; and by its very nature quite complex. It shall require a bit of patience—the third of the Six *Paramitas*/Perfections of the Mahayana. The philosophically squeamish may wish to skip it altogether.

Tibetan Buddhist Vajrayana Middle Way Madhyamaka, the 4th Buddhist tenet system, is divided into two sub-schools, as we have just seen. These are the Svatantrika (Autonomy) school which itself has two sub-schools, Yogachara Svatantrika Madhyamaka (Yogic Autonomy) of Asanga, Vasubandu, Bhavaviveka, Shantirakshita; and the Sautrantika Svatantrika Madhyamaka (Sutra Autonomy) school. "Autonomy" here means the autonomous existence of "valid cognition" (*pramana*) arguments which ostensibly prove their metaphysical assertions.

The Metaphysical Idealism of Yogachara Madhyamaka views objective reality in the mode of Chittamatra/Mind Only (the third tenet system), with no relative nor ultimate existence at all. Yet, on the basis of Mind Only stuff does indeed exist, but only as mental processing, as ideas in the mind. Sautrantika Svatantrika views relative reality in the manner of Sutra Sautrantika (the 2nd tenet system)—objective reality really exists—not as conceptually abstract universals—but as concrete particulars.

The other Madhyamaka school is Prasangika, the Middle Way Consequence school of Nagarjuna, Buddhapalita, Chandrakirti, and Tsongkhapa. So, the two main sub-schools of Middle Way Madhyamaka are: Svatantrika (with its two schools), and Prasangika. Well and good.

Both Prasangika Madhyamaka and Yogachara Svatantrika Madhyamaka are concerned to address the teaching in the Buddha's Second Turning of the Wheel of Dharma, to wit, no-self/ *anatman*, and emptiness/*shunyata* (*Ch. II*). We have seen that the *Rangtong-Shentong* deliberation—with polemical antecedents in earlier Sutrayana—is wholly a Tibetan invention; and thus extends our concern to the Third Turning, the ontological status of Buddha nature, and of the luminous clear light primordial wisdom gnosis (*jnana, yeshe*).

Both Yogachara and Prasangika assert that the objects of the domain of Relative Truth are absent and empty of any Ultimate Truth reality. The ultimate nature of relatively appearing reality is *shunyata*/emptiness, beyond our reifying conceptual imputations. This of course is a conceptual assertion. But it is an "enumerated" or provisional and approximate assertion about ultimate truth. For Madhyamaka, the "unenumerated" Ultimate Truth is the ultimate reality that is, when no one is thinking, or talking about it.

Prasangika Madhyamaka, the Middle Way Consequence school is, as we've seen, the venerated tradition of Nagarjuna, Aryadeva, Buddhapalita, Chandrakirti, and Shantideva. Prasangika Madhyamaka was founded by 5th century Buddhapalita upon Nagarjuna's (d. 55 AD) proto-Prasangika teaching in his lapidary *Fundamental Wisdom of the Middle Way* (*Mulamadhyamakakarika*). Jamgon Kongtrul Lodro Thaye explains Prasangika thusly:

> Apparent reality is whatever mind imagines. It is asserted following relative worldly tradition. Genuine ultimate reality is inexpressible and inconceivable. This is the middle way consequence school's tradition (*Treasury of Knowledge*).

We've seen in some detail above in "The Middle Way" that Prasangika means "using the consequences" of "making no assertions" (or negations) as to the ultimate nature of reality itself; refraining from attaching to or defending any conceptual position regarding the existence or nonexistence of appearing phenomena. Why? Because ultimate reality is beyond any and all conceptual cognitive processing. Yet, relative spacetime reality grasped by the conceptual intellect has profound relative, conventional value. After all, this is the dimension in which we *choose* to practice the buddhadharma, and the ethical precepts of precious *bodhicitta* conduct.

Thus does Prasangika tread a fine "middle path" between the Buddha's Two Truths—relative and ultimate. We accomplish the nondual Ultimate Truth of liberation through the dualistic Relative Truth of the Path. We practice these two as the prior and present wisdom unity that they always already are. "Practice these two as a unity" (Padmasambhava).

Moreover, Prasangika avoids the metaphysical extremes of eternalist, substantialist Materialism; and of nihilistic Absolute Idealism. Nagarjuna told it well (*Mulamadhyamakakarika*):

Existence is the view of realism. Nonexistence is the view of nihilism. Therefore the wise abide neither in existence nor nonexistence...Those who assert neither existence nor nonexistence are refuted by no one.

Because all physical and mental phenomena arise in dependence upon interdependent causes and conditions (*pratitya samutpada*) they have no intrinsic existence from their own side, and are thus absent and empty (*shunya*) of self-existence (*svabhava*)—empty of self (*anatman*), and empty of ultimate existence; though once again, apparitional appearing phenomena do indeed possess a nominal, conceptually imputed relative-conventional existence. How else could we practice dharma? This is the middle way between the metaphysical extremes of absolute existence (Materialism), and absolute nonexistence (Idealism).

For Madhyamaka, ultimate reality embraces and subsumes relative reality, beyond our concepts about existence and non-existence. Thus is the ontic prior, and epistemic present unity of the Buddha's Two Truths this *one truth*, invariant throughout our entire human cognitive processional—perceptual, conceptual, contemplative, and perfectly subjective nondual.

The contemplative, meditative realization of ultimate emptiness/*dharmakaya* is the full *bodhi* of liberation, enlightenment, and Buddhahood. How do we accomplish this? Assiduous practice of the Path under the enlightened guidance of the master, of course.

This moment to moment continuity of our *relative* practice is an always present awareness portal into the already present *ultimate* Buddha love-wisdom mind Presence that we are now.

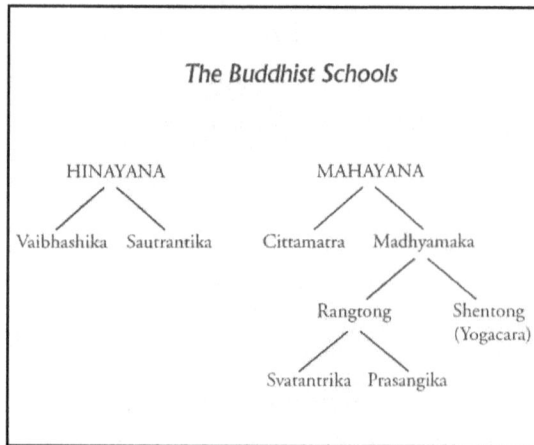

The Buddhist Schools

```
         HINAYANA                        MAHAYANA
          /    \                          /     \
Vaibhashika   Sautrantika      Cittamatra    Madhyamaka
                                              /     \
                                        Rangtong     Shentong
                                                     (Yogacara)
                                         /    \
                               Svatantrika   Prasangika
```

This concludes our exploration of Buddhist philosophy.

The Fundamental Two Truths: Relative Form, Ultimate Emptiness

Truth is one. Many are its names.

—*Rig Veda*

Because neither of the two truths has an independent nature, they are neither permanent entities, nor nihilistic voids.

—Longchenpa

Gautama Buddha told of the nondual indivisible unity that is the profound dialectic of the fundamental Two Truths of all arising reality—form or conventional Relative Truth, and all embracing Ultimate Truth, *buddic* boundless emptiness itself. These two reality dimensions are our two ways of being here—the singular one truth of the unbounded whole that is reality being itself.

In his lapidary, nondual (*advaya*) *Heart of Wisdom Sutra* (*Prajnaparamitahrdaya*), the spirit of the Buddha speaks on the *perfection of wisdom* through noble Avalokiteshvara, the great bodhisattva mahasattva:

> Form is empty (*shunya, stongpa*);
> emptiness (*shunyata, stongpa nyi*) is form.
> Form is not other than emptiness;
> Emptiness is not other than form...
> Thus all dharmas are emptiness.
> There are no characteristics.

There is no birth (being) and no
cessation (non-being). There is no
purity and no impurity. There is no
decrease and no increase. Therefore,
in emptiness there is no form, no feeling,
no perception, no formation, no consciousness...
no suffering, no origin of suffering, no
cessation of suffering, no path, no wisdom,
no attainment, and no non-attainment.
Therefore, the bodhisattvas abide by means
of *prajnaparamita.* Since there is no obscuration
of mind, there is no fear. They transcend
falsity and attain complete awakening. All the
buddhas of the three times, by means of
prajnaparamita, fully awaken to unsurpassable
true, complete enlightenment. Therefore the
great mantra that calms all suffering should be
known as truth, since there is no deception:
OM GATE GATE PARAGATE
PARASAMGATE BODHISVAHA
(Gone, gone, gone utterly beyond to the perfect
wisdom. So be it.) Practice the profound
prajnaparamita and all the *tathagatas* will rejoice.

Thus is the Mahayana *Prajnaparamita* the perfection of the wisdom
of emptiness—vast primordial whole, basic space of *dharmadhatu.*
This numinous, luminous nondual wisdom Heart is mother of all
the Buddhas of the three times—past, present, and future. "And
the child knows the mother". *Prajnaparamita,* the perfection of
wisdom, is the foundation of Buddhist Middle Way Prasangika
Madhyamaka, which is the foundation, on the accord of H.H.
Dalai Lama, of *Dzogchen* View and praxis.

Nyingma *Dzogchen* Master *rigdzin* Jigme Lingpa (1730-1798)
essentialized omniscient Longchenpa's (1308-1364) profound
Heart Essence of the Vast Expanse, the "gateless gate" to primordial

wisdom—prior unity of vast emptiness/*shunyata* and luminous clarity of our always already present clear light love-wisdom Buddha mind. This resplendent Buddhist teaching remains the authoritive expression of the *Dzogchen* Great Perfection wisdom transmission (*Ch. VIII*). The following brief but sublime wisdom homage is found in a Jigme Lingpa commentary on an homage by the Buddha's brother, Rahula:

Homage to Mother Wisdom

Homage to *Prajnaparamita*, primordial wisdom,
Inexpressible through thought or speech;
Very nature of unborn, unceasing boundless space;
Always present ground of self-aware wisdom and
Buddha Presence, basis of precious bodhicitta.
Mother of all Buddhas of the three times,
I bow down to you, perfect Wisdom Mother.

Middle Way Madhyamaka founder Nagarjuna, on this innermost secret nondual wisdom Presence that is the very Buddha nature of mind (*Mulamadhyamakakarika* XVIII, v. 9, author's translation):

Not known through anything, deep peace.
Not defiled by conceptual pretention,
Not thinking, free of identity and difference,
That is the empty nature of mind.

It is told in the Buddhist sutras that Siddhartha Gautama, erstwhile prince of the *Shakya Clan*, became a Buddha when he accomplished the full *bodhi* realization of the prior and always present unity of these Two Truths of the timeless empty boundless whole of interdependently arising reality itself. Here the Buddha cognized directly, beyond concept and belief, the nondual simultaneity and complementary unity of the perennial Two Truths that are relative form and its ultimate emptiness.

The Teaching of the Buddha: Being Happy Now. That is the title, and the titular promise of this little book. "Practice the profound *Prajnaparamita* and all the *tathagatas* (Buddhas) will rejoice". And so will you. (*Appendix A*)

A brief note on the *Prajnaparamita sutra* corpus is in order. This heart of the Mayayana teaching is a collection of the Buddha's wisdom teaching of about forty Indian sutra texts dating from about 100 BCE to 500 CE. *Prajnaparamita* (*praja* is wisdom; *paramita* is perfection) refers to both the wisdom of emptiness/*shunyata* that is the wisdom way of seeing ultimate reality itself, and to the corpus of the forty sutras that describe this way of seeing, and of being.

Prajnaparamita is personified as the Great Mother (*Yum chenmo*) of wisdom of all the Buddhas, and the fearlessly compassionate (*bodhicitta*) bodhisattvas with their ten levels (*bhumis*) of training in skillful means. The most familiar of these texts include our above much beloved nondual (*advaya*), trans-conceptual *Heart of Wisdom Sutra* (*Mahaprajnaparamita hridaya sutra*), and the Diamond Sutra (*Vajracchedika Prajnaparamita sutra*). The entire *Prajnaparamita* corpus is considered by most scholars to be based in the 2nd century 8000 verse *Ashtasahasrika sutra*.

The *Prajnaparamita* sutras, like Nagarjuna's prose, follow an apophatic or via negativa rhetorical, even ironic style—"neti neti", not this, not that—"A is not A; therefore it is A". The Indian Nyaya multi-valued logic (MVL), unlike Aristotle's limited Western two-valued, (true-false) logic, A may be *both* A and not-A (Boaz 2021a). Just when we're convinced of the truth, or of the absolute reality of a relative, conventional conceptual this or that, its ultimate existence is negated. Rude awakening indeed. Such discomfiting moments are step functions of the wisdom Path.

For example, the nondual *Heart of Wisdom Sutra* negates the Buddha's great teaching of the Four Noble Truths thusly: "There is no suffering, no origin of suffering, no cessation of suffering, no path, no wisdom". Then the Buddha negates the Five Aggregates (*skandhas*) of form—physical and mental existence: "In emptiness there is no form, no feelings, no perceptions, no mental formations, and no consciousness". No wonder some of the bodhisattvas in his retinue had heart attacks! In The Diamond Sutra: "All dharmas are dharma-less. That is why they are called 'all dharmas'".

In this ironic way is the primordial unity of Buddha's Two Truths—relative form and ultimate emptiness—revealed by negating our conceptual attachment to ultimately illusory "concealer" relative truths, so that Ultimate Truth may be non-conceptually understood, then realized. Then, if we're lucky, we awaken to the prior and present nondual unity of relative form and ultimate emptiness "just as it is", and has always been. Told the Buddha, "Rest your weary mind and let it be as it is; all things are perfect exactly as they are". "And all the *tathagatas* will rejoice" in your *prajnaparamita* awakening. And you will be happy, even in the face *samsaric* adversity and the constant presence of our death (*anitya*). (*Appendix A*)

This unified one truth that is the identity of form and emptiness is, as we have seen, invariant throughout the entire awareness-consciousness processional of human cognition—1) pre-conceptual bare attention; 2) exoteric, objective, conceptual; 3) esoteric, subjective, contemplative; and 4) perfectly subjective nondual. Awakening to this ultimate identity of The Buddha's Two Truths is our Buddha *bodhi* mind potential of direct, non-conceptual experience (*yogi pratyaksa*) as the always present clear light Presence of our indwelling luminous primordial love-wisdom Buddha mind (*buddhajnana*). The imperfect dualistic practice of wisdom and method—the wisdom of emptiness with the skillful means of *bodhicitta*—makes it so.

The primary obstruction to our omniscient *bodhi* mind that cognizes the primordial unity of the Two Truths at once is the false deep background cultural belief that self and phenomena appearing to it concretely, inherently, ultimately exist (*svabhava*).

The Buddha's wisdom of emptiness is the universal antidote to such ignorance (*avidya*) and delusion (*moha*). From this adventitious ignorance arises the afflictive emotions and their hostile ego defenses that make earthly relative existence mostly *samsaric* suffering—human alienation, despotism, and war.

Suppressing and repressing our troubling emotions, thoughts, and unfinished psycho-emotional business, whether by sublimating them through work, play, or through our wonderful meditation practice, doesn't work for long. The wisdom antidote from the great physician Buddha neutralizes the destructive emotions that cloak our already present clear light Buddha mind, that we may feel and know and act as Happiness Itself. Waking up to this repressed stuff requires real honesty, and a bunch of courage.

To be sure, the peace and bliss of sustained meditation results—in due course—in profound relative human happiness. Surely, this is the goal of spiritual practice of the Path. But it is not so. Although mindfulness and penetrating insight meditation are powerful relative contemplative antecedents to full *bodhi* awakening, such an ultimate liberation from worldly suffering must not be conflated with mere relative contemplative yogic bliss. That this is so too often presents a problematic obstruction to a "middling yogi" on the Path, namely, self-centered attachment to meditative bliss. That said, many yogis of lesser or middling capacity might wish to enjoy such a problem.

The Buddha was reticent to teach the wisdom of the ultimate emptiness of form. He taught it only to yogis and yoginis of superior capacity. His concern was that this very subtle truth would be misunderstood by the mass mind socio-cultural ideology that "I" and all this stuff inherently exists as it appears—"It's all just physical", and it is foolish to consider any alternative reality view; or, conversely, the nihilistic misunderstanding that the meaning of emptiness is that nothing at all exists, "It's all just an illusion"—so why bother with the Six Perfections/*Paramitas* of the Path: generosity, moral virtue, patience, diligence, meditation, wisdom?

The not so surprising Middle Way view is that spacetime stuff exists, but not as it appears to our senses. Under penetrating wisdom analysis objective things have a nominal, relative conventional, conceptually imputed existence, but not a permanent, absolute or ultimate existence. Buddha's "middle path" between these two blatant conceptual extremes is centrist Madhyamaka.

This does not mean that we should abandon discursive thinking and philosophical analysis, and only bliss out in mindless contemplative space. Because science, philosophy, and Buddhist dialectics cannot describe things precisely as they are perceived, we can understand that things do not appear as they are directly perceived. Physical and mental phenomenal appearance is always filtered by our deep background cultural "global web of belief".

Analytical meditation has been an important facet of Mahayana Buddhist study and practice for 2000 years, since Nagarjuna first stirred us from our obsessive conceptual doctrinaire slumbers. This is perhaps even more pronounced in the subtler or "higher" Buddhist tenet systems, especially the Mahayana Middle Way Madhyamaka systems of *Yogachara Svatantrika,* and the Gelug *Prasangika* of Je Tsongkhapa and H.H. Dalai Lama. But such analytical meditators must still engage the calm abiding (*shamatha, sati*) of quiescent mindfulness meditation with the penetrating insight of *vipashyana* meditation. It's good to know that these two contemplative modalities are a prior and ever present unity.

As to the Buddha's concern that the subtlety of the wisdom of emptiness may cause confusion in course minds, nothing has changed in this regard 25 centuries later. Most of us, practitioners or otherwise, still firmly believe that self-ego-I and its physical and mental phenomenal experience absolutely, ultimately exist (*svabhava*). That this is so is readily evidenced in our attitudes and action of body, speech, and mind, and the semiotic (logical syntax, semantics, pragmatics) idiom, ideology, and ethical conduct that arise there from to fill our minds with self.

Therefore, many Buddhist masters believe that only those with a more or less bias free, natural, open disposition—the "*Dzogchen* disposition" of Zen Mind/Beginner's mind—are suitable candidates for this radical Two Truths teaching of the nondual wisdom of emptiness. "In the beginner's mind there are unlimited possibilities; in the expert's mind there are few" (Suzuki Roshi, *Zen Mind Beginner's Mind*, 1970, Wisdom Press, 2000). The untrained mind, brimming with the false certainty of its biases and beliefs, has little space for new possibilities, nor for its already present, indwelling love-wisdom Buddha mind.

So, the main point of the practice of the Buddhist Path is non-conceptual direct yogic perception (*yogi pratyaksa*) of the subtle complementary interdependence—the prior and present unity of the Two Truths—that are relative appearance (form), and its ultimate emptiness "groundless ground". From this practice spontaneously, effortlessly arises our natural, altruistic *bodhicitta*, the primary cause of human happiness. Perhaps being happy now is simpler than we may have imagined.

From the profound *Kunjed Gyalpo, The Supreme Source*, the principle tantra of the *Dzogchen semde* (mind series) teaching cycle (*Ch. VIII*).

> The inseparability of the two truths, absolute and relative,
> is called 'primordial Buddha'.

Neo-Vedanta master Ramana Maharshi speaks of nondual Ultimate Truth:

> The ultimate truth is so simple. It is nothing more than being in the pristine state of presence. This is all that need be said.... Only mature minds can grasp this simple truth in its nakedness.
> —*The Spiritual Teaching of Ramana Maharshi*

The activity of the human mind—perceptual, conceptual, contemplative, and innermost nondual—cognitively ambulates in the "primordially pure" unity of these Two Truth dimensions—relative form, and ultimate emptiness. It is the present recognition, then realization of our "supreme identity" with that indivisible one truth unity that is the Supreme Source of every-thing that is; and our very source of liberation from suffering. Our "pristine state of presence" of that source is who we are. Who Am I? *That* I Am!

In short, relative mental and physical form arises and appears, abides, and returns again to ultimate *dharmakaya*, whose very essence is the profound fullness of emptiness/*shunyata*. Indeed, physical and mental form have never departed the primordial embrace of the all inclusive whole that is *dharmakaya*, by whatever name. That is the non-conceptual Buddha love-wisdom mind Presence that we always already are. We learn to relax into, and rest in That.

Strange Interlude. Hence, through the practice of the Path, we maintain our attentional awareness in selfless primordial Ultimate Truth—bright Presence of That—in the very midst of all kinds of delusion and confusion of the dimension of impermanent Relative Truth continuously arising and embraced within it. Thus do we enjoy the peace of mind and happiness that enhances our engaged natural *bodhicitta* practice—the compassionate thought, intention, and action for the benefit of living beings—which is, as we have so often seen in these pages, the foundational cause of human happiness.

Such happiness is therefore "already accomplished from the very beginning" (Garab Dorje). Happiness is already the case! We need no longer seek it through all of our fruitless ego centric seeking strategies—material or spiritual.

Yes, it's that simple. But it's not so easy. Maintaining our atten-tion upon our love-wisdom *bodhi* mind Presence in this constant presence of fear of our death requires assiduous practice. And that takes intelligence, courage, and ego strength. Recall, it is the self-ego-I who *chooses* to establish a real practice, and so enter the love-wisdom Path. So, it is unwise to denigrate the intractable ego. As we learn to love our prodigal selves, like the mother loves her only child, then do we rest in our Buddha nature—and recognize

245

it in everyone, and in everything. *Buddha mind sees Buddha in every thing. Course mind sees mostly trouble.*

Therefore, we take refuge in the precious Three Jewels—the Buddha as the Lama, the dharma, and the *sangha*. But when is the right time to do it? After work, when I'm not so distracted? In the morning when I'm not so tired? Later, when the kids settle down? Maybe next year on vacation? We know the answer. *Now* is always the time to enter into this bright Presence that you always already are.

So, right here and now, go ahead and do it for a minute or two. Whatever your "normal" practice may be, place it in temporary abeyance. Sit up straight and place your attention upon the breath in your belly. Breathe normally. Give thanks for the great gift of your life just as it is now. Breathe quietly for a few seconds.

Now close your eyes and raise your eyebrows as you gently place your awareness behind your forehead, in your forebrain (prefrontal cortex). Feel the very subtle stirring and expansion of your focused awareness as you produce high amplitude alpha, gamma, and theta brain rhythm—your "peace response". Now partially open your eyes. Continue, relax and enjoy.

As thoughts, questions and feelings naturally arise, briefly greet them; then label whatever arises—positive or negative—"distraction", and allow it all to dissolve on the out breath. No need to grasp at, or reject any of it. Watch as whatever arises drifts by, like a cloud in the vast empty sky, leaving no trace.

Return attention again and again to the breath. Remain close to the breath. Notice the refreshing absence of thinking and the stress it produces. *Feel* and enjoy this luminous state of Presence of your always present primordial love-wisdom mind (*Brief Course, Appendix A*).

Now, arise in peace and be kind to somebody. Do some good. It will make you happy.

The Madhyamaka Middle Way View of the Two Truths. We have seen that Mahayana Middle Way Madhyamaka (Prasangika and

Yogachara) views the Two Truths—form and emptiness—as the heart and soul of Buddha's teaching on emptiness. For H.H. Dalai Lama the Prasangika Madhyamaka of Nagarjuna (2nd century), Chandrakirti (8th century), and Tsongkhapa (14th century)—conceptual foundation of nondual *Dzogchen*—is the correct Buddhist view as to the *ultimate* nature of arising physical and mental reality. It is recognized, then realized through the *relative* practice of the view and practice of the Path (*Ch. V*).

For Middle Way founder Nagarjuna (from his *Fundamental Wisdom of the Middle Way*, (*Mulamadhyamakakarika, Chapter XXIV*):

> The dharma taught by all the Buddhas
> is precisely based upon the two truths:
> the worldly conventional level of truth,
> and the ultimate level of truth.

Thus, ultimate liberation from suffering, not to mention the full *bodhi* awakening of primordial enlightenment, or buddhahood, is only ever accomplished from a subtle and complete, "innermost secret" understanding—conceptual, contemplative, and nondual—of these foundational Two Truths of the Buddha's definitive *Heart of Wisdom Sutra* teaching.

For 25 centuries both philosophical realist and philosophical idealist *interpretations* of the Buddha's Two Truths have arisen in the context of Buddhist metaphysics, as we saw in Chapter V.

Madhyamaka is the Buddha's teaching of the Middle Way, practiced by the Madhyamikas who advocate it. The primary *mahasiddhas* of Prasangika Madhyamaka, after its late 2nd century founders Nagarjuna and his heart son Aryadeva, were Buddhapalita in the 5th century, and Chandrakirti in the 8th century, as we have seen.

Nagarjuna's accomplishment lies in his essentializing of the great *Prajnaparamita Sutra*. He utilizes the deductive logical dialectic of *reductio ad absurdum* argument to prove the fallacy of any opponents' argument. "I make no assertions" as to existence or nonexistence of phenomena. He "proves" the Buddhist notion of emptiness/*shunyata* by demonstrating the fallacy of his interlocutor's assertions as to the existence or nonexistence of appearing form while avoiding positive assertions altogether.

Moreover, he teaches of the relativity and complementarity of form and emptiness, and of all such opposites, which are necessarily mutually dependent upon one another for their meaning. Therefore, all arising entities are merely relative and conventional, empty and absent any intrinsic essence (*svabhava*) or ultimate existence. We learn to regard such apparitional appearances without the drama of a permanent self.

The common human presumption is that the ultimate essence of anything must be eternal, permanent, and changeless; but the nature of the relative dimension of spacetime stuff and beings is destruction and extinction. It shall all pass away (*anitya*). Thus does nonlocal, nondual emptiness/*shunyata* connote, not the nonexistence of phenomena, but the lack of any essential or ultimate existence of phenomena. Nagarjuna does not deny the relatively real existence of local space and time. So, Madhyamaka bestows the gift of a real world peopled with real sentient beings. So we have a bit of time to choose to practice the path of the Buddhadharma.

Therefore, everything that arises and appears as form does so in causal dependence upon a vast matrix of causes and conditions. So, once again, everything is dependent arising (*pratitya samutpada*). That which arises dependently is empty of intrinsic existence. Therefore everything is empty of intrinsic existence. The Buddha's *shunyata*/emptiness *is* dependent arising.

"To be or not to be" is not the question. It is logically incorrect to assert that the stuff of appearing reality either exists, or that it does not exist. The truth of the matter is that matter is not denied in Buddhism, as it is by the several Indian Metaphysical Idealism schools. Again, stuff exists relatively (Relative Truth/ *samvriti satya*), just not intrinsically or ultimately (Ultimate Truth/

paramartha satya). Thus is Prasangika the Buddhist Middle Way—the prodigious Buddhist Two Truths dominate ontic trope.

Buddhapalita (5th century), building upon Nagarjuna's Two Truths view, founded and developed the Middle Way Consequence School that is the Mahayana Prasangika Madhyamaka. Chandrakirti (8th century) rescued Madhyamaka from the idealist turn of Bhavaviveka and the Yogachara Madhyamikas by returning to Nagarjuna's view that Madhyamaka must not commit to any positive ontological position as to the absolute nature of existence, or nonexistence. Shantideva (8th century) continued this foundational view of *Prasangika*.

By the 11th century Chandrakirti's Prasangika Madhyamaka was well established in India, Tibet, China, and Japan (*Sanron School*). Dialogue and debate between the various doctrinal interpretations of Madhyamaka—*Rangtong* (intrinsic "emptiness of self"), and *Shentong* (extrinsic "emptiness of other")—continued through the 11th to 14th centuries, and by the 16th century pervaded all four of the primary Tibetan Buddhist schools—Nyingma, Kagyu, Gulug, and Sakya.

Refinements to Prasangika Madhyamaka were made in the 19th century ecumenical *Rimé* movement, especially by Nyingmapa Ju Mipham. The Prasangika Madhyamaka is alive and well in all of these schools, due in no small part to H.H. Dalai Lama's advocacy.

This great Middle Way Prasangika teaching is considered by many Tibetan Lamas to be the very foundation of the *Dzogchen* Great Completion (Great Perfection) view with its nondual *Ati Yoga* practice which, with Essence *Mahamudra*, is generally considered the pinnacle of the Buddha's teaching. It is said that the duality of the Mahayana Causal Vehicle—practice this cause now in order to have that result later—is completed in nondual *Dzogchen* view and praxis.

Thus it is, Buddha taught a Middle Way that defines the character of his Noble Eightfold Path that is the cause of liberation from suffering. In the first teaching following his full *bodhi* enlightenment at Bode Gaya, Buddha, in his *Dhammacakkappavattana Sutta* describes the Path as a Middle Way of moderation between the extremes of course sense pleasure, and "addiction to the painful austerities of self-mortification".

The *Pali Canon* also describes Buddha's Middle Path as "dependent arising", or "dependent origination" (*pratitya samutpada*), the balance that we later see in Madhyamaka between the metaphysical extremes of existence (eternalism, materialism), and nonexistence (nihilism, idealism).

In the Mahayana, Middle Way Prasangika is grounded in the "groundless ground" of *shunyata*/emptiness that balances the ontic extremes of "everything exists"; and "nothing exists".

Thus, as we have seen many times, is the Middle Way a centrist path between an idealist denial of all appearing reality, and a materialist affirmation of it; a centrist metaphysic balanced between a phenomenally necessary "real world out there" (RWOT), and a nihilistic denial of it; a middle path between the extremes of self-ego-I sensory indulgence, and ascetic self-denial; between attraction/attachment and aversion/hostility; between present and future; between survival rebirth of an eternal *Atman* Self, and absolute annihilation of the self upon death of the physical body; between being and nothingness; between relative form and ultimate emptiness; between *samsara* and *nirvana*. Buddha's Middle Way sees the complementarity of opposing conceptual opposites—their prior and present unity being here in time, in this timeless present moment now.

Resting in, and confidence in the view and practice of such a way reveals that the Middle Way is both the origin and aim of happiness and liberation from suffering; and the present moment of the practice of the Path that causes it. The stress and the dilemma of dualistic view and practice becomes peace of mind upon the breath as we cease thinking about it and settle into *vidya/rigpa* Buddha mind Presence of luminous and empty primordial clear light nature of mind—*dharmakaya* itself.

So, Buddha's "middle path" understanding of his Two Truths is nonlinear. It does not lead us from a beginning to an end; from present ignorance to future bliss; to a valorized transcendence of self in some idealized perfect future mind state. Rather, it is the always already present Presence of the imperfect happiness present in this present moment here and now—just as it is, adversity and all.

Hence, in the ultimate view, there's nothing to fear, nothing to fix, nothing to strive for. Buddha told it well, "Let it be as it is and rest your weary mind; all things are perfect exactly as they are". In the view of relative mind—self-ego-I—this is pure fantasy.

The Middle Way is the "feeling experience" of the Ultimate Truth of the matter (*nirvana*), in the midst of the slings and arrows of outrageous Relative Truth (*samsara*). Thus do we make our goal, not liberation and ultimate happiness in a future enlightened mind state, but our moment to moment relative ordinary mind practice itself. This is the beginning of *Dzogchen* view and practice (*Ch. VIII*). As Chögyam Trungpa told, "Make the goal the path". The Path is everything we experience, all that we think, intend, and do, here and now.

Well, how do we do this?: We practice the Buddha's Two Truths as the path of mindfulness meditation in the context of the *Three Jewels* of Buddhist Refuge: 1) *the Buddha* seen as the *Lama* or *Ajahn* or *Roshi*; 2) the *dharma,* the teaching of the Buddha; and 3) the *sangha* community.

In Mahayana ontology—the metaphysical concern for the true nature of being itself—the Middle Way Prasangika rejects foundational ontology in both its conventional and absolute raiment. Prasangika has attempted to avoid the metaphysical extremes of both fundamental realist, and idealist interpretative metaphysics. Here, any *intrinsic* reality, whether relative-conventional or ultimate, is categorically denied. Recall that even emptiness itself is empty and absent of any intrinsic or ultimate existence or self-nature (*svabhava*).

It is this Middle Way realist Madhyamaka Prasangika Two Truths view of Nagarjuna, Aryadeva, Buddhapalita, Chandrakirti, and Tsongkhapa that Tibetan Vajrayana scholar-masters, including H.H. Dalai Lama, have favored over the cittamatra "mind only" Buddhist Metaphysical Idealism of Madhyamaka Yogachara Svatantrika. But recall, we require a syncretic middle way between these two Buddhist Middle Way views (*Ch. V*).

Therefore, let us all too briefly survey this profound centrist view of the Mahayana Two Truths dominant trope that threads a centrist middle way between the false dichotomy of two ontic extremes: 1) "eternalism", an essentialist, realist Metaphysical Materialism of an absolutely existing "real world out there" (RWOT), and 2) "nihilism", the illusory, unreal *avidya maya* reality of Metaphysical Absolute Idealism. We have seen that there's a lot of reality in this luminous space between absolute existence and absolute nonexistence.

For Mahayana Middle Way Madhyamaka then, these Two Truths are: Ultimate Truth (*paramartha satya*), or emptiness, and the conventional "concealer truths" of Relative Truth (*samvriti satya*), or form that overlay and veil the luminous clear light mind Buddha mind Presence of the primordial ground.

H.H. Dalai Lama, in his most through *The World of Tibetan Buddhism* (Wisdom, 1995) suggests that Shantideva's 8th century *Bodhicharyavatara (Guide to the Bodhisattva's Way of Life)* is the best guide to Buddha's teaching on *bodhicitta,* and on the Two Truths.

Alan and Vesna Wallace's 1996 translation of *Bodhicharyavatara* is excellent. It is based primarily on two Sanskrit editions, Louis de la Vallee Poussin's 1901 edition, and P.L. Vaidya's 1960 edition of the *Panjika* commentary of Prajnakaramati. The profound and notoriously difficult ninth chapter reveals the nature of our two modes of knowing, relative and ultimate. From the *Panjika* (p. 170):

Conventional reality (*samvriti* or Relative Truth) is that which conceals and obscures the complete knowledge of things as they are because it obscures with a belief in an intrinsic nature (*svabhava*)...Its synonyms are ignorance (*avidya*), delusion (*moha*), and misunderstanding (*viparyasa*)...Ultimate truth (*paramartha*) is the highest, ultimate reality, the true nature of phenomena. Understanding (this nature), mental afflictions (*klesha*), karmic imprints (*vasana*) and all obscurations (*avarana*) are eliminated. Its synonyms (for Ultimate truth) are the lack of intrinsic nature (*nihsvabhavata*) of all phenomena, emptiness (*shunyata*), thusness (*tathata*), the pinnacle of existence (*bhutakoti*), and the sphere (space) of reality (*dharmadhatu*, etc.)

As to our conceptual understanding of the Two Truths the *Panjika* states (p.177):

Intellect is called conventional reality (Relative Truth) because every intellect has the nature of conceptualization (*vikalpa*) regarding an object that is (not truly an) object; and every conceptualization is of the nature of spiritual ignorance (*avidya*) because it apprehends unreality... No intellect ultimately apprehends the nature of ultimate truth.

Emptiness and The Two Truths. "Form is empty; emptiness is form". It was on the *relative existence* of form that the Buddha based his teaching that all spacetime phenomena are ultimately empty of intrinsic *ultimate existence*. Therefore, stuff exists! How else could we ponder its ultimate mode of existence? *With no form, there could be no emptiness of form.* No form; no emptiness. No emptiness; no form. Form is the basis of its own self-reflexive emptiness. So, when we deny the *ultimate* existence of form and an independently real self-ego-I who perceives it, we speak from a stable relatively real conceptual logical basis founded in the Sage's teaching.

Well, what is the ontic reality status of emptiness itself? Since the "fullness of emptiness" contains the potential of everything that appears to the senses, surely emptiness must exist. It must be really real. But it is not so. As we have seen, boundless emptiness too is, as Nagarjuna told, "empty of any shred of intrinsic existence". It is this counter intuitive perplexing irony of reality being itself that H.H. Dalai Lama, following Chandrakirti, has termed "the emptiness of emptiness". Notice that with penetrating analytical insight (*vipashyana*) there exists here no actual logical paradox. His Holiness clarifies it for us:

> It is important for us to avoid the misapprehension that emptiness is an absolute reality from which the illusory world emerges...it's not some kind of (entity) out there somewhere...emptiness must be understood as 'empty of intrinsic or independent existence'...(It is) form's ultimate nature... Emptiness does not imply nonexistence of phenomena but the emptiness of phenomena...its ultimate mode of being...the basis that allows form (to) arise as emptiness. (*Buddhadharma Quarterly*, Fall, 2002)

Therefore, for Buddhist Middle Way *Madhyamaka Prasangika* there exists no inherent, enduring, substantial, ultimate or independent essence, basis, Self, or entity-hood for all of this appearing relative-conventional stuff. Nor is emptiness itself such "an absolute reality". It too is "empty of intrinsic or independent existence". His Holiness has termed this bit of *Kosmic* irony "the emptiness of emptiness".

Yet clearly, *something* exists! There are undeniable trees and stars and embodied sentient beings ambulating here in this diaphanous dance of spacetime geometry. After all, who is it that takes birth, suffers and dies? Who is it that benefits from the altruistic kindness of *bodhicitta*? Who is it that chooses to practice the Path that realizes inherent Buddha mind happiness? There's a real somebody in here who experiences something! How shall we understand this?

Recall that the Mahayana Middle Way *Madhyamikas* do not deny empirical physical and mental form. Although these myriad forms of arising reality are absent and empty of any *ultimate* essence, Self, or permanent and independent existence, reality is *relatively* real by way of our sentient attention-perception, conceptual imputation, reification and designation. We impute and thereby create our realities via our perceptual *attention*, concept and belief—our individual and collective, mostly unconscious deep sociocultural background "global web of belief" (Quine 1969). Philosophers of mind know this cognitive truth as "ontological relativity".

In short, being is relative to, conditioned by, and dependent upon the conventional concept-belief imputations and designations of our prevailing cultural metaphysic. For Western culture that ontology is our Greek efflorescence that is monistic Scientific Materialism/Physicalism that has now entirely colonized the Western mind.

Therefore, our experience is but the causal, relative, interdependent "dependent arising" (*pratitya samutpada, tendrel*) of myriad selfless (*anatman*), impermanent (*anitya*) spacetime forms arising through their formless ultimate emptiness "groundless ground". Hence, the "fullness of emptiness". Thus is our primordial emptiness "groundless ground" not so firmly established by an observer's ordinary mind. And yes, emptiness too exists only relatively, dependently, via conceptual convention. It too is absent and empty "any shred" of intrinsic ultimate existence or self nature (*svabhava*).

One of the many realities that we, as a self-ego-I may choose to create—if we're smart and lucky—is the *choice* to establish an effective meditation practice and thereby enter in the bright numinous mind stream of the Buddha's teaching. Wisdom mind love and happiness is the choice of a relative conventional self-ego-I to connect to its indwelling innate clear light mind Presence.

It is here then, step by mindful step, that we awaken to and connect to always already present Presence of our indwelling Buddha mind/wisdom mind. Here, now and not elsewhere, we recover Buddha's truth that "Wonder of wonders, all beings are Buddha". Perhaps we are not all fully awakened Buddhas, yet we are always already this indwelling Buddha Nature. Let it be so.

Who is it that I Am? It is *bodhi* mind wisdom mind Presence who knows this great truth. Not later, after years, or lifetimes of practice, but right here now. *Tat Tvam Asi. That I Am.* Recognize and feel That upon each mindful breath, and be happy now. That is the Buddha's nondual Fruitional View (*Appendix A*, "Basic Mindfulness Meditation").

Moreover, it is this numinous wisdom Buddha clear light *nature of mind* that gradually deconstructs, then finally collapses the entire drama of *deluded mind*—mind-created self-ego-I. Human ignorance (*avidya*) and delusion-confusion (*moha*) utterly dissolve at this bright wisdom moment *(samadhi)* of recognition! Such a realization requires a strong, flexible, intelligent ego!

Again, Tulku Urgyen on this wondrous and ironic "collapse of confusion":

> Buddha nature has lost track of itself and created samsara, but it is also buddha nature, recognizing itself, that clears up the delusion of samsaric existence. The moment of recognition is like the spirit (demon) leaving. All of a sudden the possession vanishes. We can't even say where it went.

Now, for Shantideva, there are two embodied modes of *prajna*, or relative discriminating wisdom that may ponder this conceptually vexed emptiness dilemma: 1) a wisdom which discursively discerns the stuff of the Relative Truth dimension of form; and 2) a wisdom that utilizes both mindfulness (*shamatha*), and analytical direct penetrating insight (*vipashyana*) to probe the emptiness dimension of Ultimate Truth that transcends yet embraces its many relative conventional instantiations. It is 2) that surpasses even the most scintillating discursive scientific and philosophical intellect.

Further, according to Shantideva (1997) there are two types of persons corresponding to these two types of discriminating wisdom:

> Two kinds of people are to be distinguished:
> The contemplative and the common person.
> The conceptual view of the common person
> is refuted by the contemplative person.
> —*Bodhicharyavatara,* Ch. 9, Verse 3

So yes, the understanding of Mahayana Buddhist emptiness is founded upon the centrist *Madhyamaka* Two Truths—relative form, and ultimate emptiness. However, once again, ultimate boundless emptiness (*shunyata*) is not a logocentric, absolutely existing deeper physical or metaphysical ground or base of arising and appearing spacetime reality, although it is too often construed as such. Emptiness is not a more real transcendent reality source or absolute ground of stuff existing in a classical Newtonian container of absolute time and space.

Rather, emptiness is a selfless, non-essential relativized absolute, a "groundless ground" arising *interdependently*—"dependent arising", or "interbeing"—a timeless, formless infinitely vast matrix of interconnected causes and conditions, boundless whole itself (*mahabindu*), the very emptiness essence and nature of primordial *dharmakaya.*

We have seen that philosophers of mind call such interdependence "ontological relativity". Emptiness is relative to our deep background conceptually imputed sociocultural "global web of belief".

Thus it is, diaphanous conceptually vexing emptiness itself is free, absent and empty of any inherent qualities or attributes, including the imputed conceptual attribute of emptiness. It is utterly empty of intrinsic existence, selfless, nothing more nor less than the dependent arising of form, the very stuff of appearing reality. No form; no emptiness. No emptiness; no form. Again, both form and its emptiness base are empty and absent intrinsic, permanent self-nature.

Therefore, for Madhyamaka there is no ultimate ground! Thus is this vast expanse of the boundless whole (*dharmadhatu*, Bön *mahabindu*) that is primordial *dharmakaya*, whose very nature is emptiness, a "groundless ground" of its arising forms. Abstruse metaphysics indeed. But only to the concept mind of an all too relatively real, but ultimately insubstantial nonentity that we have come to know and love as self-ego-I.

We've seen that this seemingly paradoxical and ironic coexistence of the Two Truths that are the intrinsic unity of form and emptiness is known in the Mahayana as Nagarjuna's Madhyamaka Prasangika, a centrist Middle Way—a conceptually imperfect doctrinal balance between the false dichotomy that is the metaphysical extremes of absolute existence, and absolute nonexistence. It is mindful mantra practice that reveals the inherently trans-conceptual, directly experiential truth of the matter.

Namarupa: **Name and Form.** Nondual (unity of perceiving subject and its perceived objects) Ultimate Truth may be seen as metaphysically identical, if somewhat contextually variant, with the following Buddhist doctrinal notions: formless *dharmakaya* (*cho ku*) body of truth whose very nature is *shunyata*, boundless emptiness that is *kadag*, primordial purity of the aboriginal "groundless ground", vast expanse of *dharmadhatu*, implicate unbounded whole itself, trans-conceptual, selfless, pristine basic space (*cho ying*) of reality being itself. *Lhundrub* is the primordial Presence of *kadag*, "primordially pure" base/ground, undefiled by concept and emotion.

It is formless Ultimate Truth in which, or in whom all spacetime physical and mental form, the modes of conventional Relative Truth arise, appear and are impermanently, selflessly, and interdependently instantiated. *Dharmata* (*chos nyi*) is intrinsic nature or essence of reality, of phenomenal existence, prior to conceptual elaboration. *Dharmata* is more or less synonymous with *shunyata/* emptiness, and with *dharmakaya*. The apparitional or delusory aspect of all appearing phenomenal dharmas is *dharmin* (*chos can*) (*Ch. IX*).

How may we know, feel and finally realize this formless dimension that is Ultimate Truth in whom arises the form dimension that is Relative Truth? It is through our deepest "innermost secret" primordial wisdom mind, Buddha/*bodhi* mind, *jnana, yeshe*, gnosis—utterly free of conceptual elaboration—pristine instant open Presence (*vidya, rigpa*) of That—through which we know the prodigious Ultimate Truth of these myriad physical and mental forms of Relative Truth.

Thus are these Two Truths always an ontological unity. We recognize, then realize this prodigious unity deep within our being through the assiduous practice of the Path, under the gentle guidance of the qualified master.

The view of Indo-Tibetan Buddhism does not regard this Two Truths teaching of the Buddha as a conceptual ambiguity. Rather, the teaching is that these Two Truth dimensions, relative form and ultimate emptiness, are always already a complementary ontic prior and epistemically present unity. Once again, from Buddha's *Heart of Wisdom Sutra*: "Form is empty; emptiness is form. Form is not other than emptiness; emptiness is not other than form."

Relative Truth or *samvriti satya* (Tib. *kunzog denpa*): *satya* means truth, *samvriti* means relative and conventional, but it also means concealing or obscuring, not the whole truth. Ultimate Truth or *paramartha satya* (Tib. *don dampa*) means highest, or complete, or all inclusive whole truth—the ultimate meaning of the primordial nature of appearing spacetime form.

So, there is no inherent ambiguity here. Told Buddha, "To bring living beings to enlightenment I have taught in many ways at once." His *upaya*, or skillful means required that he teach dualistic Relative Truth to the uninitiated, and nondual Ultimate Truth to those with the capacity to understand it.

Just so, Buddhahood is endowed with the trans-conceptual pristine cognition of the vast expanse of reality itself (*dharmadhatujnana, chos ying*)—the primordially pure knowing-feeling cognizance of ultimate sameness (*samatajnana, nyam nyid yeshe*) that pervades all of samsara and nirvana. Nagarjuna told it well: "There is not the slightest difference between samsara and nirvana." The Buddha's Two Truths are always a prior and present unity. It is from that prior and always present unity that we practice his dharma teaching.

This concludes our exploration of the Buddha's Two Truths.

The Buddhist Mahayana Revolution

The revolution began in earnest in the 2nd century with Nagarjuna (d. 55), founder of centrist Middle Way Madhyamaka, and the synthesizer of the *Prajnaparamita* corpus (*Perfection of Wisdom Sutras*). This noetic wisdom Revolution profoundly altered the evolutionary course of the Buddhadharma of the previous five centuries. It changed both Buddhist metaphysics (*shunyata*/emptiness), and Buddhist ethics (the Eightfold Path). And it extended Buddhist study and practice from its exclusively monastic base to lay practice, and to social concerns (Garfield 2015, Ch. 9). Let us then first very briefly explore Buddhist metaphysical ontology.

1) *Metaphysics:* The Mahayana recast earlier *Pali Canon* (e.g. *Abhidharma*) doctrine on the Two Truths and their relation to emptiness via the doctrine that primeval ignorance (*avidya*) causes us to conceive of both persons and phenomena as existing with an innate and fundamental core essence. Under sway of such ignorance we view spacetime stuff and the self that apprehends it, is essentially and ultimately real. But it is not so.

For Middle Way Madhyamikas all phenomena are absent and empty of essential, substantial, independent intrinsic existence (*svabhava,* essential being). But most of the *Pali Canon* posits such existence. Therefore, *svabhava,* or essential inherent existence, is the Middle Way "object of negation".

Absolute, *intrinsically* real selves and real stuff are denied by Madhyamaka. Here the metaphysical extreme of monistic materialist, substantialist "eternalism" is avoided. All appearing *dharmas*, all of the phenomenal things of physical and mental reality are empty and absent "any shred" of independent, essential, intrinsic, ultimate existence.

In other words, appearing perceived objective reality by an ostensibly separate self-subject is here a nominal supposition that all of this presumed objective, *observer-independent* arising stuff of material spacetime existence has no absolute or ultimate inherent existence at all.

Well, is this an absolute negation of the existence of both perceiving subject and its intentional object altogether? Does Madhayamaka also negate arising relative, conventional *observer-dependent* phenomena? Is spacetime stuff altogether nonexistent? Is there a "middle path"?

Yes, appearing, relative, conventional arising phenomena are *ultimately* nonexistent, yet relatively, conventionally real, thus avoiding the ontic extreme of idealist nihilism—the denial of spacetime existing reality altogether. This tenet of Madhyamaka makes it a brand of Metaphysical Realism, while avoiding the eternalistic absolute monistic Metaphysical Realism of Scientific Materialism/Physicalism, and its fundamentalist proto-religious belief system known to the philosophy trade as "Scientism".

Hence, to know the emptiness of appearing reality is simply to know that spacetime stuff is relative and conventional. To know relative, conventional reality is simply to know that it is empty and absent of any essential or ultimate nature. This is the metaphysical identity of the Two Truths (*Ch. VI*). Radical ontology indeed.

But are not all great scientific and wisdom breakthroughs radical to the prevailing orthodoxy? That's the nature of the wisdom process; is it not? Cases in point: Isaac Newton's Relativistic mechanics; Einstein's Relativistic mechanics; Bohr's relativistic quantum mechanics, and the undiscovered land of a unifying mathematical quantum gravity theory which mends the vexing mathematical incommensurability of the mechanics the first three of these beautiful candidates for a prodigious "theory of everything" (TOE). (*Appendix B*)

As with Buddhist dialectics, relativistic quantum theory (QED) evolves in its dialectical process toward ever more inclusive theory and practice.

2) *Ethics:* The Mahayana Revolution also introduced the doctrine of the Bodhisattva Ideal. The goal of the Hinayana (so called "lesser vehicle") *Pali Canon* Shravaka is to become an *Arhat,* or Solitary Buddha upon completion of the Eightfold Path to the cessation of suffering—primordial enlightenment itself. All primarily for the benefit of himself. There is however an abundance of proto-Mahayana *bodhicitta* kindness and compassion in the *Shravakayana* vehicle.

However, the Mahayana bodhisattva (wisdom being) on the Path of awakening generates *bodhicitta*—wisdom heart-mind compassion (*karuna*)—through practice of the *Six Perfections*, and accomplishes Buddhahood, not for oneself, but for the benefit of all living beings, particularly those in one's sphere of influence.

(Note: *karuna* is much more than a kind emotional mind state, or a sentimental intention, or a commitment to act for others. The "kar" in *karuna* is engaged *action* to benefit others.)

Thus does *Bodhicitta* pervade and cause the bodhisattva's Path of love-wisdom awakening, and continues forever after the full *bodhi* of awakening.

Bodhicitta. For Mahayana, the Bodhisattva Ideal supplants the earlier *Pali Canon Shravakayana* goal of individual awakening, with the idea of *bodhicitta,* the compassionately engaged aspiration and action to contribute to both the relative happiness of living beings, and the relative and ultimate happiness-liberation of human beings. *Bodhicitta* may be understood as the altruistic compassionate thought, intention, and action to benefit living beings. The bodhisattva vows to accomplish the *Six Paramitas* of the Mahayana in order to fulfill the *bodhicitta* aspiration of accomplishing one's own enlightenment to that noble end.

This precious *bodhicitta* has two faces:

1) *Ultimate Bodhicitta* is the great reality gift (*jinlob*) of our being here in relative conventional spacetime form. These are the precious gifts of *bodhi*-mind Presence; along with a bit of time to awaken to the truth of *relative bodhicitta* that makes us happy, even ultimately happy. This opportunity arises only in a precious human birth. Shantideva asks the urgent question: "When will it ever arise again".

2) *Relative Bodhicitta* has two aspects. The *Bodhicitta of Aspiration* is the authentic desire to awaken oneself in order to benefit and awaken other beings, human and otherwise. It is much more than a wish, or sympathy or pity. Aspirational *bodhicitta* is the mental, emotional, and meditative contemplative preparation for the life world change that is the *engaged Bodhicitta of Action*, the prodigious lifestyle of the fully committed bodhisattva on the Path to Buddhahood.

We've seen that the definitive no-self help book on awakening *bodhicitta* through the Six Perfections of the bodhisattva's awakened life is 8th century Shantideva's *Guide to the Bodhisattva's Way of Life* (in many excellent English translations).

Review of the View. Thus it is, the Relative Truth reality dimension of impermanent, selfless, interdependently arising form, and the Ultimate Truth reality dimension of emptiness/Buddha nature are always already unified—an ontic prior, and epistemic, phenomenal present unity. Again, the relation between the Two Truths in centrist Middle Way Madhyamaka is one of metaphysical or ontological identity.

Therefore, for Madhyamaka, all physical and mental form is always only relative and conventional. However hard we may conceptually try to discover the fundamental ultimate nature, or essence, or ground of appearing phenomena, we come up empty. How is this so?

Ultimate analysis (*vipashyana, satori/kensho, direct seeing*) always reveals that there is no such essential innate foundational nature to appearing reality. Our eternal grail quest for absolute objective certainty is but a conceptual pipe dream. Indeed, there are more things in heaven and earth than are dreamt of in our materialist philosophy.

Remove all of the relative conventional qualities and attributes of a thing, or a person, and there is nothing left—no essence, no foundation; no ground; no self. Yes, form exists relatively and conventionally, but the *ultimate* nature of appearing reality is, as the sutra says, "no nature". Form, appearing both as phenomena and as a self or a person apprehending it, is fundamentally absent and empty of essential inherent self-existence, all the way up; and all the way down.

It is upon this metaphysical bedrock of the impermanent (*anitya*), selfless (*anatman*) interdependent (*pratitya samutpada*) emptiness of form that the supreme nonlocal, nondual View and Practice of the highest Tibetan Vajrayana teaching is based. Nyingma School *Dzogchen;* Kagyu School Essence *Mahamudra;* the *Mahamudra Anuttarayoga Tantra* (Tibetan *Kangyur-Tengyur Canon*) of the Gelug School; Saijojo Zen (actualized in *mujodo no taigen*) all accept these three Buddhist foundational metaphysical *shunyata*/no-self (*anatman*) principles.

*The Perfect Sphere of Dzogchen—The Great Completion—*may be seen as more or less synonymous with nondual *dharmakaya,* whose essence is luminous *shunyata*/emptiness. On the accord of Chandrakirti and H.H. Dalai Lama, Nagarjuna's Middle Way Prasangika Madhyamaka is the very metaphysical foundation of nondual *Dzogchen* View and practice. *Dzogchen* was the foundational teaching of 8th century "school of the ancient ones", the

Nyingma School, as we shall see in Chapter VIII. These oldest Buddhist teachings of India were borne to Tibet in the 8th century by Padmasambhava, Vimalamitra, and Vairochana (*Appendix D*).

Mahamudra, the Great Seal or Great Imprint of the Kagu School represents the profound truth that all appearing reality is the inseparable unity of primordial wisdom and emptiness. It connotes ultimate realization of nondual (*advaya, nyis med*) Buddha mind (*buddhajnana, mahamudra siddhi*) that is Ultimate Truth (*paramartha satya*). Definitive Essence *Mahamudra* is here considered the essence of the view and practice of the "new translation" *Sarma* (from the 11th century) teachings (Kagyu, Sakya, Gelug, Schools). H.H. Dalai Lama reveals:

> Old translation (8th century Nyingma) *Dzogchen* and new translation *Sarma* (11th century) *anuttarayoga tantra* (*Mahamudra*) offer equivalent paths that can bring the practitioner to the same resultant state of Buddhahood.
> (Gyatso,Tenzin; A. Berzin, 1997; *The Gelug/Kagu Tradition of Mahamudra*, p. 2).

Well and good. But what has arcane Buddhist metaphysics to do with all of us stuck here in spacetime suffering the slings and arrows of outrageous *samsara*?

Buddhist metaphysics here meets Buddhist practice, and Buddhist ethics. The primordial love-wisdom mind *Presence* of this great awareness-consciousness whole is, on the accord of the Mahayana Middle Way Madhyamaka, always present within each human form. Buddha mind love-wisdom Presence is already present within us! Buddha is, here and now, alive and awake within us! It is That to which we awaken self-ego-I through Buddha's original Hinayana Eightfold Path, and the Mahayana *Six Paramitas* with its ethic of wise, compassionate precious *bodhicitta*, our way to ultimate Happiness Itself. This luminous love-wisdom Presence of the empty boundless whole (*dharmadhatu*) that is reality itself has many names. Buddhists of all stripes call it Buddha nature (*tathagatagarbha*) or *bodhi*-wisdom mind, or Buddha mind (*buddhajnana*). Lama Professor Anne C. Klein (2006) has told it well:

> The unbounded whole is how and what reality is...
> Open awareness (*rigpa*, presence), fully present to
> that state of wholeness is the knowing of it.

Buddhist Dzogchen: Being Happiness Itself

Without past, present, future, empty awake mind.
— Ju Mipham Rinpoche

Fundamental Innate Buddha Mind of Clear Light. That is the inherent wisdom mind basis of *Dzogchen* View and Practice. *Dzogchen* is considered, by those who know, to be a radically simple, if very difficult path to realization of nondual primordial wisdom. How is this so?

Dzogchen Ati Yoga works *directly*—prior to conceptual Mahayana Buddhist dialectics, and to tantric deity practice—with the already present indwelling Buddha nature/Buddha mind, the very nature of mind, luminous clear light wisdom Presence of *rigpa* itself, before any arising of phenomenal appearances through its emptiness/*shunyata* ground.

It is that nondual primordial awareness essential nature of mind—the nondual state of undistracted "non-meditation" Presence that is at first "introduced", non-conceptually, to the prepared aspirant by the *Dzogchen* master. It is that luminous awareness in which we learn to rest. It is that in which we train the mind. Tsele Natsok Rangdröl:

> Mahamudra and Dzogchen differ in words, but not in meaning. The only difference is that Mahamudra stresses mindfulness while Dzogchen rests within awareness itself.

In the clear words of 20th century Nyingma *Dzogchen* master Tulku Urgyen Rinpoche:

> In short, in Mahamudra you train with outer appearances, and in Dzogchen you train with inner rigpa...All appearances are beyond benefit and harm. In this way rigpa and appearances are a unity...The word unity has great significance. Don't divide appearances as being there and awareness as being here. Let appearance and awareness be indivisible...
>
> If you recognize the essence, then when forms appear, they become the unity of appearance and emptiness... Appearing and being empty occur as a unity...The Dzogchen teachings refer to this as the unity of primordial purity (*kadag*) and spontaneous presence (*lhundrub*). Since primordial time (these two) have been inseparably united. Through Trekchö you recognize that your own essence is primordial purity. Through Tögal you realize that the nature is spontaneous presence. Neither of these has any self-nature.
>
> What is mind? Guru Rinpoche explains what is called the 'unity of emptiness and cognizance suffused with awareness'...Its essence is empty; its nature is cognizant. Its capacity is that these two cannot be taken apart. That is the meaning of unity, impossible to separate.
>
> (*Vajra Heart Revisited*, 2020, Rangung Yeshe)

Hence, in *Dzogchen* View and Practice the primordial awareness state of Presence (*rigpa, vidya*) is not dependent upon, nor distracted by external or internal appearances arising in mind. Whatever arises, the practitioner rests in the state of nondual awareness, without grasping or rejecting anything at all. But, without the direct recognition (*yogi pratyaksa*) of primordial awareness, how could one train in it? Thus the necessity of a qualified *Dzogchen* master to initiate and guide the practice of the prepared yogi/yogini aspirant.

Wonder of wonders, that *buddic* Presence is alive and awake in the mundane everyday chaos of our "ordinary mind". So, we need not seek it elsewhere, for example in the causes and conditions of buddhahood. From Garab Dorje's Three Vajra Verses, "Introduce the state of presence directly". This cannot be told in words, nor in books.

Therefore, Dzogchen View takes the Result of buddhahood as the Path. The "lower" Buddhist teaching vehicles take not the result but the *causes* of Buddhahood—dualistic practice—as the Path.

> Indian Mahayana Sutra and Tibetan Vajrayana Tantra teachings are characterized by the Path of Renunciation and the Path of Transformation, respectively. The method of the nondual *Dzogchen* teaching is the Path of Self-Liberation.
>
> (Chögyal Namkhai Norbu).

The Path of Renunciation renounces the ignorance (*avidya*) and cognitive obscurations that are the cause of the negative afflictive emotions that cause human suffering. We practice a cause (dharma practice) to gain a desired result (liberation from suffering).

The Path of Transformation is also a dualistic path wherein the practitioner proceeds from non-virtuous "impure vision" to virtue and "pure vision".

However, in the Path of Self-Liberation, there is no *concept* of impure and pure vision. In *Dzogchen* vision there is only the unity of the nondual state of self-liberation. It is from the inherent freedom of that view that we proceed upon the Path. It is from the *bodhicitta* that spontaneously arises from that view that determines the compassionate conduct.

The Buddha told that the result of such selfless altruistic motivation to act is the main cause of human happiness; and the result of self-centered negatively motivated action is the main cause of human suffering. Cultivation of compassionate bodhicitta is the only way to authentic human happiness. Without an authentic individual and sociocultural ethic of compassion it is not possible even to begin to address to prodigious problems of human beings in this relative world of pain and suffering.

The root cause of full bodhi mind awaking in all three Buddhist vehicles is the union of wisdom and compassion—these two limbs of the teaching of the Buddha. That the primordial wisdom of emptiness may result in buddhahood is due to mahakaruna—the great compassion. Just so, mahakaruna may result in buddhahood due to the wisdom that realizes mahashunyata, the great emptiness. Thus did the Buddha teach that in order to be happy being here as honored guests of this phenomenal world of time and space, we must cultivate compassionate "skillful means", and the primordial wisdom of emptiness—as a nondual unity! That is our refuge.

These two voices of the teaching strike a balance between construing emptiness as nihilistic nonexistence, wherein virtue doesn't much matter, or as eternalist material existence. The view of real, compassionate relative existence, and the absence or emptiness of intrinsic ultimate existence avoids these two metaphysical extremes that are the false dichotomy of *either* existence *or* nonexistence. That is the Buddha's Madhyamaka Middle Way teaching. Indeed, it is the ultimate emptiness of appearing phenomena that allows their relative interaction in the function of moral conduct. If our phenomenal realities were not ultimately empty of permanent existence, relative change or motion would not be possible. People, stars, galaxies would freeze in their present spacetime locations. In that case how could we change anything in the relative world through our choice to practice the Path and engage *bodhicitta* conduct? The Buddha's Path would be but a cynical exercise in futility.

Middle Way Madhyamaka Prasangika realizes this ultimate emptiness of appearing objective reality, and of a self-ego-I that apprehends it in ignorance (*avidya, marigpa*) of the truth of the matter. "In terms of that emptiness, there is no distinction between this Madhyamaka view and the *Dzogchen* view" (Lama Gen Lamrimpa 1999).

As to relative conventional objective existence, Longchenpa told, "When you examine closely, there is nothing there to recognize". Nonetheless, the conceptually and verbally imputed objects of our "real world out there" (RWOT), and this ego-I that truly believes in their ultimate existence, still show up for dinner. Fortunately, for both Prasangika and for *Dzogchen* view and practice, this cause and effect reality is still, indeed all too relatively real. So, we still have to show up for work, and arouse and engage our precious *bodhicitta* to benefit living beings. Thus, the Madhyamaka and *Dzogchen* View negate the inherent existence of the phenomenal world, while affirming its relative-conventional causal/cause and effect existence. Indeed a Middle Way. Nice *concepts*. But what makes it so?

Nondual Non-Meditation on Emptiness. It is in nondual *Dzogchen* meditation—beyond even the quasi-conceptual quiescence of shamatha meditation—that one realizes the *shunyata*/emptiness of phenomena, the very Buddha nature of mind.

Thus does the ostensible duality of relative mind (*sems*), and the nondual primordial base or ground, primordial awareness itself that is the very nature of mind (*gzhi rigpa*), together rest in the nondual unity of sameness (*samatajnana*). Nagarjuna told it well, "There is not the slightest difference between samsara and nirvana"; between relative truth and ultimate truth. The Buddha's Two Truths, relative and ultimate, are already an ontic prior, and epistemic present unity—beyond even the slightest separation of knowing subject, and its known objects.

The Nyingma school's Dodrubchen Rinpoche teaches that as primordial awareness arises, the yogi/yogini does not at all feel this absence of the primal subject-object split. Still, the all-consuming flame of the wisdom of emptiness is vividly present to contemplative experience. And that utterly trans-conceptual non-goal directed "non-meditation" is the main difference between the nondual *Dzogchen,* and the conceptual dialectical Prasangika Madhyamaka approaches. While the view of Buddha's emptiness, his Two Truths—relative compassion and ultimate wisdom—and the fruition of the Path that is buddhahood itself are the same in Madhyamaka and *Dzogchen,* there is an important difference between these two paths:

> Dzogchen practice, which is unmoved by conceptualiza-tion, is far more potent for dispelling the obscurations of the mind, and in that sense is regarded as far more profound.
>
> (Gen Lamrimpa 1999)

In *Dzogchen,* nondual, non-goal oriented direct "non-meditation" the diaphanous objects of apparitional phenomenal appearance utterly vanish into their luminous empty aboriginal "ground-less ground" as nondual *mahashunyata* arises. In the Mahayana Causal Vehicle, and in the "lower" eight vehicles of the Vajrayana, contemplative focus remains more or less on quasi- conceptual mindfulness, mantra, and deity practice. Not so in the fruitional Nyingma nondual ninth vehicle—*Ati Yoga Dzogchen*—where the prepared yogi/yogini simply rests in the Perfect Sphere of *Dzogchen,* wholly free of conceptual cognition.

We shall see below in our "Approaching *Dzogchen* Practice" that nondual *Dzogchen* non-meditation requires a deep under-standing of the primordial wisdom of emptiness, introduced and transmitted under the enlightened guidance of the *Dzogchen* master. Such preparation is required before ultimate fruitional *Dzogchen* practice can begin.

What remains for the meditator of this the radical negation of form in the emptiness/*shunyata epoché* after we surrender our habitual discursive concept mind and rest in the actual nature of mind? The non-conceptual lucent *buddic* already present Presence of this "supreme source" remains always at the spiritual Heart (*hridyam*) of the yogi/yogini. Even when we forget. It's always present! Buddha mind (*buddhajnana*) Presence makes it so.

It is said by those who know that this innate, empty, radiant clear light love-wisdom mind arises, non-conceptually, for all human beings at the moment of death, in deep dreamless sleep, in moments where waking consciousness is unwittingly suspended, in the deep meditation of highly accomplished masters, and in the conscious awareness mindstream of a Buddha.

Told the Buddha, "Form is empty; emptiness is form". Relative form—the five aggregates or *skandhas*—and their selfless ultimate emptiness are an indivisible nondual (subject-object union) unity. These are Buddha's Two Truths. Everything that arises and appears to sentient awareness is included herein (*Ch. VI*).

It is through a profound understanding of the Two Truths that we perfect the two main facets of the Buddha's love-wisdom Path—compassionate skillful means/method (*upaya*), and nondual primordial wisdom (*jnana, yeshe*). As Guru Padmasambhava told so long ago, "Descend with the (ultimate) View while ascending with the (relative) conduct. It is most essential to practice these two as a unity". This then is the prodigious *Dzogchen* View. No dilemma. No problem at all.

How then shall we understand this interdependence of wisdom and compassion that pervades the View, Meditation, and Conduct of the *nondual Dzogchen* Path?

For all three extant Buddhist vehicles—Hinayana-Theravada, Mahayana, Vajrayana—spacetime stuff and the self that perceives it is empty. Empty of what? For Madhyamaka Middle Way Buddhists (the fourth and usually considered "highest" of the Four Buddhist Tenet systems)—both Prasangika Madhyamaka and Yogachara Madhyamaka—arising and appearing form is *not* empty of existence!

Clearly, something exists! Heavy indeed is the yoke of the burden of rejoinder for those nihilist absolute metaphysical idealists—East or West—who would altogether deny this dynamic world of conventionally existing and experienced objective stuff, our "real world out there" (RWOT) that we have come to know and love. It is this all too real self-ego-I after all, who *chooses* to enter the Buddhist Path, and to act in this world of conditioned existence for the benefit of living beings. Appearing reality obviously exists. Yet, it does not exist as it appears. How then does it exist? Spacetime stuff is relative-conventionally existent, but ultimately non-existent continuously appearing phenomenal form.

For the Tibetan Buddhist Vajrayana tantric tradition, nondual *Dzogchen*, the Nyingma School Great Perfection or Great Completion is the subtle nondual pinnacle of Shakyamuni the Buddha's teaching. All four Vajrayana schools—Nyingma, Gelug, Kagyu, Sakya—agree.

The Tibetan Buddhist Middle Way Prasangika Madhyamaka of the Madhyamaka Buddhist tenet system (*Ch. V*) is the doctrinaire foundation upon which the *Dzogchen* view is established. The Yogachara Madhyamaka *Shentong* direct intuition of Buddha nature found in the Yogachara *chittamatra* tradition are equally important *Dzogchen* sources (Pettit 1999).

Middle Way Madhyamaka—with its two sub-schools that are Prasangika and Yogachara—are then the metaphysical, philosophical sources of highest *Ati Yoga* of the Great Perfection. However, *Dzogchen* ethics, and foundational practice preliminaries (*ngöndro*) are found in the yogic practices of the "lower" Mahayana and Vagrayana Buddhist teaching vehicles.

The *Dzogchen* View, Path/Meditation, and Result/Fruition presuppose the Ultimate Truth of Buddha nature (*tathagatagarbha*), our ultimate wisdom mind (*jnana, yeshe*) of the emptiness base (*gzhi rigpa*) whose essence is empty, whose nature is clear light luminosity, and whose expression is spontaneous compassionate *bodhicitta*—the thought, intention, and action for the benefit of living beings. More on this tripartite constitution of the Buddha nature of mind below.

Wisdom and Compassion. These are the two limbs of Buddha's teaching; the very bedrock of the whole of the buddhadharma.

If a thought or action is wise but not kind, it's not wisdom. If a thought or action is kind but not wise, it's not wisdom.

Tibetan Buddhist Nyingma School views the Buddha's three teaching vehicles or *yanas* of the buddhadharma—Hinayana, Mahayana, and Vajrayana—as the nine vehicles. The first eight are the Mahayana causal vehicles and are based upon the duality of cause and effect—practice this cause now and reap that happy effect later—and so are inherently incapable of liberating the yogic aspirant from the primal atavistic subject-object split. This is the prodigious false bifurcation of knowing subject and its objects known. It is this dualistic separation between self and other that is the root cause of human ignorance (*avidya, ma rigpa*) with all of its attendant suffering.

The view and praxis of the Great Perfection are grounded in the Vajrayana/Tantrayana subtle ninth non-causal vehicle—the *Ati Yoga* of *Dzogchen* which is the nondual state of *direct intuition* (*yogi pratyaksa*) of always already spontaneously present (*lhundrub*) Presence (*vidya, rigpa*) of our indwelling primordial Buddha wisdom mind nature (*jnana, yeshe, gnosis*).

The Buddha's Two Truths in Dzogchen View and Practice. The dualistic dimension of everyday Relative Truth (*samvriti satya*, Tib. *kunzog denpa*)—already embraced and subsumed in the boundless whole that is Ultimate Truth (*paramartha satya*, Tib. *don dampa*), Perfect Sphere of *Dzogchen*—is personified as, and grounded in primordial *Adi Buddha* Samantabhadra (*Tib. Kuntazangpo*), the formless *dharmakaya* Buddha in whom form (*rupakaya* as *sambhogakaya* and *nirmanakaya*) arises and is instantiated. These three dimensions constitute the Tibetan Buddhist *Trikaya of the Base* (*gzhi rigpa*)—the three buddha bodies (*kayas*) of ultimate reality itself (*Ch. IX*).

This formless, timeless primeval aboriginal dimension that is Ultimate Truth is empty and absent "any shred" of *svabhava* (*rang zhin*)—relative, conceptually imputed, permanent, independent, intrinsic, ultimate/absolute self-existence. Ultimate Buddha mind (*buddhajnana, dgongs pa*) dimension is the perfectly subjective selfless ground and potential of relative *svabhava*—omnipresent, appearing spacetime phenomenal form.

Thus it is, conditional form is relatively real, just not intrinsically, ultimately real. Stuff continuously, interdependently arising from the primordial base/ground does not exist as it appears. The stuff of our appearing realities exists only relatively, conventionally, not absolutely or ultimately. Yet here it is, all too real and full of itself throughout relative objective spacetime existence. This view is the wondrous Buddhist Mahayana/Vajrayana dominant Two Truths trope of *Dzogchen* View and Practice (*Ch. VI*).

In the *Great Perfection Aspiration Prayer of Samantabhadra*— primordial *Adi Buddha* of the Ultimate Truth *dharmakaya* dimension—this primordial ultimate ground is revealed thusly (I have taken the liberty of making slight changes to Richard Barron's excellent translation):

Ho! The entire universe of appearance and possibility, of samsara and nirvana, is one ground, two paths, two results. This is the magical display of innate intrinsic awareness, and its recognition or non-recognition. Due to the aspiration of the all noble Samantabhadra, may all beings awaken to perfectly manifest buddhahood within the palace of the basic space of phenomena! The primordial ground of all experience is un-compounded. This reflexive self-arising vast expanse of being is ineffable. There are no correct descriptions for either samsara or nirvana. If there is intrinsic awareness of this point, there is buddhahood. If there is no recognition of intrinsic awareness of the ground sentient beings wander in the suffering of cyclic existence. Therefore, may all sentient beings of the three realms be aware of the ultimate profundity of the ineffable ground of being!

The "one ground" is, as Lama Tsultrim Allione has shown us, "the base or the womb of the great mother...It is pure latency, depth radiance, an expanse of emptiness and infinite potency from which the whole universe comes, yet the ground itself is without external radiance or projective (energy/motion) aspects".

The "two paths" arise from the aboriginal, timeless, formless one ground. One of these paths is the pristine *nirvanic* "recognition of intrinsic awareness of the ground" as primordial *Presence* of one's innate, intrinsic dynamic Buddha mind, the very nature of mind that abides in an already prior and always present unity with the primordial ground—utterly inseparable from the ground itself. The *Result* or *Fruition* of this path? "There is buddhahood", already present from the very beginning.

The other path is the path we all have taken—all of us pre-enlightened beings cycling here in samsaric existence—the not so happy *Result* of "non-recognition" (*ignorance, avidya, ma rigpa* of self-ego-I) of the empty primordial "groundless ground" that is Samantabhadra (Tib. Kuntazangpo), our already present Buddha nature (*tathagatagarbha*), Buddha mind (*buddhajnana*). The usual result of this path is endless cyclic suffering of birth, old age, sickness, and death. Not a pretty picture. What then shall we do?

It is this second path that provides the opportunity to *choose* to enter in the practice of Buddha's *Pali Canon* Eightfold Path, and the Six Paramitas of the Mahayana, and through the profound teaching of these vehicles recognize, then realize the indwelling, "innate intrinsic awareness" of our Buddha mind that was, and is, as *Dzogchen* founder Garab Dorje told, "already present from the very beginning". It is that primordial love-wisdom to which we awaken.

Emptiness of Mind; Emptiness of Self. Twentieth century *Dzogchen* master Tulku Urgyen Rinpoche points out that selfless Buddhist emptiness/*shunyata*—the essential nature of the primordial *dharmakaya* ground—must be understood, not as a nihilistic, blank void of nothingness, but as "empty luminous cognizance". *"Emptiness is not empty of the kayas (buddha bodies of reality) and of primordial wisdom".*

Rather, *shunyata* is the empty absolute space (*dharmadhatu*) of *dharmakaya,* radiant clear light primordial awareness base (*gzhi*), ultimate nature of form, selfless, innate clear light Buddha nature of mind. Always present bright Presence of That. How shall we understand this?

We are told by the wise that as one *chooses* to settle the obsessively busy mind into, and then rest in *selfless* "open presence" (*rigpa*) of this "natural state of pristine awareness"—Buddha nature/Buddha mind—one realizes that the mind has no past origin, no present location, and no future destiny. The three times—past, present, future—are absent and empty of mind. Mind has no physical structure, nor mental form. It cannot be located in the brain, nor is it elsewhere. If the mind were as big as a house, we might thoroughly search the house, but we will not find the mind. Mind therefore, is a *luminous cognizant emptiness* that is inherently ineffable and ungraspable by any conceptual construct or cognitive modality—relative conventional or ultimate. Yet, here it is, brimming with our relative realities.

Just so, the self-ego-I that is so relentlessly embedded in this diaphanous apparition of self or mind, with all the virtuosity of its conceptual affordances, is also empty of intrinsic ultimate existence. It too is empty of past origin, present location or future destiny. This bizarre phantom self entity does not exist in physical body, nor in mental mind, nor elsewhere. Exhausting analytical *vipashyana* examination reveals no essential self at all. Thus is self-ego-I confirmed to be wholly empty of any whit of inherent, intrinsic existence. This is the teaching of the Buddha.

Yet, upon the arising of a strong desire (attraction), or a perceived threat (aversion), self arises like a seductive demon, or else a screaming banshee. How then shall we definitively know and feel, directly—beyond analysis—this great truth of the selfless intrinsic emptiness of form?

Approaching *Dzogchen* Practice. We tame, then train this obsessively "selfing" conceptual "wild horse of the mind" through quiescent *shamatha* meditation practice (*smriti, sati*) as taught in Sutrayana. This, with the foundational *ngöndro* practices of Tibetan Vajrayana, is the *Dzogchen* approach. In the Great Perfection the nondual indivisibility of the *Dzogchen* View and contemplative *Ati Yoga* non-meditation practice—with compassion for other beings—is axiomatic.

In beginning practice it is urgent to recognize that a naive duality between a goal-directed "gradual path", and a direct, immediate "nondual" ("not one, not two") *Dzogchen* path is, as is the conceptually contrived distinction between the Buddha's Two Truths—Ultimate and Relative—a false dichotomy that introduces a destructive duality into the *Dzogchen* View and Meditation. How then shall we enhance our view that we may feel and know the nondual truth of the matter?

We have seen that the dualistic dimension of relative-conventional, causal, physical, perceptual and conceptual truth (*samvriti satya*) is already embraced and subsumed in the nondual dimension of Ultimate Truth (*paramartha satya*). Thus exists the prior ontological and always present epistemological and phenomenological unity of the Buddha's Two Truths. This all-pervading unity is experienced non-conceptually, directly (*yogi pratyaksa*) as the experience of our indwelling Buddha nature/ Buddha mind—bright clear light Presence of That—beyond our conceptual "global web of belief" (Quine 1969) *about* it. Instant, open, knowing-feeling, *maha-ati* "pure Presence" (*vidya, rigpa*) *of* it, by whatever name, is recognition and realization of That!

What then shall we do when we inevitably become distracted and forgetful of this great truth of our here now Presence of the nature of mind. The *Dzogchen semdzins*—Vajrasattva mantra (short and long versions), the essential mantra *OM AH HUM*, and the forcefully expressed seed syllable **PHAT**—are our instant antidote, our *Ati Yoga* touchstones. It is through the *semdzin* that we return our attention to "innermost secret" Presence of the formless ground, again and again.

False dichotomy caveat: our self-ego-I concept-mind—under sway of ignorance (*avidya, ma rigpa*)—firmly believes and defends the linguistic semiotic split between dualistic and nondual Path; between Ultimate Truth and Relative Truth; between form and emptiness; between knowing subject and its objects known; between the two illusory *mayas* that are ultimate nondual selfless primordial awareness *Dzogchen vidya maya,* and relative conceptually contrived *avidya maya;* between existence and nonexistence; primordial purity and impurity; nirvana and samsara; dualistic and nondual view and meditation. All of these ultimately indivisible, yet complementary cognitive unities are cloaked in the false dichotomy of dualistic Relative Truth (*samvriti satya, kunzog denpa*) with its cognitive reticulum of "concealer" concepts and beliefs.

Thus do the two *mayas* share an identity of non-difference. Relatively they differ. Ultimately they are the same. Great 14th century *Dzogchen* master Longchenpa bespeaks (*Gyuma Galso*) the inherent nondual *unitarity* (an apropos neologism of Niels Bohr) of the two *mayas*. How is this so?

There are two kinds of human ignorance. The first is inborn and innate. The other is learned. Innate ignorance is instinctive; we are born with it. It is the instinctual view of self-ego-I, a perceiving subject inherently separate from all "other" selves and objects. The second is learned ignorance, the cognitive product of sociocultural conditioning—in Western culture the Greek materialism that has become the destructive prevailing cognitive deep cultural background mass mind ideology of Scientific Materialism/Physicalism. Both of these sad forms of ignorance are woefully short on compassion.

Dualistically appearing *avidya maya* experience is embraced and pervaded by the nondual *vidya maya* of the primordial "groundless ground" of being itself. This unity of the inherently apparitional two *mayas* arises to our experience from the nondual "primordial purity" of the aboriginal emptiness ground/base (*gzhi rigpa*) in whom all appearing reality arises and is instantiated—perfectly free and unencumbered by desire, or by conceptual fabrication and elaboration. Because, in the "*Perfect Sphere of Dzogchen*", our illusory and delusory realities are, in this Ultimate Truth view, "primordially pure" and undefiled "from the very beginning" all appearing *avidya maya* is "perfect just as it is". In the clear words of Gautama the Buddha:

> What you are is what you have been;
> What you will be is what you do now...
> So let it be as it is, and rest your weary mind;
> All things are perfect exactly as they are.

Yet, under sway of ignorance (*avidya*), and delusion (*moha*) we almost immediately conceptually interpret this selfless pristine direct attentional/perceptual experience as afflictive emotional experience—sense desire, fear/anger, greed/pride, paralyzing doubt, and the rest. The result is human suffering. The antidote is instant effortless, spontaneous non-meditation "placement of attention", again and again upon our always present Buddha mind Presence, by whatever name or concept. *PHAT*!

This is the timeless, radical *Dzogchen* View and practice.

Further, this instant, always already present open "pure presence" of the original ground are at once both origin and aim of the cognitively ambulant *Dzogchen* practitioner. "The ground is no different at the pinnacle of enlightenment than it is at the primordial base" (Adzom Rinpoche).

Caveat Auditor: Nonetheless, from the relative view, delusory dualistic *avidya maya* has a thorny thicket of bogus cognitive concepts on offer for the naively innocent obsessively thinking mind. *Avidya maya* concept-mind is a trickster. Don't be fooled. Please avoid impetuous true-false reality judgments based in habitual, skeptical, dualistic deep cultural background "global web of belief" about what is true or false; good or bad.

Yet, wonder of wonders, it is this duplicitous, dualistic concept-mind of our very own self-ego-I that reflexively recognizes *avidya maya* just as it is; ignorance, illusion, and delusion. That reflective awareness cognition is after all the first step in waking up to our selfless, luminous, clear light love-wisdom mind Presence—the primordial Buddha nature of mind—"supreme source" that is nothing less than our "supreme identity". Who am I? "That I Am!"—without a single exception.

Be That as it may, such complementary cognitive doublets may be—once the *ultimate* boundless love-wisdom whole (*jnana, yeshe*) in which they arise and abide is recognized/realized (*rtogs pa*)—useful gifts to our *relative* discriminating wisdom (*prajna*). *Prajna* facilitates spontaneous, skillful *bodhicitta* conduct—our thought, intention, and action for the benefit of living beings. And that after all is the Mahayana open secret of human happiness. The two wisdoms, ultimate and relative: Guru Rinpoche Padmasambhava advises, "Practice these two as a unity".

Popular Buddhist idiom and ideology too often sees *Dzogchen* as a shortcut to *buddic* primordial awakening. Read some books about *Dzogchen trekchö* and *tögal* practice; rest occasionally in mostly conceptualized *rigpa;* maybe even show up for a *Yeshe Lama* weekend retreat; and become fully enlightened buddhas in this lifetime. But it is not so.

This great and precious *Dzogchen* wisdom treasure is decidedly not a conceptual enterprise. It cannot be learned, let alone accomplished through books, tapes, intellectual speculation, along with a little mindfulness practice. Indeed it cannot be learned at all. Buddha told, "This cannot be taught". The non-dual primordial wisdom state of *Dzogchen* must be introduced *directly*, non-conceptually, by the *Dzogchen* master, as we shall see. Yet, study and quiescent *shamatha* "taming the wild horse of the mind" is a propitious beginning.

Although, as we have just seen, the luminous Presence of *dynamic intrinsic awareness* that is the very Buddha nature of mind abides always present in our *ordinary mind stream*—and while the Great Perfection with its nondual *Ati Yoga* is indeed a direct and expedited path to ultimate awakening to our already present innate clear light *rigpa* wisdom Buddha mind Presence—*Dzogchen* practice requires assiduous "gradualist" contemplative and behavioral, ethical conduct preparation under the guidance of a qualified *Dzogchen* master. Only then shall be revealed the trans-conceptual miracle that "it is already accomplished from the very beginning". Should you aspire to such an ultimate path, please consider well this truth of *Dzogchen* practice: From Garab Dorje's *Three Vajra Verses*:

> The nature of mind is Buddha from the beginning...
> Realizing the purity essence of all things, to remain
> there without seeking is the meditation....It is already
> accomplished from the very beginning.

"To remain there without seeking is the meditation". That is *Dzogchen* "non-meditation". Roughly speaking, in the Mahayana Causal Vehicle, meditation seeks something—peace, happiness, liberation from suffering, enlightenment. Practice this cause now, and get that payoff later, in the future. In the *Dzogchen* Fruitional View there is nothing to seek, and nothing to accomplish. That which we seek is always already present. Seeking that which we already actually are to avoid suffering, is a form of suffering.

Thus is *Dzogchen* View and non-meditation practice the non-dual Great Perfection/Completion of the dualistic preparation of the Mahayana Causal Vehicle. Without this urgent development stage Mahayana Middle Way Madhyamaka practice there is no auspicious entry into *Dzogchen*. The *Dzogchen ngöndro* foundational practices are an auspicious, difficult beginning. Effortless *Dzogchen* practice requires hard work preparation—both conceptual and contemplative.

So, first we learn basic mantra deity practice, along with mindful *shamatha* meditation. We learn to rest in this luminous spacious Presence of our Buddha mind emptiness ground that is the Perfect Sphere of *Dzogchen*, in whom everything arises. Then, with this enhanced capacity, and with the "pointing out" instruction of the qualified *Dzogchen* master, we approach the nondual *Dzogchen* View with its non-meditation on the Buddha's wisdom of *shunyata*/emptiness.

Guru Padmasambhava, in his lustrous *Natural Liberation* speaks of *Dzogchen shamatha*:

> Flawless shamatha is like an oil lamp that is unmoved by wind. Wherever the awareness is placed, it is unwaveringly present; awareness is vividly clear, without being sullied by laxity, lethargy, or dimness; wherever the awareness is directed, it is steady and sharply pointed; and unmoved by adventitious thoughts, it is straight. Thus, a flawless meditative state arises in one's mind-stream; and until this happens, it is important that the mind is settled in its natural state...Cast your gaze downward, gently release your mind, and without having anything on which to meditate, gently release both your body and mind into their natural state...Without any modification or adulteration, place your attention simply without wavering, in its own natural state, its natural limpidity, its own character, just as it is now. Remain in clarity, and rest the mind so that it is loose and free...Fine stability will arise and you may even identify (primordial wisdom) awareness.
>
> (trans. Alan Wallace 1998. See *Appendix A* below.)

In *Dzogchen* shamatha practice, naturally arising discursive thoughts, mental images, and emotions—negative or positive—are not seen as troublesome distractions to reject or enjoy. Rather, one sees them as emanations or manifestations of *dharmakaya*, primordially pure and of the same nature as the vast expanse of the ground itself, as waves are of the same nature as the great ocean.

Dzogchen is generally considered by those who know to be the most direct path to the final nondual realization of our ultimate

Buddha nature that is primordial "groundless ground" of all arising phenomenal reality, the very nature of mind and all of its experience—perceptual, conceptual, contemplative, and nondual (*advaya*; "not one, not two").

Self and all arising spacetime phenomenal reality—our beloved "real world out there" (RWOT)—are thereby dynamic, luminous, empty virtual displays of the play of this boundless whole that is primordial awareness-consciousness ground itself in which, or in whom our physical and mental experience are instantiated. We are luminous instances of That! Resting naturally in that vast spacious boundless whole (*dharmadhatu*) is the primary cause of human happiness itself. And "Wonder of wonders", "it is already accomplished from the very beginning", deep within us.

As to our open question, how do we know, and feel this? *Shamatha* and *vipashyana* meditation practice open the gate to the Path of the esoteric *Dzogchen* Great Completion of the exoteric Buddhist Causal Vehicle—always under the guidance of the *Dzogchen* master.

Nyingma *Dzogchen* Master Dudjom Rinpoche clarifies this for us:

> (*Dzogchen*), which makes the result into the path is superior to the vehicle of the transcendental perfections which makes the cause into the path (*Nyingma School of Tibetan Buddhism*, Vol. I)

Thus is the ultimate Result or Fruit of enlightenment—fully realized innate, primordial nondual wisdom *bodhi* Buddha mind (*jnana, yeshe*) that is realized as Buddhahood—taken as the "innermost" esoteric foundation of the tantric Path. Why? Because the result, Buddha nature/Buddha mind is always already present within us. So we work, relatively, with that ultimate reality, from the outset. As Guru Rinpoche told, "We discover ultimate truth only by way of relative truth". Yet, while working with relative truth we "Keep your view as high as the sky; and your deeds as fine as barley flour".

In short, we "keep the view" that we are always already Buddha. That is the nondual original nature of mind—this wondrous gift that is our here now present relative spacetime embodied, ultimately non-existent, cognizant, primordially pure and empty mind. Realizing That, we forget ourselves for a few moments and go to work to benefit living beings. It is That that makes us happy now. That is the teaching of the Buddha.

Once again, no need to seek happiness in some future perfect time or place, or mind state. Rather, we gradually awaken, through the assiduous practice of the Path, to that "supreme identity" that we already are. Who am I? To borrow a Vedic pith, *Tat Tvam Asi*. That I Am! "It is already accomplished from the very beginning" (Garab Dorje). As Gautama Shakyamuni told so long ago, "Wonder of wonders, all beings are Buddha". Thus do we "Make the goal the Path".

Conversely, the exoteric, dualistic sutra Mahayana Causal Vehicle (the dialectical vehicle) takes causality, cause and effect—practice these Six Perfections now and become a Buddha later—as the foundation of the Path. The main point here is that, although we are not yet fully awakened Buddhas, we are already Buddha! Our ordinary mind is Buddha mind from the very beginning! It is that great nondual Ultimate Truth to which we gradually awaken through the assiduous relative practice of the Path. This great Vajrayana tantric foundational premise makes all the difference in establishing the correct conceptual View (*darshana, lta ba*) from the outset. Who am I? I am Buddha from the very beginning. Good to know in approaching the *Dzogchen* path, or at any stage of the Path (*marga, lam*); especially at the beginning.

Thus it is said, *Dzogchen Ati Yoga* is the teaching pinnacle, subtlest and "highest" view and practice of Nyingma "inner tantras", and the very Fruitional Vehicle of the buddhadharma Path.

While the causal Paramitayana and the fruitional Tibetan Vajrayana are equally concerned to "accomplish" Buddhahood, unlike the skillful objective conceptual means of Sutrayana, the tantras of highest *Ati Yoga Dzogchen* of the tantric vehicle has the benefit of subjective, trans-conceptual, innermost esoteric skillful means, to wit: highly efficacious, even blissful direct and innate clear light wisdom (*jnana, yeshe, gnosis*), and mantra and deity practice meditation under the direct empowering guidance of a qualified *Dzogchen* master. Such a practice program is said to expedite Buddhahood in several lifetimes, or if you're lucky, in this lifetime, over against "innumerable *kalpas*" of rebirth for even the superior Sutrayana practitioner. Not surprisingly, those who hold the View of the Great Perfection view it as the perfect Path.

This fruitional tantric distinction is perhaps the main difference between the more or less exoteric objective and dualistic conceptual dialectics of the Sutrayana (Sautrantika) vehicle, and the esoteric Tantrayana/Vajrayana (Mantrayana) with its Middle Way Prasangika Madhyamaka teaching, the foundation of innermost esoteric, monistic panpsychic/cosmopsychic nondual *Dzogchen* view and praxis. (Boaz 2021b, *Ch. VIII*, "Primordial Consciousness: Monistic Dzogchen Panpsychism"; excerpted at davidpaulboaz.org under "Articles and Essays".)

We shall see below that in the View of the Great Perfection the *essence* (*kadag*) of all appearing physical and mental spacetime reality is boundless *shunyata*/emptiness. But emptiness is not merely a negative void because its *nature* is spontaneous presence (*lhundrub*), fullness of radiant luminosity (*prabhasa, 'od gsal*). Its *energy* is the manifested spontaneous expression in time and space of boundless compassion (*karuna, thugs re*)—great cosmic gift (*jinlob, euengelion*) of absolute *bodhicitta* whence arises the relative *bodhicittas* of aspiration, and of action. Once again, it is this precious relative *bodhicitta* that is the Mahayana/Vajrayana secret of human happiness.

These three conceptual faces—essence, nature, energy—of the Perfect Sphere of *Dzogchen* are in all ways an omnipresent, indivisible prior and present unity that is revealed through stabilized, nondual non-meditation of *Dzogchen Ati Yoga* practice.

These are some of the things we need to know when approaching the *Dzogchen* path.

The Fundamental Innate Mind of Clear Light in Sutra and Tantra. Buddha told it 25 centuries past,

> The mind is devoid of mind,
> for the nature of mind is clear light.

H.H. Dalai Lama (2000) teaches that the whole spectrum of Buddhist philosophy, ethics, and practice may be understood in terms of this one justly famous verse of the Buddha.

The first line presents the wisdom of the First Turning of the Wheel of Dharma (the *dharmachakra*), the teaching of the Four Noble Truths, and the entire meaning of Buddhist Sutrayana—of emptiness/*shunyata*, and of *bodhicitta*. The first line also introduces the wisdom of Mahayana Middle Way Madhyamaka, the Second Turning of the Wheel of the Buddha's Teaching.

The second line of the verse—"for the nature of mind is clear light"—encompasses the meaning of the Third Turning of the Wheel, namely, Buddha's teaching on our innate indwelling Buddha nature (*tathagatagarbha*)/Buddha mind (*buddhajnana*), the nondual primordial innate clear light Buddha nature of mind. The nondual *Ati Yoga* of *Dzogchen*, the Great Completion, is the practice of accomplishing this fundamental "innate mind of clear light"—non-conceptual, pristine, naked, essential Buddha mind, our indwelling open Presence of That!

For His Holiness, clear light mind nature may be understood at two levels, the Mahayana sutra teaching system, and the Vajrayana tantra teaching system. When the clear light nature of mind is understood in terms of both of these together there are two distinct references: 1) the "emptiness of the mind" which corresponds to the "objective clear light", and 2) "the essential cognizant luminous clarity and awareness" of the very nature of mind itself, which corresponds to the "subjective experience of clear light". In the clear words of H.H. Dalai Lama:

> The fundamental innate mind of clear light is considered to be the nature of mind, or the ultimate root of consciousness... This is the same experience to which Mahamudra leads, to which Dzogchen leads, and to which the union of clarity and emptiness (Sakya) leads...If you analyse them, they all arrive at the same point...As soon as there is clear and aware consciousness it is said to be permeated by the clear light rigpa...indwelling clear light, essential rigpa... When this aware aspect of rigpa is directly introduced and recognized, it can be identified even in the very thick of arising thoughts...In Dzogchen, while thoughts are active, rigpa permeates them all, so that even at the very moment when powerful thoughts like attachment and aversion are arising, there remains a pervasive quality of clear light rigpa. That rigpa you make into your practice
> —H.H. Dalai Lama, *Dzogchen*, 2000, p 168 ff.

High Dharma in a Cold Climate: *Dzogchen* View and Practice. In the ancient **Ny**ingma tradition of Vajrayana Tibetan Buddhism *Dzogchen* (*Dzogpachenpo*, Skt. *Mahasandi*) is seen as the definitive, highest teaching of Shakyamuni Buddha—the "innermost secret" teaching that he taught only to disciples of the greatest capacity and preparation.

We've seen that the *Dzogchen* (*Dzog*; complete or perfect; *chen*, great) teaching is said to have arisen from Samantabhadra (Tib. Kuntazangpo), primordial formless *dharmakaya Adi Buddha* in whom all spacetime reality form arises and appears. The teaching was then directly transmitted to Vajrasattva, *Adi Buddha* of the *sambhogakaya* dimension of light-form; then from Vajrasattva to the human *nirmanakaya* Garab Dorje (d. 55 C.E.), who recorded it for his disciple Manjushrimitra, who then classified it into the three *Dzogchen* teaching cycles—*semde, longde,* and secret *mengagde* or *upadesha*. This was then passed on to his disciple Shrisimha, then to Jnanasutra, and then in the 8th century to Tibet via Vimalamitra and Padmasambhava. In the 14th century "the omniscient" Longchenpa (1308-1364) synthesized the great teaching into a unified teaching Path. Jigme Lingpa (1730-1798) edited it into its present form as the *Longchen Nyingthig.* (For a more detailed history please see *Appendix D*: "A Brief History of the *Dzogchen* Transmission")

We've seen that for Nyingma school, the traditional three extant Buddhist teaching vehicles—Hinayana/Theravada, Mahayana, and Vajrayana—have become the *Nine Vehicles* to liberation from suffering and the ultimate clear light full *bodhi* awakening to our already present Buddha mind (*buddhajnana*). That propitious Result is buddhahood itself.

H.H. Dalai Lama teaches that the first eight of these Nine Vehicles of Nyingma utilize our reflective, relative conventional ordinary obstructed mind working as the cause and effect Mahayana Causal Vehicle to accomplish the ultimate full *bodhi* enlightenment of buddhahood. The bad news: such a path of renunciation and transformation takes countless lifetimes.

However, we have seen that in the *Dzogchen* Resultant or Fruitional Vehicle ordinary mind itself is recognized as already "primordially pure" Buddha mind "from the very beginning". This subtle, direct supreme vehicle—the *Ati Yoga* of *Dzogchen*, the nondual Great Perfection or Great Completion of the dualistic Mahayana Causal Vehicle—utilizes our already present indwelling dynamic intrinsic primordial awareness wisdom itself as the Path. Once again, this path is considered by most Vajrayana masters to be the pinnacle—with Essence Mahamudra—of all the Buddhist teaching vehicles, and may, under the most auspicious circumstances, be "accomplished" in a single lifetime. That's the good news.

This primordial awareness wisdom is the constant and "unchanging *rigpa* awareness" that is not other than Samantabhadra, primordial *Adi Buddha* of the all embracing aboriginal *dharmakaya* reality dimension. This *dharmakaya* Buddha is the "Supreme Source" (*Kenjed Gyalpo*), and represents our pristine fundamental nature, the "fundamental innate mind of clear light". It is utterly "primordially pure" and untainted by the karmic winds of dualistic conceptual thought and negative emotion.

In *Dzogchen* View and Practice luminous, numinous primordial awareness wisdom Presence—*rigpa, vidya*—is inherently present in all human beings, without a single exception. It is not something that happens conditionally—if we're good, kind, and helpful. Instant open Presence is already the case. Indeed it is who we are now.

Moreover, all of the physical and mental phenomena of relative spacetime reality arise, participate, and pass away within this vast unbounded primordial whole, by whatever name or concept. All arising reality is imbued with this primordial Buddha nature (*tathagatagarbha*). Just so, that same primordial essence is the "supreme identity" of each and every human being—bright compassionate Presence of That. On the accord of H.H. Dalai Lama:

> The most important way to understand the Great Perfection is in terms of essence, nature and compassionate energy according to which the essence is primordial purity (*kadag*) and the nature is spontaneous presence (*lhundrub*)... All the phenomena of samsara and nirvana and the path are, by their very nature, the *rigpa* awareness that is the primordial buddha Samantabhadra, and they are never outside of the primordial expanse of buddhahood...This is the fundamental innate mind of clear light.
>
> —H.H. Dalai Lama, 2007, p. 78

In other words, according to 19th century Nyingma *Rimé* polymath Ju Mipham:

Within the essence original wakefulness which is primordially pure (*kadag*) manifests the nature, a radiance which is spontaneously present (*lhundrub*).

Thus it is, in the *Dzogchen* view, the fundament of clear light ground luminosity is the *Trikaya of the Base* or the three Buddha bodies—*dharmakaya, sambhogakaya, nirmanakaya*—that is our "supreme source" (*cittadhatu, kunjed gyalpo*), ultimate reality itself (*dharmata, cho-nyid*), the very nature of mind (*sems-nyid, buddhi*): its *essence* is emptiness/*shunyata*; its *nature* is luminous clarity (*gsal-ba*); its *energy* continuously emanates as the compassionate *Kosmic* gift (*jinlob*) of ultimate *bodhicitta* that is our home as esteemed guests of this spacetime phenomenal dimension of light/motion/form (*tsal, rolba, E=mc²*).

This *jnana prana* energy naturally, selflessly expresses itself in human conduct as relative *bodhicitta*—compassionate wisdom (*thugs re*)—the thought, intention, and action to benefit living beings. Herein abides our own true happiness as individual and social beings.

So, infinite, empty vast expanse of basic space (*chos ying*) that is the unborn, uncreated, boundless whole (*dharmadhatu*) is our nondual ultimate reality ground itself (*dharmakaya*). From that unbroken whole interdependently arises (*pratitya samutpada*) relative form from its ultimate emptiness "groundless ground". As Buddha told, "Form is empty. Emptiness is form".

Ultimately, these complementary Two Truths of the vast whole are realized as a *one truth* prior and present unity that is, as we have seen, invariant throughout our entire human awareness-consciousness cognitive processional: 1) pre-conceptual direct perception; 2) exoteric, objective, conceptual cognition; 3) esoteric, subjective, contemplative cognition; 4) "innermost secret", perfectly subjective nondual cognition. Clearly, our wondrous, sometimes scintillating conceptual knowledge in no way exhausts this great whole that is our inherent human intelligence.

Therefore, the Buddhist Two Truths share a relation of identity. How is this so? The all inclusive nondual dimension of Ultimate Truth embraces, subsumes, and pervades the dynamic dualistic spacetime dimension of Relative Truth arising therein.

It is our always already present open awareness Presence (*vidya, rigpa*)—fully present to that primordial wholeness ground state—that knows and feels the truth of this great reality process. The practice of the Path with the living *Dzogchen* master and the *sangha* spiritual community opens the heart and mind of the yogi and yogini to receive the love, wisdom and deep inner ease and peace of it. And that is the very secret of both relative and ultimate human happiness. Earthy, pragmatic soteriology indeed.

Great 14th century *Dzogchen* master Longchen Rabjam (Longchenpa, 1308-1364), synthesizer of the entire previous *Dzogchen* wisdom transmission speaks of this, our conceptually unelaborated, "innermost secret" state of awareness Presence of the great unbounded whole itself:

> Naturally occurring timeless awareness—utterly lucid awakened mind—is marvelous and superb, primordially and spontaneously present. It is the treasury from which comes the universe of appearances and possibilities, whether samsara or nirvana. Homage to the unwavering state, free of conceptual elaboration.
> —Treasury of the Basic Space of Phenomena (2001)

Please consider Longchenpa's mind to mind transmission to us of this primordial awareness wisdom (*jnana, yeshe, gnosis*), the "fundamental innate mind of clear light", the very Buddha nature of mind (*citatta, sems nyid*), *dharmakaya* emptiness ground of the great whole of all our arising realities (*dharmata, cho nyid*):

> Self arising wisdom is *rigpa* that is empty, clear and free from all conceptual elaboration, like an immaculate sphere of crystal...It does not analyze objects...By simply

identifying that non-conceptual, pristine, naked *rigpa*, you realize there is nothing other than this nature...This is nondual self-arising wisdom...Like a reflection in a mirror, when objects and perceptions manifest to *rigpa*, that pristine and naked awareness which does not pro-liferate into thought is called the inner power (*tsal*), the responsiveness that is the ground (*gzhi*) for all the arising of things...For a yogin who realizes the naked meaning of *Dzogpachenpo*, *rigpa* is fresh, pure and naked, and objects may manifest and appear within *rigpa*, but it does not lose itself externally to those objects.

—Longchen Rabjam, *Treasury of the Dharmadhatu* (Commentary), Adzom Chögar edition

The Supreme Source. What is perhaps the primary *Dzogchen* tantra, *The Kunjed Gyalpo (The Supreme Source),* must surely be con-sidered one of humankind's great spiritual treasures. According to *Dzogchen* master Chögyal Namkhai Norbu, this prehistorical supreme nondual teaching—by whatever name—has been trans-mitted from master to disciple directly, heartmind to heartmind, for thousands of years.

However, historical *Dzogchen* wisdom dates from the teaching of Garab Dorje (d. 55 CE), as we have seen. The *Kunjed Gyalpo* tantra arises in the 8th Century and is the fundamental tantra of the *Dzogchen semde* (mind) teaching cycle. This reading of the great nonlocal, nondual primordial *Dzogchen* teaching is derived from Buddhist Vajrayana/Tantrayana understanding of the ultimate nature of mind, yet its truth essence runs like a golden thread through the grand tapestry of humankind's great nondual Primordial Wisdom Tradition.

Kunjed Gyalpo, The Wise and Glorious King is Samantabhadra (luminous clarity) and Samantabhadri (boundless emptiness) in inseparable *yabyum* embrace—androgynous skylike primordial *Adi Buddha*—the union of luminous clarity and emptiness that is none other than our original Buddha nature, supreme source, basis, primordial womb of everything. Samantabhadra, formless *Dharmakaya* Buddha descends into the realm of light and speaks to the *Logos,* Vajrasattva, Buddha of the *Sambhogakaya* dimension:

> The essence of all the Buddhas exists prior to samsara and nirvana…it transcends the four conceptual limits and is intrinsically pure; this original condition is the uncreated nature of existence that always existed, the ultimate nature of all phenomena…It is utterly free of the defects of dualistic thought which is only capable of referring to an object other than itself…it is the base of primordial purity…Similar to space it pervades all beings…The inseparability of the two truths, absolute and relative is called 'primordial Buddha'…If at the moment the energy of the base manifests, one does not consider it something other than oneself…it self-liberates…Understanding the essence…one finds oneself always in this state…dwelling in the fourth time, beyond past, present and future…the infinite space of self-perfection…pure dharmakaya, the essence of the vajra of clear light.
>
> —Chögyal Namkhai Norbu, 1999

Thus do the sutras and the tantras of Buddha's teaching, and all of the bivalent dualities and dialectics of the Buddhist path—objective-subjective, existence-nonexistence, form and emptiness, self-no-self, observer-data, true-false, relative truth-ultimate truth—abide "utterly free of the defects of dualistic thought", in the prior unity of the interdependently arisen Perfect Sphere of *Dzogchen,* the Great Perfection. This perfect reality sphere is nothing less than our ultimate mind nature, luminous innate clear light wisdom mind that is always already the unity of awareness and emptiness, of clarity and emptiness, and of bliss and emptiness.

Who is it, that I am? All the Buddhas and *mahasiddhas* of the three times have told it. This infinite vast expanse of the primordial awareness wisdom tantric continuum, "supreme source", boundless all embracing whole itself—bright indwelling Presence of That is who we actually are!

Recall our ancient Vedic locution, *Tat Tvam Asi*. That, I Am! *That* is our "supreme identity"—by any name—great completion of our always present Buddha nature, deep heart-seed Presence of ultimate happiness that is both origin and aim of all our urgent, dualistic, happiness seeking strategies. All the wisdom masters of the three times have told it: that which we seek is already present, deep within us. Chögyal Namkhai Norbu on this primordial supreme source:

> In terms of the source, the root of all phenomena, there is no such thing as an observer and an object to observe. All the phenomena of existence, without exception, abide in the supreme source in a condition of birthlessness... As the supreme source, Samantabhadra, pure and total consciousness, I am the mirror in which all phenomena are reflected. Although lacking self-nature everything exists clearly; without need for a view, the nature shines clear. Understanding the essential unborn condition is not an object to observe dualistically. This is the great understanding!
>
> —Chögyal Namkhi Norbu, 1999

Basic Space: The Innate Mind of Clear Light. Recent Tibetan *Dzogchen* ecumenical *Rimé* master Tulku Urgyen Rinpoche teaches that the two innermost principles of *Dzogchen* are basic space (*dharmadhatu*, Tib. *chos ying*) and primordial awareness presence (*vidya, rigpa*). Basic space is fecund luminous *shunyata*/emptiness, the innate clear light luminosity (*'od gsal*) itself. In the *Dzogchen* view the "innermost secret" realization of basic space is *klong*, infinite vast expanse of all embracing primordial reality itself, transcending any conceptual elaboration or limit, judgment or bias, beyond even the subtlest subject-object duality, beyond objective and subjective emptiness, beyond ground and path luminosity.

> As space pervades, so awareness pervades...like space, rigpa is all-encompassing...Just as beings are all pervaded by space, rigpa pervades the minds of beings...Basic space is the absence of mental constructs, while awareness is the knowing of this absence of constructs, recognizing the complete emptiness of mind essence... The ultimate dharma is the realization of the indivisibility of basic space and awareness (that is) Samantabhadra.
> —Tulku Urgyen (*As It Is*, Vol. I, 1999, and *Rainbow Painting*, 1995)

Therefore, basic space (*dharmadhatu*) and primordial awareness wisdom (*jnana, yeshe*) are an indivisible prior ontological, and present epistemological and phenomenal unity. Emptiness and our innate clear light Buddha wisdom mind share this *Kosmic* relation of identity.

On the accord of the Third Dodrupchen, Jigme Tenpe Nyima (quoted in H.H. Dalai Lama *Dzogchen*, 2000): "The *rigpa* taught in the Nyingma *Dzogchen* approach and the wisdom of clear light (*Mahamudra/Anuttara-yoga-tantra*) are one and the same":

> In *Dzogchen*, on the basis of the clear light itself, the way in which the clear light abides is made vivid and certain by the aspect of *rigpa* or knowing. That is free of any overlay of delusion and from any corrupting effect due to conceptual thoughts that will inhibit the experience of clear light...It is not accomplished as anything new, as a result of circumstances and conditions, but is present from the very outset...an awareness that can clearly perceive the way in which basic space and wisdom are present. On the basis of that key point, the realization of clear light radiates in splendor, becoming clearer and clearer, like

a hundred million suns...Here the aware aspect of clear light or effulgent *rigpa* (arising from essential *rigpa*) is stripped bare and you penetrate further into the depths of clear light...even as objects seem to arise...It is on the basis of this that you train your mind.

This poetry of the *Dzogchen* view was beautifully expressed by a great Tang Dynasty Chan/Zen Chinese master who had never heard of *Dzogchen*. His name was Haung Po (d. 850 CE):

All the Buddhas and all sentient beings are nothing but the one mind, beside which nothing exists. The one mind alone is Buddha. There is no distinction between Buddha and sentient beings....This one pure mind, the source of all things, shines forever with the radiance of its own per-fection...like the sun rising through empty sky illuminates the whole world...Still your mind and it is here....Human beings are attached to forms and so seek externally for Buddhahood. It is by this very seeking that they lose it (*Ch'uan-hsin Fa-yao*).

Lovely dharma poetry. Beautiful words indeed. And how shall we ordinary folks directly connect to and know this always already present Presence of our innermost clear light wisdom Buddha mind? How indeed. That is the question that the *AtiYoga* of *Dzogchen* answers directly.

We first establish an effective "real practice" under the guid-ance of a qualified *Dzogchen* meditation master. We must ask for direct transmission if we truly desire it. If we have already done this, we make the *goal* of this precious gift of all encompassing practice, not seeking enlightenment in some divine future mind state, but our ordinary, difficult everyday path itself—step by step, "brief moments many times"—natural continuity of clear light wisdom awareness of That that is already present deep within us, here and now.

Verily, everything, all of our cognitive experience—physical, emotional, mental, and spiritual, objective, subjective, contemplative, and perfectly subjective nondual—is the practice of the Path. That is our already present Buddha mind Presence (*Appendix A, The Brief Course*).

The Three Vajra Verses. Here are H.H. Dudjom Rinpoche's luminous Comments on Garab Dorje's *Three Vajra Verses* or *The Three Essential Points* that are the *Dzogchen* Base, View, Path, Meditation, Result, and Conduct (translated by John M. Reynolds):

Verse I: Recognize your own true nature (through direct introduction/transmission by the *Dzogchen* master). (The Base and View). "This fresh immediate awareness of the present moment, transcending all thoughts related to the three times (past, present, future), is itself that primordial awareness wisdom *(yeshe)* that is self-originated intrinsic awareness *(rig pa)*."

From this Base and View arises the *Dzogchen Semde* (mind) teaching cycle.

Verse II: Choose the state of presence, beyond doubt (The Path and Meditation). "Whatever phenomena of *samsara* or *nirvana* may manifest, all of it represents the play of the creative energy or potentiality of one's own immediate intrinsic awareness presence *(rig pa'i rtsal)*. One must decide upon this unique state for oneself, and know that there exists nothing other than this."

From This Path and Meditation arises the *Dzogchen Longde* (space) teaching cycle.

Verse III: Continue in the state with confidence in liberation (The Result and Conduct). "Whatever gross or subtle thoughts may arise, by merely recognizing their nature, they arise and self-liberate simultaneously in the vast expanse of *Dharmakaya*, where Emptiness and Awareness are nondual and inseparable *(gsal stong gnyis med)*."

From this Result and Conduct arises the *Dzogchen* "innermost secret" *Upadesha (Mengagde)*, or heart essence *(nyingthig)* teaching cycle.

The Six Vajra Verses of Vairochana.

These *Three Essential Points* (*The Three Vajra Verses*) of the essence, nature and energy of the Base, and of the Path, and of the Fruition/Result is contained in *Dhyani* Buddha Vairochana's early *Dzogchen* tantra, the *Six Vajra Verses*, or "Cuckoo of the State of Presence" (*Rig-pa'I khu-byug*), luminous Buddha mind Presence (*vidya, rigpa*) of intrinsic awareness that each human being is.

The cuckoo is the sacred bird of *Bönpo* founder Shenrab Miwo and is considered in the aboriginal *Bön* tradition as the king of birds, harbinger of spring and bearer of the primordial wisdom from vast empty space of *dharmakaya*. These early *Six Vajra Verses* of Vairochana, and the hundreds of *Dzogchen* tantras and texts that issue from it are but commentaries on Garab Dorje's above *Three Vajra Verses* or *The Three Essential Statements* (*The Three Points That Strike the Essence*).

The Six Vajra Verses (translated by Chögyal Namkhai Norbu):

Verse 1 & 2: The Base (View): The nature of phenomena is nondual (*gnyis med*), and each one, its own state, is beyond the limits of the mind (*Dzogchen semde* or mind meditation cycle).

Verse 3 & 4: The Path, Way of Practice (Meditation): There is no concept that can define the condition of "what is," but vision nevertheless manifests: all is good (*Dzogchen longde*, or space meditation cycle).

Verse 5 & 6: The Fruit, Result, Way of Being in Action (Conduct): Everything has already been accomplished, and so, having overcome the sickness of effort (spiritual seeking), one finds oneself in the self-perfected state: (*Dzogchen mengagde/upasheda*, or secret essence meditation cycle.

And from 18th century *Dzogchen* master Jigme Lingpa—great unifier of Longchenpa's syncretic corpus, and author of the *Longchen Nyingthig: Heart Essence of the Vast Expanse*—on the nondual Great Perfection *Dzogchen* view:

> No Buddhas, no beings, beyond
> existence and non-existence
> intrinsic awareness itself is absolute
> Guru—Ultimate Truth. By resting
> naturally, beyond fixation in that
> inherently free perfect innate *Bodhi*-
> mind, I take refuge and actualize
> Bodhicitta.
> —Jigme Lingpa, *Longchen Nyingthig*

"The perfect explanation of *Dzogchen*", according to Chögyal Namkhai Norbu is voiced in these perfect words of Gautama, our historical *Nirmanakaya* Buddha:

> All that arises
> is essentially no more real
> than a reflection,
> transparently pure and clear,
> beyond all definition
> or logical explanation.
>
> Yet the seeds of past action, karma,
> continue to cause further arising.
> Even so, know that all that exists
> is ultimately devoid of self-nature,
> utterly nondual.

Nondual Non-Meditation: Undistracted Ordinary Mind. Please consider this: In the luminous, numinous space between, and within, and throughout our relative perceptions, thoughts, feelings and beliefs already abides our ultimate primordial innate clear light love-wisdom mind—profound innermost Presence of That. Connect to That, moment to moment. That is the great happiness *Dzogchen* teaching.

We've often seen in these pages that our Buddha mind Presence is transpersonal/trans-ego, non-conceptual and trans-rational; that is, it utterly transcends our deep cultural background realist/ materialist "scientific" paradigm—our reality constituting "global web of belief" as to its objective existence or nonexistence. Yet, our Buddha mind is right here now, upon each mantra breath! All the masters of the three times have told it: your *bodhi* mind wisdom mind Presence is always already present! But don't *believe* this. It's beyond belief. As Buddha told, "Come and see".

Undistracted Ordinary Mind. In the most subtle nondual view and practice of Vajrayana *Dzogchen,* and of definitive Essence *Mahamudra,* mindfulness meditation practice is already simply present now in "undistracted ordinary mind"; the "primordially pure" natural state of spontaneously aware Presence—empty luminous awareness that is always present right here and now, in the midst of all kinds of thinking, feeling, and physical distractions. "Without past, present, future; empty awake mind" (Ju Mipham Rinpoche).

This nondual, innermost esoteric teaching on the nondual primordial nature of mind unfolds "from the top" as the "immediacy of the View", while the dualistic Path ascends from below. Guru Rinpoche, Padmasambhava teaches: "Keep your view as high as the sky; and your deeds as fine as barley flour...Practice these two as a unity".

Thus is confidence and certainty of the *View* established through the nondual *Meditation,* and the compassionate *Conduct* of the *Path*—View, Meditation, and Conduct/Action.

Recall the *Dzogchen Three Vajra Verses*: 1) Recognize your own true nature (by direct introduction/transmissiom from the *Dzogchen* master); 2) Choose the state of Presence beyond doubt; 3) Continue in the state with confidence in liberation". That is *Dzogchen* View and Meditation Practice.

As Lord Buddha's teaching enters the West the immediacy of the nondual View, along with the Lama's "pointing out instruction" is introduced directly by some Vajrayana Tibetan Lamas at the beginning of the process of the Path, before the student's accomplishment of the daunting preliminary practices of *ngöndro,* and "development stage" practice, which may or may not be done later as the View and Path become more established, and the unruly mind more stabilized. Why do *Dzogchen* Lamas do this?

A basic working understanding of the View—and the profound relative, conventional everyday peace and happiness that arises from it—is always here now, from the very beginning! Such immediate happiness is already present! Happiness—bright Presence of That—is already the case. It is not at all dependent upon later "advanced practice". Human happiness is always right here now in our *undistracted ordinary mind.* That is the miracle of radical *Dzogchen* truth.

So, having direct happy experience of Presence, we gradually learn to manage distractions. That is the *Dzogchen* View. There is no need to believe this. Ultimately, it is just more words. And it is assuredly beyond belief. Thus do we open to receive it *directly* (*yogi pratyaksa*). As Buddha told so long ago, "O monks, do not believe what I teach out of respect for me. Come and see."

That now said, we must, through the Buddha's basic "mindfulness of breathing", and with basic mantra prayer (e.g. *OM AH HUM*) begin to "bracket" our deep cultural background skepticism and doubt—our dubious materialist "global web of belief"—and open our heart-mind to receive. That is how we manage the natural endless painful distractions.

But the goal is not to block or to end the distractions. The goal is not to end life's inevitable adversity. Adversity happens! It's how we *choose* to respond that matters; is it not? So, we simply connect to our already present Presence—moment to moment—through the mindful mantra breath. Anxiety and impatience lose a bit of their power. We learn to go easy on and forgive ourselves, and so others, especially those we love.

We've seen that the outer and inner seeking strategies for such happiness doesn't work. So, we stop seeking and simply relax into, and rest in our already present wisdom mind Presence—"brief moments, many times". Our relief need not be some mystical "advanced practice". Our immediate touchstone is here upon the mantra breath—our ongoing instant connection to that.

Hot Tip! If you have not already done so, get a Lama in your life. If you have done so, remember again and again that you are always already now that Lama/Guru Presence. The outer Guru only mirrors your inner Guru. Bright Presence of That. "Lama walks always with loma".

Most surprising to our concepts and beliefs *about* the path of meditation—with the introduction by the Lama of *undistracted ordinary mind* to the prepared "ripe" student—there is no need to change anything! No need to seek some paradigmatic ideal "perfect meditation", or contemplative accomplishment. No need to try to do something, or not do something. No need to block thoughts and feelings; nor to indulge frustration about such distractions. No need to worry; to feel guilty and regretful. No need to *fix* this natural process of primordial arising of appearance from its emptiness primordial Buddha "groundless ground", the perfect sphere of *Dzogchen*; the perfect imprint/ seal of *Mahamudra*. Buddha told, "Leave it alone; it's perfect as it is". You can't improve it! Connect to that Buddha mind love-wisdom through mindful *shamatha*, and through your stainless, if less than perfect, *bodhicitta* conduct. It will make you happy now. That is the Path.

The lamas tell that in this nondual view and spontaneous non-meditation practice, all arising unfolding appearance already enfolded in vast unbounded whole that is nondual reality itself is always untainted, undefiled, and perfect just as it is. This basal aboriginal emptiness "groundless ground" is inherently "primordially pure" and uncontaminated by distracting dualistic thought or existence of any kind. Good to know.

Just so, the spacetime forms which arise and exist through the ground, because there is never a whit of separation from it, is equally inherently perfect as it appears. Radical teaching indeed. And fortunately, utterly beyond belief. So, it must be *directly* experienced.

Therefore, wonder of wonders, distractions—thinking, feeling, perceiving—negative or positive, are but mere appearances— waves of the primordial natural state upon the vast ocean that is present luminosity of our *undistracted ordinary mind*. There is no *essential* difference! "Form is empty; emptiness is form".

Hence, once again, as Buddha told so long ago, "Rest your weary mind and let it be as it is; all things are perfect exactly as they are". This is the radical nondual View, Meditation, and Practice of the *Dzogchen* Path, whether it is introduced at the beginning, or after years of dualistic "development stage" practice. It is this beautiful, difficult dualistic practice that makes it so.

Yes, *undistracted ordinary mind* is simply letting natural mind be as it already is, here now, without adding judgments about distractedness. It's pristine and perfect just as it is, distractions, imperfections and all. Yes, that is the radical nondual *Dzogchen* teaching. And so we still have to show up for work, and take out the trash, and be kind even to "difficult people".

Far from an idealized vacant and void state of mindlessness, undistracted ordinary mind is lucid, awake, vivid, and clear. This then, is nondual, uncontrived, unelaborated *Dzogchen* "non-meditation". As *Dzogchen* founder Garab Dorje told twenty centuries ago, "It is already accomplished from the very beginning", deep within *your* heartmind. It is that profound truth to which we awaken—step by mindful step—upon the mindful mantra breath.

And yes, it takes a bit of peaceful, lucid undistracted mindfulness meditation practice—foundational *shamatha* and mantra prayer under the guidance of a qualified lama—to recognize this not always so quiescent, already present state of *vipashyana* Presence; and to sustain it.

So now, settle into and rest in your familiar state of mindful *shamatha* upon the breath as you receive these kind words of sixteenth century great *Mahamudra* Master Dakpo Tashi Namgyal:

> Look directly into your conscious mind. It is a wakefulness for which no words suffice. It is not a definable entity, but at the same time, it is a self-knowing aware emptiness that is clear, lucid and awake. Sustain this without distraction... Next, examine a particular thought or perception...look into it directly and investigate...No matter what kind of thought occurs, its experience is, in itself, something unidentifiable—it is unobstructedly aware and yet not conceptualizing... As for perceptions, they are a mere impression of unobstructed presence, which is insubstantial and not a clinging to a solid reality. Without distraction then, simply sustain this aware emptiness that is unidentifiable awareness, also referred to as a perceiving emptiness that is perception devoid of a self-nature.
>
> —Namgyal, *Clarifying the Natural State*, 2001, p. 29 ff.

Now, naturally aware mindful Presence and your very own natural mind are one and the same (*samatajnana*). There is no separation. It has always been thus. Feel that! Then rejoice in this miraculous non-meditation of your *nondual undistracted ordinary mind*! *Emaho*!

What "Undistracted Ordinary Mind" is Not. It is not total quiescence wherein the gross and subtle phenomena of sense perception utterly cease. Nor is it a mindless inert state ("blank Zen") that excludes both sensory input, *and* discursive discriminating wisdom. It is not a vacant mind state between the arising of thoughts; not empty of sensory experience; not empty of all thinking; not an aversion to perceptual and conceptual experience of any kind.

In short, wonder of wonders, this mildly spooky nondual "non-meditation" meditation of undistracted ordinary mind does not exclude the dualistic experience of ordinary mind! Perceptual and conceptual experience is not the enemy of mindful meditation. Thoughts and feelings, negative or positive, are not the antagonist in this comic play of the mind. And non-thinking is not the goal. Let us not complicate it. Relax a bit and "Let it be exactly as it is". That is the *Dzogchen* non-meditation. Let it be so.

The Witness Presence. So now, just for a moment, place your attention upon your breath, and simply witness your awareness. Be meta-cognitively, reflexively aware of your present awareness; just as it is now. Observe what arises. No need to change it, direct it, evaluate it, think about it, grasp at or reject anything at all. And when grasping/rejecting thinking arises, just witness that. Let it be as it is. Simply feel it. *Feel* the feeling of being you being present here and now. Feel the deep *I Am prana* life current flow of *buddic* Presence of you in this precious moment now.

This primordial Presence cannot be created or fabricated. Why? It is always already present—whether you choose to believe it, or like it, or not. What is, just is. So, feel your connectedness to it, and to all living beings, and to everything that is. That is who *you* are. Rest in That, and be happy now.

Although the untrained mind, in its waking state, is brimming with relentless concepts and feelings, this undistracted ordinary mind of ours excludes any *distraction* from the "primordial purity" of *bodhi* mind Presence, always present to any and all arising distractions. All embracing primordial wisdom mind Presence is always "primordially present" throughout all of our myriad distractions. No need to believe this. Let it be as it is.

That, Dear Reader, is the actual nondual nature of mind; Buddha nature of mind—beyond our concepts and beliefs *about* it. As thoughts and feelings arise, without judgment, return to the bright undistracted state, always upon the mantra breath (*OM AH HUM*), again and again. Or, momentarily shatter a troubling constellation of thoughts/feelings by shouting out *PHAT* to return the mind to its peaceful natural state. "It's perfect just as it is". *That* is Human Happiness Itself. Rest a few moments in That! You can think about it later.

Yes, the pristine, undistracted mind state that is liberated from discursive thinking is the moment to moment non-meditative meditation. But a *goal* of utter non-movement of thought, and of perceptual and feeling experience is itself a distraction. Seeking a goal of contemplative, meditative happiness as an antidote to suffering is a form of suffering. Wisdom mind/Buddha mind seeks nothing at all. It is complete in itself. That is the meditation. "Make the goal the Path".

Therefore, for human beings being here in time, the origin of our discontent is not distracting thoughts and emotions. This is not the real problem. The origin of our suffering is, as Buddha told long ago, primal ignorance (*avidya, ma rigpa*) of our always present selfless Buddha nature/Buddha mind. Thoughts are just thoughts. Emotions are just emotions. They have no inherent power over us that we do not *choose* to give them. Everything is already embraced by clear light undistracted ordinary mind. So, "Leave it alone and let it be as it is". "This cannot be taught" (Gautama the Buddha). So, relax the need to understand it intellectually. Not so easy is it?

Thus is the nondual *Dzogchen* View and Meditation the Result/ Fruition of both relative happiness (*eudaimonia*, human flourishing), and ultimate human happiness (*mahasukkha, paramananda, beatitudo*)—liberation/enlightenment. "It is already accomplished from the very beginning". It's too simple to believe; but to present to be doubted. Please consider well this nondual *Dzogchen* View.

Once again, the goal of the practice of the Path is not the yogi's bliss, nor some perfect nondual happiness mind state; nor is it liberation from suffering. Goals can be future-looking distractions. And the future never shows up! It's too busy becoming the present moment. So, the goal is simply the practice. Abiding in this vast empty unbounded whole that is the already present all embracing *Perfect Sphere of Dzogchen* is always only here now. It's like coming home.

This concludes our exploration of *Dzogchen*, The Great Perfection/ Completion

The Three Kayas and the Foundational Buddhist Mantra Prayer

Truth is One: Many Are Its Names.

—*Rig Veda*

Let us now further explicate this sometimes obscure, ironic and profound philosophical notion of Buddhist emptiness/*shunyata* with its three root metaphysical emptiness principles—impermanence, selflessness, and interdependence—by way of the great foundational Vajrayana/Secret Mantra Buddhist mantra prayer *OM AH HUM*. We shall then see how it is that these three seed syllables are the three Buddha bodies, *kayas*, the three vajras, or reality dimensions of the vast expanse of the primordial Base/Ground, unbounded whole itself. These three dimensional realms are *dharmakaya*, *sambhogakaya*, and *nirmanakaya*—visualized as white *OM*, red *AH*, and blue *HUM*.

Etymologically, "mantra" means "to protect the mind". How is this so? Great mantra vibrational Voice (*Vak, Voici*) instantly connects us to our trans-conceptual empty and awake, indwelling and always already present primordial Buddha mind/wisdom mind—luminous, numinous blissful heartmind Presence of That. Here the mind is sheltered from the stormy waves of samsaric existence.

The integration of vibrational mantra prayer instantly connects to and enhances the movement of life-force *jnana prana* energy, with its great capacity to release negative energy from the body-mind, and as well to surrender and immediately self-liberate obstructive mind created distractions, over against mindful breathing alone. Mantra instantly connects to Presence!

OM AH HUM. Broadly construed, *OM AH HUM* is, respectively, the Body, Voice/Speech and Mind (heartmind) of all the buddhas, wisdom masters and *mahasiddhas,* avatars, saints and sages of the basic space that enfolds all beings and phenomena in the boundless whole itself (*dharmadhatu, cho ying*). This vast aboriginal ground continuously unfolds as trees, people, and stars as it arises in the "three times"—past, present, future—of this precious world system that we have come to know and love.

OM AH HUM mantra prayer is the "three gates" to both the relative happiness that is relative human flourishing (*eudaimonia*) and to ultimate happiness that is liberation from suffering, enlightenment, Happiness Itself, the ultimate happiness (*mahasukha, paramananda, beatitudo*) that causes no harm, and so creates no karma; the happiness that cannot be lost. Thus do Vajrayana/ Mantrayana Buddhists view the seed syllables *OM AH HUM* as representing the three unified and inseparable Buddha bodies (*kayas*) or reality dimensions of the *trikaya* of the base (*gzhi rigpa*), all embracing primordial "groundless ground" that is vast boundless whole (*dharmadhatu*)—awareness-consciousness being itself. (*Dharmata* may be seen as the dimension of *living beings* arising in the *dharmadhatu* whole.) The three dimensions of the *Trikaya* of the Base/Ground is symbolized by the spiraling *gankyil*.

The *Trikaya* is our *selfless* "supreme identity", primordial wisdom mind Presence of That, that we always are, our natural base condition, free of a conceptually imputed, reified "higher" Atman Self overlay. How do we instantly connect to these three Buddha bodies of the whole of reality itself? *OM AH HUM.* If you have not yet practiced this, please do so now. Give it two minutes, or more, on the mindful breath (*Appendix A*). Conceptual understanding alone will accomplish very little.

Moreover, this selfless primordial wisdom mind (*jnana, yeshe*) Presence (*vidya, rigpa*) is always present in our human cognitive processional of all four human cognitive levels of meaning: 1) Pre-conceptual, direct perception; 2) exoteric/outer, conceptual, objective; 3) inner/esoteric, subjective, trans-conceptual, contemplative; and 4) "innermost secret" perfectly subjective nondual direct yogic perception (*yogi pratyaksa*).

***OM AH HUM* is Selfless.** Buddhism is seen by most Buddhists as a selfless deep wisdom response to the Hindu *Sanatana-dharma* doctrine of a permanent, independent, eternal Atman, or "Supreme Self". Siddartha Gautama began his own wisdom path as a Hindu steeped in Vedic wisdom. Upon his full *bodhi* awakening he adopted the Hindu doctrine of karma and rebirth. But he declined to accept the Hindu doctrine of an ultimately real, continuing and enduring Atman Self. Buddha taught *anatman*, or no-self.

It is wise, but difficult not to conceive our primordial Buddha mind/wisdom mind Presence as some kind of exulted Self, a really cool upgrade, even a divine version, of our prideful self-ego-I.

However, the Sage taught that wisdom Presence is not a kinder gentler ego-I—a "supreme identity" of oneself. Buddha mind Presence is not a self identity at all. For Vajrayana Middle Way Madhyamaka, open instant Presence (*vidya, rigpa*), always present to the boundless whole itself, is inherently selfless, transpersonal and trans-conceptual. Yet, when we choose to be fully present to it in our relative-conventional life world, we spontaneously act for the benefit of living beings, which is the root cause of our own relative, and even ultimate happiness. *Mahasukaho!*

We recognize and connect to our selfless present moment Buddha mind Presence instantly through *shamatha*—mindfulness meditation upon the prana wind of the breath, combined with the quite amazing power of mantra prayer—*OM AH HUM*, or other mantras. But as we become a bit more comfortable with the notion of *shunyata*/emptiness, constant mindful introspective, metacognitive, reflexive awareness of our awareness is required to check our habitual tendency to superimpose (*vikshepa*) a distracting, conceptual, permanent reality upon our pristine arising direct and selfless experience, and this *ultimately* nonexistent relative self-ego-I who experiences it. *Vipashyana* is the selfless immediate seeing *samadhi/satori* of That. We train the habitually, conceptually reifying and imputing "wild horse of the mind" in That.

Emptiness and the *Trikaya* of the Base. *OM AH HUM* presents as the Three Primordial Wisdoms that are the three faces of nondual primordial wisdom mind itself (*jnana, yeshe, gnosis*). These three are, respectively, the *essence, nature and energy* of this nonconceptual primordial base/ground of all existence/experience.

In other words, *dharmakaya/OM* is like space, formless emptiness *essence* reflected in *sambhogakaya/AH* which is like the sun, luminous *nature*, clarity, clear-light bridge continuously mirroring, manifesting, expressing and illuminating form—*energy*—*nirmanakaya/HUM*. These three "Buddha bodies of existence" are ultimately a prior nondual unity, utterly nonexistent as relative conceptual imputations and beliefs.

Thus is luminous clear-light *dharmakaya/shunyata*/emptiness so much more than a mere negative, nihilistic void. Thus is this prodigious emptiness potential, the primordial "groundless ground" that is the "emptiness of emptiness"—also the "fullness of emptiness"—potential of all arising matter-energy form. Emptiness/*shunyata* embraces and subsumes all of form. Yet, as we have so often seen in these pages, emptiness itself is empty of any whit of inherent, independent existence. It is established by relative conventional conceptual minds, and is absent any more profound existence beyond that.

Therefore, emptiness exists! The proper question is: How does emptiness exist? It exists relatively, but not ultimately. *The relative existence of something is required in order to deny its ultimate existence.* In other words, for something to be nonexistent it must still exist in some modality for it to be considered a candidate for nonexistence.

Therefore, form exists in a relative, logically necessary complementary relation to emptiness. No form, no emptiness. No emptiness, no form. In the ultimate view that interdependent, dependently arising (*pratitya samutpada*) logically and ontologically necessary relation is one of sameness or identity (*samatajnana*). To be sure, "Form is empty"; yet, "emptiness is also form". Buddha continues: "Form is not other than emptiness; emptiness is not other than form" (*from the Prajnaparamita The Heart of Wisdom Sutra*). This seminal teaching is known as the Buddha's "Fourfold Profundity".

In *shunyata* abides the very potential and possibility of form. Emptiness—the *absence* of the intrinsic or ultimate existence of form—is the Ultimate Truth of all of the forms of Relative Truth that arises as instantiations of/through it. This *absence* of the inherent ultimate nature of form exists! Absences exist. Absent the absence of an elephant in the room, there would be at least one elephant in the room. Therefore, emptiness exists!

From his lapidary nondual *Heart of Wisdom Sutra*, Buddha's clear words arise again,

> Form is empty (*shunya, stong pa*);
> Emptiness (*shunyata, stong pa nyi*) is form.
> Form is not other than emptiness;
> Emptiness is not other than form.

These two reality dimensions, form and emptiness, constitute the Buddha's Two Truths—Relative Truth (*samvriti satya*), and Ultimate Truth (*paramartha satya*) that embraces and includes it (*Ch. VI*).

Nirmanakaya (*HUM*) is the clear-light bliss of luminous *sambhogakaya* manifesting as light *energy* of spacetime form as primordial Buddha mind/wisdom mind (*buddhajnana*) for the benefit of all living beings in physical and mental form. All of the physically embodied buddhas, *mahasiddhas* and bodhisattvas incarnated into form are *nirmanakaya* beings arising for our benefit from the *sambhogakaya* dimensional realm, this light bridge from timeless formless *dharmakaya/OM* into the relative conventional array of time and form.

Just so, the tantric meditational deities of Tibetan Vajrayana are *sambhogakaya* dimensional presences—qualities, ornaments—of our selfless, formless actual ultimate identity descended into relative spacetime physical and mental form to guide us on the relative Path. However, all of this—Buddha nature, primordial wisdom (*jnana, yeshe*), the three *kayas*, the deities—are *vidya maya*, beautiful dharma ornaments, but *ultimately* illusory. That is the *Rangtong* Prasangika Madhyamaka, foundation of the *Dzogchen* view (cf. *Rangtong* and *Shentong, Ch V*).

OM AH HUM may be seen as a foundational or root mantra in whom other Buddhist mantras arise and participate. Occasionally voicing it while abiding in the "calm abiding" of *shamatha* awareness provides an instant connection to trans-conceptual primordial wisdom mind of the Buddhas, already present deep within each human form. Once again, chanting mantra prayer instantly liberates and focuses *prana* life force energy where mindful breathing alone may not. Mantra adds the vibrational power of voice/speech/breath to the mindful practice of the Path.

So it is, relatively construed, these three *kaya* dimensions or Buddha bodies—the *Trikaya* of the Base—are, respectively *dharmakaya/OM, sambhogakaya/AH,* and *nirmanakaya/HUM*.

D*harmakaya/OM,* (*cho ku, kadag*) is for Vajrayana/Secret Mantra Buddhism the all-embracing dimension of Ultimate Truth (*paramartha satya*), utterly free of conceptual elaboration, the ultimate truth body, nonlocal, timeless formless buddha body of reality itself.

What are the three faces of the primordial Base or Ground? Let us now hearken back to the three primordial wisdoms, the three aspects of nondual primordial wisdom (*jnana, yeshe*)—Essence, Nature, and Energy.

D*harmakaya* is the primordial Base or Ground, aboriginal vast expanse that embraces the implicate order the of the boundless whole itself; formless basic space of *dharmadhatu* that subsumes and pervades all spacetime phenomenal form. The *Essence* of *dharmadhatu*, and of *dharmakaya* is *shunyata*/emptiness (*dharma* connotes existing stuff, *dhatu*/basic space is emptiness); its *Nature* is luminous clarity, infinite potential of form; its *Energy* is continuous manifestation of light-motion-form (*tsal/rolba*, $E = mc^2$) descending from *dharmakaya* ground for the benefit of beings.

In human conduct this primal energy is expressed as the precious *bodhicitta*—the skillful unity of wisdom and compassion (*thugs re*), spontaneously and skillfully expressed through the Four Boundless States (*Brahma-Vihara, Apramana*). These limitless mind states of *bodhicitta* are: boundless kindness (*maitri*); boundless compassion (*karuna*), boundless empathetic joy (*mudita*); and boundless equanimity (*upeksha*), in which the first three states spontaneously arise.

Dharmakaya is therefore the very Buddha nature of mind and all of its experience. Heady wine indeed. So many words for that singular, invariant, nonlocal, nondual one truth of the matter.

Selfless primordial wisdom mind Presence (*vidya, rigpa*) may be seen as the always already present timeless noetic (body, mind, spirit unity), nondual (subject-object unity) state of *knowing/feeling* experience of this ground, "supreme source"; our transpersonal, trans-ego-I *selfless* "supreme identity" of That—our love-wisdom Buddha mind. Recall here that the spontaneous Presence (*lhundrub*) manifestation of nonlocal intrinsic emptiness of *dharmakaya/kadag* is not a self-reified supreme state or condition, or "higher self" of a local self-ego-I, try as we may to conceptually reduce it to that.

Yes, many words for That which is utterly beyond words and concepts; beyond the discursive reach of our linguistic, semiotic sociocultural "global web of belief" (Quine 1969).

No-Self Help: Bringing Your Meditation Practice Home. It seems to me that heady conceptual understanding of the buddhadharma is little more than intellectual self-stimulation until it becomes unified with trans-conceptual *direct* (*yogi pratyaksa*) love-wisdom mind Presence, and the compassionate *bodhicitta* expression of that Presence in one's lifeworld conduct.

Again, we accomplish this great process step by mindful step through Buddha's "mindfulness of breathing"—*shamatha* enhanced by mantra prayer and the penetrating insight of *vipashyana*—"brief moments many times". This joyous, simple but difficult practice continues imperfectly, moment to moment, as mindful continuity of our own awareness Presence, always embracing the constant distractions, most of the time—breath by mindful breath!

So clearly, none of this works without the non-conceptual contemplative *practice* of it. Reading and talking cannot accomplish much of anything. *Straight talk*: should you *choose* to further your practice of the Path, you are well advised to actually do so. Please become aware, if you are not already aware, that all excuses for avoiding the relationship that is the practice of your *present awareness* are equally lame. It's wise to take total responsibility for them. The most utterly mindless of them all? *"I don't have time"*. Or shifty, inauthentic variations on that theme. As most aspiring yogis and yoginis succumb here and there to this egocentric stalling tactic, what's a serious practitioner to do?

We all must breathe. *Your meditation practice is breathing with mindful awareness now!* Learn to be present to your moment to moment awareness as it rides the breath; to be reflexively present and aware of your awareness—whatever is now present—vast space of this very moment now.

Myriad thoughts, judgments, feelings, and bodily sensations arise and fall away continuously. Be aware of the bright spaciousness that pervades this whole objective/subjective diaphanous display of your present awareness—personal drama as well the loving kindness. Awareness may present as positive, negative, or neutral. No need to think about or evaluate it. No need to change it at all. No need to grasp at, or reject any of it. *Be gently present to your awareness just as it is here and now—moment to moment.* As Buddha told, "Let it be as it is".

Thus is your entire lifeworld practice—it's all practice—condensed to this precious present moment now. Past is a present memory. Future is a present anticipation. Even the present is illusory for it abides timelessly between nonexistent past and future. Yet, there is this luminous cognizance upon the mantra breath. Bright awareness Presence of That. That is the real. That is always present. It is That upon which we place our attention now. Yes, meditation is awareness management—our choice of *present placement of awareness*—self-ego-I, or our always present Buddha mind Presence. That is the practice of the Path made simple. As Albert Einstein told. "Spacetime reality should be made as simple as possible, but not simpler".

As we become familiar, then comfortable with this ironic feeling of apparitional empty absence of a solid, inherently existing *objective* "real world out there" (RWOT), we come to realize that this knowing subject—self-ego-I—that perceives it is itself equally absent and empty of any whit of intrinsic *ultimate* existence, even as *relatively* real spacetime stuff trespasses self-awareness constantly. This is the Buddha's seminal teaching of *anatman*, or no-self: emptiness of self; emptiness of phenomena appearing to a self.

But wait! If self and the world are utterly illusory, why bother to practice the Path? What does it matter? Who is it that gets liberated? Who is it that acts in an illusory world to benefit illusory living beings? Who is it that is acting out all of these nonexistent nouns? And doesn't such a nonexistent reality violate the Mahayana/Vajrayana Middle Way *samaya* to avoid the ontological extremes of *either* eternalist, materialist existence, *or* nihilist, idealist nonexistence? Plenty of impudent questions. The easy answer is this: our conceptually nonexistent, but ultimately already present Buddha mind Presence is always here and now. How do we connect? By now you know.

Let's consider these impertinent questions in their larger context.

The relationship of the Buddha's Two Truths—Ultimate emptiness and Relative form—"Form is empty; emptiness is form"—bestows the great gift of a relatively real, but not ultimately real, cause and effect spacetime reality, a RWOT in which we have the great gift of time, and freedom of choice to enter the Path of awakening to this great one truth that is the ontic prior and phenomenally present unity of these Two Truths of our appearing spacetime realities (*Ch. VI*).

It is through the Two Truths that the dualistic drama of *relative* experiencing subject and its experienced objects are unified in the *ultimate* primordial boundless whole itself (*dharmadhatu*). The prodigious subject-object split—self and a separate other—with all its suffering is healed at last. And then we see that this unity has always been thus. There has never been a split. The prior unity of self/subject and other/object is always already the case. But now we can feel, and know that great primordial truth. What a relief! *Emaho!*

Whether you are a novice or "advanced" practitioner, refine more and more your awareness so that you remain present even in distractions. Practice that, most of the time. Sitting, walking, sleeping; working, playing, loving; happy, anxious, pissed off—your mantra breath is always right here. Remain present to presence of primordial *prana* life current that pervades your whole being with each breath. *OM AH HUM*. That is the great gift of your own present awareness now. Bright Presence of That. It's like coming home.

So, let us now more deeply penetrate this mysterious *trikaya* of the base, the three Buddha bodies that are relative form embraced by ultimate emptiness. To accomplish this task we must quite artificially and unnaturally divide the inherently indivisible *trikaya* into its three individual buddha bodies/*kayas* that we may better understand the nondual whole. As we perform this rather unnatural dualistic conceptual exercise, let us remain clearly present to the nondual Presence of the non-conceptual, post-empirical vast implicate order of the whole itself. How shall we do this? *OM AH HUM.*

1) **Dharmakaya** (*cho ku*), truth body, is *ultimately* trans-con-ceptual, nonlocal (not located in spacetime), and nondual (non-separate subject-object unity), beyond the grasp of *relative*, conventional logical syntax of language that defines the limit of human discursive concept-belief understand-ing—and well beyond the linguistic semiotic (logical syntax, semantics, pragmatics) reach of the intellectual virtuosity of even the best scientific, philosophical, and buddhalogical minds of our species.

Yet, this apparent cognitive gulf between self-ego-I and its selfless "supreme source" is not at all unbridgeable. Indeed, as we have seen, in the ultimate view, local self *atman* and nonlocal no-self *anatman* are already a prior *ultimate* nondual ontologi-cal and present phenomenological unity. Relative subject and its ultimate object are separate by conceptual convention only. There is no ultimate ontic nor epistemic separation. In the ul-timate view self/no-self is a false dichotomy. With this nondual understanding, there is, as Zen Master Suzuki Roshi told, "No problem whatsoever in this world".

Further, as the objective emptiness of the inherent existence of form becomes gradually revealed and accepted, the luminous emptiness of inherent existence of the knowing subject/self shines clear. And yes, we remain present to the unfolding of this great primordial truth through mindful breathing and mantra prayer.

Moreover, and most happily, it is the incorrigible, blatantly resistant self-ego-I who *chooses* to establish the *relative* love-wisdom practice connection to always present *bodhi* mind wisdom mind Presence of that wondrous primordial unity. Propitious *Kosmic* irony indeed. So be kind to your unruly self-ego-I.

D*harmakaya* is seen in Hinayana and Theravada Buddhism of the early *Pali Canon* as the totality of Buddha's dharma discourses, both provisional and definitive. Here the metaphysics of Mahayana and Vajrayana *dharmakaya* are nearly absent.

However, in Vajrayana/Secret Mantra, formless *dharmakaya*, and the primordial unity of the unified *trikaya* itself is *recognized* by the assiduous practitioner via the discriminating wisdom of *prajna*, much as we are doing here. It is *realized*, then compassionately expressed via the nondual primordial wisdom of *jnana/ yeshe* through instant open Presence (*vidya, rigpa*) as taught in the subtlest Buddhist paths of *Dzogchen*, Essence *Mahamudra, Definitive Madhyamaka,* and *Saijojo* Zen. All of these paths bespeak the very truth of timeless, essenceless, transpersonal unity of these three buddha bodies that are primordial *Trikaya* of the Base. Bright cognizant Presence of That (*tathata*, thatness, suchness, Hindu *Tat/Sat*).

As we have seen, the vast expanse of *dharmakaya* embraces and pervades the basic space of *dharmadhatu* (*cho ying*). *Dharmadhatu* and *dharmata* are more or less synonymous with Buddhist emptiness/*shunyata*, Buddha nature (*tathagatagarbha*), nature of all arising dharmas, basis or primordial "groundless ground" of everything. (*Dharmata* refers to the human face of *dharmadhatu*.)

In the *Dzogchen/Ati Yoga* view (the Great Completion or Great Perfection) *dharmakaya* may be seen as the *Perfect Sphere of Dzogchen*. So many names for the nameless groundless, primordial ground of all the worlds. In whom does this all arise? Who is the supreme source? Who is it that I Am? To borrow a Hindu (and Judaic-Christian) pith, *Tat Tvam Asi!* That Thou Art! That I Am!

According to 20th century Tibetan *Dzogchen Rimé* master Tulku Urgyen Rinpoche, the two innermost principles of *Dzogchen* are basic space (*dharmadhatu, cho ying*), and awareness (*vidya, rigpa*). This basic space is pregnant womb of luminous emptiness, the unity of emptiness (*shunyata*) and innate clear light luminosity ('*od gsal*); the prior and present unity of appearance and emptiness, and of bliss and emptiness.

In *Dzogchen* view and practice the innermost secret realization of basic space is *klong*, the infinite "vast expanse" of reality itself, transcending all conceptual elaboration, dilemma, judgment and bias, beyond even the subtlest subject-object duality; beyond both objective and subjective emptiness; beyond ground and path luminosity.

Tulku Urgyen explains,

> As space pervades, so awareness pervades...like space, rigpa is all-encompassing...Just as beings are all pervaded by space, rigpa pervades the minds of beings...Basic space is the absence of mental constructs, while awareness is the knowing of this absence of constructs, recognizing the emptiness of mind essence...The ultimate dharma is the realization of the indivisibility of basic space and awareness (that is) Samantabhadra.
> —Tulku Urgyen, *As It Is*, Vol. I, 1999; *Rainbow Painting*, 1995

Thus are basic space and primordial awareness a prior ontological and present phenomenological unity. Emptiness and the clear light of primordial awareness are a unity. "The *rigpa* taught in the *Nyingma Dzogchen* approach, and the wisdom of clear light (*Essence Mahamudra, Anuttara yoga tantra*) are one and the same" (Third Dodrupchen Jigme Tenpe Nyima).

> In *Dzogchen*, on the basis of the clear light itself, the way in which the clear light abides is made vivid and certain by the aspect of *rigpa* or knowing. That is free from any overlay of delusion and from any corrupt effect due to conceptual thoughts that will inhibit the experience of clear light...It is not accomplished as something new, as a result of circumstances and conditions, but is present from the very outset... an awareness that can clearly perceive the way in which basic space and wisdom are present. On the basis of that key point, the realization of clear light radiates in splendor, becoming clearer and clearer, like a hundred million suns...Here the aware aspect of clear

light or effulgent *rigpa* (arising from essential *rigpa*) is
stripped bare and you penetrate further into the depths
of clear light...even as objects seem to arise... It is on the
basis of this that you train.
—Third Dodrupchen Jigme Tenpa Nyima (quoted in
H.H. Dalai Lama, *Dzogchen*, 2000)

Dharmakaya, whose essence is emptiness, is the prior and always
present unity of emptiness and primordial wisdom—*samatajnana*,
primordial Buddha mind (*buddhajnana*), Buddhahood itself. It
bears repeating: Buddhist emptiness is not a great transcendental
absolute *thing* or object or deeper reality behind the appearances
of empirical phenomenal reality. Emptiness is not to be conflated
with any transcendental theistic godhead, West or East. It is not a
great transcendent reality ground whence space and time emerge,
though it is too often construed as such.

We have also seen that *dharmakaya* is sometimes referred to
in the Mahayana/Vajrayana as a "groundless ground" whose *ultimate* reality is "empty of intrinsic existence", and whose wisdom
mind Presence is profoundly devoid and absent any sense of an
experiencing self-ego-I. Eighth century Prasangika Madhyamaka
master Chandrakirti has termed this subtle understanding the
"emptiness of emptiness". Fortunately, all of these *ultimate* non-
entities admit of real *relative* conventional existence. So we still
have to manage the kids, and our parents.

Yes, Buddha told: "Form is empty; emptiness is form". No
form, no emptiness. No emptiness, no form. Emptiness is no more
nor less than the selfless, impermanent, interdependent arising
of relative, conventional spacetime form. Once again, Buddha's
emptiness/*shunyata* does not exist independently, ultimately. It
exists relatively, as Buddha's dependent arising or interbeing
(*pratitya samutpada*). Emptiness and dependent arising are metaphysically identical.

The really good news? Human beings are, in each and every
moment, always already primordially awakened to this great truth

via our indwelling, innate Buddha nature, luminous wisdom mind Presence of That. And it is through the assiduous practice of the Path—mantra, mindfulness meditation, *vipashyana*, deity practice, and compassionate *bodhicitta* conduct—that we realize this ultimate happiness in our lives; step by mindful step upon the *prana* wind of the mantra breath. It takes a little time, and a lot of self acceptance, not to mention real courage, to realize that "it is already accomplished from the very beginning" (Garab Dorje).

Dharmakaya No-Self Help: Bringing It Home. Therefore, please consider well the profound Vajrayana *Dzogchen* fruitional view that the *goal* of the Path is not enlightenment, nor release from suffering, nor personal peace, happiness, bliss, nor physical and mental health, nor general well-being, nor freedom from anxiety, anger and the afflictive pathological emotions, in some *future* mind state. How shall we conceptually understand this *Kosmic* irony?

The future never shows up! It remains in the future. Fortunately, it spontaneously becomes the present in this eternal moment *now*. Happiness, liberation from suffering, enlightenment happens only in this present moment now. As we have seen, our past is gone, but a present memory. Our future has not yet arisen, but a present anticipation. So, we cannot *become* happy later. But we can *be* happy here now. Happiness is always only now. Everything only happens in the present moment now. So, the goal of the Path is your practice, not later, but right here and now. As Chögyam Trungpa Rinpoche told, "Make the goal the Path".

Still, as we saw in our all to brief introduction to Zen Master Dōgen, this eternal present moment now exists in a causally interdependent relation to a past and a future. Being here in time is always a simultaneous array of these "three times"—past, present, and future. We must learn from the past, without regret or guilt. We must learn not to fear the future. We must learn that both of these domains are closed, and loaded with the suffering of regret and fear, so it's wise to invest very little of our precious time and life energy there. This present moment now is so significant because our entire past and future are enfolded within it, all the while simultaneously unfolding in this timeless continuum of ever present "eternal now".

Thus are the Three Times unified in the primordial happiness of Now. But most of this is just concepts. How then shall we bring *dharmakaya* home? As mindful mantra prayer fills the troubled mind with already present Buddha mind *dharmakaya* Presence, very little space remains for the causes of suffering—the afflictive emotions of fear and anger, greed and pride (*Appendix A*).

Therefore, make your happiness goal not some future happy mind state. Make your goal the moment to moment practice of the Path itself, your selfless here now present mind state; your moment to moment love-wisdom practice itself.

Mindful breathing with mantra prayer is your cognitive touchstone. That is the body-mind location of human happiness—the location of your love-wisdom Buddha mind Presence. Place your attention upon That, "brief moments, many times", and be happy now. When your attention wonders, gently return it to your always already present wisdom mind Presence—again, and again. Happiness rides the mindful mantra breath. Remain close to your mantra breath.

Thus is happiness a choice, always the result of your present mind state—wherever you choose to place your attention right now. From such peace of mind spontaneously arises your *bodhicitta*—thought, intention, and action for the benefit of living beings. And that, after all is the real secret human happiness—*your* happines now!

Now you know how to be happy. It's not so complicated after all. And yes, it requires a bit of relative, non-goal directed practice in being, and remaining here now. "To remain present without seeking is the meditation" (Garab Dorje).

Yes, human happiness is an awareness management skill set! In a very real sense happiness arises from mindful management of your *present awareness. OM AH HUM* upon your mindful breath is your immediate always present touchstone. Now arise from yourself and do some good. It will make you happy now.

Hence, on this Mahayana Buddhist view, your mindfulness mantra practice is not merely about you, the ongoing drama of your self-ego-I. Your happiness, both relative flourishing and ultimate liberation from suffering is the result of *bodhicitta*, your compassionate thought, intention and action to benefit, not just yourself, but "other" living beings. Take it a step at a time. That is the primary cause of your happiness. That is the real work. Paradoxical? Ironic? To your concept-mind, yes; but not to your wisdom mind. Always present primordial Presence of That! Wonder of wonders, That is who we actually are, without a single exception.

The Dharmakaya Buddha. We've seen that in the Buddhist *Tibetan Canon* the iconographic primordial *Adi* Buddha of this vast, empty, formless realm of *dharmakaya* potentiality is, for the Old Translation Tibetan *Nyingma* School (8th century) Samantabhadra (Tib. *Kuntuzangpo*). For the New Translation (*sarma*) Schools (12th century) of Tibetan Buddhist Vajrayana— *Gelug, Kagyu, Sakya*—this primordial *Adi* Buddha is Vajradhara (*Dorje Chang*). These two *Adi* Buddhas are metaphysically or ontologically equivalent, representing and embodying boundless *shunyata*/emptiness as primordial awareness-conscious itself, experienced by the yogi or yogini as pure luminous cognizance, the already present noetic (body mind spirit union), nonlocal, nondual nature of mind (*sems nyid*) in whom we, and all reality are always already instantiated.

For the yogi or yogini who accomplishes the state of *dharmakaya*— the state of primordial *Adi* Buddha—is to accomplish primordial liberation-enlightenment itself, full *bodhi* of Buddhahood.

It is Vajradhara in whom arises the *Mahamudra* Father tantras (*Guhyasamaja, Yamantaka, Kalachakra*, etc.) of the *Gelug* and *Kagu* Schools. From Primordial *Adi Buddha*—by whatever name or concept—manifest the Five Wisdom Buddhas—the *Dhyani* Buddhas of the Vajrayana Path.

This concludes our brief engagement with the *dharmakaya* buddha body dimension.

2) **Samghogakaya**/*AH, longku,* devotional formless "body of delight", wisdom mind bliss/peace of enlightenment arises constantly, directly and spontaneously from *dharmakaya;* clear light bridge into form. Here the proto-light-forms of arising reality appear with or as luminous clarity; clear light "ground luminosity" that is pure awareness/cognizance itself. The *Adi* Buddha of this formless realm is, for *Nyingma* School, the logos Vajrasattva. The many *sambhogakaya* buddhas of the three times—past, present, future—establish the timeless endless buddha fields of the *sambhogakaya* reality dimension.

In the Tibetan Buddhist Vajrayana or Secret Mantra path the practice deities—peaceful or wrathful—manifest from this bright *sambhogakaya* Buddha body of light dimension. It is these indwelling, non-separate but relative practice deities, introduced via direct transmission from the Vajra Master, that guide us on this difficult, joyous Path.

3) **Nirmanakaya**/*HUM,* transformation body, energy manifestation of *dharmakaya/OM* in time and human form as embodied primordial love-wisdom mind—the wisdom of emptiness—luminous Buddha mind love-wisdom Presence, spontaneously and skillfully expressed by the bodhisattva masters and Buddhas as *bodhicitta* conduct for the benefit of living beings.

HUM is the utter inseparability of the Two Truths, Relative and Ultimate Truth, ultimate *bodhicitta* physically and mentally embodied in the dimension of Relative Truth space and time by

Gautama Shakyamuni (sage of the *Shakya Clan*), the historical Buddha, and by Padmasambhava, the "second Buddha", and by all of the Buddhas, bodhisattvas, and avatars of the Three Times—past, present, future—who have incarnated into space-time form to teach the way of love and wisdom, and thus to ease the suffering of sentient beings.

The direct trans-conceptual prior and always already present complementary unity of the Two Truths—Relative Truth (*samvriti satya, kunzog denpa*) and Ultimate Truth (*paramartha satya, don dampa*)—is fully realized and compassionately expressed in conduct by such Buddhas, and their heirs, the beloved bodhisattvas. A bodhisattva is one in whom precious *relative bodhicitta*—the fully engaged compassionate thought, intention, and action for the benefit of all sentient beings—has taken root, and is continuously manifested in kind, compassionate (*karuna*) action-conduct in this relative world of time and form, realm of the suffering of *samsara*.

More generally, *HUM* is primordial Buddha nature of *OM*, the basal, empty primeval "groundless ground", always already present Presence of That, indwelling in all beings and in all spacetime form.

Thus is nonlocal, nondual *OM* realized locally in time as *HUM*, primordial *Bodhi*-Buddha mind/love-wisdom mind Presence (*vidya, rigpa*). The prior and present unity or utter non-separateness of the Two Truths—Relative and Ultimate—and of the *Trikaya of the Base* of these three Buddha bodies/dimensions is sometimes called *svabhavikakaya,* the essence body.

Therefore, arising spacetime phenomenal existence is always this complementary and ultimately indivisible unity of the Two Truths—relative form/appearance and ultimate primordial boundless *dharmakaya* in whom it all arises, abides, and returns. "Form is empty; emptiness is form". Realization of this nondual unity is the full *bodhi* of liberation, and then enlightenment.

It is this wisdom of emptiness as already present, unelaborated, trans-conceptual selfless state of Presence—*nirmanakaya bodhi* mind love-wisdom mind Presence—that is coemergent great bliss fruition of the Buddhist Path. Thus is timeless unity of the primordial ground with fruition of the Path realized. Told *Dzogchen* Master Adzom Rinpoche, "The fruit is no different at the pinnacle of enlightenment, than it is at the primordial base".

In this "already accomplished" fruitional view of Vajrayana *Nyingma* school's *Dzogchen* path, this natural unity of the Two Truths is always already the "mandala of nondual primordial purity (*kadag*), and its spontaneous presence (*lhundrub*) at the Heart; the prior and present "unity of *samsara* and nirvana"; the "mandala of the ultimate nature, and its compassionate expression", the "mandala of the three vajras" (body, speech, mind).

Failing this subtle nondual understanding we "miss the mark" (*hamartia*/sin, *avidya*) of the already present luminous mandala of the base/ground, spontaneous wisdom mind Buddha mind Presence of That. In this way do we miss the very essence of Tibetan Buddhist Vajrayana's fruitional vehicle, namely that Buddha mind/wisdom mind is, as *Dzogchen* founder Garab Dorje told 2000 years ago, "already accomplished from the very beginning", deep within us. The mindful Secret Mantra practice of the Path awakens us to this great non-conceptual, nondual truth.

OM AH HUM*: In Summary. *OM is *dharmakaya* dimension: basal, formless, "vast expanse" of unbounded whole, infinite basic space of *dharmadhutu*, primordial "groundless ground" or base (*kadag, gzhi rigpa*) of all arising and appearing spacetime phenomena. *Dharmakaya/OM* is this skylike basic space of reality itself. *Sambhogakaya/AH* is the luminous spiritual sun who illumines the *rupakaya* bodies of form. *Nirmanakaya/HUM* is reflected, embodied manifestation of that spiritual sun in spacetime physical and mental form.

OM/dharmakaya is timeless, formless, nonlocal, nondual body of Primordial *Adi Buddha Samantabhadra, mahashunyata,* great boundless emptiness, vast formless, selfless whole of *dharmadhutu* (*mahabindu*), analogous to *Nirguna Brahman*, Tao, trans-theistic, nondual God the Primordial Father (*Abba, En Soph, godhead, Yahweh*) in whom all of this luminous spacetime *prana* life energy of form is an arising, participating, interdependent, manifest instantiation.

The non-conceptual, direct, contemplative knowing-feeling wisdom Presence (*yogi pratyaksa*) of this formless *OM* body, by whatever name or concept, is enlightened *Bodhi* mind/wisdom mind, *vidya*, *rigpa*—bright Presence of That—always dwelling deep within our human spiritual Heart (*hridyam*).

AH is *sambhogakaya* dimension: mirror-like reflection of sky-like *dharmakaya* basic space, Voice (*Vak, Speech, sound*), clear light bridge of luminous cognizance/awareness descended from timeless formless *OM* into light-energy of form. Form is *HUM*, spacetime, $E=mc^2$, subtle *prana* wind and gross matter/energy of embodied form, which instantiates our very being here as guests of this ultimate *bodhicitta* gift of spacetime reality.

Being in form, our precious human birth, gives us time to open to receive this wondrous gift (*jinlob*) of our life, just as it is now. Self acceptance of this great gift of life, exactly as it is, with the precious *bodhicitta*, are the primary causes of human happiness.

HUM is *nirmanakaya* dimension: life energy manifestation of *OM* embodied in spacetime human form—the Buddhas, bodhisattvas, mahasiddhas, tulkus; indeed all of the love-wisdom avatars, masters, saints and sages who have come to earth to show the way to freedom from the ignorance (*avidya, marigpa*) that is the very cause of human suffering.

Some of the names for this embodied selfless *nirmanakaya HUM* Presence (*vidya, rigpa*) of boundless primordial *dharmakaya/OM* are: Buddha Nature; *bodhi*/Buddha mind; *Atman* that is Brahman; *I Am That I Am Presence* of Moses and the Prophets, and of Jesus—*Christos/logos/gnosis*—that is our innermost Christ Nature; Hebrew *Shekhinah*, innermost nondual Presence of Godhead. Told Jesus, "That which you seek...the Kingdom of God...is already present within you...and it is spread upon the face of the earth...but you do not see it" (Luke 17).

The "not seeing it" is ignorance/confusion/delusion (*hamartia*/sin, *avidya, ajnana, marigpa*), the ignoring of our own radiant love-wisdom mind Presence. This ignorance then produces attraction/attachment and aversion/hostility with all its individual and collective afflictive pathological emotion: fear and anxiety, anger and hatred, ego desire, greed and pride, shame/blame, guilt, and the rest. Such ignorance is the cause of human suffering.

This embodied already present *buddhic* Presence known as *HUM* is our light-form gift of human life-consciousness, our utterly selfless "supreme identity" with formless *OM*—boundless whole—all-embracing primordial awareness-consciousness being itself in whom this all arises, abides, and passes away. Thus is realization of mindful Presence of *HUM* the end of human suffering.

HUM is thus selfless primordial wisdom mind, the unity of the mindstream of all the *nirmanakaya* Buddhas and *mahasiddhas* given for us to ease the suffering of beings in time and form. *HUM* is indivisible unity of embodied skillful compassionate objective means/method with subjective indwelling, nondual wisdom mind Presence in the practice of the Path that is ultimate liberation from the ignorance, delusion and obscuration, the very cause of human suffering.

Yes, it is told by the love-wisdom *nirmanakaya*s of our Great Wisdom Tradition that the fruition/result of this Path is Happiness Itself, ultimate happiness that does no harm; the happiness that cannot be lost.

HUM is spontaneously expressed as *bodhicitta*, wise, kind, skillful compassionate thought, intention and action arising effortlessly for the benefit of all beings—Christ/Buddha Wisdom Mind—outshining realization in human conduct of this Great Compassion gift of our life, inherently always already present being here in form. All That is *HUM*.

OM AH HUM. Yes, these three reality dimensions, these three gates to liberation and enlightenment are always and forever a prior and present unity. *OM AH HUM* is a *relative* lifting, a protective mantra touchstone that instantly connects us to our indwelling always present *ultimate* Buddha mind Presence. Thus are Buddha's Two Truths unified in nondual primordial Presence within the human heartmind, for the immediate benefit of living beings.

This nondual unity of boundless emptiness and luminous awareness is revealed to the Buddhist practitioner, step by mindful step, through practice of mindful breathing, deity practice, the great power of mantra prayer, and compassionate *bodhicitta*. As Buddha told so long ago, "Let it be as it is and rest your weary mind; all things are perfect exactly as they are". This vast reality process is perfect just as it is. We cannot improve it. We follow it imperfectly, joyously through resting in our own innermost Presence of it.

So, give thanks for the profound gift of your *ultimate* nonexistence, and your *relative* embodied existence, just as it is now. It's the only way we can be truly and authentically happy here. And that happiness is already present deep within us. Be present to That! Thus it is. So be it.

SARVA MANGALAM

Postscript: Now What?

There is much more to be told. And experienced. And compassionately expressed.

Should you enjoy this peaceful "innate intrinsic awareness wisdom mind Presence" now present within you, if you have not already done so, enhance it by finding a teacher/guide who can introduce you to a living wisdom master, and a community of like-minded folks to share it with. The benefit to you, and others in your sphere is immeasurable.

All of the love-wisdom masters of the great Primordial Wisdom Tradition of humankind have told it: our human realities being here in time are always only this present spacious, timeless presence of *now*. So, "Rest your weary mind and let it be as it is".

Rest now in indwelling primordial wisdom mind Presence of that "groundless ground" of the vast boundless whole of everything arising within it. That is who we actually are, without a single exception. Do this often through "placement of attention" upon the mindful mantra breath (*Appendix A*). Then *be* the change you wish see.

"When we understand, there is no problem whatsoever in this world", said Suzuki Roshi. It's like coming home. So, now arise and do some good. It will make you happy.

Thus it is. So be it.

David Paul Boaz Dechen Wangdu: info@coppermount.org; davidpaulboaz.org

Appendix A: Brief Course
Let It Be: Basic Mindfulness
Meditation

Enjoy the space between your thoughts.

Happiness Arises From Your Present Mind State!

So, *train your mind* in happiness: peace, free of the habitual thinking of self-ego-I with its unhappy fear, anger, and pride. Meditation is after all a conscious finite portal into infinite peace—spacious, boundless primordial whole of everything arising therein—bright love-wisdom Presence of That, always already present within you *now*. Train your mind in *placement of awareness/attention* upon that aspect or imprint, or Presence of you, in this present moment now. "Mindfulness of breathing" is the meditation that accomplishes this open secret of human happiness. Below are Ten Steps that could change your life.

It's easier than you think. Begin by sitting in a chair, your back straight, hands in your lap, legs uncrossed, feet flat on the floor. Or sit on a cushion, legs crossed.

1. Thank You

Experience deep thanks for the great gift of your life, just as it is now. Accept yourself—all your positive and negative experience—exactly as you are, here and now. Feel your selfless good will intention to benefit all living beings. This is the primary cause of human happiness!

Lower your gaze so that your neck is straight. Relax jaw, neck, gut. Feel the breath in your belly. Now *place your attention* behind your forehead. Close your eyes, raise your eyebrows. This will produce alpha brain rhythm, the peace response, replacing stressful "fight or flight" beta rhythm. Feel a subtle focused fullness in the forebrain. Let the crown of your head open as light streams in from above and meets the *prana* life-force energy rising upon each breath. *Feel* it pervade your entire body-mind—and deep into the earth.

2. **Attention!**

*Now, gather the "wild horse of the mind" by **placement of attention** on your breath. Be present to your breath as it arises in your belly.* Let your mantra prayer begin. Softly recite *OM AH HUM* (see below). This then is your "alpha mantra breath": 5 seconds in; 7 seconds out through pursed lips (12 seconds). Do it 3 to 9 times (36 to 108 seconds). Let your mantra prayer continue, either consciously, or in the background, day and night.

Each breath feel your busy mind settle into its quiet natural state of wakefulness; your clear light love-wisdom mind Presence—that aspect of you that is utterly one with the great source of everything—your safe place, beyond all thoughts, concepts, beliefs; free of judgment, fear, anger, guilt, pride; free of self-ego-I. No need to think about it. Open and feel it! Be that stillness. Now say to the busy mind, "Peace, be still". Say to the grasping self, "Peace, I Am".

Thoughts, questions, feelings naturally arise. Briefly greet them. Negative or positive thinking, planning, wandering, worry/anxiety, anger: label whatever arises "distraction". Then surrender it all on the out-breath. Or let it flow by on vast empty space of the sky, like a bird, leaving no trace. *Again and again return attention to the breath.* After 3-5 minutes open your eyes slightly and breathe normally, mouth closed.

As you settle into, and rest in your selfless *wisdom mind Presence*, your breath will naturally be slow and gentle. Enjoy this feeling of delight within you. Feel your connectedness to everything. No need to create it; or grasp at it. Mindful Presence upon the breath is always already present—your "Supreme Identity". Who Am I? *That I Am!*

3. **In-Breath**

Open to receive luminous purifying "life-force energy", sustainer of all life. It has many names. In the East this energy is *prana* or *ch'i* (spirit/breath). For the West it is *pneuma*/Holy Spirit, the very "breath of life", "bio energy", the subtle face/voice of gross physical light/energy/form ($E=mc^2$) arising from formless, non-conceptual, spacious unbounded whole; vast primordial awareness-consciousness ground itself in whom this all arises. *Breathe,* you are alive! Open and receive. Feel it pervade every space of your body-mind.

4. **Out-Breath**

Release thoughts, feelings, past, future, all self-ego-I grasping. Feel your stability deep in Mother Earth. Whatever arises—thoughts, feelings, doubts, happy or not—release it all on the out-breath. Surrender it all. Witness it all dissolve as you return to your breath, again and again. *Let it be just as it is* in this peaceful luminous sky-like space of the mind.

Please consider this well: Thoughts are only thoughts. They come and they go in dependence upon your present mind state. Thoughts are not a solid reality! You are now learning to choose *your realities by choosing your present mind state. All of the love-wisdom Masters of our great Primordial Wisdom Tradition have taught this great liberating freedom to be happy right here now.*

So, more or less absent thoughts, *feel* your selfless, natural clear-light *Wisdom Mind Presence*—subtle peace, clarity, bliss. From this natural spacious mind state the kind, compassionate *activity* of love spontaneously arises in your mind stream—the very secret and primary cause of human happiness. Place your *attention* on that. Let it be so now.

Thus it is, that deep peace which you desire rides the breath. Remain close to the breath. When distracted by anxiety/anger or self-judgment—simply return to already present Presence upon your breath, again and again. When your mind is filled with light of love-wisdom mind Presence, there is no room for the negative stuff. Practice that and be happy.

5. **Presence**

Here, now, breathe. Open your heart and mind and feel your always present indwelling love-wisdom mind Presence of vast boundless whole in whom this all arises. It's right here! That you are now! Subtle Presence of That may be directly *experienced, prior to thinking, as luminous clear-light mind essence—the very Christ-Buddha nature of mind, beyond any name, concept, or belief.*

Now experience this *prana/spirit* life-energy at the crown of your head. Feel it stream in from above upon each breath. Open your heart to receive. Feel it pervade your entire body-mind. Let it flow downward throughout your head, throat, chest, back, *hara* center in the belly, pelvis; then deep into Mother Earth. Feel your fearless stability in earth.

Let this energy of Presence penetrate any discomfort—that self-contraction from your natural life-energy flow: physical tension and pain, sense desire, grief, doubt, guilt, fear/anxiety, anger/hostility, harsh judgments of self and others. Patient love and wisdom heal fear and anger. Your alpha mantra breath is your touchstone to being That now.

Now experience the emotional lift as any and all presently activated "attachment and aversion" are inundated by Presence of this clear light life energy. *Be* for a moment with whatever arises—attractive or aversive. Then surrender it all on the out-breath. Know now you are free of it. Let this light penetrate and pervade space of your entire emotional and physical body-mind: brain, nervous systems, heart, organs, cells, the very atomic structure of your physical/emotional/spiritual being. Now, rest in this feeling of delight within you.

"Let it be as it is, and rest your weary mind, all things are perfect exactly as they are" (Buddha). "That which you seek...the Kingdom of God...is already present within you...and it is spread upon the face of the world, but you do not see it" (Jesus the Christ).

With each breath *feel* healing life energy Presence fill and overflow into your subtle energy field, this light of you that embraces and pervades your whole body-mind. Awaken to this "basic goodness" that you are, prior to our cultural skeptical "global web of belief". But don't *believe* this. Open, *feel* it. Now self-ego-I is tamed, at peace. Rest fearlessly in That.

6. **Wisdom Mind is a Choice**

"What you are is what you have been; what you will be is what you do now" (Gautama the Buddha). This bright basic space upon the breath is your natural wakefulness—your primordial love-wisdom mind Presence. *Choose* to be that space/peace, here and now, beyond ego: no past nor future; no attachment nor aversion; no true nor false; no judgment at all—just for this moment. No need to think, try or do anything. *Know that your clear-light mind is already awake, kind and wise. Rest in That, each breath. Let it be as it is; calm and clear.*

Love-wisdom mind *practice* is your Path to liberation from ego-centric ignorance and delusion, root cause of human suffering. Stay with it. Your self-ego-I may resist. Notice the bogus excuses. This *choice* is Happiness Itself: kind *relative* human flourishing that does no harm; and *ultimate* happiness-liberation from suffering; the happiness that cannot be lost.

Thus is human happiness very much an awareness management skill set! Happiness arises, not so much from desirable stuff, but from the choice of your *placement of awareness/attention* upon your breath, in this present moment now! No belief, no leap of faith, no authority but your own is required. Simply settle your mind, open your heart, and be fully present to your alpha mantra breath now. That is your *connection* to peace and happiness already present within you. That is the foundation of your love-wisdom mind practice of the Path.

7. **Refuge**

Now you know this precious space/peace of your *Christ-Buddha Mind Presence*. Take refuge in it often. Breath by breath purify, pacify, stabilize, beautify your mind; a most courageous act; your most urgent activity. Make mindful breathing a priority, *"brief moments; many times"*, all day and all night. Soon it becomes a conscious continuity of awareness. Who am I? Feeling *Presence* of that vast whole—"*Tat Tvam Asi*; That I Am*", without a single exception. You have never been separate from That! Feel That, breath by breath. *That is the View. That is the Teaching. That is the Practice. It's like coming home.*

8. Compassion Meditation

By this good generated by each mindful breath make this aspiration for the benefit of all living beings: "*May all beings be free of suffering, and the causes of suffering. May all beings have happiness, and the causes of happiness*". This powerful mantra prayer is as well, your *Compassion Meditation* when practiced for a few minutes. "Come and see" what it does for your present heart-mind state of happiness.

Is not your happiness already linked to the happiness of others? We're all in this reality boat together. Accomplish your own happiness through compassionate thought, intention, and action to benefit other beings. It's called altruism. In the East it's *bodhicitta*. It's the magic metric for a good life. So arise, and do some good. It will make you happy *now*.

9. Real Practice

Practice requires patience and courage. Patience is the antidote to anger, which arises from fear. It takes courage to face fear. Practice 20-30 minutes or more upon rising; 10-20 minutes upon retiring; and many "36 seconds of bliss" alpha mantra breaths during the day. Peace is always here, between your thoughts, each mindful breath.

Take refuge in your love-wisdom mind Presence often. Feel it at your heart before sleep; and all night long. Be present while eating, walking, working, loving. Lovingly accept yourself as a mother accepts her child. No blame. Anxious, angry? No time? *Take three OM AH HUM belly breaths right now!* Go ahead and do it now. Your goal is *not* peace and happiness in some ideal future mind state. *Make the practice itself your goal*—each mindful breath. "Mindfulness of breathing is the foundation of all wisdom and happiness" (Buddha).

10. **The Five Benefits of Mindfulness Meditation Are Always Already Present**

1) Body-Mind relaxation experienced as profound peace, forgiveness, healing.
2) Non-conceptuality: beyond self-ego-I thinking, concept, belief, fear/anger.
3) Clarity: mental and perceptual acuity, luminosity, vividness, wakefulness.
4) Deep appreciation and acceptance of your life, and yourself, just as you are.
5) Wisdom Mind Presence: happiness expressed as kind, compassionate action.

The Power of Voice

Use ancient mantra prayer *OM AH HUM,* a touchstone, during practice—it's all practice—to instantly connect to and protect your primordial *love wisdom mind* Presence. Let it be always in your awareness foreground, or background. Free your mind by reciting daily 108 mantras while walking, or sitting. Get a 108 bead mala.

Good Sleep

Engage your alpha mantra breath for a few minutes as you sit on the side of your bed. Now continue to recite *OM AH HUM* silently, on your back, hands over your heart, or at your side, palms down. Settle into your clear light love-wisdom mind Presence.

Now begin your *full body scan. Feel* the gentle peace of *prana spirit wind* life energy throughout your entire body mind. Your crown center is open. Step by mindful step receive life energy flow from above through your crown and throughout your head; then neck, shoulders, chest, arms and hands; then belly and back, pelvic area, legs and feet.

Relax into the light. Let any obstruction to energy flow—tension, pain, worry, anger—flow away on the out breath, and out through your feet and hands. "Rest your weary mind and let it be as it is". Feel life energy *prana* peace pervade your entire body-mind. Now say quietly, "May all beings be free of suffering and the causes of suffering. May all beings be happy, and have the causes of happiness."

As your breath naturally becomes slow and regular, let mantra prayer arise into your awareness background as you assume your normal sleeping position. Let this spirit breath of yours be your love-wisdom lullaby and goodnight.

OM AH HUM?

These three reality dimensions are one prior and present *unity*. *OM* is formless empty space, primordial ground of all phenomena, vast unbounded whole itself. *AH* is like the sun; selfless clear light awareness—light bridge into form. *HUM* is non-conceptual *love-wisdom mind* Presence of *OM,* always already present now within you; light-form gift naturally expressing itself as skillful loving *bodhicitta*—thought, intention and action to benefit living beings. *Who am I? I Am OM AH HUM*: three gates to happiness—body, voice, mind of all the Buddha's and wisdom masters—your instant connection to That! Feel it purify your cause/effect karma. *The benefit of mindful breathing is immeasurable.*

Now you know the "innermost secret" of human happiness. Please consider it well. If you desire it, then practice it. Now arise and do some good. It will make you happy now.

David Paul Boaz Dechen Wangdu:
coppermount.org; davidpaulboaz.org

Appendix B:
Quantum Emptiness and Buddhist Impermanence

> Whenever we try to pick out something by itself, we find it hitched to everything else in the universe.
>
> —John Muir

All the buddhas, and most quantum cosmologists agree, in the fullness of time all physical and mental forms shall pass away into primordial quantum/*buddic* emptiness; then arise again in a never ending cycle of countless, timeless eons. Physical and mental cosmic form *relatively* arising from the nondual (subject-object unity) *ultimate* aboriginal *Kosmic* whole *(dharmadhatu)* of its emptiness/ *shunyata* ground is inherently impermanent *(anitya)*, and utterly absent and empty *(shunya)* of any intrinsic, ultimate existence. Yet, in this spacetime relative conventional world the all-pervasive suffering of living beings exists. What shall be our response?

It is luminous non-conceptual primordial awareness Presence of that great whole in whom we and all of this arises and abides that is metacognitively, reflexively instantiated in human cognizance, always already present at the Heart (hridaya) *of the human being-by whatever name or concept. Nondual contemplative meditative practice of the Path makes it so-makes it real. All of the love-wisdom masters of the three times-past, present, future-have told it: awakening to this intimate, indwelling Presence is the cause of altruistic* bodhicitta *conduct the primary cause of human happiness,*

As to Buddhist impermanence (*anitya*), human and other beings upon the earth shall pass. Our precious Mother Earth shall pass. Our solar system and our home galaxy, the Milky Way shall, in due course, merge cataclysmically with our sister galaxy Andromeda. Many solar systems will perish. The great galaxy super-cluster in which this new galaxy abides shall as well pass away. The physical and mental universe itself, and indeed all of the universes of the endless, infinite cyclic multiverse shall all expand into quantum/*buddic* emptiness and quite naturally cease to exist, as matter energy entropy thermodynamically peters out in this universe of ours in a "Big Chill" heat death. All energy-motion is here *kaput*! Understanding that dark truth, there is nothing solid in heaven nor in earth to which living beings may cling. That is the impermanence of quantum suffering writ large!

But wait! We've already seen that the buddhas and recent quantum cosmology have both told that from the emptiness of the vast expanse of nearly empty space, and the zero motion of seemingly random non-physical "zero point energy" (ZPE) quantum vacuum field fluctuations similar to "partless space particles" of Buddhist A*bidharma*-spontaneously arise proto-matter as new form. Hope for spacetime stuff springs eternal!

Well, what does "quantum zero point energy" mean? The total energy density of this universe equals zero because the total mass of the universe is positively charged; and the total gravity of the universe is negatively charged. The positive charged mass exactly, cancels the negative charged gravity, equaling zero energy density. Therefore, the total energy of this universe is zero. Sounds almost mystical; a conclusion resisted by both Buddhism and physics.

This endless process of the arising of physical form from its primordial quantum/*buddic* emptiness zero ground state is a continuity (the meaning of tantra) of infinite gravitational attraction and repulsion. Great gravity is thus, in the gloss of the Hindu *Bhagavad Gita*, the awful "creator and destroyer of worlds".

According to quantum pioneer Werner Heisenberg's Principle of Uncertainty, all matter particle fields, and every point in space undergoes random quantum fluctuations, even in its zero point energy "ground state". From this virtual ground, sooner or later new matter/mass will fluctuate into existence. There is an eternity in which this happens; brief moments, many times.

Einstein's equivalence of mass and energy, described by his illustrious Special Relativity Theory (SRT) equation $E = mc2$, means that any zero point in space that has quantum energy potential has mass. So, every point in space has potential mass to spontaneously give rise to quantum fluctuations of new "virtual particles" of physical form. From such an ostensibly uncaused random event springs new inflationary universes, new inflationary Big Bang singularities—spacetime form arising ex nihilo, from nothing, from quantu*m/buddic* emptiness, an infinity of universe occurrences—a multiverse, endlessly and forever arising and passing away—all of this explicate order subsumed and embraced in the nondual infinite, implicate order of the whole.

Thus, there is virtual motion/form inherent even in zero point emptiness; even at the zero atomic/molecular motion of absolute zero, at the end of time when all matter of this particular universe has finally lost its motion to the all-consuming vacuum of empty space. Then, from this nearly empty vacuum of space "somewhere" arises a new universe. How is this so?

The properties of this continuously arising matter-mass then, are nothing less than quasi empty uncaused random quantum vacuum fluctuations of the zero point energy field. In physics it is assumed that there can be no "perfectly empty vacuum". Empty space cannot be perfectly empty. "Virtual particles" enter and exit spacetime existence continuously. Quantum Field Theory (QFT) predicts them, and their effects are observable.

Scientists have often said that "nature abhors a vacuum". Perhaps our primordial Mother Nature prefers form to emptiness.

It seems that utter emptiness may indeed "be" nonexistent, other than as an empty concept.

Some fine day, somewhere, a new universe instantly inflates into existence from a near empty quantum fluctuation—again and again as the cyclic multiverse, by whatever name or concept, endlessly creates and destroys cosmic worlds.

A word is now in order about this cyclic multiverse of recent cosmology—and of the Hindu and Buddhist cosmologies—the infinite complex of coexisting "parallel universes".

In the great Primordial Wisdom Tradition of humankind the cyclic arising and falling away of multiple universes is alive and well. Just so, the relativistic quantum cosmology of the 21st century "multiverse theory" is gently becoming the new scientific cosmology orthodoxy.

Scientific theories once considered empirically and experimentally unknowable—the heliocentric solar system; electromagnetism; curved spacetime, quantum super-positions; black holes—are no longer beyond the pale of science. Such abstract notions were more metaphysical than physical. Yet, step by empirical step such radical ideas entered the embrace of accepted "scientific method". Multiverse theory now teeters rather precariously on the cusp of such scientific orthodoxy.

The good news? Multiverse theory is founded in the relative stability of mainstream relativistic quantum mechanics (QFT, QED); and most of its protocols now qualify as scientific method. That is to say, multiverse theory makes empirical predictions, and at least some of it can be empirically falsified. "Multiverse theory can be tested and falsified even though we cannot see the other universes" (Max Tegmark).

Quantum cosmologists have identified four levels of "parallel universes" that constitute the endless infinite cyclic multiverse. Cosmologist Max Tegmark has holistically engaged these four in his excellent *Scientific American* article of May 2003. (Reprinted in *The Best Science and Nature* Writing, 2004)

All four of these timeless levels of cosmic being in spacetime are entirely dependent upon purely conceptual mathematical reasoning. These four universe levels—with mathematical variations on the theme—are presumed to exhaust our human cognitive capacity for understanding both the relative, *and* ultimate nature of not only this universe of ours, but the entire admittedly ineffable multiverse! O Human Hubris! Are there not more things in heaven and earth than are dreamt of in our mathematical philosophies? Let's see.

Historically, culturally, there are two general mathematical paradigms—Aristotelian and Platonic. These two are ancient Greek cognitive products of two ostensibly different metaphysical or ontological paradigms as to the ultimate nature of appearing physical and mental reality-our deep cultural background Western "global web of belief (Quine 1969)—in short, Aristotelian and Platonic.

The traditional distinction between the ontic views of the seminal Greek philosophers Plato and Aristotle emphasizes Plato's otherworldly, transcendental ideal, and *a priori* (prior to experience) noetic view of our human knowledge of ultimate reality—over against Aristotle's concern for earthly natural phenomena, including the nature of human reason, and of ethics.

Aristotle (383-321 BCE) was a realist metaphysician of physical form. Plato (427-346 BCE) was an idealist metaphysician of his archetypal Platonic Forms. Together they constitute the very foundation of the Western mind.

So, the Aristotelian view is of an ultimately physical/material fundamental appearing reality that mathematics attempts to explain. Mathematics is relative and conventional, not transcendental and absolute, as Plato would have it. For Aristotle here is nothing of much interest beyond the physical dimension. The metaphysics of Aristotle is a metaphysics of matter. Aristotle's science, with his logic, which is based in his Three Laws of Thought—while superseded by today's predicate calculus, quantum logic, and multi-valued logical systems (MVL)—have provided the foundation for Western modern science with its dominant metaphysical trope, Scientific Materialism/Physicalism.

However, the Platonic mathematical paradigm views mathematics, as did Plato himself, as an ideal, archetypal, transcendentally perfect Form or Idea—abiding beyond spacetime reality—a *universal* that a *particular* human mind may only mathematically approximate. This paradigm sees the entire K*osmos*—objective and subjective—as inherently, ultimately mathematical in nature. The conceptual rub is just that we human observers conceive of it imperfectly.

Modern physics and cosmology is profoundly mathematically Platonist. Mathematics penetrates the secrets of the universe so unreasonably well, so it is said, because the universe is *inherently* mathematical in both its relative *and* ultimate nature. What possible reason could there be to seek the ultimate truths of reality elsewhere? That is the modern physics cognitive bias (confirmation bias). Still, as we shall soon see, what is, *is*—far beyond our mere concepts and belief*s about* it.

Can these heady truths of mathematics be truly reduced to something physical? Can the dualistic (subject-object separation) conceptual structures of mathematics that exist in the human mindscape be so easily reduced to mere physical structures and functions ? Max Tegmark:

> I have suggested that complete mathematical symmetry holds: that all mathematical structures exist physically as well...Any self-consistent fundamental physical theory can be phrased in some kind of mathematical structure" (*Sci. Amer.* 2003).

Notwithstanding the circular reasoning, this is a typical example of the prevailing metaphysical bias of Greek Aristotelian Metaphysical Materialism/Physicalism, "scientific" reductionism: to wit, all appearing physical and mental reality—love, goodness, beauty, truth, ethics, spirituality, and the rest—are ultimately reducible to merely physical/mathematical conceptual phenomena. To question this scientific metaphysical dogma is taboo. One could lose tenure! Given our all too human propensity to cognitive bias, perhaps it is better to have questions that can't be answered, than to have answers that can't be questioned.

Thus has our Greek materialist legacy colonized the Western mind and spirit. And, as I have argued in these pages, at considerable expense to the multidimensional truth of our appearing realities, and thus to our human happiness.

Is this relentless objective conceptual rational cognition all we are? Must the boundless whole of reality itself be reduced to the mere conceptual objective dimension of this vast reality?

Clearly, human awareness enjoys at least four self-evident experiential cognitive dimensions: 1) exoteric, objective, conceptual; 2) esoteric, subjective, intuitive, non-conceptual; 3) greater esoteric, subjective, contemplative, spiritual; and 4) perfectly subjective, "innermost secret" nondual, the noetic primordial wisdom unity of knowing subject and its known object—just prior to the odious subject-object split, with all its human suffering. These four cognitive awareness-consciousness dimensions are then, always already an ontologically prior, and epistemologically, phenomenally present unity!

Therefore, let us add to the four multiverse levels/dimensions of recent cosmology, a fifth dimension, a *Level V Multiverse*—an all-embracing post-mathematical, post-empirical, trans- conceptual, yet contemplatively directly known (*yogi pratyaksa*) sphere of pristine nondual primordial awareness-consciousness itself in whom all of the stuff of the "many mansions" of arising and appearing reality are blissfully instantiated.

Level V Multiverse indeed. What then shall we name it? This many dimensional *Kosmic* all inclusive infinite boundless emptiness whole in whom cosmic physical form arises, evolves, and participates has for thousands of years been known to the prodigious Primordial Wisdom Tradition of our species by such names as *Parabrahman, Samantabhadra, dharmakaya, dharmadhatu, Tao, Ein Sof, Yahweh,* and many others. "What's in a name? That which we call a rose, by any other name would smell as sweet" (Juliet Capulet).

Back to the present. In 1929 astronomer Edwin Hubble, with the aid of his observatory janitor and brilliant part-time cosmologist assistant Milton Humason, discovered that the non expanding static "Steady State Model" of our universe of early 20th century physics is actually expanding! Then, in 1998 future (2011) Nobel laureates Saul Perlmutter, Brian Schmidt, and Adam Reiss and their teams, working independently, discovered that Hubble's expanding universe is actually accelerating! What hath God wrought!

The most reasonable explanation for an expanding, *accelerating* universe is a global *positive* repulsive quantum ZPE vacuum energy, an anti-gravitational force which counteracts the natural attractive-contractive force of gravity by impulsing the matter of the universe "outward".

The vacuum energy soon received the prosaic name *dark energy*. This mysterious, intuitively unnatural cosmic stuff quickly became identified with Einstein's cosmological constant lambda Λ of 1917, when Einstein first predicted dark energy as he began to apply his GRT field equations to the curved structure of space-time. But at the time he refused to believe it! Thus did the ZPE vacuum energy, which became dark energy, become Einstein's new constant of nature Λ. This new constant of nature is the energy density inherent in the boundless whole of spacetime that is described by Einstein's General Relativity Theory (GRT) field equations.

In 1917 Einstein executed "my greatest blunder" by inserting his cosmological constant lambda Λ into his scintillating 1915 GRT field equations to "hold back the universe" expansion predicted by these original equations. He needed to conform to the static, non-expanding "steady state universe" of Bondi, Gold, and Fred

Hoyle—the waning ideology of pre-Big Bang cosmology of the early century. In his heart of hearts he knew better.

In 1931, after Hubble's 1929 discovery that the universe was actually expanding, Einstein blundered again by retracting the untidy new constant Λ from his GRT field equations. Of course he couldn't know it, but his lambda constant was, 67 years later, to become the very dark energy that propulses this accelerating universe of ours.

Had Einstein trusted his initial GRT field equations he would perhaps have discovered the expanding universe long before Hubble. But he was steeped in the ideology of the time and could not free his mind from the "confirmation bias" that blinded him to the truth present in his original GRT field equations.

Moreover, Einstein became aware in the late 1920's that he had erred in failing to accept what Georges Lemaitre, Alexander Friedman, Willem DeSitter, and others had pointed out in the decade prior, that his cosmological constant lambda Λ insertion into the GRT field equations did not at all provide the stable "steady state" universe that he intended. Indeed, this discomfiting appendix would surely result in an unstable readily collapsible cosmos! Einstein rebuffed them all.

Now, as if the cosmic irony were not already thick enough, Einstein's early static, non expanding model of the universe has been recently incarnated into quantum cosmology in a new effort to explain away the nagging problem of a physically impossible, fine-structure constant (α) busting Big Bang singularity—a quite problematic whole lot of stuff from a whole lot of nothing. Some daring, *tenured* cosmologists are now pursuing an "emergent universe" that inflates from a static pre-cosmological constant Einsteinian universe. (Ellis and Maartens 2004, Class. Quant. Grav. 21:223-230)

Perhaps Albert Einstein should have been known as the greatest physicist of all time (Einstein and the buddhas deny the ultimate/absolute existence of time), instead of the second greatest, behind Isaac Newton. But as Shakespeare's Dogberry told in *Much Ado About Nothing,* such "comparisons are odious". (For the cosmology of GRT see Sean Carroll's excellent *Spacetime and Geometry: An Introduction to General Relativity,* 2003. For the intriguing drama of 20th century physics and cosmology see Boaz 2021a, excerpted at davidpaulboaz.org)

Dark energy has no known cause. It has been for 20 years both mathematically and observationally utterly inscrutable.

Still, dark energy is the foundation of the current Concordance Lambda Λ Cold Dark Matter (ΛCDM) Standard Model of cosmology. Quantum Field Theory (QFT) explains this vacuum ground state as a vast ensemble of constantly fluctuating zero point energy quantum particle fields present everywhere in spacetime. These quantum ZPE vacuum fluctuations contribute to the overall value of anti-gravitational dark energy cosmological constant which causes the acceleration of the cosmos.

So, the ZPE vacuum energy offers a reasonable explanation for the readily observed cosmological data—but at the cost of a most unnatural physical parameter. *Why is ZPE so much smaller than QFT predicts?* ZPE should be orders of magnitude larger than the observed data. Why do tiny stubborn quantum vacuum energy fluctuations refuse to produce the huge "natural" vacuum energy density that QFT demands? The prodigious quantum theory is after all always correct, "the best predictive tool in the history of physics"! Thus arises the supremely vexing "cosmological constant problem". No one has a clue how to explain this huge discrepancy between quantum theory and cosmological observation.

In other words, when quantum calculations are performed on the expected energy density of the universe we get an enormous value for the actually observed small ZPE vacuum energy—a ludicrous 120 orders of magnitude greater than the tiny values revealed by cosmological observation! This devastating discrepancy between theory and observation—between the large theoretical vacuum energy predictions of QFT, and the small values of cosmological observation—has been called by Steven Weinberg "The worst theoretical prediction in the history of physics".

This curious, most discomfiting "quantum vacuum catastrophe" has yet to be explained. It has cast a pall over one of the greatest intellectual achievements of humankind, namely, the cosmology that is the Lambda Cold Dark Matter (ΛCDM) Cosmological Standard Model of 20th century physics and cosmology.

This massive theoretical gap between quantum theory and cosmological observation and experiment represents one of the two primary conundrums of modern physics; the other main problem being the inherently vexed incommensurability of objective classical General Relativity Theory (GRT) with post-classical non-objective Quantum Field Theory (QFT). This present state of cosmic ignorance has precluded a consistent Quantum Gravity Theory (QGT) that unifies these two foundational pillars of physics. (Boaz 2021a; excerpted at www.davidpaulboaz.org)

Moreover, the dimension of physical spacetime form with all its relatively existent fermion (quarks and leptons) and boson (photons and gluons) quantum fields are *non-gravitating* zero point energy fields. Zero mass equals zero gravity. Great gravity of the "participatory universe" of gravitational physicist John Wheeler in summarizing his pal Einstein's GRT: "Spacetime tells matter how to move; matter tells spacetime how to curve".

So, here the gravitational plot thickens. Zero point vacuum energy is not subject to Einstein's gravity! The dark energy that is accelerating the universe to its final entropic thermodynamic Big Chill "heat death" demise at the end of time is usually explained by this non- gravitating vacuum zero point energy, Einstein's cosmological constant Λ. Can gravity be so easily dismissed? It is Λ after all which precludes the gravitational contraction of the universe all the way back to a "Big Crunch"; then a reflexive new "Big Bang". With the 1998 evidence of the acceleration of Hubble's expanding universe to its ultimate dissolution in timeless quantum/*buddic* emptiness—the old Big Chill-Big Bang/Big Crunch cosmology has fallen on hard times.

What if this gravity defying universe-accelerating dark energy of the cosmological constant Λ is emotionally unstable and decides to rapidly, or even exponentially increase its acceleration? Such a bipolar manic increase in dark energy density, should it occur, is said to be caused by a very disturbed, Hubble Parameter busting "phantom energy". This scenario is even worse for any beings still hanging out in embodied form. Here, the ultimate fate of the universe is that all matter is instantly torn asunder, right down to its quarks and leptons—a karmic *Kosmic* "Big Rip"! Not good for embodied minds. Even disembodied minds require a bit of spacetime stuff to mentate upon.

Thus is impermanent *(anitya)* samsaric spacetime existence loaded with cosmic suffering for sentient beings. Even for presumably inanimate matter—if we can ignore the panpsychic notion that all matter has some degree of consciousness—it still somehow desires to be. "Desire is the creator and destroyer of worlds" *(Bhagavad Gita)*.

Well, where is quantum cosmology headed, conceptually, in light of our quantum vacuum discrepancy problem? Clearly we must again consult Great Gravity. There are several interesting theories on offer that do not require a modification of Einstein's orthodox GRT gravity theory.

The most promising notion in this regard is that ZPE vacuum energy is precisely zero, and that dark energy is something entirely different, a nearly constant but non-zero *dynamical* energy field—in a word *Quintessence*—a radically new bosonic (photons and gluons) field of nature whose energy density does not much increase or decrease throughout the accelerating expansion of this universe toward its ultimate oblivion a few trillion years hence (give or take a trillion).

It has now become scientifically acceptable to seriously question mainstream physics' insistence on the purely *physical* existence of the quite problematic, diaphanous, altogether unfindable "dark sector"—dark matter and dark energy. What is it? No one knows.

The existence of dark energy has, as we have seen, not been detected directly. It is but a probable abductive *inference to the best explanation* based upon present data. It is therefore possible that GRT is incomplete and needs to be modified—a most unhappy thought for our cosmological GRT orthodoxy.

Clearly, GRT is extremely accurate at solar system, and even at intra-galactic time/distance scales. But if General Relativity is deceiving us at vast intergalactic time/distance scales, then perhaps we do not need the presently unscientific, non-empirical ghostly dark energy to fathom the acceleration and fate of the universe. Dark energy is after all inferred from the *global* gravitational motion of the vastness of this entire universe, even beyond the "future visibility limit" of our observable universe.

Due to the finite nature of the velocity of light we have no light signal access to most of the universe. The greatest distance we can observe is the distance that light has traveled in the 14 billion years since the proverbial Big Bang singularity that began the expansion of our universe Our visibility limit then is this "Hubble volume", or "horizon volume" limit. Considered from this greater view, gravity may well be inadequate to the task of divining causes of the behavior of mass/energy at such vast cosmic scales. Thus arises the heretical possibility of modifying Einstein's hitherto almost sacrosanct gravity (G) field equation.

Great gravity is no longer sacrosanct. Physicists have known almost since the early 20th century inception of the quantum theory that GRT breaks down on quantum gravity *micro-scales* near the inconceivably tiny Planck scale; for example during the first second after the Big Bang, and at minute black hole temperature scales where Hawking radiation is measured in billionths of a degree kelvin. Perhaps then, GRT breaks down on great inter-galactic scales as well. Evidence from quantum cosmology is now beginning to demonstrate that this is probably so.

Be that as it may, any tweaking of GRT is quite problematic for the Concordance Lambda Cold Dark Matter (ΛCDM) Standard

Model orthodoxy of modern physics. Still, there is significant work on "modified gravity" theories—for dark matter, and dark energy—presently under way.

Well, what if the huge "natural" vacuum density predictions of QFT are actually true? What would that mean for our perfect "galactic habitable zone", our *Kosmic* "Goldilocks Zone" where nothing is too hot nor too cold, and everything is a perfect middle way—"just right" for beings to arise and evolve the smarts to ask questions like, "What is the correct vacuum density of Λ to permit the acceleration of the cosmos?" What are the physical parameters required for this great "spiritual" *Kosmic* gift—our cosmological middle way that gives us time to open and receive the nondual truth of the matter? As Plato told so long ago, "No small matter is at stake. The question concerns the very way that human life is to be lived" (*Republic* Book I).

The formally spooky, but now respectable *Cosmological Anthropic Principle* states that any conjecture as to the origin and end of the universe is constrained by the necessity to allow for the existence of sentient beings who may evolve to ask such impudent questions. Such cosmic "environmental selection" has become a cogent explanation for the observed quite problematic value of the cosmological constant Λ. How is this so? If the ZPE quantum vacuum energy were to actually have its "natural" QFT predicted large value, there would be no smart beings here in spacetime to question it!

Life forms could not arise in a universe with anything close to such a large cosmological constant. If Einstein's dark energy/vacuum energy constant lambda Λ were large and negative the universe would almost instantly collapse. If Λ were large and positive the universe would almost instantly expand exponentially such that atomic structure could never form, let alone galaxies, stars, solar systems, planets, and impudent people.

Therefore, the vacuum energy of the universe could not be much different than its current small observed value, or we would not be here to observe and ponder it. So, it is ontologically necessary—so the Anthropic Principle Argument goes—that the actual

ZPE dark energy of the cosmological constant Λ is relatively small when compared to its huge "natural" QFT predicted value. But the Anthropic Principle Argument, whether in its strong (SAP) or weak (WAP) forms, is a philosophical argument. And most physicists are intimidated by philosophy.

Thus is this important cosmological reasoning consideration often given an unscientific, unsympathetic dismissal. Confirmation bias again. (Confirmation bias is the near universal human cognitive propensity to interpret new information as supporting one's current "web of belief". It is one of a set of cognitive biases by which we not so supremely "rational" human beings deceive ourselves.) This unwholesome trend of Anthropic Argument bias is diminishing as physicists begin to dialog with philosophers of physics, philosophers of mathematics, and even with Buddhist scholar-practitioners.

Still, in an ensemble of the many universes of infinite multi-verse only a universe that includes the physical parameters that permit life to arise can select an environment (environmental selection) in which intelligent sentient beings can evolve to question the nature of our being here. Let us then thank our lucky stars for this great *Kosmic* anthropic gift that is our being here now in relative spacetime form—whether or not we fully understand it conceptually or mathematically.

The inherent incompleteness of physics and physical cosmology necessitates moving beyond our present cognitive limits toward post-physical, post-empirical, trans-conceptual, even contemplative technologies. Thus is the new knowledge paradigm that is the 21st century Noetic Revolution in matter, mind, and spirit now upon us. (Boaz 2021b, excerpted at davidpaulboaz.org)

Thus it is, by the lights of both Buddhist metaphysics and astrophysical metaphysics, spacetime stuff really exists, at least relatively and conventionally, and it is (almost) empty of inherent existence—just as Gautama the Buddha told so long ago. From quantum/*buddic* emptiness spacetime form continues to arise; abide; then return again to emptiness, without ever departing its infinite *Kosmic* primordial awareness-consciousness formless emptiness ground in whom physical cosmic forms arise and evolve continuously, and forever.

Once again, the trans-conceptual contemplative certainty of this intuitively obvious all- ground—by whatever name or concept—is always present in the nondual, direct experience *(yogi pratyaksa)* of our already present Presence of it, at the love-wisdom Heart of the human being. Einstein, Planck, Bohr, Heisenberg, Schrödinger, and many other great physicists understood this great physical/spiritual truth, at least conceptually. Many of them wrote about it. Some practiced it in prayer and meditation.

There is much more to be said on the matter. Still, "Form is empty; emptiness is form". The Buddha understood the subjective emptiness nature and impermanence of relative physical spacetime form 25 centuries before the relativistic quantum mechanics of Einstein and Heisenberg.

This concludes our brief excursus into relativistic quantum emptiness that is the Buddhist impermanence and emptiness of form.

David Paul Boaz davidpaulboaz.org info@coppermount.org

Appendix C:
Varieties of Buddhist Experience:
Dzogchen and Quantum Emptiness

Ontological Extremism, a Middle Way, and the Light of the Mind. In Buddhism the *Abhidharma* of the *Sarvastivada* and *Vaibhashika* Schools, along with Democritus and his master Leucippus, and Western functionalist Material Realism (Metaphysical Scientific Realism/Scientific Materialism/Physicalism), all hold the realist atomist position wherein reality consists of indivisible, physical/material atomic baryonic matter particles (atomism) that have an ultimately physical, objectively real, permanent, even absolute and eternal existence. This is the ontology of Physicalism. Appearing reality is ultimately only physical.

We shall see that this Modernist European Enlightenment paradigm known as Scientific Materialism, is a failed paradigm that not even post-Standard Model particle physicists and quantum cosmologists take seriously, at least theoretically; although most are still ideologically committed. Paradigm shifts take a couple of generations.

So some Buddhist schools believe that atoms are eternal; and some particle physicists believe that electrons and protons within these atoms are eternal, that they do not decay. In the case of recent particle physics, the existence of ordinary atomic baryonic matter (our beloved protons and neutrons) is believed to be *observer-independently* arising from the "empty space" of the quantum vacuum potential, the zero point energy field (ZPE), apart from any perceiving, experiencing, experimenting consciousness, or mind. Such realists, whether Theravada Buddhists, most Hindus or physicists, are *essentialists*, believing that reality exists essentially and *independently*—just as it appears from its own side, of its own power, independent of any observer consciousness. A tree in the forest exists when there is no one about to observe it. This view is known as "common sense realism".

On the other hand, Mahayana *Madhyamaka* Buddhists argue that physical and mental reality arises *interdependently*, as a result of an infinite sequence of prior causes and conditions. Appearing stuff is observer-dependent. It is an observer consciousness that reifies and imputes reality.

In other words, the essentialist view is *observer-independent*. The world of stuff is a separate "real world out there" (RWOT), whether or not it's observed by a sentient consciousness. So, the Middle Way *Madhyamaka* view is *observer-dependent* or ontologically relative—relative to our linguistic semiotic deep cultural background "global web of belief". For this view, stuff exists not independently, but relative to the consciousness of an observer/perceiver.

On the essentialist, usually realist and materialist/physicalist view, reality as it appears to our senses is a perfect "mirror of nature" (Rorty), a kind of "immaculate perception" that represents an eternal barrier between inherently unitary human consciousness and an essentially separate Platonic RWOT. This observer-independent, theory-independent, realist/materialist view is opposed by the epistemological idealism of the Hindu *Sanatanadharma*—the hoary Vedas, the Upanishads, and the dualistic Vedanta of Madhva's *Dvaita* Vedanta.

It is also opposed by Buddhist Idealists, the *Yogachara/Chittamatra* or "Mind Only" school of Asanga and Vasubandhu, and as well by Western Objective Idealists—Bradley, Royce, McTaggart—who broadly construe arising material objective reality as unreal, a subjective apparition or illusion of a sober, sentient perceiving consciousness. For *Chittamatra* Idealism, appearing relative-conventional physical spacetime reality is relative and illusory (*avidya maya*) as it arises from our *concept* of its basal nondual ultimate "groundless ground" (*vidya maya*).

For Middle Way *Madhyamaka Prasangika* Realism, both form and emptiness are mere illusory *concepts*. As Shakyamuni Buddha told in his nondual *Heart Sutra*: "Form is empty (*stong pa, shunya*) ; emptiness (*stong pa nyi, shunyata*) is form...all dharmas are emptiness; there are no characteristics. There is no birth and no cessation...in emptiness there is no form...no ignorance, no end of ignorance...no path, no wisdom, no enlightenment, and no non-enlightenment..."

Well, ontologically speaking, what *is* there then? What indeed? Buddha asks us to "abide by means of *Prajnaparamita*", bright indwelling *presence*, always already present primordial wisdom, and thereby "fully awaken to unsurpassed, true, complete enlightenment". And yes, it takes a bit of trans-conceptual practice to understand the prior ontic unity of the epistemic Two Truths—Relative and Ultimate—as utterly empty of essence; or as Nagarjuna told, without "a shred of inherent existence". Yet form is *relatively*, conventionally real.

And for *Chittamatra*, this appearing phenomenal reality is "mind only." There can be no objectively knowable real things in themselves. Again, for realistic *Prasangika*, spacetime phenomena do indeed exist relatively, conventionally, just not absolutely or ultimately. This then is the great *Madhyamaka* Middle Way, a fine balance between the nihilistic non-existence of Indian Idealism, and the substantialist eternalist permanence of existing stuff of Scientific Realism and Scientific Materialism.

Kant's Transcendental Subjective Idealism—a duality of realist, material objective *phenomena*, and the perfectly subjective and unknowable, utterly transcendent *noumenon*—is a Western (Platonist) version of our Primordial Wisdom Tradition's "Two Truths" duality—objective relative and subjective ultimate—and parallels the "Neutral Monism" of William James.

Kant's incipient middle way idealism also parallels the non-essentialist, yet pragmatically realist centrist Buddhist Middle

Way *Madhyamaka Prasangika* view of Nagarjuna and Chandrakirti. As we have seen, here reality arises and appears interdependently (Buddha's "Dependent Arising" (*pratitya samutpada)*, is ontologically relative and observer-dependent, that is to say, our realities are dependent upon the semiotic "global web of belief" (Quine 1969) of the consciousness of a reflexively self-conscious observer.

Is such a middle way between these perennial Two Truths of relative form and ultimate emptiness/boundlessness cognitively realizable? Is there a centrist position between our seemingly competing paradigms, the epistemic extremes of descending, substantialist, objective Science (form) and the ascending idealism of subjective Spirituality (emptiness)?

Yes. Between these two philosophical extremes—the realist/materialist reification of a permanent, absolute, substantial, eternal and independently existing physical and mental phenomenal reality "out there", and the idealist nihilistic negation of it—abides the mean that is the Madhyamaka prasangika, the centrist Nalanda Buddhist Middle Way Consequence School (H.H. The Dalai Lama 2009).

Prasangika is the complementary theoretical basis, according to Longchen Rabjam (2007), and His Holiness the Dalai Lama (2009) of the utterly nondual view and praxis of Buddhist *Nyin gma* School's *Dzogchen*, the Great Perfection, that acausal, transconceptual "correction" or completion of the inherent duality of the Two Truths trope that is Middle Way *Prasangika,* and indeed of the entire great Buddhist Causal Vehicle (Klein 2006; Boaz 2015). Indeed, His Holiness advises that *Prasangika* is the Middle Way foundation of the great nondual *Dzogchen* teaching (2009).

Thus, in *Dzogchen* we have not only a centrist *Prasangika* synthesis of the Two Truths—Relative and Ultimate—that are exoteric Realism/Materialism (matter), and esoteric Idealism (mind/spirit), but an optimistic and freeing soteriology—an "innermost secret" or greater esoteric view and praxis for an expedited human liberation/enlightenment, ultimate happiness itself. Indeed, this is the happiness that cannot be lost.

But human happiness is only here and now. We cannot *become* happy or enlightened in the future; we can only *be* happy here now. Why? The future never shows up! It is always too busy becoming the present moment.

Further,wonder of wonders, as *Dzogchen* founder Garab Dorje told, "It is already accomplished from the very beginning", deep within us, here and now. Our inherent happiness abides in the Presence of the primordial ground, nondual whole itself, by whatever name or concept.The spiritual path is our trans-conceptual awakening to That! And 500 years before, Shakyamuni Buddha told: "Let it be as it is and rest your weary mind, all things are perfect exactly as they are".

As things are far from perfect in the spacetime dimension of Relative Truth, he was describing the realm of Ultimate Truth. And these are always already an ontic prior, and epistemic present unity. As Nagarjuna told, "There is absolutely no difference between *samsara* and *nirvana*".

Leibnitz' view of such a perfect "best of all possible worlds"; and recent cosmology's tautological but non-trivial Anthropic Principle (both weak and strong versions), point out that our unlikely universe with its highly improbable super-"fine-tuned" physical constants that favor life forms must necessarily exist in order that human consciousness arise to reflexively observe and ponder it all. Both Leibnitz and the Anthropic Principle suggest that a nondual noetic (no *essential* subject-object separation) view of this otherwise ineffable perfect subjectivity is necessary.

On the accord of Buddhist Vajrayana epistemology, this perfect understanding is Buddha mind (*samatajnana*), the Great Perfection of *Dzogchen*, the mind of Ultimate Truth. Indeed, this is the very nature of mind. And that is who we actually are. Heady wine indeed to dualistic concept mind ensnared as it is in the prodigious quest for absolute objective certainty within this dimension of merely realist/materialist "concealer" Relative Truth.

It is perhaps a bit sobering to remember that all of this heady conjecture is but self-stimulating concept mind. Yet, there is this unreasonable brightness of the mind that is always present.

"Everything that exists lacks an intrinsic nature or identity" asserts Alan Wallace (2003) explicating Nagarjuna's Buddhist selfless (*anatman*) centrist *Madhyamaka* ontology. The appearance of objects arising from the basal primordial ground (the unbounded whole or *mahabindu, dharmakaya, chittadhatu*) are interdependently related, that is, their reality is dependent upon other related events and processes in a vast matrix of "prior causes and conditions."

Moreover, human discursive mind conceptually imputes, designates, then reifies these appearances into independent, objectively "real" physical/mental spacetime existent realities in accordance with our atavistic, deep background cultural assumptions. Thus arises what WVO Quine (1969) terms our deep background socio-cultural "global web of belief", the cause of it all.

We then habitually reduce our bright subjectively real original noetic direct experience to objectified discursive cognitive entities abiding in an emblematic, seemingly separate "real world out there". With a bit of mindfulness practice we may learn to *choose our reality*; that is, we learn to maintain the initial nondual noetic purity of our basal primordial wisdom ground as it arises spontaneously through ordinary direct perception, prior to conceptual intervention and judgment. With a bit more practice we can do this simultaneously with our parallel conceptual dualistic relative-conventional dimension of a RWOT.

So we live in these two worlds—objective real/material, and subjective mental/spiritual—at once; whether we are cognizant of this unity, or not. Is not our soteriological imperative the recognition, realization then compassionate expression of the prior unity of these two? To reduce or not to reduce, that is the epistemic question of nondual enlightened awareness. Hence, from the epistemology you choose, arises the ontology you deserve.

The Two Truths and Dōgen's Being-time. Dōgen, perhaps Japan's greatest Zen master, spoke of this arising, descending dimension of relative time and its phenomenal contents—the spacetime dimension of Relative Truth (*samvriti satya*)—as "a being-time moment flashing into existence" from the vast spacious expanse of the basal, non-logocentric, primordial emptiness (*shunyata*) base or ground, unbounded whole that is nondual reality being itself—the all-embracing dimension of Ultimate Truth (*paramartha satya*).

This "Ultimate Truth" is nothing less than his *Ugi,* or Being-Time. Dōgen's *Ugi* is the here now, always already present prior and present unity of the Buddhist *Madhyamaka* "three times"—past, present, future. So there is no beginning, and no end to this vast expanse of reality itself. The dimension of spacetime Relative Truth, including us, instantiates this vast primordial "groundless ground" of everything that arises and appears to sentient participating consciousness. Yes, we are luminous primordial awareness instantiations of *That*(*tat*). Human consciousness necessarily intends *That.*

For Dōgen (and Padmasambhava), the eternal present exists for us only relative to a past and a future. Being-Time/*Ugi* is a simultaneous array of all three. Thus we live in a single vanishing instant now. Yet, this precious moment now derives its meaning from the inter-subjective context of a personal and even collective past, and of a possible future. This momentous moment now is significant because all of our past and future are interdependently, causally enfolded within it, while always unfolding in the timeless continuum of this present moment now. Yes, we live in the moment, but not only in the moment. To live only in the moment now, without awareness of past and future (karma) is to "make our life meaningless". Not to live in the moment now, is "to lose reality itself".

Philosophers of physics and cosmology, if not always physicists and cosmologists, are now discovering a post empirical *kosmic* being-time in Dōgen Zenji's syncretic view of the prior epistemic unity of our two faces—objective and subjective—of this inherently reflexive consciousness, an unbounded whole (*mahabindu*) that is reality being itself, the very nature of mind with all that arises within it—our actual "supreme identity".

Dōgen's great insight is that prior to the superimposition (*vikshepa*) and intervention of conceptual cognition, ordinary direct perception bestows the inherent (*sahaja*), immediate, luminous, "primordially pure" noetic nature of mind, the ultimate ground of relative mind, all its relative conventional experience. Here, in the "bare attention" of basal "naked awareness"—ontologically prior to subject/object separation and habitual conceptual imputation and reification—abides trans-rational nondual noetic reality itself. This pristine awareness is our very aperture to that primordial wisdom ground. It is our intrinsic awareness Wisdom Mind, Suzuki Roshi's "Big Mind", Buddha mind that always already knows this great truth.

Such immediate perception, an instant prior to conception, is pure perception. And we all do this, all the time, with every perception! Wonder of wonders, we are all "primordially awakened" (*bodhi, vidya*) to this always "already accomplished" innate and perfect clear light mind. That is our actual "supreme identity". The rub? We must recognize, realize and awaken (*bodhi*) to this great "perfectly subjective" truth. How do we do this? We consult the experts and follow their injunctions, of course. As H.H. The Dalai Lama (2009) told, "The clear light mind which lies dormant in human beings is the great hope of humankind".

Hence, there is always, through all of our cognitive states—perceptual, conceptual, emotional, and transpersonal transconceptual contemplative—an ontic prior unity of past, present, future, always being here now. We can learn to be present to the nondual noetic *presence* of That. And yes it takes a little selfless transpersonal mindfulness (*shamatha/vipashyana*) contemplative practice. Who am I? As Buddha told, "Don't believe what I teach, come and see".

Toward an Integral Noetic Science of Matter, Mind and Spirit. Physics and cosmology are quantitative. "The qualitative" (value, volition) is active yet largely suppressed and denied in the common orthodoxy of the physical sciences. Let physics now recognize and strategically develop the qualitative dimension in science!

What is urgently required is an integral noetic ontology and a centrist epistemology and methodology that accounts for a trans-rational, yet contemplatively knowable nonlocal subjective ultimate or universal trans-physical reality matrix emptiness base or "groundless ground"—the unbounded whole and "supreme source" of our wisdom traditions—in which objective physical relative spacetime particulars (energy, mass, force, charge, waves, particles and people) arise, interact and participate. Mereologically, the panpsychic prior ontic unity that is this great whole subsumes yet embraces its parts, while the parts participate in the whole.

Clearly, such a noetic science requires a methodological, "post empirical" relaxing of the adventitious limits of the obsessively objective positivist view and praxis that is "old paradigm" Scientific Realism and Scientific Materialism/Physicalism. Such a Kuhnian scientific revolution is now upon us (Boaz 2021b).

The basal quantum zero point energy (ZPE) vacuum energy field (constant density dark energy, Einstein's cosmological constant Λ) of Quantum Cosmology's "lambda CDM Standard Model", with the parallel premodern wisdom of Buddhist boundless emptiness (*shunyata/dharmakaya/kadag*) in which this energy vacuum arises, is a good beginning.

The physical quantitative spacetime ground that is the empty ZPE vacuum field is itself thereby grounded in a subtler, all subsuming trans-quantitative, even trans-rational primordial emptiness base in which, or in whom it arises and participates. This of course requires noetic contemplative research methodologies that utilize both quantitative objective third person data sets, and the qualitative, though still objective data sets of personal, subjective, introspective, even contemplative first person reports of highly experienced meditation masters.

Thus are the Mahayana Middle Way *Madhyamaka Prasangika* Two Truths—spacetime Relative Truth, and post-empirical, post-Standard Model Ultimate Truth—unified in the Buddhist "perfect sphere of *Dzogchen*", unbounded whole (*dharmadhatu*), nondual ultimate reality itself in which this all arises and participates. Mereologically, multiplicity, the particular parts are necessarily subsumed by the greater all embracing whole.

The Copenhagen Interpretation of Relativistic Quantum Field Theory (QFT); Stephen Hawking's 2010 Model Dependent Realism (MDR) view of QFT; Dirac's unification of Einstein's Special Relativity with Bohr's early quantum theory, that resulted in quantum electro dynamics (QED); and recent Quantum Bayesianism (QBism) interpretations of QFT are Science's inchoate *relative* cognitive architecture for accomplishing such a middle way centrist methodology. It must now be integrated with the trans-physical *ultimate* whole itself—nondual primordial *Dzogchen*.

The immeasurable challenge is this: that greatest of human intellectual achievements, the prodigious Standard Model of particles and forces, with its recent Λ-CDM Standard Model of Cosmology still clings to the orthodox, old paradigm dogmatic materialist metaphysic that is extreme objectivist Realism—Physicalism/Materialism of a classical Newtonian cosmos of "real" purely physical objects permanently and eternally existing in an absolute, objectively relatively real spacetime; although this is quickly changing. A purely objective spacetime has fallen on hard times. Physicists are at last beginning to hear Einstein on time who told that, "Time is an illusion; but a very persistent one". With new work on QED, many physicists have thrown out space as well (Boaz 2019).

Be that as it may, the notoriously perverse mathematical incommensurability of QED with Einstein's General Relativity Theory (GRT)—required to unify these two great pillars of modern physics—the two will continue to remain separate and contradictory without a continuing ideological softening of Modern Science's hyper-objectivist monistic Metaphysical Materialism/Physicalism, now considered by most philosophers of physics a failed ontology. How is this so? It contradicts the inherently random trans-causal and therefore non-objectivist quantum theory, to wit, QED.

We desperately need a unifying theory of quantum gravity to heal this epistemic split between the minute micro realm of the Planck scale quantum, and the vast large scale cosmic dimension ruled by gravity.

Quantum mechanics has subsumed three of the four fundamental forces/particles of the wondrous Standard Model of particle physics, namely Electromagnetism, the Strong Nuclear Force that atomically binds the worlds, and the Weak Nuclear Force of radioactive decay. Only Einstein's "Big G" gravity "force" remains to be tamed by the sublime quantum theory.

Because the quantum theory clearly obtains in both dimensions—the three forces of the very small, and large scale gravity, we need a propitious new theory of the *relative in the quantum*. Where does gravity become quantum?

In short, we a new quantum spacetime that reveals how the hitherto smooth non-quantized gravity continuum of Aristotle, and of Einstein's GRT may be quantized—course grained into discrete quantum bits, "lightquanta" as Einstein called these discrete foundational qbits, like photons, or gravitons.

Einstein himself failed to accomplish this syncretic consummation, though he predicted the discrete gravitons of his continuous gravity waves. None of the twenty or so epistemic interpretations of QED have done any better. What in heaven and earth would a qbit particle of space possibly be? We might visit Buddhist *Abidharma* and explore their "space particles".

What *is* certain is that at the tiny Planck scale, spacetime continuity is kaput, a new scientific paradigm emerges, and the old objectivist, Greek materialist paradigm finally becomes scientific history.

The bad news is that at the empirically and even logically impossible Planck scale, time and distance are immeasurable.

How then may we determine which of the several quantum gravity theories are tenable? Here the spooky subjectivist quantum anomalies of nonlocality/entanglement and the logically defying quantum superposition—a point like particle existing in two places at the same time—will continue to play an important role. If gravity can be shown to possess either of these theoretically related quantum properties, then it is quantum in nature.

Richard Feynman, QED researcher and creator of Feynman diagrams, suggested that if gravity, the warping of spacetime, is indeed quantizable a superposed particle arising in its logically absurd two locations at the same moment in time must produce two co-existing entangled spacetime gravitational fields simultaneously. If this subjective superposed eigenstate does not collapse into an objective reality state, then it must be entangled revealing that gravity is indeed a quantum phenomenon. Experiments are now under way to settle the matter. However, should gravity prove to be subject to quantization, we still need a correct theory of quantum gravity to show how (Boaz 2021a, *The Collapse of Objective Reality: Quantum Nonlocality and Buddhist Emptiness, Ch. VIII*).

What if quantum theory is in need of modification? What if it breaks down in the gravitational extremes of neutron stars and black holes? What if it is QED that must be adapted to General Relativity as a few microphysicists believe? Time will tell. And so it goes.

Our understanding of gravity was greatly enhanced by Einstein's GRT. Kuhnian scientific revolution or no, what is painfully slow to change is science's cultural zeitgeist, namely classical, objectivist Platonic Scientific Realism, and Realism's epistemic handmaid, monistic physicalist Scientific Materialism/Physicalism. Notable exceptions to this unwholesome course may be the antirealist, ontologically relative quantum views of Bohr, von Neumann, Wheeler and Barbour.

Of the many physicists and cosmologists in recovery from this afflictive obsessive "scientific" physicalist/materialist view, relativistic physicist and cosmologist Stephen Hawking's story is perhaps the most inspiring. Upon analysis of Kurt Gödel's two 1936 incompleteness theorems Hawking became disabused of his grail quest for a logically impossible Theory of Everything with its realist/materialist presumption, and embraced an antirealist view. This epistemic reversal of his hitherto ardent Scientific Realism of *A Brief History of Time*, became an ever so reticent antirealist Model Dependent Realism (MDR) ontology revealed in his excellent book, *The Grand Design* (2010). Such rare intellectual openness and honesty in a great mind is indeed a joy to behold. Stephen Hawking, you will be missed!

Well, what might the culture of old paradigm Modern Standard Model physics and cosmology, and post-Standard Model physics—Supersymmetry/M Theory, Multiverse Theory, dark sector vacuum energy—look like with this methodological enrichment of the ontology, psychology and contemplative science of Premodern Buddhist Middle Way philosophy? Let particle physicists, cosmologists, neuroscientists and Buddhist scholar-practitioners dialogue over pizza and ale.

There is now in the West an auspicious, inchoate union of Buddhism and science arising. This unified integral noetic ontology, with its emerging science of consciousness, presents a propitious opening for the new noetic science of matter, mind and spirit of our emerging Noetic Revolution; and the healing wisdom that abides therein (Boaz, *The Noetic Revolution: Toward an Integral Science of Matter, Mind and Spirit*, forthcoming 2021).

David Paul Boaz davidpaulboaz.org info@coppermount.org

Appendix D:
A Brief History of the Dzogchen Transmission

In Uddiyana (Orgyen) in the second century CE, **Garab Dorje** (b. circa 55 CE), the human founder of the primordial *Dzogchen* teaching, in his *Sambhogakaya* form, having received it directly from primordial *dharmakaya* Adi Buddha Samantabhadra (*Tib.* Kuntazangpo), transmitted the great teaching to his heart son **Manjushrimita** (*The Three Essential Statements* or *The Three Vajra Verses*) who then classified these precious texts (*The Dzogchen Nyingthig*), and then transmitted them to **Jnanasutra, Guru Padsambhava** or Guru Rinpoche (*The Khandro Nyingthig*), **Vimalamitra** (*The Vima Nyingthig*), and then to **Virochana** (*The Cuckoo of the State of Presence*).

Vimalamitra and Padmasambhava then carried the teaching from Uddiyana to Tibet in the 8th century CE, at the invitation of Buddhist practitioner **King Trisong Detson.** In the 14th century the entire *Nyingthig corpus* was synthesized and essentialized by Nyingma luminary **Longchenpa** (Longchen Rabjam 1308-1364) as *The Seven Treasures (Dzodun), The Trilogy of Finding Comfort and Ease, The Trilogy of Natural Freedom,* and *The Three Inner Essences.*

In the 18th century Nyingma master **Jigme Lingpa** (1730-1798) rediscovered the complete *Dzogchen Nyingthig,* which includes all of the above treasure texts, as a root mind *terma (gong ter)* and condensed its essence as The *Yonten Dzod,* which is now known as The *Longchen Nyingthig.*

In this form the *Dzogchen* teaching was transmitted to the masters of the 19th century ecumenical *Rimé* (unbiased) movement, the effort to overcome the doctrinal sectarian strife of the various schools that began with the 8th through 11th century confrontation between the *Bön* Tibetan indiginous religion and the introduction of Indian Buddhism in Tibet. *Rimé* masters actually supported the *Bön* teaching. The *Rimé* movement founder was Sakya School Jamyang Khyentze Wangmo. Its primary actors were Jamgon Kongtrul, Patrul Rinpoche, and Nyingma *Dzogchen* master Ju Mipham Rinpoche.

This innermost esoteric *Longchen Nyingthig* is generally considered the authoritative expression of the Nyingma School's great nondual fruitional *Dzogchen* tradition—the Great Perfection or Great Completion (*chen*/great, *dzog*/perfect or complete)—studied and practiced at all levels of the teaching—from foundational *Ngöndro* practice, through *Yeshe Lama* practice, to the *Trekchö* and finally the *Tögal* teaching series.

Nyingthig means heart-mind essence. Esoterically, the *Longchen Nyingthig*, the *Heart Essence of the Infinite Expanse*, contains the precious heart essence of the aboriginal primordial *Dzogchen* view and praxis. It contains the innermost secret pith instructions—the *upadesha* (*mengagde*)—and is transmitted from *Dzogchen* Master to prepared disciple directly, non-conceptually, from heartmind to heartmind. The "innermost secret" practice of *Dzogchen* is the highest or subtlest nondual yoga of the Nyingma ten vehicles of enlightenment, namely, *Ati Yoga*.

The "ripe" disciple prepares to receive this sacred nondual Ultimate Truth teaching by completing the *Longchen Nyingthig* foundational practices (*ngöndro*) before entering in the secret pith instruction of the *upadesha/mengagde* that includes preparatory *Yeshe Lama*, then the *Trekchö* and finally the *Tögal* teaching cycles.

It is said that the *nirmanakaya* Buddha Garab Dorje initially received the primordial *Dzogchen* teaching, in its entirety, as a direct transmission from the *dharmakaya* Buddha Samantabhadra (*Tib.* Kuntazangpo), primordial *Adi* Buddha, through the *sambhogakaya* dimension Buddha Vajrasattva, from whom emanates all space-time historical *nirmanakaya* buddhas. Indeed, it is taught by some *Dzogchen* masters, including 20th century master Tulku Urgyen, that the timeless *Dzogchen* teaching was transmitted to its human founder Garab Dorje by none other than our historical *nirmanakaya* Buddha Gautama Shakyamuni, the twelfth of the twelve great *Dzogchen* masters, in his *sambhogakaya* form as *sambhogakaya* Buddha Vajrasattva (Tulku Urgyen, 1995).

Now, from a more relative, conventional historiographic and doxographic view, early Nyingma *Dzogchen* was formatively influenced primarily by certain Indian Buddhist tantras, but as well by Taoist *Chan*, indigenous Tibetan *Bön*,Tibetan Nestorian Christianity, and Kashmiri Shivaism (Chögyal Namkhi Norbu 1996; John Reynolds 1996; Boaz 2020).

The preceding historiographic evidence is based upon extant texts from the 8th through 10th centuries CE, and from recently discovered texts at Tun Huang, China—the *Rig P'ai khu byug* and the *Bas P'ai rgum chung*. However, according to certain *Dzogchen* tantras the *Dzogchen* linage includes the timeless *Twelve Teachers of Dzogchen* (Dodrupchen Rinpoche, *Tantric Doctrine According to the Nyingmapa School*).

Not all of these twelve buddhas were of the local spacetime human dimension. Some of these stellar prehistoric beings predate even the ancient *Bön Dzogchen* Master Shenrab Miwoche (Tonpa Shenrab Miwo) who transmitted the *Dzogchen* teaching cycles in Olmo Lung Ring (Central Asia) circa 1600 BCE (Reynolds 1996). From there the teaching spread to Orgen (Uddiana)/Zhang Zhung, then to Tibet, then to the rest of the world.

Indeed, the *Grathal gyur tantra*, and other such texts teach that the great nondual primordial *Ati Yoga Dzogchen* teaching, by whatever name or form, has appeared in inhabited star systems throughout the kosmos for many kalpas, long before the arising of our solar system; and will continue long after its death.

Thus it is, for the Nyingmapa, and many other Buddhist schools, and for non-Buddhists as well, the nonlocal, nondual primordial *Dzogchen* teaching represents the pinnacle of all love-wisdom teaching of the three times—past, present, and future.

Dzogchen view and praxis is therefore most relevant to the great wisdom task that is now upon us, the real work of unifying our two seemingly incommensurable knowledge paradigms—objective Science and subjective Spirit/spirituality—as we embark upon our 21st century Noetic Revolution in science, religion and culture (Boaz 2021, excerpted at davidpaulboaz.org).

David Paul Boaz davidpaulboaz.org info@coppermount.org

Bibliography

Ajahn Brahm. 2006. *Mindfulness, Bliss, and Beyond.* New York: Wisdom.

Almas, A.H. 2008. *The Unfolding Now.* Boston: Shambala.

Allione, Lama Tsultrim. 2018. *Wisdom Rising.* New York: Simon and Schuster.

Anam, Thubten. 2009. *No Self, No Problem: Awakening to Our True Nature.* Boston: Shambhala.

Begley, Sharon. 2007. *Train Your Mind, Change Your Brain.* New York: Ballantine.

Boaz, David Paul. 2021a. *The Collapse of Objective Reality: Quantum Nonlocality, and Buddhist Emptiness* (forthcoming). San Diego: Waterside.

___. 2021b. *The Noetic Revolution: Toward an Integral Science of Matter, Mind and Spirit* (forthcoming).

___. 2020. *Mindfulness: 36 Seconds to Bliss.* San Diego: Waterside.

Bohm, David and Basil Hiley. 1993. *The Undivided Universe.* New York: Routlege and Kagen Paul.

Bohr, Niels. 1934. *Atomic Theory and the Description of Nature.* New York: Cambridge Press.

Carroll, Sean. 2003. *Spacetime and Geometry: An Introduction to General Relativity.* NY: Addison.

Chalmers, David J. 1996. *The Conscious Mind.* New York: Oxford Press.

Chögyam Trungpa. 2015. *Mindfulness in Action.* Boston: Shambhala.

Cozort, Daniel. 1998. *Unique Tenets of the Middle Way.* New York: Wisdom.

Dōgen Zenji. 1986. *Shobogenzo* (trans. Thomas Cleary). Univ. Hawaii Press.

Dowman, Keith. 2010. *Maya Yoga* (Longchenpa's *Gyuma Ngalso*). Kathmandu: Vajra Publications.

Dzogchen Ponlop Rinpoche. 2006. *Penetrating Wisdom*. New York: Snow Lion.

Dudjom Rinpoche. 1991. *The Nyingma School of Tibetan Buddhism*. Boston: Wisdom.

Garfield, Jay. 2015. *Engaging Buddhism: Why It Matters to Philosophy*. New York: Oxford Press.

Gen Lamrimpa; Wallace, Alan. 1992. *Calming the Mind: Tibetan Teachings on Cultivating Meditative Quiescence*. New York: Snow Lion.

Gunaratara, Henepola. 2011. *Mindfulness in Plain English*. Boston: Wisdom.

Gyamptso, Kenpo Tsultrim. 2001. *The Two Truths*. Auckland: Prajna Editions.

Herbert, Nick. 1985. *Quantum Reality*. New York: Anchor.

His Holiness the Dalai Lama. 2007. *Mind in Comfort and Ease*. (Longchen Rabjam's *Finding Comfort and Ease in Meditation on the Great Perfection*). Boston: Wisdom.

_____. 2000. *Dzogchen*. New York: Snow Lion.

_____. 2005. *Essence of the Heart Sutra*. Boston: Wisdom.

_____. 2009. *The Middle Way*. Boston: Wisdom.

Heisenberg, Werner. 1958. *Physics and Philosophy*. New York: Harper.

Hopkins, Jeffrey. *Meditation on Emptiness*. Boston: Wisdom.

Jomgön Kongtrul. 2005. *The Treasury of Knowledge* (Book Six, Part Four). New York: Snow Lion.

Klein; Lama Anne C. 2006. *Unbounded Wholeness: Dzogchen, Bon, and the Logic of the Nonconceptual*. New York: Oxford.

_____. 1998. *Knowledge and Liberation*. New York: Snow Lion.

Lamrimpa, Gen. 1999. *Realizing Emptiness* (trans. B. Alan Wallace). New York: Snow Lion.

Longchen Rabjam. 2007. *Precious Treasury of Philosophical Systems* (trans. Richard Barron). Padma.

_____. 2001. *Precious Treasury of the Basic Space of Phenomena* (Autocommentary): Padma.

Mipham, Jamgon. 2007. *White Lotus*. Padmakara Translation Group. Boston: Shambhala.

Nagarjuna. 1995. *Fundamental Wisdom of the Middle Way* (trans. Jay Garfield). New York: Oxford.

Namgyal, Dakpo Tashi. 2001. *Clarifying the Natural State*. Hong Kong: Rangjung Yeshe.

Newland, Guy. 2008. *Introduction to Emptiness*. New York: Snow Lion.

Norbu, Chögyal Namkhai. 1999. *The Supreme Source*. New York: Snow Lion.

Nyoshul Khenpo. 1995. *Natural Great Perfection* (compiled by Lama Surya Das). New York: Snow Lion.

Penrose, Roger. 2004, 2007. *The Road To Reality: A Complete Guide to the Laws of the Universe*. Vintage.

Pettit, John, W. 1999. *Mipham's Beacon of Certainty*. Boston: Wisdom.

Porges, Stephen. 2014. *Polyvegal Theory*. New York: Norton.

Quine, Willard Van Orman. 1969. *Ontological Relativity and Other Essays*. New York: Columbia.

Reynolds, John M. 1996. *The Golden Letters*. New York: Snow Lion.

Scientific American. November 2014.

Schrödinger, Erwin. 1958. *Mind and Matter*. New York: Cambridge Press.

Shantideva. 1997. *Guide to the Bodhisattva's Way of Life* (translated by B. Alan and Vesna Wallace. New York: Snow Lion.

Sheng, Chuan, Ed. *Exploring Buddhism and Science*. Singapore: Buddhist College of Singapore.

Siegel, Ronald D. 2013. *Mindfulness and Psychotherapy, Second Edition*. New York: Guilford Press.

Sogyal Rinpoche. 1992. *The Tibetan Book of Living and Dying*. San Francisco: Harper.

Surya Das, Lama. 1992. *Awakening the Buddha Within*. New York: Broadway.

Suzuki Roshi. 1970. *Zen Mind, Beginner's Mind*. New York: Weatherhill.

Thanissaro Bhikkhu. 2015. *The Karma of Mindfulness.* Valley Center, CA: Metta Forest Monastery

Thich Nhat Hanh. 2001. *Miracle of Mindfulness.* New York: Beacon Press.

Wallace, B. Alan. 2007. *Contemplative Science.* New York: Columbia Univ. Press.

_____. 2009. *Mind in the Balance: Meditation in Science, Buddhism, and Christianity.* New York: Columbia Univ. Press.

_____. 2012. *Meditations of a Buddhist Skeptic.* New York: Columbia Univ. Press.

Wilber, Ken. 2017. *The Religion of the Future.* Boston: Shambhala.

_____. 2006. *Integral Spirituality.* Boston: Shambhala.

www.ingramcontent.com/pod-product-compliance
Lightning Source LLC
Chambersburg PA
CBHW031231090426
42742CB00007B/156